PSEUDOSCIENCE
AND THE
PARANORMAL

PSEUDOSCIENCE
AND THE

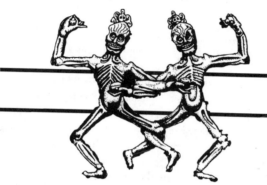

PARANORMAL

A Critical Examination of the Evidence

TERENCE HINES

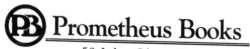 Prometheus Books

59 John Glenn Drive
Amherst, NewYork 14228-2197

Published 1988 by Prometheus Books

Inquiries should be addressed to
Prometheus Books, 59 John Glenn Drive, Amherst, New York 14228–2197.
VOICE: 716–691–0133, ext. 207.
FAX: 716–564–2711.
WWW.PROMETHEUSBOOKS.COM

03 02 01 00 99   7 6 5 4

Library of Congress Card Catalog No. 87–043318
ISBN 1–87975–419–2

Printed in the United States of America on acid-free paper

This book is dedicated to the memory of
Norman Guttman.

Contents

Preface

When I began teaching the "Parapsychology and the Occult" course at Pace University's Pleasantville, New York, campus in the spring of 1984, I quickly realized that no textbook covered all the areas I wanted to include in the course. An obvious solution was to write a textbook of my own—and so the idea for this book was born. The literature that critically examines paranormal claims and phenomena is widely scattered over different disciplines and can be very difficult to track down. Because of this I wanted the book to be not only a textbook but also a reference volume that would serve as a guide to the critical literature. To this end, an abundance of references is provided, so that papers and books containing further details on any topics discussed can be tracked down. Books and articles that would be of special interest to readers seeking additional information are specially marked in the reference list.

I also wrote this book out of a firm conviction that it is not enough merely to debunk paranormal beliefs; another interesting and equally important issue is why people continue to believe in paranormal and occult claims in the face of clear empirical evidence that these claims are invalid. Platitudes about a "will to believe" are inadequate explanations. Rather, explanations for continued belief must be based on knowledge about how humans process information and about the nature of human memory and perception. For example, it is well known that both perceptual and memory processes are subject to powerful illusions that can convince people that they have seen a flying saucer or have had their future predicted with great accuracy by a psychic. These perceptual and cognitive illusions rather than some ill-defined "will to believe" account in large part for the continued belief in the reality of paranormal phenomena. Of course, other factors—especially uncritical reports in the media—also play a role.

This book is aimed largely at the student who will use it in a course. However, it has been written so as to require no background in psychology or other fields. There are two reasons for this. First, many courses that use a book such as this have no prerequisites. Second, I wanted the book to be accessible to a general audience of those interested in the critical analysis of paranormal claims.

Approximately half of the manuscript for this book was completed during the summer of 1985 when I was a Visiting Scholar in the Psychology Department at Dartmouth College. I thank all the members of the department for helping to make that summer so pleasant and productive. Dr. William Smith's comments were especially helpful.

Many other colleagues have helped in ways large and small, from answering specific questions to reviewing sections of the manuscript. I thank them all, especially Stephen Barrett, MD, who made useful comments on the section of the manuscript that became chapters ten and eleven, and Philip J. Klass, whose discussions about UFO abduction cases added greatly to chapter eight. Of course, I alone am responsible for any errors that remain.

I also want to thank those involved in the actual production of the manuscript and book. Theresa Markley, Maria Carovinci, and Melanie Roberts all typed various sections of the manuscript with speed and accuracy. Lys Ann Shore edited the entire manuscript with skill and interest, and the final book has benefited greatly from her efforts.

Finally, I must thank my wife, Mary, who not only read and made valuable suggestions on many chapters, but who has been loving and supporting during the two years when the writing of this book took so much of my time.

1

The Nature of Pseudoscience

What is pseudoscience? It's difficult to come up with a strict definition. In the real world things are not clearly delineated but surrounded by gray areas that doom any hard definition. As the term implies, a pseudoscience is a doctrine or belief system that pretends to be a science. What distinguishes pseudoscience from real sciences? Radner and Radner (1982) and MacRobert (1986) have discussed criteria for separating real science from pseudoscience and for helping to decide whether a new claim is pseudoscientific.

The most common characteristic of a pseudoscience is the non-falsifiable or irrefutable hypothesis. This is a hypothesis against which there can be no evidence—that is, no evidence can show the hypothesis to be wrong. It might at first seem that such a hypothesis must be true, but a bit of reflection and several examples will demonstrate just the opposite. Consider the following hypothesis: "I, Terence Michael Hines, am God Incarnate, and I created the universe thirty seconds ago." Now, you probably don't believe this hypothesis, but how would you go about disproving it? You could argue, "You say you created the universe thirty seconds ago, but I have memories from *years* ago. So, you're not God." But I reply, "When I created the universe, I created everyone complete with memories." We could go on like this for some time and you would never be able to prove that I'm not God. Nonetheless, this hypothesis is clearly absurd!

Creationists, who believe that the biblical story of creation is literal truth, often adopt a similar irrefutable hypothesis. They claim that the world was created less than 10,000 years ago. As will be seen in chapter twelve vast amounts of physical evidence clearly refute this claim. All one has to do is point to something older than 10,000 years. Backed into a corner by such evidence, creationists often rephrase the creationist hypothesis in an irrefutable form. They explain the clear geological and fossil evidence that dates back millions of years by claiming that God put that evidence there to test our faith. An alternative version is that the evidence was manufactured by Satan to tempt us from the true path of redemption. No evidence can refute either of these versions of the hypothesis, since any new piece of geological or fossil evidence can be dismissed as having been placed there by God or Satan. This does not make the hypothesis true—it makes it trivial. That is, such a hypothesis contributes nothing to our understanding of the physical world.

Another example of an irrefutable hypothesis comes from a doctrine not usually considered a pseudoscience (but it meets the criteria, as will be seen in chapter five)—psychoanalysis. Freud believed that all males had latent homosexual tendencies, but that in most males these tendencies were repressed. Clearly, homosexual males have homosexual tendencies. But what about heterosexual males? To determine whether the hypothesis that all males have repressed homosexual tendencies is false, you could give some sort of test for homosexual tendencies. What if you failed to find such tendencies? The standard Freudian reply is that the tendencies have been so completely repressed that they don't show up on the test. Given this irrefutable hypothesis, no test could show that heterosexual males don't have latent homosexual urges. No matter how sensitive the test, the reply can always be made that the urges are so deeply repressed that they don't show up on the test.

Those who are skeptical about pseudoscientific and paranormal claims are frequently accused of being closed-minded in demanding adequate evidence and proof before accepting such a claim. But who is really being closed-minded? As a scientist, I can specify exactly the type of evidence that would be required to make me change my mind and accept the reality of astrology, UFOs as extraterrestrial spacecraft, or any other topic considered in this book. But the believer, who likes to paint him or herself as open-minded and accepting of new possibilities, is really extremely closed-minded. After all, the irrefutable hypothesis is really saying "There is no conceivable piece of evidence that will cause me to change my mind!" *That* is true closed-mindedness.

One more point should be made about irrefutable hypotheses: Although they are nonfalsifiable, they are not nonverifiable. That is, they could be shown to be true. The Freudian hypothesis about males' latent homosexual urges could be verified if all males did show such urges on some sensitive test of sexual preferences. So, irrefutable hypotheses are only that—irrefutable. They could be verified, if the evidence to support the hypothesis existed. Of course, the promoters of irrefutable hypotheses have been forced to fall back on them precisely because no evidence exists to support them. Thus, an irrefutable hypothesis is a sure-fire sign of a pseudoscience.

A second characteristic of pseudoscience is proponents' unwillingness to look closely at the phenomenon they claim exists. That is, careful, controlled experiments that would demonstrate the existence of the phenomenon if it were real are not conducted. The reality of the phenomenon is uncritically accepted, and the need for hard data and facts is belittled. MacRobert (1982) gives an excellent example in the work of George Leonard (1976), who believes that official photographs from the National Aeronautics and Space Administration (NASA) show that "somebody else is on the moon." Leonard contends that he has discovered this secret and is trying to inform the public about it in spite of a massive conspiracy of silence. Leonard's evidence consists of low-resolution NASA photographs, many of them poor reproductions, not the crisp originals. The objects Leonard sees, such as huge bridges and construction equipment of various types, are all just at the limit of resolution of the photos he uses. MacRobert (1982, p. 47) points out that "when he had a chance to get better photos and see the terrain more clearly, he didn't. One of his pictures is supposed to show miles-long bridges. The photo is a very distant shot, and the bridges are the vaguest smudges. Equally good close-ups have been taken of the bridge areas, and if the bridges were there, they would reach from one side of the photos to the other like a wall poster of the Golden Gate. For some reason Leonard did not get those particular close-ups, readily available from NASA. He was unwilling to look carefully." Oberg (1982) has discussed Leonard's errors in detail.

It will be seen throughout this book that there is a general unwillingness on the part of promoters of pseudoscientific claims to look carefully at the evidence they put forth to support their claims. This contrasts, of course, with the behavior of scientists who are extremely careful in examining evidence.

What Radner and Radner (1982) term "looking for mysteries" is another common feature of pseudoscientific claims. Here the proponent searches for allegedly unexplained phenomena and says, in effect, "There, Science, explain that." If science can't fully explain the phenomena, reasonable explanations are ignored or dismissed, and the proponent concludes that his pseudoscientific theory is supported. This type of accumulation of stray events is best illustrated by "UFOlogists," who claim that unidentified flying objects (UFOs) are extraterrestrial spacecraft. Proponents of such claims compile almost endless files of UFO sightings and other UFO-related phenomena. The skeptic is then told that unless he can explain away *every single* report, the theory that UFOs are extraterrestrial craft must be true. In other words, the burden of proof is placed on the skeptic to disprove the claim.

In reality, the burden of proof should rest squarely on the one who is making the extraordinary claim. This is because, as we have seen, it is often impossible to disprove even a clearly ridiculous claim. Consider the claim that Santa Claus is a real, living person: What evidence might one offer for such a claim? The proponent might point to the hundreds of children who say every year that they have seen Santa Claus. They can't all be lying, can they? Surely there is some grain of truth in all these reports. And didn't the astronauts on Apollo 8 report sighting Santa Claus from space when they were between the earth and the moon? Skeptics will say that was just a Christmas joke, but NASA could be hiding evidence from the public. And how about packages that appear under the Christmas tree on Christmas morning inscribed something like "To Susan from Santa"? Where did they come from? The skeptic will point out that the vast majority of such inscriptions are written by parents to maintain their children's belief in Santa, but what about the small number of cases that cannot be explained away so simply? They really do exist, of course, and are due mainly to packages getting mixed up in the mail. But the skeptic will never be able to explain away every single piece of evidence that the proponent puts forth as evidence of the physical existence of Santa Claus. This inability to explain away every bit of evidence should not, of course, convince one of the truth of the "Santa Claus is real" hypothesis. The burden of proof must rest on the proponent. He or she must bring forth clear, acceptable evidence that Santa Claus is real and not simply demand that skeptics explain away miscellaneous reports to prove that Santa *doesn't* exist.

This may seem like a silly example, but the type of "evidence" listed above for the existence of Santa Claus would be more than sufficient to convince many proponents of pseudoscience that a real phenomenon exists. In fact, it was just such evidence—the testimony of two little girls and some photographs that they faked—that convinced none other than Sir Arthur Conan Doyle, the creator of fictional detective Sherlock Holmes, that fairies really existed in the English countryside. The story is important because it illustrates how reversal of the burden of proof can lead to the uncritical acceptance of the most absurd claims.

The story starts in Cottingley, England, in 1917. Two girls—Elsie Wright, thirteen, and a cousin, Frances Griffiths, ten—claimed to have taken two photographs of fairies who played with them. Three more photos were apparently taken in the summer of 1920 (Sheaffer, 1977-78). It was Doyle who brought the photos to the public's awareness, and he later wrote a book arguing for the real existence of fairies, based largely on these photos (Doyle, 1921). The photographs, one of which is shown in figure 1, have always looked fake. But neither this nor the inherent absurdity of the claim has stopped many people, in addition to Doyle, from taking the existence of fairies seriously. As Sheaffer (1978) points out, UFOlogists have been interested in fairy sightings, believing they may be related to the UFO phenomenon and extraterrestrials. Various reports of fairies, leprechauns, and the like are all brought together to argue that maybe there really is some substance to the reports. And, again, the skeptic is challenged to explain away each and every report. Just as in the case of the Santa reports, however, it's impossible to explain every case. For example, we can never expect each child who has reported seeing fairies to admit lying. But the Cottingley photos can be explained. They were—and this should come as no great surprise to the reader— a hoax. The "fairies" were cutouts from a children's book of the time, and many years later Frances and Elsie admitted the hoax (Cooper, 1982). Finally, Sheaffer (1978) has subjected the photographs to computer enhancement and found evidence of a string that was used to hang the cutouts from shrubs while the photos were taken. So, what began as a hoax and concerned a clearly absurd hypothesis—that fairies really exist— turned into pseudoscientific belief that required sixty years and much effort to put to rest. And none of this would have happened if the burden of proof had been on the proponents in the first place to provide adequate evidence of their claim—such as a fairy or a leprechaun in a cage. Instead, the burden was shifted to the skeptics who were told, "If you can't explain away every photo and every report, then fairies must exist."

Proponents of pseudoscience often complain that skeptics are unfair in demanding more proof for pseudoscientific claims than for the claims of "establishment" scientists. This is both true and reasonable, under the circumstances: extraordinary claims demand extraordinary proof. For example, consider the following two claims about transcendental meditation (TM): (1) TM can make you feel better; (2) TM can teach you how to defy the law of gravity and float in the air at will. Most people would accept the validity of the first claim based simply on the testimony of several people who felt better after they learned how to meditate. Clearly one would demand more proof for the second claim. Most people wouldn't accept statements from several people that they knew how to levitate at will. Additional evidence would be needed. Pictures wouldn't do, because the TM movement has been known to fake photos of people levitating (Randi, 1980). You'd probably demand that someone actually levitate right in front of you. And you'd want a professional magician present as an observer to ensure that no trickery was involved. In short, you would demand more rigorous confirmation of the second claim than of the first. So, not only is the burden of proof on the proponents of pseudoscience to prove their claims, but the burden on them is greater than on someone making a claim that does not challenge the bulk of known facts.

Proponents of pseudoscience often use myth and legend as support for their claims. After all, they reason, myths and legends have been around for a long time, so they must contain a kernel of hard truth. In fact, myths are primitive attempts to explain natural phenomena in a way that the culture using the myth could understand (Barnard, 1966; Vitaliano, 1973). Myths should never be taken literally. Thus, one can trace the modern Santa Claus myths back through Christian thought to Saint Nicholas, and the customs surrounding the giving of gifts at Christmas time (Revzin, 1986). Nowhere, of course, is it ever suggested that the current image of Santa Claus, complete with sleigh and reindeer, is or ever was a real being. But anyone who took the modern myth literally would be fooled into believing that such was the case. Many proponents of pseudoscience have been similarly fooled.

Another characteristic of most pseudosciences will be considered here. This is the failure of proponents of pseudoscience to change or update their theories in the light of new evidence. For example, in 1950 Immanuel Velikovsky put forward his theory of "worlds in collision" (see chapter nine). Knowledge of the solar system in particular and astronomy in general changed vastly in the thirty-two years between 1950 and Velikovsky's death in 1982. Yet, not once did Velikovsky change his theories during that period to reflect this new knowledge. Like many proponents of pseudoscience, he felt the theory was written in stone. It was, so to speak, revealed truth not to be changed by mere facts. If the facts don't fit, the proponents of pseudoscience prefer to ignore the facts. The theory must be preserved at all costs.

This is rather ironic, as I suspect that the general public's impression is that scientists are conservative, closed-minded stodgy folk who rarely change their minds. In fact, nothing could be further from the truth. In the last 30 years all areas of scientific investigation have undergone radical changes. New theories have appeared, been useful for a time, then given way to even newer theories as new data and facts demonstrate that the old theories were inadequate. Science changes so rapidly, it is frequently difficult to keep up with the changes even in one's own field. This is in contrast, of course, to the pseudoscientists whose theories almost never change. Again, if one looks at the actual *behavior* of scientists and pseudoscientists, it is clear which is really the more open-minded of the two groups.

The characteristics of pseudoscience discussed in this chapter may not permit one to determine with precision whether a specific claim or belief system is a pseudoscience. But they do offer some useful guidelines. As applied in the following chapters, which examine various areas of pseudoscience, these criteria should help readers evaluate other pseudoscientific claims.

The Paranormal

The paranormal can best be thought of as a subset of pseudoscience. What sets the paranormal apart from other pseudosciences is a reliance on explanations for alleged phenomena that are well outside the bounds of established science. Thus, paranormal phenomena include extrasensory perception (ESP), telekinesis, ghosts, poltergeists, life after death, reincarnation, faith healing, human auras, and so forth. The explanations for these allied phenomena are phrased in vague terms of "psychic forces," "human energy fields," and so on. This is in contrast to many pseudo-scientific explanations for other nonparanormal phenomena which, although very bad science, are still couched in acceptable scientific terms. Thus, chelation therapy, a currently popular bit of medical quackery (see chapter eleven), is said to remove calcium from clogged arteries when the chemical ethylenediamine tetraacetate (EDTA) is given. The specific claim is that EDTA binds to calcium, thus destroying material blocking arteries. Binding of one substance to another is a real and very important biochemical process. However, the claims of the chelation therapists are simply wrong (Bennett, 1985; Richmond, 1985-86; Yetiv, 1986), and the therapy is not effective. Thus, the claims for chelation therapy are pseudoscientific, but not paranormal.

However, the boundary between paranormal and nonparanormal pseudosciences is often fuzzy. Different individuals may give different types of explanations for the same alleged phenomena. Thus, the claims that UFOs are extraterrestrial spacecraft is generally a pseudoscientific one (see chapters seven and eight). But some UFOlogists, such as Vallee (1975), now argue that UFOs are really some sort of psychic projection. This transforms the phenomenon into a paranormal one.

Another example concerns biorhythms (discussed in chapter six). The pseudoscientific explanation of these alleged effects is that the rhythms are set at the moment of birth in the individual's brain (Mallardi, 1978). Attempts are then made to tie the claims for biorhythms in with what is now known about biological rhythms in humans and animals (Gittleson, 1982). On the other hand, a "biorhythmist" in Oregon explained that the concept of biorhythms works because "it concerns itself with rhythmic flows of energy, relating to the conscious levels of our being, to the subconscious levels of creativity and intuition, and to superconscious levels that relate to the spiritual tendencies of the human condition" (Holden, 1977, p. 5). I would classify this as a paranormal explanation.

Scientific Mistakes: N-rays and Polywater

The stories of N-rays and polywater are classic examples of scientific mistakes. In both cases, initial claims for the existence of a new phenomenon seemed to garner impressive experimental support. Much interest was thereby generated until it became clear, on further experimentation, that neither phenomenon had ever really existed. Once this was clear, scientists expended no further effort investigating either phenomenon. Instead, these scientific dead ends were abandoned.

The N-ray and polywater stories are important for a discussion of pseudoscience and the paranormal for several reasons. First, they demonstrate once again, this time in a scientific context, that attempting to shift the burden of proof to the skeptic is not a legitimate means of defending otherwise untenable hypotheses. Second, when contrasted with claims about ESP (discussed in chapter four), these cases show how most incorrect ideas in science are handled. Finally, they show that, under some circumstances, scientists who become strongly attached to a particular claim will resort to some of the same techniques used by proponents of pseudoscientific claims, such as nonfalsifiable hypotheses. The following discussion of N-rays is based on the excellent articles by Klotz (1980) and Nye (1980). The discussion of polywater is based on the book by Franks (1981). The reader should refer to these sources for much more detail on these fascinating episodes in the history of science.

René Blondlot (1849-1930) bears the dubious distinction of being the "discoverer" of N-rays. Blondlot was an outstanding physicist at the University of Nancy in France. He made many important contributions to physics in the late 1800s. The late 1800s and early 1900s were an exciting time in physics. In 1895, X-rays had been discovered and in the next few years other types of radiation were found: alpha, beta, and gamma rays. Thus, as Klotz (1980, p. 168) points out, when Blondlot made known his discovery of N-rays (named after the University of Nancy) in 1903, physics was "psychologically prepared" for the discovery of another new type of radiation. Such a discovery had, at the time, ample precedent, a precedent that it would have lacked even ten years previously.

One of the properties of N-rays that Blondlot reported in his 1903 paper was that they increased the brightness of an electric spark. Blondlot used subjective judgments of spark brightness as a measure of the presence of N-rays in later experiments. No instruments were used that could have given objective measures of brightness. Blondlot's reputation in physics was such that, once he had reported N-rays, other physicists rushed to study this new phenomenon. In the next few years a stream of papers appeared, largely from other French laboratories, confirming that N-rays did, in fact, exist and detailing additional properties. Blondlot's own laboratory, as might be expected, led the research effort. By this time, Blondlot had adopted a new method for determining the presence of N-rays. A screen was painted with a chemical that became more luminous when N-rays were projected onto it. Again, the judgments of luminosity were purely subjective; Blondlot even specified that observers should "not look directly at the screen" (Nye, 1980, p. 132), but observe it out of the corner of their eye.

In the course of further investigation, it was found that the sun, flames, and incandescent objects were all sources of N-rays. Another French investigator, Auguste Charpentier, found that the human nervous system emitted N-rays, and this finding was soon "confirmed" in Blondlot's laboratory. Further, when a portion of the nervous system was active, that portion was said to emit more N-rays. Blondlot also discovered "secondary" sources of N-rays. These were sources that absorbed N-rays and then re-emitted them. The fluids of the human eye were alleged to be such secondary sources and, amazingly, when the eye was exposed to N-rays, it became more sensitive to dim illumination. Text that could not ordinarily be read in dim light could be read after the eye was exposed to N-rays.

Here, then, was an important new phenomenon, confirmed by dozens of independent studies in many different laboratories, many of the studies conducted by well-known and highly respected scientists.

Other physicists, especially those working outside France, were skeptical about the existence of N-rays. They objected to the conclusions of Blondlot and others who based their results on subjective judgments of brightness. Such judgments are liable to be influenced by the observer's beliefs and so are poor sources of data. One experiment allegedly showing that N-rays increased visual sensitivity was faulted as being due to nothing more than dark adaptation—the phenomenon that accounts for the increase in ability to see in dark rooms the longer one spends in such a room. More devastating to the claims about N-rays was the failure of other physicists outside France to repeat Blondlot's results. These failures were most striking when objective as opposed to subjective measures of brightness were used. Nye (1980) chronicles the numerous failures to replicate Blondlot's results in the few years following his initial report.

One of the most telling pieces of evidence against the existence of N-rays came in 1904 when American physicist Robert W. Wood decided to visit Blondlot's laboratory to see for himself whether Blondlot's experiments were valid. Wood was an extraordinary man, with many interests outside physics (Seabrook, 1941). One of his interests was exposing fraudulent spiritualist mediums; Wood's experiences in this endeavor must have helped him when he came to evaluate Blondlot's N-ray experiments.

Blondlot had found that N-rays were blocked by lead. Wood observed demonstrations of N-ray effects in Blondlot's laboratory and concluded, as had other critics, that the reported changes in brightness that Blondlot used to argue for the reality of N-rays were figments of Blondlot's imagination and a result of his desire to validate the existence of N-rays. N-ray experiments had to be carried out in a darkened laboratory, so the changes in brightness due to the rays' presence could be observed. This gave Wood an opportunity to make several observations that proved Blondlot's judgments of brightness changes were a function of his beliefs, and not of the presence or absence of N-rays. In one experiment, Wood was to block an N-ray source by inserting a sheet of lead between the source and a card with luminous paint on it. Blondlot, acting as observer, made judgments about the paint's brightness and, therefore, about the presence or absence of N-rays. Without telling Blondlot, Wood changed the experiment in one slight but vitally important way. He would indicate to Blondlot that the lead sheet was blocking the N-ray source when it really wasn't, or vice versa. If N-rays really existed, Blondlot's judgments of the brightness of the luminous paint should be a function of whether the lead screen really was between the card and the N-ray source and should have no relationship to whether or not he believed the sheet was blocking the source. In fact, Wood found that Blondlot's judgments depended on whether he believed the screen to be present or not. For example, if he believed the screen was present (blocking N-rays), but it wasn't, he reported the paint to be less luminous. If he was told the screen was not present (allowing N-rays to pass), but it really was, he reported the paint to be more luminous.

Similarly, in two other situations, Wood showed Blondlot's subjective brightness judgments to be a function of his belief. Blondlot had claimed that an aluminum prism would produce a spectrum of N-rays of different wavelengths, just as a prism produces a spectrum of visible light of different wavelengths. Wood found he could remove the aluminum prism from the path of the N-rays without interfering with Blondlot's ability to see the N-ray spectrum. Later, when Blondlot's laboratory assistant became suspicious of Wood, Wood pretended to move the prism, while leaving it in place. This caused the assistant to report that the N-ray spectrum was not present. Finally, Wood performed a similar substitution in an experiment designed to show that N-rays increased visual sensitivity in dim light. An N-ray source was placed near a subject's eyes. The "subject of the experiment assured Wood that the hands of a clock, which were normally not clearly visible to him, became brighter and much more distinct" (Klotz, 1980, p. 174) when the N-ray source was held near. Wood then replaced the N-ray source with a similarly shaped piece of wood, a substance that was not an N-ray source. Nonetheless, as long as the subject was unaware of the switch, he continued to report that objects were brighter and more distinct when the piece of wood, which he believed to be an N-ray source, was close to his eyes.

Wood's report, published in the British journal *Nature* in 1904, along with the failures of other laboratories to verify the existence of N-rays, led to the conclusion that N-rays do not exist. No further papers appeared on the topic after about 1907. Only Blondlot, convinced until the end that N-rays were real, pursued his research on the topic until he died in 1930.

At the height of the debate over the existence of N-rays, proponents adopted a nonfalsifiable hypothesis to account for critics' inability to observe the rays: The critics' eyes weren't sensitive enough. When Wood initially told Blondlot that he couldn't see any brightness difference on a screen when the rays were or were not present, he was told "that was because my eyes were not sensitive enough, so that proved nothing" (Seabrook, 1941, p. 238). Years later, one of the early proponents of N-rays made a similar point: "If an observer (who is not convinced) sees nothing, you conclude that he does not have sensitive eyes" (Becquerel, 1934, cited in Nye, 1980, p. 153).

It is vital to note that Blondlot and the other proponents of N-rays were not lying when they reported that they saw a brighter spark or luminous screen when they believed that N-rays were present. Sparks and luminous screens vary in brightness from moment to moment for several reasons. Random changes in brightness that confirm an observer's belief are much more likely to be noted than those that go against the belief. Numerous similar instances where a belief can profoundly change the way in which someone perceives a stimulus will be noted throughout this book.

The case of N-rays also illustrates how science handles the burden of proof. (Compare this to the discussion of academic studies of ESP in chapter four.) Assume that someone wished to argue, today, that N-rays really do exist. To bolster the case, he goes back to the physics journals of 1903-1907 and assembles all the papers that argued that N-rays are real. The proponent then challenges the skeptic to explain in detail what was wrong in each of the published papers favorable to the existence of N-rays. Could the skeptic meet this challenge? Certainly not—there is simply not sufficient detail in the papers to pinpoint precisely what led the author to mistakenly conclude that N-rays exist.

Does the fact that the skeptic cannot pinpoint the methodological errors in each and every experiment supporting the existence of N-rays mean that the existence of the rays should be accepted? Of course not. The general explanation for the favorable results—such as reliance on subjective measures—along with the failure of well-designed studies to validate the existence of N-rays is more than enough to justify the conclusion that N-rays do not exist. Unlike proponents of pseudoscientific claims, science places the burden of proof on the individuals who make extraordinary claims. Blondlot and his colleagues failed to provide valid evidence for the existence of N-rays.

Polywater, initially known as anomalous water, was "discovered" in the early 1960s by a Russian scientist named Fedyakin, working at a laboratory about one hundred miles from Moscow. This form of water had several extremely strange qualities. It boiled at a temperature well above water's normal boiling point and froze at a point well below water's normal freezing point. Further, polywater was said to be a more stable form of the H_2O molecule. This led to at least one scientist making the dire prediction that, if even the smallest amount of polywater was allowed to contaminate natural water supplies, natural water molecules would spontaneously change into the more stable polywater form, thus ending all life on earth due to the radically different characteristics of polywater. (Readers familiar with the work of Kurt Vonnegut, Jr., will recognize at once the similarity between polywater and the mythical substance "ice nine" created in Vonnegut's story "Cat's Cradle.")

Russian research on polywater quickly moved from the provinces to a prestigious laboratory in Moscow. At first polywater attracted little attention in western scientific circles. However, when it did, there was an explosion of papers on the topic in numerous scientific journals. Between 1962 and 1975 several hundred papers on polywater appeared.

For various technical reasons, polywater could be produced only in minute quantities inside sealed glass tubes with equally minute diameters. The debate over the existence of polywater turned on one crucial point— whether the water produced in these tubes was pure H_2O, or whether it was impure, the impurities leaching out of the glass and changing the properties of the pure water. Proponents of polywater claimed they had produced pure polywater, with no impurities. That is, the substance was pure H_2O in a new and different molecular configuration. Skeptics who tried to produce polywater in their laboratories consistently ended up with nothing more than impure water of the normal molecular configuration. The proponents responded, as might be expected, that the reason the skeptics couldn't produce true polywater was that they hadn't learned how to do it just right. While such a rejoinder was appropriate at first, it quickly became little more than a nonfalsifiable hypothesis that proponents used to explain away every failure by the skeptics to produce "true" polywater.

As the 1960s faded into the 1970s, it became clear that polywater did not exist and claims for its reality were, in fact, based on impure water, as the skeptics had argued from the first. By the mid 1970s, polywater was a dead issue.

The similarities between the N-ray and polywater episodes are instructive. One striking similarity was the use by proponents of both phenomena of nonfalsifiable hypotheses in the defense of their claims. Thus, such techniques for defending untenable claims are not limited to pseudosciences and the paranormal. They appear in legitimate science in those—happily rather rare—situations where commitment to the reality of a certain phenomenon is stronger than the data on which that commitment is based. The much more common use of nonfalsifiable hypotheses in pseudosciences and the paranormal is due simply to the near-total lack of real phenomena in these areas to begin with.

As was the case with N-rays, it would probably be impossible to pinpoint the exact procedural errors made in every experiment that seemed to produce evidence of polywater. We know, of course, the general nature of the errors made, but that is different than an exact explanation for every case on record. However, as in the case of N-rays (and as will be noted again in the chapters on UFOs and ESP), it is not necessary for the skeptic to explain away every seemingly positive instance of a claimed phenomenon before rejecting the phenomenon. In the polywater case, as well as in the case of N-rays, the total failure of careful experimentation to turn up evidence for the reality of the phenomenon, combined with a general explanation for what went wrong, was more than sufficient for scientists to reject the existence of the phenomenon.

The same principle of rejecting a finding even if no scientific flaw can be found in the experiment, on the ground that the result cannot be replicated, is universal in science. Science is littered with experiments reporting some particular result that, upon later attempts, fails to replicate.

A personal example makes the point. My master's thesis (Hines, 1976) examined a particular question in the field of hemispheric asymmetries in the human brain. In one of the experiments, I obtained the results that I expected. I was quite excited by this, considering that two other experiments in the thesis had failed to provide the results I strongly expected. I went ahead and wrote the thesis. Then I went back and tried to replicate the findings. Two replications failed. To this day I have no idea why the initial experiment succeeded in providing the anticipated results. However, the two failures to replicate, along with similar failures that were later reported in the literature, convinced me that the initial, positive result was incorrect.

Why Study Pseudoscientific Claims?

The serious examination of pseudoscientific and paranormal claims by scientists and scholars who are skeptical about the existence of such phenomena is not a recent development. In the late nineteenth and early twentieth centuries the claims of spiritualists were carefully scrutinized by several scientists (see chapter two). A new interest in evaluating pseudoscientific claims arose during the early 1970s as scientists and educators became concerned with the uncritical acceptance by the public of almost every type of pseudoscientific claim. This resulted in the formation in 1976 of the Committee for the Scientific Investigation of Claims of the Paranormal (CSICOP). The members of CSICOP, including scientists, writers, educators, journalists, and philosophers, founded the organization because of the concern about the "uncritical acceptance by wide sections of the public of many claims of 'paranormal' phenomena as true, even without testing" (Kurtz, 1976-77, p. 6). The objectives of CSICOP include critical, nonbiased, objective research into pseudoscientific claims, the publication of the results of these studies, and a commitment not "to reject on a priori grounds, antecedent to inquiry, any or all (paranormal) claims, but rather to examine them openly, completely, objectively, and carefully" (Kurtz, 1976-77, p. 6).

This is very different from the usual approach of scientists and scholars, whose typical response to pseudoscientific claims is simply to dismiss them as nonsense. This latter is a most unfortunate attitude. It is important to examine these claims objectively for at least four reasons. First, the claim may, in fact, be true. Failure to examine it would then delay the acquisition of new, perhaps important, knowledge. Second, if the claim is false, the scientific community, which is heavily supported by the public through taxes, has a responsibility to inform the public. Ignoring a claim and not testing it leaves the field to the promoters of such claims and deprives the public of the information needed to make informed choices. Third, several important psychological issues relate to the study of pseudoscience and the paranormal. Why, for example, do people so strongly believe in theories that not only have no evidence to support them but also have been shown time and again to be flat wrong? Fourth, and finally, the unthinking acceptance of pseudoscientific claims poses real dangers. Believers may act on their beliefs and cause physical harm, even death, to themselves and others. In addition, as our society becomes more dependent on science and technology, we are all threatened by an increase in the uncritical acceptance of clearly incorrect nonscientific superstitions and related beliefs. The rest of this section will consider in detail these reasons for the study of pseudoscientific claims.

The claims might be true

There are several examples in the history of science of phenomena that were once considered to be pseudoscientific or paranormal in nature but were eventually shown to be real, verifiable phenomena of considerable theoretical and practical interest and importance. Perhaps the best example is hypnotism. Hypnotism was first called "mesmerism" after the Viennese physician Franz Anton Mesmer who popularized it in the 1700s. For about one hundred and fifty years hypnotism was generally considered to be a paranormal phenomenon and was therefore ignored by establishment science and medicine. It gained some respectability in the late nineteenth century through its use in psychotherapy. In the twentieth century, especially in the recent decades, the scientific study of hypnosis has expanded greatly. In fact, there are now several journals and many books devoted to the topic. (For a review, see Hilgard, 1977.) As is frequently the case when a pseudoscientific phenomenon is studied carefully and shown to represent a real phenomenon, some initial claims for the phenomenon are found to have been overstated. This is certainly the case with hypnosis, as will be seen in chapter eight. The point here, however, is that there is a true hypnotic phenomenon that is well deserving of study.

A second example of a phenomenon once scorned but then studied and confirmed scientifically is the case of meteorites. "Stones falling from the skies? Absurd! Ridiculous!" was the common attitude well into the eighteenth century. Hall (1972) has pointed out that reports of stones falling from the skies were treated by the scientific community of the day with much the same contempt that is now reserved for reports of UFOs. And yet, meteorites are clearly real. Might UFOs be real, too? To find out, one has to study the phenomenon, not just dogmatically insist that it is "impossible."

A final example is acupuncture, the ancient Chinese technique for reducing pain that gained considerable western attention after then-President Nixon renewed relations between the United States and the People's Republic of China in the early 1970s. The first reports of this technique certainly sounded unlikely—after all, how could sticking needles in someone reduce the perception of pain? However, experimental work since the early 1970s has established that acupuncture for the relief of pain is a real phenomenon, although, again, initial reports of its effectiveness were rather exaggerated. By now, much is known about the physiology of acupuncture. Briefly, for reasons as yet unknown, acupuncture causes the release of endorphins, substances produced by the brain that cause, among other effects, a reduction in pain sensitivity (Han and Terenius, 1982). Liebskeind (1976) has shown that endorphins reduce pain sensitivity by modulating the firing rate of pain-sensitive neurons in the spinal cord, slowing the rate of firing in response to painful stimuli. Endorphins may also be released under various stressful and emotional conditions (Watkins and Mayer, 1982); the attendant pain reduction may account for some seemingly miraculous effects that will be discussed in chapter ten.

In all of these examples, phenomena that were initially considered to be pseudoscientific and unworthy of study have been shown to be real. These cases alone would justify the study of other pseudoscientific and paranormal phenomena, although it must be realized that the "hit rate" in this type of endeavor is very low. Of the numerous paranormal claims considered in the remainder of this book, the vast majority will be found to have no scientific support.

Responsibility to inform the public about the truth of paranormal claims

A glance at the occult books section in any moderately large bookstore is all that is needed to convince one of the huge market for pseudoscientific and paranormal claims in this country. A 1975 Gallup poll (Culver and Ianna, 1984) revealed that 15 percent of Americans believed in astrology. *Linda Goodman's Love Signs*, a book claiming to predict sexual attraction and compatibility through astrology, was on *The New York Times* bestseller list for months when it was published in 1982. Every kind of pseudoscientific claim finds eager buyers. Psychics, palm readers, tarot card readers, mediums, and the like rarely lack for victims willing to shell out fifteen, twenty-five, or even one thousand dollars for a reading. Those claiming that the earth has been visited in historical times by ancient astronauts, or that there is a mysterious area off Florida's east coast where ships and planes have disappeared, or that they can bend keys with sheer mind power make millions from books, films, and the lecture circuit. In short, the public spends a lot of time and money supporting the proponents of pseudoscience and the paranormal. As will be seen in the following chapters, there is not one bit of evidence to support these pseudoscientific claims, and much evidence exists that flatly contradicts them. This being the case, the continued claims by proponents of pseudoscience constitute nothing short of consumer fraud. And it is a massive fraud that costs the American public billions of dollars each year. In this situation, scientists have a strong responsibility to investigate pseudoscientific claims and to speak out vigorously when those claims are shown to be false. Unfortunately, communication of the real data on the truth of pseudoscientific claims is often hampered by the media. Television and radio programs and newspapers are frequently more interested in presenting sensational claims than in carefully evaluating the truth of such claims. The media, both print and electronic, have often acted with extreme irresponsibility in covering pseudoscience and the paranormal. In the case of uncritical coverage of faith healers and psychic surgeons, this lack of responsibility on the part of the media has resulted in injury and death.

The case for speaking out is even clearer in the case of modern health and nutrition quackery, which is a $10 billion a year problem in the United States (Pepper, 1984). The quacks' and charlatans' victims are most likely to be those least able to defend themselves—the desperate, the elderly, the poor.

Only through careful evaluation of pseudoscientific claims and seeing that the results of those evaluations are reported by the popular media can the public be fully informed. The proponents of pseudoscience and the paranormal, who make vast sums of money selling their wares, are unlikely to provide the public with accurate information. Scientists, then, have a responsibility to inform the public.

Psychological issues

Ethical issues aside, several important psychological issues are raised by the study of pseudoscience and the paranormal and people's belief in them. The major issue is why people come to believe in such claims in the first place. What is it that convinces them, for example, that astrology is a valid way to guide their lives? Or that biorhythms really predict when they are most likely to do well or badly on an exam? Second, why do these beliefs persist so strongly in the face of clearly contradictory evidence? The answers to these questions will be discussed throughout the remainder of this book. Suffice it to say here that research on perception and especially memory has demonstrated the importance of cognitive illusions that are in many ways analogous to visual illusions. These cognitive illusions provide the basis for both initial and continued belief in pseudoscientific and paranormal claims, although other factors, also to be discussed, are important.

Dangers of paranormal beliefs

Skeptics are often asked, "Who cares if there really isn't anything to astrology? What does it hurt if someone believes in it?" I've found that this question is frequently asked by proponents of pseudoscientific claims when they have been backed into a corner by the evidence. The answer can be made at three levels. At a philosophical level, most people would agree that it is harmful to hold invalid beliefs and that, generally speaking, one should base one's life on a correct view of how the world operates.

To do otherwise is to be deluded. On a more practical and personal level, one can consider pseudoscientific and paranormal claims in the context of consumer fraud. People are being induced through false claims to spend their money—often large sums—on paranormal claims that do not deliver what they promise. Presumably no one would ask, "What's the harm if the label says the cereal box contains sixteen ounces but it really only contains thirteen ounces?" The situation is the same for paranormal claims except that the box is empty. The personal damage done by uncritical acceptance of paranormal claims can be most clearly seen in faith healing and psychic surgery (see chapter ten). People go to these fraudulent healers and often are convinced, incorrectly, that they have been cured. Thus, they may not seek legitimate medical help. By the time they realize that they have not, in fact, been cured, they may be beyond even medical help. Nolen (1974) has documented such cases. Of all the proponents of pseudoscience, faith healers and psychic surgeons are the most dangerous—they kill people.

Finally, from the point of view of society at large, uncritical acceptance of paranormal belief systems can be extremely damaging. The classic example is the witchcraft craze that swept Europe between approximately the middle of the fourteenth and the start of the eighteenth centuries. During that period, well over two hundred thousand people were burned, tortured, or hanged as witches (Robbins, 1959). The belief in the reality of witches is a classic example of a paranormal belief. It shared many characteristics with modern-day paranormal belief systems. We will see, for example, in chapters seven and eight that proponents of the reality of UFOs as extraterrestrial spacecraft argue that some of the strongest evidence for the reality of UFOs is the many reports of UFOs that have been seen and reported by reliable, trained, sane observers. Yet even a short perusal of the literature on witchcraft will reveal hundreds of similar reports of witches turned in by reliable, trustworthy witnesses. Of course, not one of these reports was true.

Another similarity between the belief in witchcraft and the belief in numerous modern pseudoscientific claims is the presence of an irrefutable hypothesis as a cornerstone of the belief system. For the poor individual accused of being a witch, the irrefutable hypothesis spelled a slow and lingering death. There was no possible piece of evidence that could show that the accused was not a witch. Once an accusation was made, no matter how flimsy the grounds for it, the accused was arrested. At this point, the accused was asked to confess to the charges. If the confession was not made, the accused was tortured. If a confession was still not made, the torture continued. Johannes Junius, the burgomaster of Bamberg, made this point in his last letter to his daughter before he was executed as a witch in August, 1628. He described the several days of torture he endured without confessing and then says, "When at last the executioner led me back into the cell, he said to me, 'Sir, I beg you, confess something, whether it be true or not. Invent something, for you cannot endure the torture which you will be put to; and even if you bear it all, yet you will not escape, not even if you were an earl, but one torture will follow another until you say you are a witch'" (Robbins, 1959, pp. 292-93). There was no way out. If one confessed without torture to being a witch, one was executed. If one did not confess at once, one was tortured until one did and was then executed. If one confessed and later recanted the confession, the torture started anew. To make matters worse for the accused, who might be willing to confess at once simply to escape torture, one was asked to name acquaintances who had engaged in witchcraft. If names were not forthcoming, they were extracted, again, under torture. These other individuals were then rounded up and tortured into confessing and naming still more "witches," and so the horrible cycle went on.

The witch delusion also provides what is presumably one of the first reported cases of "special pleading" for a pseudoscientific claim. Proponents of pseudoscience often claim that the usual rules of science are too strict (tacitly admitting that their evidence is scientifically inadequate to prove their claims) and that less stringent criteria of proof should be allowed for this or that pseudoscientific claim. In this vein, Robbins (1959, pp. 3-4) notes a "distinguished professor of law at the University of Toulouse [who] advocates the suspension of rules in witch trials, because 'not one out of a million witches would be accused or punished, if regular legal procedure were followed.'"

An even more terrible pseudoscience, the phony racial theories of the Nazis, has in the twentieth century resulted in loss of life on a scale vastly greater than that caused by the witchcraft delusion. Although the role of the occult, per se, in the rise of Nazism has been overestimated, it is clear that the racial theories upon which Hitler built the Holocaust were pure pseudoscience.

Another commonly heard defense of paranormal claims goes like this: "Reality is relative. If I decide to believe in astrology, then it becomes real in my own reality and works for me." In other words, belief determines the structure of reality. An extreme version of this rather silly position is held by many parapsychologists who try to explain their critics' repeated failures to find any evidence confirming the existence of ESP by saying that the critics don't believe the phenomenon to be real and, therefore, for the critics, it isn't. We'll see in chapter four that a much better explanation is that the critics conduct better, more tightly controlled experiments than do the believers. In any event, this position that belief determines reality puts its proponents in a rather unpleasant position. In Nazi Germany millions of people really believed that Jews were sub-human. If belief determines reality, then this belief must really have been true. This is an absurd position and those who hold that belief determines reality have never bothered to think their notion through to the repellent consequences of its logical conclusions. The point is that truth is independent of belief. When the proponents of a pseudoscientific claim maintain that belief determines reality, it's a safe bet that they can't prove their point using legitimate rules of evidence.

The examples of the witch delusion and the Nazi horrors show the great damage done by the uncritical acceptance of pseudoscientific claims. Both might well have been avoided if the public had been educated in critical scientific thinking and had simply asked, "What evidence is there that what you are telling me is really true?"

Of course, not all pseudosciences have the vast potential for damage of the witch mania and the Nazi racial theories. However, if one accepts faulty evidence, intellectual shoddiness and fraud, and twisted logic in the case of relatively benign pseudosciences, it will be much easier to accept the same type of evidence when it is presented in support of much more damaging pseudosciences.

2

Psychics and Psychic Phenomena

The term "psychic phenomena" conjures up an image of Jeane Dixon fore-telling the future with great accuracy, of a psychic crime fighter leading police straight to where a body has been hidden, of a spiritualistic medium contacting the dead and relaying to the living information only the dead could have known, of an ordinary individual having a dream that later turns out to have correctly predicted an important event. This chapter will discuss the origins of spiritualism and examine contemporary claims for such phenomena. (The somewhat more scientifically respectable study of ESP, clairvoyance, and psychokinesis in parapsychological laboratories will be discussed in chapter four. Chapter four will also discuss the well-known psychic Uri Geller, as his alleged abilities have been extensively tested in parapsychological laboratories. That Geller could equally well have been discussed in the present chapter points up the often fuzzy distinction between spectacular psychic claims and laboratory parapsychology.)

Spiritualism

Scientific investigation of alleged psychic phenomena began in the mid-1800s as a result of the worldwide interest in spiritualism. Spiritualism was born in 1848 in a small New York town south of Buffalo. Two sisters, Kate and Margaret Fox (eleven and thirteen years old respectively), produced strange knocks and rapping in their home which were interpreted as messages from the dead. The effects were produced by various simple tricks, as the sisters later admitted (Kurtz, 1985b; Brandon, 1983). An older sister took the young girls on tour, and a nationwide interest in spiritualism and communication with the dead sprang up in their wake. This interest quickly spread overseas. As the interest in spiritualism grew, so did the number of spiritualistic mediums, individuals who claimed to be able to contact the spirit world and communicate with the dead. Mediums could be found in every city.

Communication with the dead took place at a seance, in which the medium and "sitters" would hold hands while seated around a table in the dark. Various phenomena occurred during the seance, varying from rather mundane rappings and knockings through table tipping (in which the table seemed to move of its own accord) up to the most spectacular seances where "ectoplasm" would flow from the medium's body, "actual spirits" would appear, and objects would materialize out of thin air, presumably "apported" from the spirit world. Photographs of disembodied spirits floating near the medium were also produced in some quantity. It was these sorts of phenomena that convinced so many people of the truth of spiritualists' claims and of the reality of communication with the dead.

The rage for spiritualism attracted the attention of some of the period's leading scientists. Most were highly skeptical and critical of spiritualism, but several attended seances and came away convinced of the reality of spiritualistic phenomena. A few then instituted often impressive studies of individual spiritualists which, they claimed, gave solid scientific support to the claims of spiritualism. This type of research and interest led in 1882 to the founding in England of the Society for Psychical Research (SPR). The goal of the SPR was scientific investigation of spiritualistic and other "psychic" phenomena. As such, it represented an alliance between the spiritualists and the small portion of the scientific community that accepted their claims. As time passed, however, the alliance weakened and finally, later in the 1880s, split. The split came about not because of doubt on the part of the scientists who belonged to the SPR, but because of a fundamental difference with spiritualists over the correct interpretation of the phenomena that took place at seances (Cerello, 1982). The spiritualists felt that these phenomena proved the existence of an afterlife and the reality of the individual soul, and demonstrated that they were in communication with the dead. For the spiritualists, these claims did not have any particular religious implications— and hence spiritualists were attacked as vehemently by organized religion as by organized science, perhaps more so. Their claims, however, were still too nonmaterialistic for many of the scientists in the SPR. As Cerello (1982) points out in his excellent history of the development of psychical research in Britain during this period, the SPR came more and more to interpret spiritualistic phenomena in terms of telepathy (what would now be termed ESP) and psychokinesis (PK). Thus, if a medium told someone at a seance something that medium could not have known through normal channels, she (most mediums were female) was not getting the information from the spirits of the dead, but rather through her own power of ESP. Similarly, when an object was apported during a seance, it was not being transported from the "other side" by spirits, but was being moved by the medium through PK. This latter explanation for spiritualistic phenomena prevailed in the SPR, and is still accepted in parapsychological research to this day. Thus, these phenomena constitute the first pieces of evidence for the reality of paranormal claims. It is the nature of that evidence that will be considered here.

The debate over the validity of spiritualistic phenomena, however they were interpreted, raged well into the early twentieth century. Some of the most famous names in science, literature and the arts were involved, including Michael Faraday, discoverer of electromagnetism, Sir Arthur Conan Doyle, and magician Harry Houdini. Brandon (1983) has written an excellent account of the history of spiritualism and the debate surrounding it. (Modern spiritualists, who still exist and who still claim to be in communication with the dead, will be considered later in this book.) Much of the material in the following sections is drawn from Ray Hyman's (1985a) "A Critical Historical Overview of Parapsychology."

Probably the most famous scientist to become involved in the investigation of spiritualistic phenomena was Michael Faraday. Faraday investigated table moving, which was frequently observed at seances. The table at which the seance was held, and on which the sitters rested their hands, would move about, seemingly under its own power. When the seance was conducted by a professional medium, it was easy to attribute the movement to conscious shoving of the table by the medium—one of many types of cheating practiced by mediums. What made table movement so convincing and fascinating, however, was that it commonly took place at informal, private seances where only a group of friends was in attendance and cheating could usually be ruled out. It was even possible for a single individual to sit at a table and have it move about—yet the individual would swear that no conscious attempt had been made to move the table.

The key word here is "conscious." Through several ingenious experiments, Faraday (1853, cited in Hyman, 1985a) demonstrated that the movement of the table was due to consciously imperceptible muscle exertions on the part of sitters. After satisfying himself that the table movements were not due to any type of electromagnetic forces, Faraday constructed special tables that would reveal unconscious muscle exertions. Hyman (1985a, p. 10) describes one such experiment, in which Faraday

> placed four or five pieces of slippery cardboard, one over the other, on the table top. The pieces were attached to one another by little pellets of a soft cement. The lowest piece was attached to a piece of sandpaper that rested on the table top. The edges of the sheets overlapped slightly, and on the under surface Faraday drew a pencil line to indicate the position. The table turner then placed his hands upon the upper card and waited for the table to move in the previously agreed upon direction (to the left).

When the sheets of cardboard were examined after the table movement, it was found that the top sheet had moved to the left relative to the sheets under it. This indicated that the movement was caused by the hands pushing on the table. If the table had moved to the left of its own accord, the top sheet would have moved to the *right* relative to the lower sheets, as the table dragged the hand along with it.

Faraday also demonstrated that, when a feedback device was arranged that showed the subject he was exerting a force to make the table move, the table promptly ceased to move "of its own accord."

Unconscious muscle movements are also responsible for another spiritualistic phenomenon, the Ouija board. This is a board marked with the letters of the alphabet and special "yes" and "no" locations. Users put their hands on a planchette that is supposedly guided by the spirits around the board to spell out answers to questions. In fact, the planchette is guided by unconscious muscular exertions like those responsible for table movement. Nonetheless, in both cases, the illusion that the object (table or planchette) is moving under its own control is often extremely powerful and sufficient to convince many people that spirits are truly at work. Such unconscious muscular movements are also responsible for dowsing (water witching), as explained in chapter twelve.

The unconscious muscle movements responsible for the moving tables and Ouija board phenomena seen at seances are examples of a class of phenomena due to what psychologists call a *dissociative state*. A dissociative state is one in which consciousness is somehow divided or cut off from some aspects of the individual's normal cognitive, motor, or sensory functions. These states can be found in differing degrees of severity and underlie such nonparanormal phenomena as hypnosis, hysterical disorders, and the rare psychiatric disorder of split or multiple personalities. The dissociative state also explains several other impressive phenomena associated with the seance.

Many, probably the vast majority, of mediums were out-and-out frauds who faked everything associated with their seances, including the trance that they entered to contact the spirits of the dead. Some mediums, however, experienced genuine trances. During such a trance, the medium is in a dissociative state. Other "personalities" emerge and take control of the medium's body. These other personalities are interpreted, by both the medium and the sitters at the seance, as genuine manifestations of spirit control. Viewing a medium in a genuine trance state is compelling. The medium's voice may change dramatically as different "spirits" take control. The medium's facial expression may also change. It is obvious that *something* is happening in such situations. The important question as far as paranormal claims are concerned is whether whatever is going on provides evidence for the paranormal. The answer is no. Mediums who experienced genuine dissociative trance states were no better able to provide valid proof of their contact with the dead than were other mediums. If the true dissociative state did put the medium into contact with the dead, one would expect the spirits of the dead to be able to provide evidence of their identity. While the spirits often claimed to be famous people, they were unable to provide evidence to support such claims.

The case of one famous medium clearly shows the close association between the dissociative state found in the psychiatric disorder of split personality and that found in the mediumistic trance. This is the case of Hélène Smith (for additional details, see Zusne and Jones, 1982), a French medium who was active near the turn of the century. Smith had numerous spirit guides who took over her body while she was in a trance. One of her most famous guides was the "spirit" of someone who could not possibly have existed. For a considerable period, she was said to be under the control of the spirit of a dead Martian. When this Martian was in control, she would speak and write in "Martian" and produce drawings of Martian landscapes.

The Hélène Smith case illustrates two important points. First, there is a striking similarity between the behavior of a medium in a true trance state and the individual with multiple personalities. In the latter, more than one personality is found in the same body. One personality will be in control at one time, while another personality will emerge to take control at other times. There may be several different personalities and they may be strikingly different in their moods, temperaments, and interests. Some of the personalities may not be aware of the others, while some will be aware that others exist. Individuals suffering from the disorder do not have to go into a trance for the different personalities to emerge.

The second point illustrated by the Smith case is that other manifestations of the dissociative state exist than simply speaking as if a different personality is in control. Smith also wrote while in her trances, allegedly under the guidance of the spirit control. This is known as automatic writing; it can be produced by some individuals who are not in a trance state. The arm, in such individuals, seems to write "on its own" and it is easy to understand how the feeling could develop that the arm was "possessed," perhaps by a spirit of the dead. In fact, automatic writing is an example of a milder form of dissociative state.

Phenomena that took place at seances run by professional mediums were sometimes extremely spectacular and were not so easily put to the test as table moving. For example, Alfred Russel Wallace, a co-discoverer with Darwin of the principle of natural selection, reported (Wallace, 1878, quoted in Hyman, 1985, p. 20) that at a seance he attended with five close friends, the entire seance table became covered with "fresh flowers and ferns" while the sitters carefully watched. The flora appeared from nowhere, and "the first thing that struck us all was their extreme freshness and beauty. The next that they were all covered, especially the ferns, with a delicate dew." Clearly, unconscious muscular exertions will not do as an explanation here. Thousands of other individuals were deeply affected by similar spectacular personal experiences with mediums that convinced them beyond any doubt that spiritualism was real.

One prominent scientist who was convinced of the reality of spiritualistic phenomena on the basis of the events he observed at seances was the American chemist Robert Hare. To further test the reality of spirit communication, Hare designed an experiment in which tipping and movement of a table at which a medium sat caused a pointer to indicate letters on a wheel that was out of sight of the medium. Hare would ask the medium questions, the table would move, and the answer to the questions would be spelled out. The results were very impressive, as shown in the following quotation from Hyman's (1985a) description of Hare's experiment, reported first in Hare (1855):

> Hare then began by asking if any spirits were present to indicate so by causing the letter Y to be under the pointer. Immediately the pointer moved to the letter Y. Hare next asked, "Will the spirit do us the favor to give the initials of his name?" The index pointed first to R and next to H. Hare immediately asked, "My honoured father?" The index pointed to Y. After a few more tests such as these, the onlookers urged that Hare admit the reality of spiritual agency. Hare must have still shown some hesitation, because the index spelled out, "Oh, my son, listen to reason!"

This type of report seems convincing. Highly trained scientists, some conducting complex experiments that seemed to verify their initial impressions, concluded that spirit communication was real. The evidential value of these impressions and experiments is destroyed, however, when it is revealed that mediums accomplished their seeming miracles by cheating and using magic and sleight of hand at every possible opportunity.

Remember that the reports of what occurred at seances—the reports that convinced so many of the reality of spiritualist phenomena—were eyewitness testimony. Such testimony is unreliable even when the object of the testimony is not making conscious and skillful efforts to deceive, mislead, and distract witnesses from what is really taking place. Of course, mediums were doing just that, so eyewitness reports of what happened at seances, given by individuals totally unfamiliar with the deceptive techniques used, are even less reliable than most eyewitness reports.

The literature on spiritualism is replete with stories of mediums being caught "red handed" during a seance, cheating to produce some wonder or another. One of the greatest exposers of mediumistic fraud was the famous magician and escape artist Harry Houdini who wrote of his experiences in his classic 1924 book, *A Magician Among the Spirits*. Here Houdini described in detail the methods used by many mediums. Brandon (1983) and Dunninger (1967) also describe some of the techniques that have been used by mediums to produce their effects.

Houdini deserves special mention here. Perhaps more than any other single person, he was responsible for the decline in public acceptance of spiritualistic claims. The public recognized both his name and his expertise as a magician and uncoverer of fraudulent mediums. That he never found a single genuine medium was very powerful evidence against spiritualism. Houdini himself was a skeptic who badly wanted to be able to believe, but the constant string of frauds he saw prevented him from doing so. His desire was to communicate with the spirit of his mother, whom he loved (Brandon, 1983). Even in death, Houdini continued to expose the sham of spiritualism. He died suddenly in 1926 at the age of 52. Houdini had arranged a secret code with his wife that he would transmit from the spirit world. If she received it, this would prove that the medium giving the code was truly in contact with Houdini's spirit. In spite of years of searching, no medium was ever able to give the code, although many claimed to be in contact with the great magician.

Some mediums confessed their fraud. An apparently very accomplished medium wrote the anonymous *Confessions of a Medium* in 1882. Margaret Fox herself confessed, in 1888 (the confession is reprinted in Kurtz, 1985b), that the origins of spiritualism were fraudulent. The mysterious rapping at the Fox home in 1848 had been produced by Kate and Margaret tying an apple to a string and bouncing it up and down on the floor in order to frighten their mother. Margaret Fox stated that those, and all subsequent phenomena she and her sister Kate had produced, were fraudulent.

The methods used by mediums were many and varied. At some seances seemingly disembodied voices would move about the room, responding to the medium's or the sitters' questions. This was easy to accomplish as seances were almost always held in the dark. An assistant of the medium, or sometimes the medium in person, completely dressed in black clothing, head covered, would move invisibly about the darkened room. This general gimmick could be adapted to have the black-clothed individual hold some bright object that would then appear to float mysteriously about the room. On more than one occasion, a skeptical sitter would spring out of his chair and grab the "spirit," only to find that he had grabbed a very angry and embarrassed medium. Cumberland (1888/1975) reports spraying red dye in the face of the spirit and later discovering the very same dye on the face of the medium. So-called spirit photographs, in which the head or the entire form of a spirit seemed to float about the medium, were easily produced by trick photography—usually double or multiple exposures of the same plate. They seem astonishingly crude today and were easily duplicated. Some female mediums went so far as to conceal in their vagina or anus objects to be "apported" during the seance and gauzy fabric that would become "ectoplasm" during the seance. These were places that Victorian gentlemen, no matter how skeptical, were highly unlikely to ask to search.

Does the critical literature on mediums and spiritualism contain an explanation for every single apparently wondrous phenomenon reported by sitters at the thousands of seances held over the years? Of course not. Many reports, such as medium D. H. Home's levitation (Brandon, 1983, pp. 71-73), the dewy flowers reported by Alfred Russel Wallace, and the results of Hare's (1855) experiments, remain to my knowledge without specific explanations. Should the lack of such explanations convince anyone that spiritualistic phenomena and claims are valid? Certainly not. The burden of proof must rest on the so-called psychic, and not on the skeptic. This conclusion is strengthened by the fact that, when rigorous experimental conditions were imposed on mediums that truly excluded cheating, no spiritualistic phenomena were seen (Houdini, 1924; Brandon, 1983).

What of the scientists like Hare and Wallace who were convinced by what they saw at seances? Were they incompetent scientists, dupes, or just plain gullible? The answer is none of the above. They had simply ventured out of their own area of expertise—an often fatal mistake. They assumed, as did their critics in the scientific community, that if one is a good observer in the laboratory, one is also qualified to observe in the seance. This is simply not true. Mediums were known to cheat, using the magicians' tricks of sleight of hand and distraction. Magic is a skilled trade requiring years of experience and practice. The training of a chemist, physicist, or psychologist confers no ability to spot magicians' tricks. To detect such cheating requires a magician. This is one of the most important requirements in research into paranormal claims. In the investigation of any type of psychic, only a magician can spot the tricks that mediums and other pyschics so often use. This is, of course, why Houdini was so successful in exposing mediums. He was a magician and knew exactly what to look for. In addition, a magician will be of immense help in any psychic investigation in designing procedures to eliminate trickery and sleight of hand.

The repeated revelations of fraud and trickery on the part of even the most famous mediums had surprisingly little immediate effect on believers in spiritualism. One common response, which presaged the responses of believers in psychic phenomena to similar revelations in the 1970s, was to admit that a particular medium did cheat sometimes, but that at other times the phenomena were real. This argument, of course, was an attempt to shift the burden of proof back to the skeptic by requiring that the skeptic explain away every single allegedly miraculous event before a medium, or spiritualism in general, would be considered discredited.

In the past few years a new, simpler, form of mediumship has become quite popular. Known as *channeling*, it dispenses with the sleight of hand and other gimmickery associated with classical mediumship. There are no floating, disembodied apparitions, no apported objects in channeling. The medium simply sits and allows some entity to speak through him or her, becoming a channel for the entity's communication. Depending on the channel, the entity may be from the past, the future, another planet or even another dimension. Mrs. J. Z. Knight, a California channel highly thought of by Shirley MacLaine, channels Ramtha, who conquered the world 35,000 years ago. Ramtha was born on Atlantis. Mrs. Knight certainly doesn't channel for free. A session of listening to Ramtha costs $400. The fee is $1500 for a two day seminar (Gardner, 1987a). What sort of wisdom do the channels impart? It consists largely of platitudes about getting in touch with yourself, loving yourself and the lack of reality of reality.

Psychic Readings

Repeated exposés of fraud had a cumulative effect over the years, and spiritualism was largely discredited by the 1920s. Classic mediumistic spiritualism is, however, still with us, although it now has a much smaller following. Proponents support a number of spiritualist "camps" such as Camp Chesterfield in Chesterfield, Indiana, and Camp Silver Belle in Ephrata, Pennsylvania. The term "camp" here is somewhat misleading—a better term would be resort, as the camps have all the amenities of a resort. Just as youngsters might go to a tennis camp to improve their tennis game or to a computer camp to learn how to program computers, thousands of elderly people go to spiritualist camps to communicate with their dead relatives and friends. M. Lamar Keene was for years a leading medium at Camp Chesterfield. He revealed the inner workings of modern spiritualism in his 1976 book (coauthored with Allen Spraggett), *The Psychic Mafia*. Spiritualism has become big business, raking in millions of dollars annually from the lonely, the elderly, and the bereaved who believe that they are being put in touch with the spirits of their loved ones. As Keene makes clear, spiritualism is a lucrative racket. He reports that he and his partner took in between $10,000 and $20,000 "in one night of services" (p. 68) at their small spiritualist church in Tampa, Florida. Another time, "I collected one Sunday $18,000 in contributions, most of them cash, for our building fund" (p. 71) Of course, there never was any plan to build anything with the money other than Keene's personal bank account. Keene states that "one woman, who wasn't particularly well off, gave more than $40,000 to the church—to my partner and me—during the four years or so she attended" (p. 69). Sitters would leave money to Camp Chesterfield in their wills, one man leaving $100,000 and another estate more than $500,000.

Keene (1976) reveals in detail the tricks of the medium's trade, several of which are worth repeating here. One of Keene's specialties was apporting lost objects during a seance, or having the spirits tell the sitter where a lost object would be found, even if the sitter wasn't aware that the object was missing. Imagine sitting at a seance and having the college ring you lost weeks ago fall onto the table. Or having the spirits tell you that the earring you lost will be found at a particular place in the local shopping mall where, you are told, you lost it. You go to the specified location and find the earring. A miracle? Not quite. Here's how it's done.

The spiritualist hires an accomplice to deliver a bouquet of roses to someone, usually a widow, who is a sitter at the spiritualist's seances. The ultimate object is to get the victim to increase the contributions to the spiritualist's "church." The flowers are lovely; the card with them indicates that they are from an anonymous admirer. Such a lovely and mysterious gift will thrill most people. At this point, the phony delivery man makes his move. By any of a number of ruses, he gains access to the victim's home. One technique that almost always works is to ask permission to use the bathroom. Few people will refuse such a request, especially considering that the fellow has just brought such a pleasant surprise. While the victim puts the flowers in a vase, the accomplice quickly scans the bathroom and the bedroom—which is frequently located near the bathroom—looking for any small piece of jewelry, ideally one that is likely to be of more sentimental than monetary value. The item is pocketed and the accomplice leaves. Why not take something of monetary value? The victim is likely to report such a loss to the police, the last thing the spiritualist wants. Loss of items of little monetary value, even if they have great sentimental value, is much less likely to be reported to the police. However, it is quite likely that the victim may ask the spirits for help in finding the object. Once the spiritualist has the object, a number of variations can be worked on this basic theme. In one, the object is apported at a later seance, to the victim's amazement. In another, the object is hidden somewhere and the spirits tell the victim where to look for it.

An especially effective technique is to have the accomplice simply hide the object somewhere in the house, behind a loose baseboard, for example. Later the spirits tell the victim where to look in his or her own house. The reader can probably think of other variations on this technique.

Once you know how it's done, the whole thing seems extremely simple. But almost no one, unless they were familiar with the methods of spiritualists and similar con artists, would figure out on their own what happened. They are much more likely to attribute it to the powers of the spirits and the spiritualists. As a result, they may increase their donation to the spiritualist.

Another favorite spiritualist trick, used when facing large groups, is "billet reading." The basic technique is familir to anyone who has seen Johnny Carson's "Amazing Carnak" routine. It's called the "old one ahead" in the trade. The idea is to convince the congregation that the spirits are providing the spiritualist with information that the spiritualist would otherwise be unable to obtain. At the start of the spiritualist service (not a seance but a service similar to those in established churches), the people present are asked to write a question for the spirits on a card and then seal it in an envelope. These sealed envelopes are then collected. Later in the service, the spiritualist holds them up one at a time and, without opening them, reads the question, the question presumably being communicated to him by the spirits. At this point, someone in the congregation will usually exclaim that that was his or her question. The spiritualist then answers the question, tears open the envelope to satisfy himself that the spirits communicated the correct question and answer, then picks up the next envelope and continues. Again, it's a simple trick, once you know how.

Before the "reading" starts, the spiritualist opens one of the envelopes and memorizes that question. There are several ways of finding out what is in one envelope, even if the envelopes are in full view of the audience at all times (see Corinda, 1968 for a detailed discussion of these techniques as used by legitimate stage magicians). Once the spiritualist has memorized the first question, the rest is easy. The spiritualist picks what the audience thinks is the first envelope (it's really a second envelope), holds it up, recites from memory the first question, answers it, then rips open the envelope he's holding. The audience thinks the spiritualist is simply verifying that the envelope really contained the question he just obtained from the spirits. In fact, the spiritualist has just opened the second envelope and is reading a second question. He then picks up a third envelope (the audience thinks it's the second) and reads off the question that was in the previous envelope. A simple trick, but very effective if done well.

In addition to the use of stage magic techniques, spiritualists and psychics use other, more mundane techniques to convince their victims that they have extraordinary powers. For example, most spiritualists and psychics don't just see anyone who walks in off the street; instead, new clients must make an appointment. This allows time for the accumulation of information. One way of obtaining information about a new client is through a private detective. A detective is especially likely to be used when the victim is wealthy enough to justify the expense involved. However, a great deal of information about an individual can be obtained through other, less expensive sources. For example, in many states, one's driving record and driver's license abstract are public information, available for a fee of a few dollars. These records may contain information on age, exact birth date, accident record, insurance company, driver's license and policy number, and so forth. The individual's address gives information about the neighborhood he lives in and, hence, his income level, ethnic background, and perhaps religious background. A slow drive past the house will reveal much—the type of house, the color, the number and type of cars in the driveway, the presence of children's toys on the lawn. All this information, available essentially free, can be fed back to the victim who will likely be amazed that the psychic could know such details about his or her life. The victim will almost always accept the psychic's knowledge of this information as proof of his or her powers.

Modern spiritualists and psychics keep detailed files on their victims. As might be expected, these files can be very valuable and are often passed on from one medium or psychic to another when one retires or dies.

Even if a psychic doesn't use a private detective or have immediate access to driver's license records and such, there is still a very powerful technique that will allow the psychic to convince people that the psychic knows all about them, their problems, and their deep personal secrets, fears, and desires. The technique is called *cold reading* and is probably as old as charlatanism itself. The technique has been described in detail by Hyman (1976-77).

In a cold reading, the reader begins with a "stock spiel," a set of general statements that will apply to almost everyone. Because the majority of human problems fall into one of three general categories—sex, money and health—the reader already has some idea of the nature of the victim's problem. Of course, the nature of the problem can, to some extent, be predicted by carefully observing the age, mode of speech, style of dress, and physical appearance of the victim. If the victim is young, health problems are not likely to be the reason for the consultation. Sex or personal problems are much more likely to be the reason for the visit. If the victim is a college student—this can be ascertained by simply asking during prereading chitchat, another extremely valuable source of information, or by noting a college ring or fraternity pin—concern about grades is also a strong possibility. In any case, information obtained by careful observation of the victim is then used to guide the reading toward the most likely problem area. For example, if a woman comes in wearing an expensive dress and lots of jewelry, money is probably not the problem she's come to talk about. Elderly people are more likely to have health problems, and many of these can be spotted simply by looking at the victim—the tremors of Parkinson's disease, the hobbling caused by arthritis, the types of paralysis caused by some strokes, can all be readily observed.

As an exercise, put yourself in the position of a cold reader and see what you make of this: A middle-aged man, good looking and well dressed, walks in. During idle chat before the reading, you discover he's in town for a week or so on business. You also note that there is a white area of skin at the base of his ring finger. What do you conclude?

Students often answer that the fellow has been recently divorced and thus no longer wears a wedding ring. A logical response, and perhaps right, but there is another, somewhat seamier, possibility: Perhaps the man is playing around while he's away from his wife and that's why he's not wearing his ring. How do you tell which alternative is true, or whether neither is true? (After all, his wife could have died recently.) Finding out is simple—you ask, but in such a way that he's not aware you're asking and isn't aware he's given you the information. You then, later in the reading, feed the information he's given you back to him, and he's probably amazed at your psychic powers.

One of the most powerful sources of information for a cold reader is vague statements in the form of leading questions. For example, you could say something like, "I see a recent loss in your life," and inflect the end of the sentence like a question. Because of the inflection, the victim will almost always respond as to a question. He may answer right out, "Yes, my wife just died," or "My wife and I were separated last month." Or the response may be more subtle and almost unconscious—a nod of the head, for example. Even such subtle responses confirm that you're on the right track. If you get a puzzled look and a shake of the head, you know you're on the wrong track. He hasn't suffered a recent loss, so the "fooling around" hypothesis is more likely. At this point, don't come out and say, "I see you cheating on your wife." Never make a specific statement like that in a cold reading. For one thing, it may get you a fist in your face. For another, it may start the victim wondering how you obtained such specific information, and he *may* be able to figure it out for himself. Instead, make it a bit vague: "The spirits point to less than total satisfaction with the woman in your life." Note that you don't say "your wife" here. By being vague, you're protecting yourself: you may be wrong after all. Maybe his wife *did* just die. How embarrassing it would be for you to say "your wife" and use the present tense.

In any event, when you make the comment and watch for the victim's response, you'll learn more. Let's assume the victim's response is a sigh and a nod. This is evidence that the "fooling around" hypothesis is correct. But again, don't make a specific statement. In fact, a good strategy at this point would be to drop the topic and move on to other areas, perhaps doing a little fishing about financial matters. Later, when the victim has probably forgotten the details of your comments about his marital affairs, vague as they were, pop in something like, "I'm getting part of a word or a name. Frank? Frank something? Does that mean anything to you?" Note that you're asking him, not telling him, but that won't be noticed. Let us assume, for this example, that several notorious pick-up bars in town are on "Franklin Avenue" so, if your "fooling around" hypothesis is right, the partial name "Frank" will mean something to him. (A good cold reader must keep up on the locations of such places, and much else besides.)

If you're good, this fellow will leave wondering how you knew he was planning to go to that pick-up place on Franklin and hoping that his wife never develops psychic powers, of which he has just seen such an impressive demonstration.

Another technique used by psychics is the *multiple out*. The basic idea is to make statements or predictions that are vague and nebulous, so that they can be interpreted, often after the fact, to fit almost any outcome. Thus one of the great powers of the cold reading is the very vagueness of the statements the reader makes. In the above example, the victim would be just as impressed with the reader's "psychic" powers if he were planning to go to Franklin Avenue that night, if he had thought about going but decided against it, if he had gone some previous night or during a previous trip. In other words, because of the vague nature of the reading, there are numerous real-life situations that are consistent with it, and the reader gets credit for being psychic if any of them have taken place, have been thought about, or occur in the future. This characteristic of the cold reading is actively enhanced by the reader, who will often preface the reading by saying something like, "the messages I get are often symbolic and have to be fitted into your particular life."

One sometimes hears of people who have consulted psychics and claim to have been told extremely specific facts about themselves and their friends that the psychic "couldn't possibly have known." Again, it's simple, once you know the gimmick. The reader asks questions about initials and common names: "I see the initial J—is there an important J in your life?" If not, little is lost, but since the victim has been instructed to interpret what the reader says, he or she will search around in memory for someone with a first or last name beginning with J. Note also that "important" is itself a vague term. Important how? A lover, a colleague, a fellow-student, a child, a friend? There are dozens of possibilities.

The reader can run the same trick with a full name: "Does the name Fred mean anything to you?" To which the response will often be something like, "My God, Fred Black, how did you ever know about him? Why, I haven't seen Fred since that football game back in college." Of course, the reader didn't know about Fred Black, the football game, or college. But the victim is now convinced that he did and will swear that the psychic told him about Fred Black, even though he had no way of knowing about him. Sometimes it's not even necessary to supply the name, the victim will do it himself. A statement like "I see in the cards that you're not happy with your personal relationships" can elicit the response, "How did you ever know that Sally and I were having problems?" The reader didn't know, but the victim will have missed that.

What does the reader do next? A good cold reader tells victims what they want to hear: "Don't worry, the tea leaves tell me that it will all work out for the best in the end." This doesn't really mean anything, but the victim, convinced of the psychic's powers, will believe the reader has foretold a pleasant outcome. It's likely that the victim will be back again, money in hand, the next time he or she has a problem.

Tarot cards have been in use since at least the fourteenth century (Hargrave, 1930/1966) and are widely used by cold readers. Susan Blackmore (1983), a parapsychologist with "eight years experience of using the cards for divination" (Blackmore, 1983, p. 97), performed a study of the accuracy of personality readings given using the cards. She found that when she gave the reading "face to face," subjects rated the reading as highly accurate. However, when asked to pick their own reading from among nine others, subjects were unable to do so and "tended to choose readings which were most general."

One of the most fascinating effects of cold readings is that they not only convince the victim that the reader has paranormal powers, they can also convince the reader of the same thing. Ray Hyman, a psychologist who studies why people believe in the paranormal, became interested in the issue when, as a student, he became convinced that he really could divine amazing information from the lines in people's palms. Let Hyman (1976-77, p. 27) tell the story in his own words:

> One danger of playing the role of reader is that you will persuade yourself that you are really divining true character. This happened to me. I started reading palms in my teens as a way to supplement my income from doing magic and mental shows. When I started I did not believe in palmistry.

But I knew that to "sell" it I had to act as if I did. After a few years I became a firm believer in palmistry. One day the late Dr. Stanley Jaks, who was a professional mentalist and a man I respected, tactfully suggested that it would make an interesting experiment if I deliberately gave readings opposite to what the lines indicated. I tried this out with a few clients. To my surprise and horror my readings were just as successful as ever. Ever since then I have been interested in the powerful forces that convince us, reader and client alike, that something is so when it really isn't.

Psychics are also practitioners of what might be called "sleight of tongue," fast talking that gets them out of erroneous statements so fast that few will notice, unless a transcript of what they said is examined. A performance by Doris Stokes, a well-known and respected British medium, as analyzed by Hoggart (1984, pp. 21-22) in the following passage, provides an excellent example. The performance Hoggart is describing appeared on the BBC television program "40 Minutes."

I looked closely at one typical example of her style, transcribed here from the show. She began by asking whether anyone in the audience of several hundred knew of a 'little Daniel.' A youngish woman came forward and said: 'I've got a Daniel.'

Doris Stokes: Little Daniel?

Woman: Very little.

DS: You know, a baby Daniel? Did he have to go back into hospital, love?

Woman: Yes, he had to go back into hospital.

DS: But he's all right now, love.

Woman: No . . . well, he might be all right on your [i.e. the spirit] side, but we've lost him.

DS: Yes, that's what they're saying, he'll be all right now, love. And they said 'We've brought little Daniel, and he went home and then he had to go back into the hospital.' And he never went home again, but they said 'He's all right now.' And he's about three now, lovey?

Woman: Yes, he has.

DS: I can see him, he's got auburn hair, love.

Woman: Yes, he has.

DS: Yes, he's here, looking at the flowers.—'Yes, Daniel, you can, love'—he says 'Can I have some flowers for my mum? [Audience sighs.] So when you go tonight, lovey, will you take some flowers?

Woman: He wasn't my baby.

DS: No, but you know his Mum.

Woman: Yes.

DS: No, I didn't say to you . . . he said, 'Can I have some flowers for my Mum, 'cos she'll never believe I'm here,' and he's a beautiful child . . . Just a minute, Daniel . . . He had a defect [Woman nods] with his heart, darling, and they tried to repair it, and it didn't work, but he's growing up and he's nearly three he said, and he's talking away. . . .'

Those who believe in Mrs. Stoke's ability to hear spirit messages from beyond—and there are many—or those who think vaguely that there must be *something* in it, might be greatly impressed by that exchange. After all, she had scored several hits. The boy had to go back into hospital, he had a heart defect, he had auburn hair, and he would have been three years old. She also got agreement for saying 'he's a beautiful child,' though the woman was hardly likely to reply 'No, he was a revolting little brute.'

Horrid old skeptics, such as members of CSICOP, see the exchange slightly differently. It's a fair assumption that the woman was distressed about the child Daniel, and this would almost certainly imply illness and so a return to hospital. Heart disease is a common killer of infants (and earlier in the same session Mrs. Stokes coped bravely when she wrongly announced that a man had died of a heart attack—he turned out to have died of cancer. 'He did have a heart attack at the very end, he tells me,' she riposted. Conveniently, the spirits are sometimes on hand to correct the living).

She is right about the child's age, and right about his hair color—though neither is particularly surprising. The woman told her he was 'very little,' and the description 'auburn' could apply to almost any hair except blonde or jet black.

But, most remarkably to a skeptic, she is entirely wrong about the two most important facts of all: in spite of her smooth recoveries, she clearly thinks she is addressing Daniel's mother and she believes at the start that the child is still alive. Is this because, as she says, that listening to spirit voices is as confusing as listening to five phone conversations at once? Or is it because she was thrown by the woman's first remark: 'I've *got* a Daniel,' in the present tense?

Time and again, Mrs. Stokes is right about a few small details and wrong about the important ones. Sometimes this has hilarious results. 'She adored those kids,' she says of a deceased grandmother. 'Well, she never actually saw them . . . in this life,' adds the mother, anxious to let her off the hook. Giving a hearing to a bereaved family Mrs. Stokes apparently knows that their lad knew someone called 'Gary' (a fairly common name among working-class teenagers) but has to be told that their boy had shot himself. Learning this, she is able to inform them that he was 'moody.'

Another factor plays an important role in convincing reader and victim that the cold reading is accurate. This is known as the *P. T. Barnum effect*. It permits victims to believe that a vague stock spiel, with few or no specifics, is an accurate description of their own individual personality. The Barnum effect (so named because of P. T. Barnum's famous quip "There's a sucker born every minute") can be demonstrated easily in a classroom. The instructor gives a personality test to each student, telling the class that the test results give an accurate picture of an individual's personality. About a week after the students have taken the test, they receive typed personality sketches, complete with their names at the top, based on their test responses. Students are then asked to judge how accurate the sketches are as a description of their own, individual, personality and how accurate they would be if applied to the "average" person. Invariably, the sketch is seen as a very accurate portrayal of the individual's personality, but a very poor portrayal of the personality of the "average" person (Hyman, 1976-77). This would be unsurprising, except for one thing: there really was no personality test. All the students were given the same personality sketch, differing only in the name typed at the top of the page. Thus, the belief that the nonexistent personality test is valid results in the acceptance of the sketch as highly accurate, even though all the students rate it as applying to them alone.

Psychics, astrologers, graphologists who claim to be able to determine personality from handwriting, and tarot card readers all benefit greatly from the Barnum effect. The vast majority of their clients are already, to some extent, believers. Thus, even a vague description that applies to nearly anyone will be seen as highly specific to the individual. The psychic will then be given credit for amazing, perhaps even paranormal, insights.

Some typical stock spiels that have been shown to be effective illustrate just how vague such statements really are. The following two are taken from Hyman (1976-77) and Snyder and Shenkel (1975), respectively.

> You appear to be a cheerful, well-balanced person. You may have some alternation of happy and unhappy moods, but they are not extreme now. You have few or no problems with your health. You are sociable and mix well with others. You are adaptable to social situations. You tend to be adventurous. Your interests are wide. You are fairly self-confident and usually think clearly. (Hyman, 1976-77, p. 23).

> Some of your aspirations tend to be pretty unrealistic. At times you are extroverted, affable, sociable, while at other times you are introverted, wary and reserved. You have found it unwise to be too frank in revealing yourself to others. You pride yourself on being an independent thinker and do not accept others' opinions without satisfactory proof. You prefer a certain amount of change and variety, and become dissatisfied when hemmed in by restrictions and limitations. At times you have serious doubts as to whether you have made the right decision or done the right thing. Disciplined and controlled on the outside, you tend to be worrisome and insecure on the inside.

Your sexual adjustment has presented some problems for you. While you have some personality weaknesses, you are generally able to compensate for them. You have a great deal of unused capacity which you have not turned to your advantage. You have a tendency to be critical of yourself. You have a stong need for other people to like you and for them to admire you. (Snyder and Shenkel, 1975, p. 53).

When one is forewarned about the vagueness of these spiels, the ploy becomes fairly obvious. Why is the vagueness overlooked when the victim is not forewarned? The answer lies in the active role victims adopt when they consult a psychic. The psychic is likely to say that the readings are symbolic and that clients must try to apply what is said to their own life. Thus, when victims are told, "Your sexual adjustment has presented some problems for you," they are likely to recall a specific instance of this sort. They then credit the psychic with telling them, not the vague statement, but the details of the specific instance.

A good stock spiel will have what are called "double-headed" statements (Dickson and Kelly, 1985). For example: "Often extroverted and outgoing, you are sometimes retiring and unsure of yourself in social situations." The stock spiel is not totally flattering. Flattery in a cold reading should not be overdone. Everyone has some bad points, and if the reader makes vague statements that seem to match some of them, the victim won't think, "Well, I'm just being flattered." In other words, putting negative points into the spiel enhances its credibility even further.

Psychic Predictions

The psychics currently most in the public eye are those who, like Dorothy Allison, Jeane Dixon, and numerous others, claim to be able to foretell the future, find missing persons, and help the police solve crimes. Their exploits and predictions appear endlessly in supermarket tabloids like the National Enquirer and on the local television evening news. The most famous such psychic was Michel Nostradamus (1503-1566), whose predictions have been the topic of numerous books and a television documentary, "The Man Who Saw Tomorrow," narrated by the late Orson Welles.

Nostradamus was certainly a most prolific prophet. His prophecies fill more than 175 pages in Edgar Leoni's (1961/1982) Nostradamus and His Prophecies. This is by far the most scholarly work on Nostradamus. Leoni provides not only the English translations of all Nostradamus's prophecies, but also the original French text, along with a biography and bibliography of Nostradamus. The English translations of Nostradamus's predictions in this chapter are all taken from Leoni.

Nostradamus has been credited with predicting nearly every major historical event to take place since his death, and many minor events (Hoebens, 1982-83; Randi, 1982-83b). Among his alleged correct predictions have been the rise of Napoleon, the rise and fall of Hitler, World Wars I and II, the invention of fighter aircraft, the atomic bomb, the deaths of John F. and Robert Kennedy, to name a few. He is even said to have *named* Hitler, getting his name correct to within a single letter.

However, these prophecies are only seen to be accurate *after the fact.* No one has ever used them to make correct predictions about what is going to occur before it occurs. Rather, after an event occurs, people go back to Nostradamus's thousands of predictions and find a passage that seems, now that the event is known, to have foretold its occurrence. For example, after World War II, many people claimed that Nostradamus had foreseen the details of that war. But no one had been able to see such predictions in his writings before the war.

Nostradamus's prophecies are far from the sharp, clear predictions most people believe them to be. He left a total of one thousand verses, divided into ten "centuries," each with one hundred verses, as well as some additional predictions. Each of the one thousand verses can contain multiple predictions, so there are literally thousands of prophecies. In the best traditions of the "multiple out," the verses are vague, sometimes to the point of being little more than gibberish. A few examples will give a flavor of these verses:

An Emperor will be born near Italy,
One who will cost his Empire a high price:
They will say that from the sort of people who surround him
He is to be found less prince than butcher.
(Century I, verse 60)

Ruin for the Volcae [people of southern France]
     so very terrible with fear,
Their great city stained, pestilential deed:
To plunder Sun and Moon and to violate their temples:
And to redden the two rivers flowing with blood.
(Century VI, verse 98)

Dyers' caldrons put on the flat surface,
Wine, honey and oil, and built over furnaces:
They will be immersed, innocent, pronounced malefactors,
Seven of Borneaux smoke still in the cannon.
(Century IX, verse 14)

Such vague passages can be interpreted in many ways. The first one quoted above has been seen as a prediction of the rise of Napoleon, but, as Randi (1982-83b) points out, it applies as well to Hitler and Ferdinand II, a Holy Roman Emperor. In fact, it applies to any European ruler born "near" (an extremely vague term) Italy during the fifteenth through the twentieth centuries (and beyond) who associated with unsavory individuals and involved his country in any sort of costly adventure, whether war or some sort of economic disaster that resulted from poor policy. As such, it probably applies, with enough creative interpretation, to almost any ruler of this period. In short, Nostradamus was predicting that at some unspecified time, in some unspecified European country, there would be a ruler in some way involved in killing people and whose policies would somehow prove costly to his country.

What about claims that Nostradamus predicted specific developments that have taken place in the twentieth century, such as fighter aircraft and the atomic bomb? Consider the verse (Century I, verse 64) said to predict both of these:

> They will think they have seen the Sun at night
> When they will see the pig half-man:
> Noise, song, battle, fighting in the sky perceived,
> And one will hear brute beasts talking.

This is certainly a far cry from any truly specific prediction of fighter aircraft and atomic weapons!

Nostradamus's greatest, and most specific, prediction is said to be his almost perfectly accurate naming of Adolph Hitler. In fact, the word *Hister* does occur in the prophecies three times. It is clear, however, that this in no way refers to Adolph Hitler. *Hister* is the Latin name of the lower Danube River. The translations of the three verses with *Hister* make it clear that Nostradamus was not accurately predicting Adolph Hitler's rise and fall, for they are more or less gibberish:

> Beasts ferocious from hunger will swim across rivers:
> The greater part of the region will be against the Hister,
> The great one will cause it to be dragged in an iron cage,
> When the German child will observe nothing.
> (Century II, verse 24)

> In the place very near not far from Venus,
> The two greatest ones of Asia and of Africa,
> From the Rhine and Lower Danube [Hister]
>   they will be said to have come,

Cries, tears at Malta and the Ligurian side.
(Century IV, verse 68)

Liberty will not be recovered,
A proud, villainous, wicked black one will occupy it,
When the matter of the bridge will be opened,
The republic of Venice vexed by the Danube [Hister].
(Century V, verse 29)

Again, these are not the clear predictions claimed for Nostradamus by those more interested in selling sensational paperbacks and misleading television pseudodocumentaries than in correctly informing their readers and viewers.

While Nostradamus has been improperly credited with predicting numerous historical events, one such event is said to have been foreseen by many psychics: the sinking in April 1912 of the ocean liner *Titanic* after it struck an iceberg in the North Atlantic. A short novel, part of another novel, several short stories, and even several poems written in the period between 1890 and 1912 contain the theme of a great passenger liner sinking after it strikes an iceberg (Gardner, 1986). Some of these stories contain what may seem to be impressive correspondences with what actually happened to the *Titanic*. For example, Morgan Robertson's 1898 novel— reprinted in Gardner's (1986) detailed analysis of the claim that the *Titanic* disaster was foreseen—was titled *The Wreck of the Titan*. The sinking of the *Titan* is similar in many respects to the actual sinking, years later, of the *Titanic*. Both the fictional and the real ship, for example, sank with loss of many lives after striking an iceberg in the North Atlantic in April. Neither had adequate lifeboats.

But these correspondences are not due to any paranormal predictions. In the era of the great passenger liners, running into an iceberg at night was a constant danger. Recall that radar was then unknown. Further, an iceberg was just about the only thing that could sink such a ship, short of enemy action in war. Thus, if one were going to write a story about a large passenger liner sinking, an iceberg practically had to be involved. The requirement that the fictional ship strike an iceberg further constrained where and when the accident could take place. After all, a ship isn't likely to run into any icebergs when sailing from Marseille to Rio de Janeiro in July.

Examining the predictions of twentieth century psychics reveals a plethora of vague prophecies characterized by multiple outs and a large number of very specific predictions that are also very wrong. Further, psychics have been totally unable to predict any of the numerous unexpected major news stories of the last fifty years.

No psychic ability is required to make obvious predictions like "there will be continued trouble in the Middle East during the year," but psychics often claim after the fact that they made much more specific predictions. Almost no one, least of all the media that report these psychic wonders, ever bothers to check out their claims, which thus go unchallenged. In recent years, however, skeptics have begun to follow up psychics' claims; the results show a consistent pattern of either outright failure or distortion of vague predictions.

It was a vague prediction, retroactively made much more specific, that launched the success of Jeane Dixon, probably the best-known contemporary psychic. Dixon and her admirers claim that she correctly predicted not only John F. Kennedy's 1960 election to the presidency but also his assassination (Montgomery, 1965). Impressive, if it were true—but it's not. Dixon's actual prediction appeared in the May 13, 1956, *Parade* magazine. It stated, "As for the 1960 election, Mrs. Dixon thinks it will be dominated by labor and won by a Democrat. But he will be assassinated or die in office, 'although not necessarily in his first term.'" Now that prediction covers a lot of ground. The portion about a Democrat winning the election would have about a 50 percent chance of coming true. There are numerous possible outcomes that would be consistent with the second portion of the prediction, regarding assassination or dying in office. The president, whose name is never mentioned, could be assassinated in his first or his second term. He could die during his first or second term. Dixon would undoubtedly have claimed a hit if Kennedy had had a serious illness during either the first or the second term, or if an assassination attempt—whether or not the President had been injured—had taken place during the first or second term. However, the coup de grace to Dixon's claim to have foretold the Kennedy assassination is that in 1960 she predicted that "John F. Kennedy would fail to win the presidency." (Tyler, 1977).

Another way to make a prediction seem surprisingly accurate is to make the entire, specific prediction after the event has taken place and then try to con the public into believing that it was made before the event. The best-known, and most blatant, example of this psychic technique took place in 1981 when Los Angeles psychic Tamara Rand claimed to have predicted the attempt on President Reagan's life. Her "prediction" included the details that the assassin would have the initials "J. H.," which John Hinkley did, and that the last name would be something like "Humley," which is pretty close to Hinkley. She further "saw" that the President would be shot in the chest in a "hail of bullets," and that the assassin would come from a wealthy family and have sandy hair. All of these descriptions are correct. She even got the time of the assassination right, saying it would take place in the last week of March or the first week of April, 1981. The attempt actually took place on March 30, 1981. These predictions were said to have been made on a talk show taped on January 6, 1981, on KTNV-TV, Las Vegas.

Such astonishingly accurate predictions were impressive stuff, and ABC, NBC, and CNN all broadcast the videotape of the January 6 program on April 2, 1981, four days after the assassination attempt. Alas, these major newsgathering organizations made no attempt to verify the accuracy of Rand's claims before broadcasting her videotaped "predictions." In fact, the tape was a fake. Rand and KTNV talk show host Dick Maurice had conspired to produce the fake tape, which was actually filmed in the KTNV studios on March 31, the day *after* the assassination attempt (Frazier and Randi, 1981-82). The hoax was exposed when Associated Press reporter Paul Simon, who was skeptical of the story, investigated and turned up the truth.

One important point should be noted here about the nature of Rand's phony predictions. She took pains to make her predictions less than perfect. She did not say,"I foresee that on March 30 an attempt will be made on the life of President Reagan by a man named John Wayne Hinkley. Hinkley will attempt to assassinate the President as he emerges from the Sheraton Washington Hotel at 1:48 P.M." No one would have believed such a specific prediction. So Rand purposely made her "prediction" somewhat vague, although consistent with what had happened.

When one examines the specific predictions psychics have made before the predicted event is supposed to take place, one finds a dismal record of failure. Several compilations of psychic predictions have recently been made (Saxon, 1974; Frazier, 1982-83; 1983-84; 1984-85; 1985-86). The record of what psychics predicted that didn't happen and what they didn't predict that did happen makes amusing reading. A selection of failed predictions for 1982 from the *Weekly World News* (WWN) of December 1, 1981; the December 1, 1981, *Star;* (S1); the June 29, 1982, *Star* (S2): and the June 22, 1982, *Globe* (G) includes the following:

Startling new evidence of pyramids and massive statues on Mars will convince scientists that life flourished there millions of years ago. (WWN)

A sensational scandal involving money from casinos and organized crime will rock Monaco and even threaten Prince Rainier's crown. (WWN)

Cuban President Fidel Castro is overthrown in a major uprising. (WWN)

Linda Ronstadt and California Governor Jerry Brown will marry in 1982. (S1)

The latter part of 1982 will see gasoline supplies getting tighter and prices rising still higher. (S1) (Gasoline prices dropped during the last half of 1982.)

On the economic front, 1982 will be one of the worst years for the U.S. since 1929. The stock market will crash. (S1)

Sugar Ray Leonard will fight again. (S2) (This one and the next were made by Jeane Dixon.)

An impeachment effort will be launched against one or more Supreme Court justices. (S2)

A controversy will break out when it's discovered that a man-made explosive device sank the *Titanic*. (G)

Of course, psychics failed to predict any of the truly surprising events of 1982, such as: the death of Grace Kelly; the stock market hitting an all-time high on November 3; the death of Soviet Premier Brezhnev and the succession of Andropov; the arrest of Bulgarians in the 1981 assassination attempt on the Pope; the pro football strike; Edward Kennedy's statement that he would not run for President in 1984; implantation of the world's first artificial human heart; and the attempt to blow up the Washington Monument. The story is the same for 1983, 1984, 1985, and 1986. Psychics constantly make wildly incorrect predictions and totally miss the events that do take place.

In view of psychics' dismal record of failed predictions, why do so many people continue to take their claims seriously? There are several reasons. First, until recently no one has been "keeping score" on psychics' predictions. The tabloids certainly don't run a column at the end of the year detailing the fact that the psychic predictions they ballyhooed so vigorously earlier have all turned out to be wrong. In short, failed predictions are not news and are forgotten. On the other hand, when a psychic does manage to be correct, either by being trivial ("I foresee continued trouble in Lebanon") or by claiming that a prediction was much more specific than it really was, that prediction gets plenty of media attention. Thus, the public is selectively exposed to "correct" predictions and almost never hears about the thousands of failures.

A second, and related, reason for the continued belief in psychics is simply that one hears so much about them. Psychics and their predictions fill the tabloids and turn up frequently on television and radio talk shows and local television news. It is natural to assume that, if one hears a great deal about a particular topic, there must be something to it. Most readers and viewers will thus assume, incorrectly, that there must be some validity to psychic claims simply because these get so much media attention.

Finally, continued belief is often a result of personal encounters with psychics. People are convinced by the psychics' cold reading abilities and other forms of trickery outlined above. They reason that, since one or two individual psychics were so "accurate" in foretelling events in their personal lives, they are also accurate when predicting news events.

Psychic Crime Detection

Many people believe that psychics can help police solve crimes and find missing persons. Certainly, psychics' claims in these areas attract considerable media attention. When examined, however, these claims turn out to be as groundless as claims to predict the future.

One of the most famous psychic "crime fighters" is Dorothy Allison of Nutley, New Jersey. She claims to have helped dozens of police forces solve crimes, including the string of murders of black children in Atlanta in 1980-81. She appeared on the Phil Donahue television program in 1981, and this resulted in the citizens of Atlanta bringing pressure on the police force to invite her to try her hand at solving the children's murders. Allison's trip to Atlanta was widely covered on the local television news in both New York and Atlanta, as well as many other cities. The results of her trip, however, received much less coverage. A Sergeant Gundlach of the Atlanta police force, quoted by Randi (1982-83a), revealed that Allison produced a total of forty-two different names for the murderer or murderers—she believed that there were two murderers. Thus, she was of no help whatever in solving the murders.

In another case, Allison went to Columbus, Georgia, to help solve a string of murders of elderly women. According to Columbus Police Chief Curtis McClung, in the space of two days, "she said a whole lot of things, a whole lot of opinions, partial information and descriptions. She said a *lot*. If you say enough, there's got to be something that fits" (*Skeptical Eye*, 1980).

The multiple out is the heart of Allison's method. She produces so many "feelings," "impressions," and "hunches" that, after the fact, some are bound to have been correct. This effect is accentuated by the fact that she often takes a Nutley, New Jersey, detective with her to "interpret" what she has said. With sufficient "interpretation," almost anything can be transformed after the fact into a "correct" prediction. An excellent example of this technique is Allison's prediction in the case of a missing teenager whose parents turned to Allison for help (*Skeptical Eye*, 1980).

She sadly informed the parents that the boy was dead and would be found "near an airport." Now, that sounds pretty specific. After all, dead is dead—except when psychics are trying to cover up their blunders. The teenager had, in fact, joined a religious cult and was living in New York City's Pan Am Building. Allison claimed she was right because the boy was "emotionally dead" and there is a heliport on the roof of the building. With such leeway, it's almost impossible to imagine any statement about the boy that couldn't be made to fit the situation, after the fact.

Allison blundered in another famous case in the New York area. In 1979 Etan Patz, a five-year-old boy, disappeared while walking to school in the Greenwich Village section of Manhattan. To date, the boy has never been found. His disappearance set off the national concern over missing children in the early 1980s. In 1980 Allison was prominently featured on at least one major New York television station predicting that little Etan would be found "alive and well in six months." Obviously, she was flat wrong, but what one did *not* hear six or seven months, or a year later, on that television station was a story that started: "Dorothy Allison, the famed New York psychic, was wrong in her prediction about Etan Patz made on this program last year."

The Dutch clairvoyant Gerard Croiset, who died in 1980, was another famed psychic crime fighter. Pollack (1964) recounts many of his exploits, relying for his information on Dutch parapsychologist, Professor W. Tenhaeff, who was a promoter of Croiset. Hoebens (1981-82a, 1981-82b) reviewed the claims made for Croiset, both in Pollack's book and in the European literature. He found that the claims are not supported by the facts. For example, Pollack (1964) describes a 1953 case in which Croiset allegedly saw, psychically and in detail, what had happened to ten-year-old Dirk Zwenne. Pollack's account, taken from Tenhaeff, contains many specific statements and predictions that Croiset is said to have made, which were said to have come true. In fact, Croiset never made such statements. Hoebens (1981-82a) tracked down the original report of the Zwenne case and found that Croiset made the same type of vague statements that we have called the multiple out. In addition, several of his statements were simply wrong. At one point, Croiset said the body would be found at a particular location. When taken to a second location to see if he "saw" anything there, he indicated that he did not. The body was found at this second location, not the first. Croiset also said that when discovered the body would bear a fatal wound on the left side of the forehead. There was no such wound. Of course, these errors are not mentioned in Pollack's book. The Zwenne case is just another example of psychics, or their promoters, claiming great accuracy and slyly changing the predictions after the fact.

In another instance, Tenhaeff claimed (1980, cited in Hoebens, 1981-82a) that Croiset identified an arsonist who had been setting fires in a Dutch city. Tenhaeff stated that Croiset described the arsonist as someone who "sometimes wore a uniform," "lived in an apartment building," and had "something to do with toy airplanes." Further, the "toy" airplanes could be "model" airplanes. The arsonist turned out to be a policeman who worked with model airplanes—an impressive hit for Croiset, especially since Tenhaeff claimed that his statements had been made to State Police Commander Eekhof and had been videotaped and that a transcript of the videotape had been made, verified, and signed by Commander Eekhof.

Hoebens (1981-82a) interviewed Commander Eekhof and found that the truth was much different. Croiset had never mentioned a uniform. That detail had been added later by Tenhaeff, after the arsonist had been caught. Nor had Croiset mentioned "toy airplanes." He had spoken of "'airplanes'—'sitting in airplanes,' 'airfields,' and 'airplane construction.' When asked by Commander Eekhof whether it could be model airplanes, Croiset first said yes, maybe, but then retracted and said, 'No, these are big airplanes'" (Hoebens, 1981-82a, p. 36). So, once again, vague statements become—after the fact—precise predictions, and statements that were never made are credited to the psychic to show his amazing powers.

Hansel (1966, 1980) has debunked another Croiset claim. In this instance, Croiset is said to have solved an assault on a young woman. But the police involved reported that, while Croiset did make comments on the case, his comments were useless.

Reiser, Ludwig, Saxe, and Wagner (1979) have studied whether, in a controlled situation, psychics can provide any information about a crime. They examined twelve psychics, eight professionals who make all or part of their living from selling psychic services and four amateur psychics. Physical evidence from four crimes, two solved and two unsolved, were presented to the psychics, who were to give their impressions of the crimes. The psychics were told nothing else about the crimes. The psychics, either individually or as a group, scored no better than chance on any of the four crimes. They showed very poor consistency in their impressions of the same crime and made flagrant errors. The most common error was to believe that the crimes had something to do with the "Hillside Strangler" murders which were taking place at the time in Los Angeles, where the study was conducted. In fact, none of the cases had anything to do with the "Strangler" series of killings.

Ted Serios's Thought Pictures

Ted Serios, another phony psychic, caused quite a stir in parapsychological circles when he claimed, in the 1960s, to be able to project a picture onto film in a Polaroid camera through psychic powers (Eisenbud, 1967). This feat was accomplished by the use of a little sleight of hand and a fairly clever gimmick. Usually, Serios would use what he called a "gizmo," a tube of paper rolled up and placed against the camera lens. He said this helped him to focus his mental energy and direct it toward the film. He also used something he didn't tell anyone about—a tiny tube, about one inch long and one-half inch in diameter. This tube had a tiny magnifying lens at one end. In the other end one could insert a piece cut from a standard 35mm slide. Lined up properly, this device projected the image on the cut piece of transparency onto the film of the Polaroid camera. The device was small enough to be concealed in the palm of the hand and so could be used even when the larger paper "gizmo" wasn't around to conceal it. Serios's method of producing his pictures was revealed in Reynolds (1967), Eisendrath (1967), and Randi (1980). It was a magician working with Reynolds and Eisendrath who spotted Serios's method.

The media's response to Serios was sadly typical. *Life* magazine, in spite of knowledge that Serios was a fake (Randi, 1980), published a story (Welch, 1967) that supported his claims. All mention of Serios's use of sleight of hand was edited out of the story.

As might be expected, given the technique Serios used, his pictures were not of the highest quality. They were frequently fuzzy and out of focus. If Serios really had the ability to project his thoughts onto film, it would be reasonable to expect that, if asked to think about, say, a dog, he could obtain a recognizable picture of a dog. That's not the way it worked, however. The pictures usually bore little or no relationship to the object that Serios was asked to project onto film. Unless, of course, one was allowed to "interpret" the resulting image. Dr. Jule Eisenbud (1967), a strong supporter of Serios's claim, unwittingly gives a lovely example of how believers will support their preconceived beliefs with the most tortuous "interpretations." Serios was asked to produce a picture of the sunken nuclear submarine *Thresher*. Instead, he produced a picture that looks very much like Queen Elizabeth II. How did Eisenbud explain that one? The Queen's name in Latin is "Elizabeth Regina" and the last two letters of *Elizabeth* and the first two of *Regina* are *thre*, the first four letters of *Thresher*. Further, the sea is symbolically mother of life and Queen Elizabeth is a mother figure. It also seems that Serios is very fond of his mother, whose name is Esther. Take the *t* out of *Esther*, drop the first *e* and you're left with *sher*, Adding that to *thre* from the name of the Queen, gives *Thresher*, which was what Serios was asked to produce a photo of in the first place. As Randi (1980, p. 222) comments, "Isn't parapsychology just grand, folks?" The reader should remember that this sort of reasoning is often taken very seriously in parapsychology, as we will see in chapter four.

Prophetic Dreams and Hunches

Many people become convinced of the reality of psychic phenomena because of some seemingly psychic personal experience they have had. Going to a psychic who does a good cold reading can also be very convincing, as mentioned earlier in this chapter. Having what seems to be a prophetic dream is especially convincing. Many people can relate dreams that they, a friend, or a relative, have had that later "came true." In some rare instances, the dream contains detailed information about the event that later takes place, information that the dreamer really had no way of knowing. Take a hypothetical example: Late one night John is awakened by a nightmare in which his beloved great-aunt Petunia is driving a brand-new shocking pink Porsche down the San Diego freeway. Suddenly, an engine of a 747 flying over the freeway to make a landing at San Diego airport falls off and crushes the Porsche, killing Aunt Petunia instantly. Shaken by the dream, John writes it down and then goes back to sleep. He is stunned to learn later that day that, in fact, Aunt Petunia was killed in just the way he had dreamed a few hours after he had had his dream.

Is such a dream not compelling evidence that, at least sometimes, dreams can psychically foretell the future? Most people would answer yes to that question. But I will argue that such dreams are simply coincidences. That argument may sound quite implausible at first, simply because most people are unaware of the vast number of dreams that take place. Sleep and dreaming have been the target of a great deal of research over the past twenty-five years (see Arkin, Antrobus, and Ellman, 1978, for a good review). Much has been learned about dreaming from this research. What is relevant here is that dreaming does not occur throughout the night, but only during periods of REM (rapid eye movement) sleep. There are five such REM periods in the normal night's sleep. Each REM period lasts about fifteen to twenty minutes in adults. In a single REM period, there are upwards of fifty dream "themes"—snippets of more or less (often less) coherent "story." Thus, a normal individual will have at least two hundred fifty (five REM periods times fifty dream themes per period) dream themes per night. That may not sound like many, but multiply that figure by the approximately 225 million people in the United States, as of the 1980 census. This means that there are 56 billion, 250 million dream themes dreamed every night in the United States. In one year there are 20 trillion, 531 billion, 250 million dream themes dreamed in the United States alone. World population is about 5 billion. Using that number, there turn out to be 456 trillion, 250 billion dream themes dreamed across the world each year. That is an unimaginably vast number. The mathematical Law of Large Numbers states in essence that if an event is given enough opportunities to occur, sooner or later it will occur. Thus, if you flip a coin long enough, sooner or later you will have a run of twenty heads, even though the probability of that event is tiny. Similarly, with the huge number of opportunities for dreams to come true afforded by the vast number of dream themes that occur each year some will turn out to be impressively "prophetic" by chance alone.

The convincing nature of prophetic dreams is enhanced by the fact that we don't remember the vast majority of our dreams. In fact, some people never remember any dreams. But they do dream. When these individuals are brought into a sleep laboratory and awakened during a REM period, they report normal dreams. The dreams that are most likely to be remembered are ones that take place just before awakening in the morning or, more to the point of the present discussion, those that "come true." If a dream doesn't "come true" there is very little chance that it will be remembered. We have all had the experience of awakening and not remembering any dreams. Then, sometime later during the day, something happens to us, or we see or hear something, that retrieves from our long-term memory a dream we had had, but which, until we were exposed to what is called a *retrieval cue*, we were unable to recall voluntarily. Of course, if we had not been exposed to the retrieval cue, we would never have been aware that the dream had occurred. Thus, the nature of memory for dreams introduces a strong bias that makes dreams appear to be much more reliably prophetic than they are—we selectively remember those dreams that "come true."

Another familiar factor works to make dreams appear more prophetic than they are—the multiple out. People will frequently count a dream as "coming true," even if the events in the dream and the events in real life are only somewhat similar. A personal example: When I was living in Boston, one night I had a dream about a horrible accident on the Boston subway system's Green Line. In my dream the accident took place underground (a large part of the Green Line is above ground). There were many dead, much blood, and a great number of injured. I mentioned the dream to a friend. A few months later, there *was* an accident on the Green Line. A car empty of passengers was traveling on the section of track above ground. It derailed and rolled down a small embankment. No one was hurt and, since it was a Saturday, no one was really very much inconvenienced. Yet my friend was convinced that my dream had been a psychic prophecy that had come true. She was a bit miffed that I didn't immediately agree that psychic phenomena were real.

Of course, the accident in my dream and the real-life accident were entirely different. To count the two as a "match" and classify my dream as prophetic would mean my dream almost had to come true: Sooner or later, some type of accident, large or small, will occur on any subway line. Further, dreams don't come with little disclaimers at the end stating "this dream invalid for purposes of prophecy in thirty days." Thus, they have practically an endless amount of time to come true. Given this, it's hardly surprising that some do.

Alcock (1981) reports an experiment that shows that eliminating the opportunity for multiple outs in dreams eliminates their seemingly prophetic nature. He is often confronted by people who report that their dreams *"always* come true." I have had people make similar reports to me. Alcock simply asks these people to keep a dream diary, in which they write down their dreams upon awakening. When this is done, the dreams all at once stop being accurate. The diary is a written record of the dream and it prevents the dreams from being "misremembered" as more accurate than they really were.

Hunches, intuitions, and "feelings" that something is going to happen seem to be accurate more often than would be expected by chance, for similar reasons. We forget the hunches that don't come true, but remember the ones that do. I used to own a secondhand Pinto automobile. I often had hunches that something would go wrong with the car. Not surprisingly, eventually one of the hunches came true. Consider how multiple outs can operate to inflate the "hit rate" of hunches. A wife has a strong feeling that her husband has been involved in a serious car accident and becomes very worried. Upon returning from work, she finds her husband in perfect health. Was the hunch wrong? A believer in the prophetic power of hunches would be very likely to count the hunch as a hit if: (1) the husband had been in a minor accident; (2) had *seen* a serious accident; (3) had *seen* a fender bender or minor accident; (4) had seen what was *almost* a serious accident. After all, the believer in the prophetic nature of hunches or dreams will tell you, these things aren't precise—they must be interpreted to make them meaningful. The intepretation always place takes place after the fact.

Seemingly amazing coincidences that have convinced some people of the reality of ESP are due to similar memory-biasing mechanisms. A classic example is to be thinking of someone and, minutes later, having them call. Is this sort of instance amazing proof of direct mind-to-mind communication? No—it's just a coincidence. It seems amazing because we normally don't think about the millions of telephone calls made each day and we don't remember the thousands of times we have thought of someone when they *haven't* called.

Hintzman, Asher, and Stern (1978) have nicely demonstrated selective memory for coincidences in a laboratory setting where the coincidences were under strict control. In one experiment, subjects rated a list of nouns on various characteristics (size and attractiveness). They were not told that they would later be asked to recall the words. After a brief "filler task" designed to pass the time and occupy the subjects' attention, a set of pictures of objects was rated. Some of the pictures corresponded to some of the words that had been rated in the first part of the experiment and this correspondence was what was defined as a coincidence for the purposes of the experiment. When the subjects, without previous warning, had to recall as many of the words they had previously rated as they could, their memory was much better for words if that word's corresponding picture had been rated in the picture-rating portion of the study. This occurred even if the subject didn't notice that some of the pictures corresponded with the words.

In a second experiment Hintzman, Asher, and Stern (1978) showed that the same effect was found if the pictures were rated first. Finally, in a third experiment, it was found that the effect of the coincidence was maintained over a period of twenty-four hours. In this final study, a set of words was rated, then came a filler task, then a set of pictures was rated. Memory was not tested—again unexpectedly—until the next day. This series of experiments demonstrates that coincidences are better remembered than noncoincidences.

Related to hunches is the phenomenon of déjà vu, which means "already seen" in French. In a déjà vu experience, a place or situation seems familiar even though the person having the experience knows that they have never been in that place or situation before. Such experiences have led some people to conclude that they had visited the familiar seeming location in a past life. One need not resort to reincarnation for an understanding of déjà vu. It can be understood in terms of normal memory function. Specifically, déjà vu results when two different memory processes that normally occur together occur separately. Usually when we find ourselves in a familiar location, we have both a memory of the previous experience or experiences at that location and a feeling of familiarity. In the déjà vu situation, the feeling of familiarity is present, but the memory of previous experience is not, either because it is too weak, or because there was no previous experience. In this latter situation, the mechanism that generates the feeling of familiarity has briefly malfunctioned.

There is laboratory evidence for the dissociability of actual retrieval of a memory and a feeling of familiarity. In the "tip of the tongue" situation (Brown and McNeill, 1966; Gruneberg and Sykes, 1978) you know you know the answer to a question, that is, you are familiar with it, but you can not retrieve it. This effect is especially annoying when it occurs when one is taking an exam or playing a game. The reverse situation can also be shown to occur. People may have no consciously retrievable memory of learning, for example, a list of words, but will relearn the words faster than if they had never learned them in the first place (Nelson, 1978).

Demonic Possession and Neuropathology

Suddenly, a normally well-mannered, quiet and devout individual begins to jerk and twitch and, to his own and everyone else's horror, starts to curse and swear uncontrollably, using foul language he would ordinarily never even consider using in public. Another individual, following a sensation of profound dread and terror, appears to be thrown violently to the ground where he begins to writhe and thrash about, sometimes severely enough to break bones or even to cause death. A third individual is overcome by a shimmering, brilliant vision of a bright light, when no light is actually present. The vision may contain various shapes and structures.

In all these cases, the individual is not in control of the behaviors he or she is exhibiting and believes, correctly, that he or she has absolutely no ability to control them. This being the case, it is easy to understand how control of the behaviors would be attributed to some malign and external force, such as the devil or demons. This would be especially likely to be the explanation of the behaviors in the first two cases, where the foul language, self-injurious behaviors, and lack of control all would be easy to interpret as the work of demons. In the final case, the experience could equally well be attributed to some type of divine inspiration or message.

In fact, the three cases described above are examples, not of demonic possession or inspired visions, but of three different neurological diseases that have for centuries been taken as evidence for paranormal experiences. Beyerstein (1987-88) has traced the relationship between these three diseases and belief in demonic possession and inspired visions in an excellent paper that provided the basis for much of the following discussion. The first case is one of Gilles de la Tourette's syndrome, a rare disease that has become the focus of considerable interest in neurology recently because of its strange symptoms, including uncontrollable twitches and, in severe cases, uncontrolled swearing and use of racial and ethnic epithets. An entire monograph (Friedhoff and Chase, 1982) has been devoted to the symptoms, possible neurochemical causes, and treatments of this disease. It is clear from the work reported in that volume that Tourette's syndrome is a neurological disease, not a psychological disorder. Shapiro and Shapiro (1982) have noted that the infamous *Malleus Maleficarum*, published in 1489 as a "manual" for the witch hunters of the Inquisition, contains descriptions of behaviors said to be demonstrative of having consorted with the devil; these are similar to those seen in Tourette's syndrome. The behavior of the little girl in *The Exorcist* (Blatty, 1971) is very similar to what is seen in severe cases of Tourette's syndrome. While Blatty contends that he based the book (and movie) on a case of "real" demonic possession (see Winter 1985), Shapiro and Shapiro (1982) state that the case was actually one of Tourette's syndrome that was mistaken for possession. Such gross misdiagnoses of the syndrome are not, then, limited to the Middle Ages, but can still occur. Shapiro and Shapiro (1982) note that twenty-four of their Tourette's syndrome patients had undergone exorcism for their disorder, but none had been helped by the process. Drug treatment may provide some benefit, but the pharmacology of the disorder is not yet well understood (Friedhoff and Chase, 1982).

The second case described above is one of epilepsy, a neurological disorder much more common and well-known than Tourette's syndrome. The symptoms of epilepsy vary greatly from individual to individual. At one end of the scale are the "absence spells" where the individual is simply unresponsive to external stimuli for a minute or so and appears to be staring off into space. At the other end of the spectrum is the much more dramatic and dangerous grand mal seizure, as in the case described. Seizures are often preceded by an aura that is sometimes a feeling of impending terror and revulsion. When, immediately following this, some mysterious outside force seemingly takes over one's body and causes it to behave in self-injurious ways, the inference that demons or the devil are responsible is an easy one to make.

A detailed account of the neuropathology of epilepsy is well beyond the scope of this book (for such an account see Beyerstein, 1987-88, or Adams and Victor, 1985) but a basic understanding will be necessary for this discussion. Information transmission between nerve cells in the mammalian brain is almost always a chemical process—molecules of chemicals called neurotransmitters are responsible. Within a neuron, transmission is electrical, and it is the electrical activity of a neuron that causes the molecules of neurotransmitter to be released from one neuron to make contact with and thereby transmit information to other neurons. In epilepsy, due to various chemical and physical changes in neurons, some neurons generate far too much electrical activity. This activity spreads through the brain. The areas of the brain to which it spreads determine the exact type of aura and seizure the patient will experience. Thus, in a case of an aura of dread and fear followed by a seizure in which the patient flails about, the areas of the brain responsible for feelings of fear and dread (in the limbic system) and those responsible for normal motor control are involved. For various neurophysiological reasons, the temporal lobe of the brain and the limbic system—the set of brain structures responsible in large part for emotional behavior and feelings—are frequently the site of epileptic activity.

Strange as it may seem, epileptic seizures need not always be unpleasant events. When the brain structures within the limbic system that underlie feelings of pleasure are involved, and the areas for motor control are not involved (so there is no dangerous flailing about), the experience can produce feelings of profound joy. Such experiences are interpreted differently by different people and in different cultures, but a common factor of "transcendence" and "oneness with the universe" runs through the interpretations. The great Russian writer Dostoevski, who was very probably epileptic, was subject to sudden episodes of what he interpreted as religious ecstasy. He described the feeling in a passage from *The Possessed*, published in 1871 and quoted in Beyerstein (1987-88):

> You suddenly feel the presence of external harmony . . . you suddenly perceive the entirety of creation . . . it is a joy so great that, even if it were to last more than five seconds, the soul would not endure it and it would fade away . . . and for that I would give my whole life and not think I was paying too dearly.

Mandell (1980) has extensively reviewed the physiological and neurochemical research relevant to the brain processes underlying feelings of transcendental joy and euphoria. The basic physiological mechanisms involved in these states seem to be the same whether the state of euphoria is generated by epileptic activity or by drugs. Similar physiological changes may be brought about by the rhythmic chanting, singing, and dancing seen in the religious and conversion rituals of many cultures (Beyerstein, 1987-88; Henry, 1982). What differs in these situations is not the feeling but the cause to which it is attributed.

While epilepsy affects behavior dramatically during a seizure, it also has effects on behavior in the period between seizures. The personality of individuals with temporal lobe epilepsy is recognizably different in many cases from that of people not suffering from this disorder. The syndrome of temporal lobe epileptic personality includes "occurrence of spontaneous ecstatic episodes, religious preoccupations and compulsive, usually metaphysical, writing and preaching with a general feeling state of good-natured kindness" and a "reduction of interest in sexuality (*not* impotence)" (Mandell, 1980, p. 437). Temporal lobe epileptics are also much more likely to have had multiple religious conversions (Mandell, 1980). See Geschwind (1983) for additional discussion.

Epilepsy varies greatly in severity from individual to individual. At the extreme end of the range are individuals who, while they have never had overt seizures or even absence spells, do show signs of mild, epileptic-like temporal lobe dysfunction when their electroencephalograms, or EEGs (brain waves) are examined. These individuals show some of the personality characteristics of those with overt temporal lobe epilepsy. These personality characteristics, when seen in clinically nonepileptic individuals, have been termed "temporal lobe signs" by Persinger (1984a), who developed a questionnaire test to detect them. Makarec and Persinger (1985) found high positive correlations between the number of temporal lobe signs in a nonepileptic population and actual EEG measures of epileptic-like temporal lobe activity (ELTLA). Persinger (1984b) showed that during a "peak experience" induced by meditation, one subject had a large increase in ELTLA. Nine other meditating individuals whose EEG was also recorded during meditation showed no increase in ELTLA and reported no peak experiences, although the normal meditation-induced relaxation was found. In another case reported by Persinger (1984b), a subject who "spoke in tongues" had increased ELTLA during the period when she felt herself to be in "closest contact with the Spirit" (p. 131). Another subject who spoke in tongues showed no increased ELTLA. Persinger (1984a) found a strong positive correlation between temporal lobe signs and the tendency to have experiences that were interpreted as paranormal. Persinger and Makarec (1987) have reported similar results in a sample of some 400 college students.

Neepe (1983) has separately developed a questionnaire test for temporal lobe signs and finds that individuals who report alleged paranormal experiences score higher on his questionnaire than do those who report no such experiences. Neepe (1983) also provides some suggestion that individuals who report having paranormal experiences have higher levels of ELTLA than those who do not have such experiences. Nelson (1970, cited in Neepe, 1983) found EEG signs of temporal lobe "instability" in ten out of twelve trance mediums tested. The presence of temporal lobe signs also correlates positively with hypnotic susceptibility (Persinger and De Sano, 1986; Ross and Persinger, 1987). Along similar lines, hypnotic susceptibility has been shown to be positively correlated with a personality trait termed *absorption* by Tellegen and Atkinson (1974), who developed a test of this trait. The highly absorptive individual is one who easily blocks out distracting inputs, can "get lost" in a book, film, television show, or fantasy, and can focus attention on a given stimulus, whether the stimulus is external or self-generated. Tellegen and Atkinson (1974) suggest that such highly absorptive individuals are more likely to have a "dissociative experience." It is just this type of experience that can lead to acceptance of the reality of paranormal experiences. Davidson, Schwartz, and Rothman (1976) used an EEG measure of attention and found that subjects who scored high on absorption were better able than others to inhibit brain activity in a brain area related to a distracting stimulus. Galbraith, Cooper, and London (1972) found a similar ability in highly hypnotizable subjects, as did Spiegel, Cutcomb, Ren, and Pribram (1985). The latter authors showed that asking highly hypnotizable subjects to imagine a barrier between their eyes and a light stimulus reduced the neural response to that light. No such effect was found in the less hypnotizable subjects.

What does this welter of correlations and research reports mean? First, it provides considerable support for Persinger's (1983) hypothesis that mystical and paranormal experiences are caused by subtle abnormalities in the electrical activity of the temporal lobes or underlying neural structures. They also offer a starting point for an explanation of why there are large individual differences in the propensity to have what are interpreted as paranormal experiences. Because of mild electrophysiological abnormalities, some individuals may be less able to distinguish between reality and fantasy due to their greater ability to block out intruding reality when attending to a fantasy. It should not be thought, however, that physiological explanations can account for all acceptance of paranormal experiences as real. The more purely psychological factors such as constructive memory and perception and the fallacy of personal validation also play a strong role. Their role may be greater in those individuals who are not subject to increased ELTLA.

One final neurological disorder has been responsible for reports of paranormal events. This is the migraine headache (Beyerstein, 1987-88), the third of the diseases whose symptoms were described above. Like the symptoms of epilepsy, the symptoms of migraine vary greatly from individual to individual (Sacks, 1985). Migraine is generally caused when blood vessels in the brain spontaneously constrict and then greatly expand (Adams and Victor, 1985). The expansion results in the often excruciating pain of the migraine headache. During the constriction phase, blood supply to the brain areas supplied by the constricting vessels is diminished. Often these vessels supply the occipital lobes, where much visual function is centered. The resultant lack of blood causes striking "fortification illusions" (figure 2), so named because of their resemblance to fortresses of the Middle Ages. The fortification illusion is due to the cells in the visual cortex becoming, for a period of a few minutes, highly active in response to their lowered blood supply. Following this, they cease activity, and the result is a blind spot (or *scotoma*). The fortification illusion may be either colored or black and white, depending presumably on the specific areas of the visual cortex involved. The illusion, which is very striking, appears as a bright, shimmering, ineffable pattern that slowly grows in size as the attack continues. Showers of bright lights ("seeing stars") may also accompany the attack. Some lucky individuals, for reasons that are far from clear, experience only the illusions and not the pain. Beyerstein (1987-88) and Sacks (1985) have both pointed out the great similarity between the illusions of the migraine attack and the drawings by various religious mystics and others who claim to have had religious visions (figure 3).

3

Life After Death

The idea that the human spirit survives after the physical death of the body is probably as old as humanity and plays an extremely important role in nearly all of the world's great religions. On a more mundane level, hardly a week goes by that the supermarket tabloids don't proclaim "startling new evidence of life after death," while the occult sections of bookstores are filled with sensational paperbacks alleged to contain true reports of ghosts (Holzer, 1974). This chapter will examine several phenomena that are said to provide evidence for the reality of life, or survival of some sort, after death.

The best evidence for survival after death would be contact between the living and the spirits of the dead. Such contact was the goal of spiritualism. However, as was discussed in chapter two, the spiritualistic movement totally failed to produce even a shred of evidence for such survival. Modern psychical researchers have thus generally turned away from mediums and spiritualism and looked for evidence of survival after death in other phenomena.

Ghosts and Poltergeists

The most dramatic and seemingly convincing evidence for the existence of ghosts comes from thousands of eyewitness reports of ghosts and apparitions. Less convincing, and much more common, are the odd noises (creaks and knockings) and movements of objects (such as doors closing "under their own power") that many people interpret as due to ghosts or spirits. Reports of both types of phenomena are very much like reports of UFOs in one vital respect. In both UFO and ghost reports, eyewitness reports form the basis for considering the phenomena as genuine. As will be explained in the discussion of UFOs in chapters seven and eight, eyewitness reports are astonishingly unreliable due to the constructive nature of both perception and memory. In the case of reports of ghostly apparitions, another important factor further diminishes the credibility of eyewitness reports: hallucinations.

Ghosts are usually spotted at night by someone who has just retired to bed. After going to bed, people fall into a sort of "in between" state where they are neither fully awake nor fully asleep. During this period *hypnagogic hallucinations* are quite common. These hallucinations are distinct from dreams in that they may seem to the individual to be real. If you've ever heard your name called as you were falling asleep, but you know that no one really called you, you've had a hypnagogic hallucination. Auditory hallucinations are most common, but visual imagery is enhanced as well in this state, and highly realistic visual hallucinations, as well as combined visual and auditory hallucinations, do occur (for more details on such hallucinations, see Siegel and West, 1975). A similar type of hallucination occurs when one awakens and is termed a *hypnopompic hallucination* (Siegel and West, 1975). These two types of hallucinations are responsible for a great number of impressive reports of ghosts and similar apparitions.

As in other areas of the paranormal, such as prophetic dreams, a reporting bias exists that spuriously increases the frequency of dramatic ghostly encounters. Unspectacular hypnagogic hallucinations, such as hearing one's name called, are likely to go unreported or even unremembered. However, a spectacular hallucination of a ghost, perhaps complete with groans and other auditory "special effects," is very likely to arouse one into full wakefulness, so the hallucination will be firmly planted in memory.

Recent findings show that a very large percentage of normal individuals have experienced auditory hallucinations even when fully awake. Posey and Losch (1983-84) found that more than 70 percent of a sample of 375 college students had at some time experienced an auditory hallucination of hearing voices while they were awake. Such hallucinations may readily be mistaken for ghosts or taken as evidence of the paranormal by those experiencing them. This is especially true since the high frequency of these waking hallucinations is not a well-known finding. It is the commonness of such hallucinations, along with the relatively high frequency of hypnopompic and hypnagogic hallucinations, that acocunts for the 50 percent of Americans who report that they have had some sort of paranormal experience indicative of life after death (Greeley, 1987). Greeley's research indicates that initial belief in life after death does not make one more or less likely to have an experience that is interpreted as evidence for life after death or communication with the dead. This is just what would be expected on the basis of the high frequency of waking auditory and hypnagogic and hypnopompic hallucinations. Belief in life after death does not affect the probability of experiencing such hallucinations. However, as Greeley's (1987) research also shows, having such an experience can engender strong belief. Psychologically, then, the effects of having such a hallucination, and misinterpreting it as reality, are very similar to seeing a strange light in the sky and misinterpreting it as a flying saucer. Both experiences can result in very powerful beliefs.

Most reports of hauntings, however, derive from far more mundane phenomena. Strange moans, groans, knockings, and the like are heard. Or doors swing shut when no breeze was about. These are sometimes interpreted as being due to a ghostly presence, even if an apparition is never seen. It is certainly a giant leap from a series of odd noises or a door swinging to a haunted house. Any house, but especially older ones, will creak and groan as the temperature or humidity changes. Such noises can easily be mistaken for the sound of footsteps by those inclined to imagine the presence of a deceased tenant in their abode. A well-balanced door can be readily shut by a slight breeze, too small to be detected by the witness standing a few feet away. My own experience with these sorts of reports is that, as one mentions the many nonghostly alternatives, the report becomes more and more embellished, much like an eight-inch trout that grows to a two-foot monster as the story of its catching is told over and over.

Fraud and hoax have long played a role in reports of ghosts and hauntings, especially in the most dramatic cases. MacKay (1841/1980) describes numerous cases of faked hauntings including a 1649 case in England in which a series of dreadful ghostly occurrences drove a group of Cromwell's administrators from a palace in Woodstock. The haunting was later revealed to have been the work of a royal loyalist. In spite of the fact that the cases MacKay relates were fraudulent, hundreds, probably thousands, of people were convinced of their reality before the real causes were determined.

Two of the most dramatic and allegedly well-documented modern cases of hauntings have likewise turned out to be fraudulent. The cases in question are those of Borley Rectory in England and the "Amityville Horror" in Amityville, New York.

Borley Rectory in Essex became popularly known as "the most haunted house in England" after a book of that title was published in 1940 by Harry Price. Price's book purports to document a series of astonishing hauntings and manifestations from the time the rectory was built in 1863. The manifestations Price reported included the ghosts of a nun and several other individuals; all sorts of noises in and around the rectory that, according to Price, could not have been due to normal causes; spontaneous fires; mysterious cold spots; unexplained ringing of electrical bells that had been installed in the rectory; crockery flying through the air without any human assistance; and even mysterious messages written on the walls by the ghosts.

The phenomena Price reported in his book were said to have been witnessed by many of the inhabitants of the rectory over the years, and Price interviewed many of them for the book. He also visited the rectory on many occasions and, from May 1937 to May 1938, rented it himself, relating his own experiences at the rectory in the book.

The book was very well received and many readers found it convincing. One reader, Sir Albion Richard, K.C., C.B.E., said of the book:

> The evidence which he [i.e., Mr. Price] has collected of the phenomena which appeared there is as conclusive as human testimony can ever be and is admirably marshalled.
>
> I have not met anyone who has read the book—and it is mainly with legal friends of long experience in the weighing and sifting of evidence that I have discussed it—(many of them, like myself, previously sceptical) who has not been satisfied that the manifestations therein disclosed are proved by the evidence, to the point of moral certainty. (Quoted in Dingwall, Goldney, and Hall, 1956, p. 171).

Another famous English jurist, Sir Ernest Jelf, then Senior Master of the Supreme Court, was equally impressed with the evidence in Price's book (Dingwall, Goldney, and Hall, 1956).

The rectory burned in February 1939 but until the remains were finally torn down in 1944 people continued to visit the site and report strange occurrences. Price published a second volume, *The End of Borley Rectory*, in 1946; he died two years later, in 1948.

In the early 1950s the Society for Psychical Research in England undertook a complete investigation of the haunting. The result is a painstaking and scrupulous book, *The Haunting of Borley Rectory*, by parapsychologists Dingwall, Goldney, and Hall, published in 1956. Unfortunately the book is long out of print but a short summary can be found in Hall (1985).

Dingwall, Goldney, and Hall (1956) demolish the claim that Borley Rectory was ever haunted. They find, by comparing reports in Price's books to the actual statements that witnesses made to Price and which are still preserved, that Price distorted and embellished reports to make them much more dramatic than they actually were. Their investigation also made it clear that during the period in which the seemingly paranormal goings-on were at their peak, Mrs. Marianne Foyster, wife of the Rev. Lionel Foyster who lived at the rectory from 1930 to 1935, was actively engaged in fraudulently creating these phenomena. Price himself "salted the mine" and faked several phenomena while he was at the rectory. When such phenomena were seen by others, as in one case where a glass of water mysteriously turned to ink, they were embellished and entered Price's books as further evidence of the reality of the haunting.

Dingwall *et al.* (1956) find a nonparanormal explanation for nearly every incident reported from Borley. The very few that go unexplained do not constitute support for the reality of the haunting, any more than the "irreducible minimum" number of unexplained UFO sightings constitute evidence for extraterrestrial visitation. Rather, they are merely cases about which not enough is known to arrive at the correct explanation. In any case, as was shown in chapter one, the burden of proof should not rest on the skeptic. In their conclusion Dingwall *et al.* (1956, p. 168) state that "when analysed, the evidence for haunting and poltergeist activity for each and every period appears to diminish in force and finally to vanish away."

Harry Price was well known as a ghost hunter and psychic investigator before his first book on Borley Rectory appeared. Hall (1978) has shown that Price's regard for the truth was as poor in the other paranormal occurrences that he reported as it was in the case of Borley Rectory.

If Borley Rectory is the most famous haunted house in England, the "Amityville Horror" house in Amityville, New York, is probably the most famous haunted house in the United States. This house has a much more gruesome history than the rectory. In late 1974 six members of the DeFeo family were murdered (shot to death) by a seventh member of the family, Ronald DeFeo. In 1975 the house was purchased by George and Kathy Lutz. Within hours of their moving in, they were witness to the most astonishing and horrible hauntings in the history of parapsychology, according to Jay Anson's 1977 book, *The Amityville Horror*. It was so bad that the Lutzes stayed in the house only twenty-eight days.

What happened while they were in the house? The incidents read like the script for a horror movie—one with lots of special effects. Large statues moved about the house with no human assistance. Kathy Lutz levitated in her sleep. Green slime oozed from the walls. Mysterious voices were heard, sometimes saying, "Get out, get out." A large door was ripped off its hinges. Hundreds of flies appeared seemingly from nowhere. In fact, the book was made into a movie in 1979.

It has since been revealed that the book was a hoax from start to finish, dreamed up by the Lutzes with the sole purpose of making money. Morris (1977-78) in a long review pointed out numerous problems with the claims in the book even before it was known to be a hoax. Moran and Jordan (1978) investigated some of the incidents reported in the book and found that the events described never happened. For example, a Father Mancuse is said in the book to have attempted to rid the house of its ghosts by using holy water. He is said to have had a mysterious car accident very shortly thereafter, and to have had his hands break out in a terrible rash. His own living quarters began to reek so badly that he and other priests couldn't stand to live there. This entire story was made up, as Moran and Jordan (1978) show. Not only did none of these dramatic incidents happen to Father Mancuse, he never even entered the Lutzes' house. Other incidents reported in the book also turn out to be fictitious when subjected to Moran's and Jordan's investigation.

In the summer of 1979 lawyer William Weber, who defended murderer Ronald DeFeo, revealed the origin of the hoax. Weber had been planning to write a book about the case itself when the Lutzes contacted him regarding their experiences in the house. Thinking that these might make an interesting addition to his own book, Weber spoke with the Lutzes at length. In a United Press interview in July 1979 (see Frazier, 1979-80) Weber said, "We created this horror story over many bottles of wine that George Lutz was drinking. We were really playing with each other. We were creating something the public would want to hear about." When Weber mentioned that the murders took place about 3 A.M., Kathy Lutz said, "Well, that's good. I can say I'm awakened by noises at that hour . . . and I could say I had dreams at that hour of the day about the DeFeo family."

Owners of the house since the Lutzes moved out have not noted a single incident of anything out of the ordinary. Barbara Cromarty, who lived in the house after the Lutzes left, said, "We know everything was a hoax" (Frazier, 1979-80, p. 3). The current owners, however, are troubled by another type of manifestation: the curious people and crackpots who come from miles around to gawk or to look for ghosts.

Closely related to classical hauntings is the poltergeist, German for "playful spirit." The two are sometimes reported together, as was the case at Borley Rectory. Some of the goings on in the "Amityville Horror" house would have been classified as poltergeists, had they not been revealed as part of a hoax. The vast majority of the thousands of poltergeist reports that have accumulated over the years are of mild, even humorous, events such as objects moving about when no one is watching, breaking of crockery, spontaneous small fires, and showers of pebbles and small stones, the latter often being inflicted on some particular adult like a priest. Poltergeists, when they occur alone, are almost invariably associated with adolescent children. This association has led some parapsychologists (i.e., Fodor, 1964) to propose that the approach of puberty and attendant increase in sexual energy and feelings in adolescents causes a release of psychic energy that is responsible for the poltergeist activity. This association between adolescents and poltergeist activity causes the more skeptical to reflect on adolescents' well-known love of pranks and practical jokes—particularly when played on adults. Those who believe poltergiests are a paranormal phenomenon will quickly point to many cases, mostly decades old, that "have never been explained." This is quite true, but is merely another example of the "irreducible minimum" argument used by UFOlogists and other proponents of pseudoscience to shift the burden of proof to skeptics. And, as usual, poltergeist reports are based entirely on eyewitness testimony. The case for their reality as anything other than teen-age pranks is exceedingly poor.

In March 1984 a poltergeist occurrence in Columbus, Ohio, received nationwide and even worldwide media attention. Typically, the coverage was totally uncritical. In New York City, for example, WCBS-TV used the phrase "Poltergeist for real!" as the teaser for the story on the evening news. At the center of the incident was, predictably, a fourteen-year-old girl named Tina Resch.

Shortly after Tina, an emotionally disturbed adoptee, had seen the movie *Poltergeist*, objects began to fly about in the Resch household. This phenomenon quickly came to the attention of the *Columbus Dispatch*, which published several photos showing, allegedly, a telephone flying through the air under its own power while Tina looked on in horror. Parapsychologist William Roll of the Psychical Research Foundation in Chapel Hill, North Carolina, stayed in the Resch house to investigate the case. He concluded that "when I felt I had Tina under close observation" she demonstrated "genuine recurrent spontaneous psychokinesis" (quoted in Randi, 1984-85, p. 232). "Recurrent spontaneous psychokinesis," or RSPK, is Roll's term for the poltergeist phenomenon.

Randi, a well-known magician and Fellow of the Committee for the Scientific Investigation of Claims of the Paranormal, also came to Columbus with a team of scientists to investigate the case, but was denied entrance to the Resch house. Nonetheless, their investigation, reported in Randi (1984-85), revealed that Tina had faked the entire string of occurrences. Not only were the media easily duped by a fourteen-year-old girl, but also, in several cases, the media knew about the fraud but failed to report it.

The Resch poltergeist turned out to be so elusive that no one ever actually saw a single object even start to move of its own accord. This included the newspaper photographer who found that if he watched an object it stubbornly refused to budge. So, he would hold up his camera and look away. "While Tina sat in a soft chair with two telephones within easy reach, Shannon [the photographer] looked away. When he saw a movement from the corner of his eye, he pressed the shutter" (Randi, 1984-85, p. 224). One of the photos obtained in this way was distributed by Associated Press and touted widely as proof of the reality of the phenomenon. Examined closely, the photographic evidence in this case strongly suggested that Tina was faking the occurrences by simply throwing the phone and other "flying" objects when no one was looking. Randi's careful analysis of the other photos, many unpublished, of Tina and her flying phone strengthen the conclusion that she was faking. Interestingly, the editor of the *Columbus Dispatch*, Luke Feck, embarrassed by the revelation that he and his paper were taken in by so obvious a fake, has refused Randi permission to print the photos they had given him earlier, in an apparent attempt to suppress the evidence of Tina's trickery and the newspaper's credulity.

This refusal came only after Randi had uncovered even more direct evidence of Tina's faking: she was caught faking on videotape. A camera crew from WTVN-TV in Cincinnati had been filming in the Resch home. While the crew were packing up to leave, a camera, pointed at Tina, was accidentally left on and recording. Randi (1984-85, p. 228) describes what the camera caught: "Seated at one end of the sofa, near an end-table, and believing the camera was no longer active, she watched carefully until she was unobserved, then reached up and pulled a tablelamp toward herself, simultaneously jumping away, letting out a series of bleating noises, and feigning, quite effectively, a reaction of stark terror." This all was revealed when the tape was processed. When confronted with the evidence, Tina said she had only done it to get the television crew to leave.

Typically, this incident and Tina's explanation led some to conclude that Tina only cheated "sometimes"; the rest of the time the paranormal phenomena were genuine. For example, the reporter, Mike Harden, who first reported the poltergeist, wrote in the *Columbus Dispatch* that the same day that Tina had been caught cheating, the television crew had witnessed a true poltergeist occurrence in the form of a moving table. But WTVN crew member Robb Forest saw Tina move the table with her foot.

What of parapsychologist Roll's statement as to Tina's genuineness? It turned out that he, like others, had not actually seen any object start to move. In one incident, he was facing away from a picture when it fell from the wall. This took place upstairs in the Resch house and Tina had been up there, apparently alone, for half an hour before this event. As Roll was attempting to rehang the photograph, using a pair of pliers to drive in the nail, a small tape recorder flew some feet from the dresser where it had been left. The layout of the room shows that Roll had his back to the recorder when it made its short journey and, attending to the task of rehanging the fallen photograph, couldn't have been watching Tina closely at all. Randi (1984-85, p. 233) further points out that "Roll is myopic and wears thick glasses; he is a poor observer."

So, the Tina Resch case crashes in flames. But how many television stations and newspapers that initially reported it as verified evidence of the reality of poltergeists have informed their viewers or readers of the results of the full investigation of the case? Not many, as you might expect.

Randi (1984-85, p. 222) makes an important point in his discussion of the Resch case, saying:

> I have long believed that the major difference between the skeptic and the parapsychologist is one of expectation. The former does not believe that validation of paranormal claims is imminent; the latter depends upon that event for justification. Also, the skeptic will invoke parsimony—the simplest explanation consistent with the facts—where the parapsychologist eschews it. Personally, I find it much more reasonable, when objects fly around the room in the vicinity of an unhappy 14-year-old, to suspect poor reporting and observation rather than a repeal of the basic laws of physics.

Perception and memory being constructive, the expectations of the parapsychologist are frequently met.

Near-death and Out-of-body Experiences

Badly injured in an automobile accident, the victim is rushed to the nearest hospital emergency room. Working frantically, the doctors manage to save him. Later, after his recovery, he tells a strange story. He saw, as if from a vantage point near the ceiling of the emergency room, the entire scene as the doctors worked to save him. It was as if he were floating above his physical body looking down on it. Then, he found himself moving down a tunnel with a blazing white light at the end. As he neared the end of the tunnel, a being dressed in white, together with a dead relative, came toward him and told him his time had not yet come. During the entire experience, he felt a great sense of unity and profound understanding and a total lack of anxiety.

Reports such as this have been collected by several investigators who argue that they represent true reports of an afterlife (Ring, 1980; Moody, 1976; Osis and Haraldsson, 1977). These investigators make a point of the great similarity of these "deathbed" visions, even across different cultures. This is what would be expected if the visions were really memories of a trip to the threshold of the afterlife. However, proponents of the afterlife interpretation of these reports grossly underestimate the variability among reports. One researcher (Rawlings, 1978) found that the patients he talked to often reported visiting Hell; no other researcher in this area has elicited such reports. In Ring's (1980) reports, the tunnel imagery is rarely found.

Moody (1976, p. 87) has explicitly called attention to the great variability in the reports: "There is an enormously wide spectrum of experiences, with some people having only one or two of the elements, and others most of them." In addition, reports of this type are quite rare. Most people lying critically injured in the emergency room don't experience them.

The way in which the reports are collected poses another serious problem for those who want to take them seriously as evidence of an afterlife. Osis and Haraldsson's (1977) study was based on replies received from 10,000 questionnaires sent to doctors and nurses in the United States and India. Only 6.4 percent were returned. Since it was the doctors and nurses who were giving the reports, not the patients who had, presumably, actually had the experience, the reports were secondhand. This means they had passed through two highly fallible and constructive human memory systems (the doctor's or nurse's and the actual patient's) before reaching Osis and Haraldsson. In other cases (i.e., Moody, 1977) the reports were given by the patients themselves, but months and years after the event. Such reports are hardly sufficient to argue for the reality of an afterlife.

Near-death visions are actually hallucinations. Siegel (1980) has described the high degree of similarity between near-death visions and other types of hallucinations (such as drug-induced hallucinations) in both form and content. Thus, hallucinations caused by drugs frequently contain images of long tunnels, blinding light, otherworldly beings, friends alive and dead, and so forth. However, most of the individuals who experience deathbed visions are not drugged. What, then, is responsible for their hallucinations? The answer is *cerebral anoxia*. When the body is badly injured—especially if the heart stops, even if only for a brief period—the brain is deprived of oxygen. Even a very brief period of cerebral anoxia such as sixty to ninety seconds can result in impairment of neuronal function (Brierley and Graham, 1984).

The effects of cerebral anoxia are well known (Alcock, 1981). Initially there is a feeling of wellbeing and power. As the anoxia continues and more neurons become impaired, there is a loss in the ability to make critical judgments, reality becomes vague, and hallucinations appear.

The response of the proponents of life after death to this argument is to admit that cerebral anoxia, drugs, and brain damage can cause hallucinations that are essentially identical to deathbed visions. But the hallucination hypothesis, they claim, is not sufficient to explain the visions because not every patient who has ever had such a vision has been conclusively shown to have been anoxic, brain-damaged, or drugged. Again, the "irreducible minimum" number of allegedly unexplainable reports is thrown up as proof of the paranormal hypothesis after the initial mass of supposedly supportive evidence that the proponents started with, has been whittled down to almost nothing by careful inspection. Certainly there will always be cases in which, because of incomplete medical information, it will never be possible to show that a particular patient was anoxic or intoxicated. However, the fact that anoxia and drug intoxication are known to produce hallucinations just like the report given by the patient would suggest the rational conclusion that the patient was anoxic or drugged, not that the patient had visited the threshold of the afterlife.

When recovered, patients sometimes report comments and bits of conversation that took place while they were presumably unconscious, either due to the severity of injuries or to anesthesia. Should this be seen as convincing evidence for some sort of "astral" body being detached from the physical body and observing the situation? No. Even during unconsciousness, the brain is able to register sensory impressions. Thus, events that occur when an individual is asleep may appear in the dreams (Arkin, Antrobus, and Ellman, 1978; Foulkes, 1985). Further, the brain can discriminate between important and unimportant events while the individual is asleep (Arkin, Antrobus, and Ellman, 1978). A classic example is the new parent who is awakened by the slightest cry of the infant, but sleeps right through much louder, but less important, noises. Registration of sensory inputs also can take place while the individual is anesthetized, as general anesthetics do not block the sensory inputs to the brain. The registration of stimuli in anesthetized patients was recently demonstrated by Millar and Watkinson (1983). While patients who were undergoing surgery were anesthetized, a tape-recorded list of words was presented to them. After recovery from anesthesia their memory was tested. When asked to recall the words on the list, they were unable to do so. However, when they were asked simply to recognize which of two words had been presented to them, they were correct at a rate significantly above chance. Thus, even while under general anesthetic, the brain does retain some capacity to store new information, although it may be difficult to retrieve this information later. This is very likely the source of the snippets of conversation that sometimes turn up in deathbed visions.

Near-death experiences do seem to have psychological effects on those who experience them. The individuals may become more secure, more religious, and may adopt a generally more mystical and "spiritual" world view (Irwin, 1985). These personality changes testify to the power of the misinterpretation of what is actually happening to the individual. Similarly, although less dramatic, changes may take place in those who have experienced an auditory hallucination that they misinterpret as evidence of life after death or see an object in the sky which they can't identify at once and therefore misinterpret as an extraterrestrial flying saucer.

The personality changes and the extreme conviction with which people hold to the new beliefs engendered by a near-death experience convince many that the new beliefs are valid. It is important to remember, however, that the strength of a belief is no guide to its validity. Hundreds of people, for example, believed with all their heart that the Reverend Jim Jones was a true miracle worker (in fact he used sleight of hand to fake faith healings) who would lead them to the promised land. Many converts experienced personality changes after joining Jones's church. In spite of the firmness of their convictions, they died in the jungles of Guyana.

Out-of-body experiences (OBEs) can occur in non-life-threatening situations, and some individuals claim they can leave their physical body at will and travel through space using their "astral" body. Another term for this ability is *astral projection.* It has attracted considerable interest among parapsychologists. At least conceptually, testing for the reality of such OBEs would seem to be quite easy: you find a subject who claims to be able to have an OBE at will, place the subject in a sealed room, and ask the subject to, for example, read the serial number of a dollar bill sealed in a box in another room. Experiments similar in concept to this one have been done. They have not yielded evidence to support the reality of the OBE (Blackmore, 1982, chapter 18).

A phenomenological point is often raised to argue that OBEs really are due to something leaving the body: people reporting OBEs almost always report seeing their own body from a vantage point somewhere above it. If the OBE were nothing more than a hallucination combined with bits and pieces of memories acquired during the event, wouldn't one expect the result to be seen from the perspective of the physical body— for example, with the doctors looking down on the patient? In fact, there is nothing at all unusual about the vantage point seen in OBEs. Remember the last time you went to the beach? Or the dinner you had last night? Try to form a visual image of some such occasion. The overwhelming majority of people see the scene from a vantage point above where they actually were. They, and presumably you, "see" themselves in the scene. This is in spite of the fact that all the information used to construct the image comes from memory. As far as I know, no one has ever used this fact about mental imagery to argue that whenever we form a mental image of something that happened to us in the past, we are actually projecting our astral body back in time. But such a claim would make as much sense as the claim that, because the person is looking down on his body in the OBE, the OBE must be truly paranormal in nature.

In her book-length review of the OBE literature, parapsychologist Susan Blackmore (1982) concluded that the OBE experience, while extremely interesting from a psychological point of view, provides no evidence for any type of paranormal event. Irwin (1985), in a more recent book on the topic, reaches the same conclusion. Both Blackmore (1982) and Irwin (1985) focus on psychological differences between those who have and have not experienced OBEs (OBE-ers and non-OBE-ers). Blackmore (1982) hypothesized that OBE-ers would be better than non-OBE-ers at forming visual images and that OBE-ers would be poorer at distinguishing reality from fantasy than non-OBE-ers. Recent research on the psychological differences between OBE-ers and non-OBE-ers has strongly confirmed Blackmore's (1982) hypotheses. OBE-ers are more likely to remember dreams from a "bird's-eye perspective" and are better at forming visual images from that perspective than are non-OBE-ers (Blackmore, 1986a). It is this bird's-eye perspective that is so common in OBEs and is one of the aspects of the experience that OBE-ers find so compelling. People who have experienced OBEs are also more susceptible to hypnosis than are non-OBE-ers (see Irwin, 1985, for a brief review). OBE-ers also show greater suggestibility and become more deeply absorbed more easily than non-OBE-ers (Irwin, 1985). Individuals who can be hypnotized are more likely to experience imagined or suggested events as real, even when not hypnotized (Irwin, 1985). Thus, individuals who have become convinced that some nonphysical aspect of their personality has left their physical body differ from individuals who have not had such an experience in that they are less able to distinguish reality from fantasy.

Reincarnation

Arguments that reincarnation is a real phenomenon are based on reports of people who, either spontaneously or under hypnosis, remember past lives and details of those lives that they would have, supposedly, no other way of knowing. Cases allegedly proving reincarnation are numerous, and it has proved impossible to conduct detailed investigations of all of them. However, when the most dramatic cases are investigated carefully, evidence for the reality of reincarnation evaporates. The investigation of alleged cases of reincarnation reveals the normal sources of the information that the individuals supposedly could have obtained only in a previous life. But proponents of reincarnation often conduct very poor investigations and hence miss the true explanations.

The most famous alleged case of reincarnation is that of Bridey Murphy. In 1952 one Virginia Tighe was hypnotized. She reported details of a previous life in Cork, Ireland, as "Bridey Murphy." While hypnotized, she spoke in a distinct Irish accent that she did not have normally and described her life in Cork in great detail. Her case was reported as proof of reincarnation in Bernstein's (1956) best-selling book, *The Search for Bridey Murphy*.

The case was thoroughly investigated several years later. It was discovered that, as a child, Mrs. Tighe had had a neighbor across the street who had grown up in Ireland and used to tell her stories about life there. The woman's maiden name? You guessed it—Bridey Murphy. Further, it was revealed that Mrs. Tighe had been involved in theater in high school and had "learned several Irish monologues, which she had delivered in what her former teacher referred to as a heavy Irish brogue" (Alcock, 1978-79, p. 38; see also Gardner, 1957, for more on the debunking of the Bridey Murphy case).

Iverson (1977) reported the case of Jane Evans, among others, in a book claiming to prove the existence of reincarnation. Evans was a housewife living in Wales who, under hypnosis, gave details of six past lives. The great amount of historically accurate detail in Evans's accounts led Iverson (1977) to argue that her case was excellent proof of reincarnation. For example, in one of her past lives she was a maid of Jacques Coeur, an extremely wealthy and powerful merchant in fifteenth-century France. Evans "was able to fully describe the exteriors and interiors of Coeur's magnificent house—she even gave details of the carvings over the fireplace in his main banquet hall" (Harris, 1986, p. 21). Impressive stuff, to be sure, until it is realized that Coeur's house is "one of the most photographed houses in all of France" (Harris, 1986, p. 22), interior and exterior.

Evans's account of her life in Coeur's house contains one most puzzling, and significant, error. She says he was not married and had no children. But he was married and had five children—not the sort of thing the maid would be likely to overlook. This omission on Evans's part is most illuminating. A novel based on Coeur's life titled *The Moneyman* by Thomas B. Costain contains great detail about Coeur's life, but makes no mention of his wife or children. Harris (1986, p. 22), who has investigated Iverson's (1977) cases states that "there is overwhelmingly strong evidence" that this book provided the basis for Evans's "memories" of her life in fifteenth-century France.

Evans's tales of her other lives contained similar errors and historical inconsistencies. She also reported a life as a Jew in the twelfth century in York, England. In that life she remembered being forced to wear a badge of yellow circles denoting that she was Jewish. However, badges for Jews were not used in England until the thirteenth century and then were not made of yellow circles, but white stripes (Harris, 1986).

In yet another life, Evans was a woman living in the time of the Roman occupation of England. Her knowledge of that period was quite detailed. It was this detail that allowed Harris (1986) to trace the origin of her information. It came from a best-selling novel set in that time period titled *The Living Wood* (de Wohl, 1947). Harris (1986, p. 23) notes that *"every single piece of information* given by Jane Evans can be traced to de Wohl's fictional account. She uses his fictional sequences in exactly the same order and even speaks of his fictional characters, such as Curio and Valerius, as if they were real people."

Are cases like those of Bridey Murphy and Jane Evans hoaxes? Not in the usual sense that a conscious attempt was made to deceive. Tighe and Evans (and the hundreds of others who report past-life memories) presumably really believe that these memories come from a past life. In just the same way, people who see a strange light at night often come to believe passionately that they have seen a flying saucer, complete with all the details one would expect on such a craft. Such belief can be extremely convincing to others, even though the belief is wrong.

Ian Stevenson, a parapsychologist at the University of Virginia in Charlottesville, is a leading proponent of reincarnation. In his writings on the subject (Stevenson, 1975, 1977) he presents case studies of people who have what he considers memories of past lives that they could not have obtained in any normal way. In one report (Stevenson, 1975) he described Indian children with alleged past-life memories. Barker (1979b), a colleague of Stevenson, has investigated one of these Indian cases, the one he considered the "most authentic, evidential and thoroughly investigated" (Barker, 1979a, p. 269). He concluded that the child in the case had acquired through normal means the information that Stevenson took as evidence of reincarnation.

Stevenson's work has been widely criticized, even in parapsychological circles (see Edwards, 1987c for a fuller discussion). The major problem with Stevenson's work is that the methods he used to investigate alleged cases of reincarnation are inadequate to rule out simple, imaginative story telling on the part of the children claiming to be reincarnations of dead individuals. In the seemingly most impressive cases Stevenson (1975, 1977) has reported, the children claiming to be reincarnated knew friends and relatives of the dead individual. The children's knowledge of facts about these individuals is, then, somewhat less than conclusive evidence for reincarnation.

Many proponents of reincarnation use hypnosis to elicit past-life memories. This technique produces totally unreliable reports, because hypnotized individuals will readily agree to leading questions, make up stories, fantasize, and thus report nonexistent past lives in detail. They may often truly believe that their "memories" are evidence for past lives, but, as has been seen, the strength of a belief is a very poor guide to its truth. Even claims that hypnosis can regress an individual back to his or her own childhood are unfounded (Nash, 1987).

The same type of process may take place even when people are not under hypnosis. When asked to relax and "imagine" themselves in some past life, they begin to make up a story set in the appropriate time and place. Some fantasy-prone individuals may have difficulty separating reality from fantasy, and the self-generated past-life story may take on so much reality that they believe it to be a real past-life memory.

Proponents of reincarnation sometimes claim that individuals can speak languages they have not learned in their present life. This is said to occur especially under age-regression hypnosis. Thomason (1984), a linguist, has investigated three such cases. As far as I know, these are the only three such cases to have been investigated by a qualified linguist. In the first of the three cases, a hypnotist claimed that one of his patients was speaking Bulgarian while hypnotized. The hypnotist himself did not know any Bulgarian and apparently made the judgment based on the general "sound" of the patient's utterances. In fact, the "language" was not only not Bulgarian, but wasn't any language at all. It was merely run-together sets of syllables that had a Slavic sound. The second case was similar. A patient claimed to be speaking Gaelic and to be a fourteenth-century Frenchman. Analysis of his speech showed that it combined modern French and Latin in a hodge-podge. Further undermining this patient's claim to regression to a past life are the facts that Gaelic was never spoken in France and the patient made many historically incorrect statements about fourteenth-century France while under hypnosis. The third case was of a woman who claimed to have been an Apache in a previous life. Her speech was almost all Hollywood-style pidgin English, for example: "He ride ponies for white man. I no care. He [white man] spoil my Dwaytskem [her husband]. I no like. He scout for white man. I go to happy hunting ground" (Thomason, 1984, p. 347).

Thomason (1984, 1986-87) also comments on an earlier analysis by Ian Stevenson (1974) of a woman known as "TE" who was supposed to be able to speak Swedish, learned in a past life. Thomason (1984, p. 347) comments that "Stevenson is . . . unsophisticated about language, and TE's 'Swedish' is as unconvincing as" the Bulgarian, Gaelic, and Apache in the other cases she examined.

Descriptions of other impressive-sounding evidence for reincarnation that disappeared upon close examination can be found in Harris (1986), Edwards (1987a, b) and Wilson (1982). Edwards (1986, p. 34) comments on Wilson's (1982) book saying that in it "all the most famous reincarnation cases are minutely examined and on the basis of meticulous research all of them are found wanting." For more philosophical criticisms of reincarnation theory, the reader is referred to Edwards, 1987a, 1987b, and 1987c.

A discussion of the evidence for life after death would not be complete without some mention of the belief that the voices of the dead can be heard on tape recorders. This turns out to be a surprisingly common belief, although it is unclear how seriously it is taken by many of those who talk about it. In any event, the usual claim is that if one takes a tape recorder out to a graveyard one can record the voices of the dead. How? Put the machine in the "record" mode with a blank tape and turn the volume all the way up. Then, when you play the tape back, if you listen carefully, you'll hear the voices of the dead. They're not very clear, to be sure, but if you listen long and carefully, you can begin to make them out. It should be obvious what is happening here. The tape recorder, while it is recording, is picking up stray sounds from the environment and, especially, the sound of the breeze or wind passing over the microphone. When played back, these noises do sound strange and, at least to me, rather peaceful. If one expects to hear voices, constructive perception will produce voices. The voices, not surprisingly, are usually described as speaking in hoarse whispers. The Indians used to believe that the dead spoke as the wind swirled through the trees. The tape recorder has simply brought this illusion into a technological age.

According to the New Age movement, humankind is just on the threshold of a so-called "new age" of psychic enlightenment in which all psychic powers will be verified as real; all humans will possess such powers; people will all love one another; war, disease, and hunger will be forever banished from the earth; and, in short, the earth will be transformed into a near-paradise. A particularly bizarre element of the New Age vision is the claim that just such a world is seen when people are hypnotically sent into the future ("progressed" as opposed to "regressed"). Another claim is that people who have near-death experiences report being told of such a world by "others" during the experience. Unfortunately, as Edwards (1986) notes, those who have "progressed" have been sent far into the future, between 2100 and about 2600. Too far ahead, of course, to enable one who is "progressed" to bring back specific information with which to test the claim that he or she really stepped into the future.

4

Laboratory Parapsychology

Parapsychology is the study of extrasensory perception (ESP), precognition or clairvoyance (the ability to see into the future), and psychokinesis (PK— the ability to move or to influence objects with psychic powers). Collectively these are often referred to as *psi* or *psi phenomena*. The experimental literature in parapsychology is vast. Hyman (1985a) has estimated that it consists of approximately 3,000 experiments. These experiments have been largely carried out by competent, honest, rational investigators who are convinced that the data support the existence of psi phenomena. Nonetheless, the experimental work conducted to date has left the great majority of scientists unconvinced, to say the least, that ESP or any other such phenomenon has been demonstrated.

It is well beyond the scope of this chapter to review the entire corpus of experimental work in parapsychology, so the chapter will focus on the categories of experiments that are considered by proponents to show the best evidence for the reality of psi phenomena. Proponents might object to this approach on the grounds that it fails to consider certain specific experiments that proponents believe clearly establish the reality of ESP and related phenomena. Several points made earlier answer this type of objection. It will be recalled that in the cases of N-rays and polywater, it was not necessary for skeptics to explain away every experimental result that seemed to support the existence of these phenomena. What convinced everyone (with the exception of Blondlot himself in regard to N-rays) that these phenomena were spurious was their failure to replicate, combined with a powerful common factor that would explain, in general, the seemingly supportive results. In the case of N-rays this factor was the use of highly subjective measures of N-ray effects. In the polywater case, it was the inadequate examination of the "polywater" for impurities.

Further, the demand that every experiment in parapsychology must be considered and explained away in detail before one can reject the existence of psi phenomena is identical to the position of UFO proponents that skeptics must be able to attribute every UFO report to some known object before the extraterrestrial hypothesis of UFOs can be rejected. As will be seen in chapters seven and eight, there will always be some "irreducible minimum" number of unexplained UFO sightings. This in no way proves the claim that UFOs are extraterrestrial spacecraft; it simply means that investigators will never have all the information needed to find the known objects that caused each sighting.

Applying this logic to the parapsychological literature, the present chapter will focus on the failure of parapsychological studies to replicate, and the multiple and general procedural errors that have led to results seemingly supportive of psi phenomena. The reasons why many parpasychologists remain convinced of the reality of such phenomena, in spite of extremely poor evidence, will also be discussed.

Parapsychologists often complain that their critics use higher standards of proof for claims of psi phenomena than for other types of claims. They argue that critics reject as proof of the reality of psi evidence that they would accept as sufficient to prove more mundane claims. As was shown in chapter one, this is both true and reasonable because extraordinary claims demand extraordinary proof.

The issue of cheating and fraud also divides parapsychologists and their critics. There can be no doubt that, historically, cheating and fraud have been much more common in parapsychology than in other areas of scientific investigation. The reason is probably quite straightforward— the dearth of positive results pushes more investigators in parapsychology to cheat, compared to other research areas where positive results are obtained much more commonly. This is not to say, of course, that cheating does not go on in other areas of scientific investigation. It clearly does. It remains, however, less common than in parapsychology.

The relative frequency of dishonesty in parapsychology, by either investigators or their subjects, is no excuse for critics to fall into what Hyman (1980-81, 1985a) has termed the false dichotomy of accounting for all reports of experiments supporting the existence of psi by assuming that either the report is true or fraud was involved. There are a host of other explanations for positive reports that involve neither the reality of psi nor fraud. These explanations turn on what are often very subtle methodological flaws in experiments that can produce results that seem to support the reality of psi. As Hyman (1985a) has pointed out, it is the job of the responsible critic of parapsychology to work with parapsychologists toward the goal of eliminating such methodological errors and problems in a joint attempt to produce the best possible studies of psi. Only in this way can the critic really contribute to productive investigation of the existence of psi.

The Nature of the Evidence

Historically, the first type of evidence used to argue for the reality of ESP and related phenomena was drawn from spiritualism. As was noted in chapter two, such evidence was inadequate because of widespread fraud and the fact that witnesses who reported impressive spiritualistic phenomena were untrained in magic and sleight of hand.

In the 1930s a new, more laboratory-oriented, approach to the study of ESP gained popularity among parapsychologists. Subjects were to identify long series of hidden objects; their "hit rate" would be compared to that expected by chance. Usually, the objects to be guessed were cards or numbers. The most famous practitioners of this type of experimental parapsychology were J. B. Rhine, of Duke University in Durham, North Carolina, and S. G. Soal of England. Rhine's experiments are well known in this country, and his procedures for studying ESP have come to form the popular view of a typical ESP experiment. Rhine actually coined the term *extrasensory perception* in 1934 and popularized the use of the now-famous Zener ESP cards. These cards were named for a Duke University psychology professor, Carl Zener, who developed them when working with Rhine. Zener cards consist of a deck of twenty-five cards, five each with a different design printed on the face: square, circle, star, cross, and three wavy lines.

In the standard ESP experiment using Zener cards, the cards are arranged in random sequence, then shown—face down and one at a time—to the subject, who must identify which of the five designs is on the card. Since there are five possible designs, the rate of correct responses (the "hit rate") expected by chance is 20 percent. Hit rates significantly above chance or significantly below chance (the latter being termed *psi missing*) are taken as evidence of ESP in one form or another. We will see that numerous factors other than ESP can produce hit rates above chance.

The results of Rhine's experiments can be fairly easily summarized. For the most part, subjects scored at chance levels. That is, the hit rate when guessing which design was on the card was the 20 percent expected by chance. Occasionally, however, a few subjects were found to score significantly above chance for at least some period of time. This effect typically declined as testing of these "gifted" subjects continued.

The basic experiment can be varied in numerous ways. For example, the cards to be guessed can be shown to another person, who then attempts to send this information to the subject who is doing the actual guessing. Clairvoyance can be studied by having the subject guess the sequence of designs before the cards are randomized.

Most people, having heard about ESP and related phenomena in the popular media, tend to think there is a considerable body of scientific evidence for such phenomena. This is simply not so. The major problem in parapsychology is the lack of any repeatable paranormal phenomenon. Occasionally, seemingly impressive results pop up, but they have the curious property of not being repeatable in other laboratories—at least not when procedural, statistical, or other flaws in the construction of the experiment are corrected. Several examples of this will be discussed below. As in the case of N-rays and polywater, lack of repeatability is a sign that the alleged phenomenon is merely an artifact, the result of some experimental flaw, and not a real effect. It is this lack of repeatability of paranormal phenomena that has convinced the great majority of the scientific community that psi phenomena are non-existent.

The ubiquity of negative results has been troubling to parapsychologists as well as to their critics. Dommeyer (1975, p. 11) has commented that

> The reader inexperienced in parapsychology is likely to believe . . . that psi phenomena are relatively commonplace. The scientific investigator knows that this is not so. . . . The present reviewer, after spending the greater part of two summers in the 1960s at the Parapsychology Laboratory at Duke University, was unable to observe over those months a single identifiable instance of ESP or PK.

Crumbaugh (1966, p. 524) makes a similar point, but his experience covers a much longer period of time:

> At the time [1938] of performing the experiments involved I fully expected that they would yield easily all the final answers. I did not imagine that after 28 years I would still be in as much doubt as when I had begun. I repeated a number of the then current Duke techniques, but the results of 3,024 runs [one run consists of twenty-five guesses] of the ESP cards— as much work as Rhine reported in his first book—were all negative. In 1940 I utilized further methods with high school students, again with negative results.

Beloff (1973, p. 312) makes the same point:

> I recently completed a seven-year programme of parapsychological research with the help of one full time research assistant. No one would have been more delighted to obtain positive results than we, but for all the success we achieved ESP might just as well not have existed. . . . I have not found on comparing notes with other parapsychologists . . . that my experience is in any way out of the ordinary.

These, and additional testimony making the same point can be found in Alcock (1981).

The most common rationale offered by parapsychologists to explain the lack of a repeatable demonstration of ESP or other psi phenomena is to say that ESP in particular and psi phenomena in general are *elusive* or *jealous phenomena*. This means the phenomena go away when a skeptic is present or when skeptical "vibrations" are present. This argument seems nicely to explain away some of the major problems facing parapsychology until it is realized that it is nothing more than a classic nonfalsifiable hypothesis, like those discussed in chapter one.

It is common in parapsychology for a new method of studying psi phenomena to be reported with much initial optimism that finally a way has been found to obtain a repeatable demonstration of the phenomena. Often the initial report is accompanied by seemingly impressive results. But when attempts are made by other laboratories to use the new technique, no hint of paranormal phenomena is found. Examples of this pattern of events will be discussed in the next section. Skeptics argue that the reason for the lack of evidence for psi phenomena when an experiment is repeated are such mundane things as better experimental controls and procedures and better statistical analysis. Proponents, however, are likely to say that others failed to obtain evidence for psi phenomena because they didn't believe in them. And so, since such phenomena are jealous, they promptly went away.

A related finding in parapsychology is the oft-noted negative correlation between the quality of a parapsychological experiment (measured by the degree and rigor of controls, use of appropriate statistical tests, and so forth) and the probability of obtaining results favorable to the existence of psi phenomena. In other words, the better-controlled the experiment, the less likely it is to show evidence for psi phenomena (see Hyman, 1985b, for one example). The skeptical explanation of this correlation is quite simple: The better and more rigorous the controls in an experiment, the less the chance for artifactual findings to occur. If psi doesn't exist, then when one removes the various sources of artifacts in an experiment, evidence for psi phenomena will also disappear. The proponent who accepts the "jealous phenomena" point of view (and not all do), has a different explanation: The use of strict controls is evidence of a lack of belief in the phenomena, and this causes the phenomena to go away. This approach is used to explain even the failure of believers to obtain good evidence of psi phenomena. Even for strong believers, the use of strict controls means they have at least some degree of doubt, and that doubt causes the phenomena to vanish.

A case in point is that of Susan Blackmore, an English parapsychologist of long standing who has recently become rather skeptical (Blackmore, 1986b, 1986-87). In a 1986 article in *Fate* magazine, she outlines the reasons for her increasing skepticism. They constitute a familiar theme. In sixteen years of research in parapsychology, she was never able to obtain any evidence for psi phenomena. Another parapsychologist, Scott Rogo (author of a book called *Phone Calls from the Dead*) replied to Blackmore's article (Rogo, 1986). In his reply Rogo attributes Blackmore's continued failure to find evidence of psi phenomena not to the nonexistence of such phenomena, but to Blackmore's unconscious motives. "Is Blackmore using her own ESP to block her subjects' functioning during her tests? Is she psychically sabotaging her own experiments?" he asks (Rogo, 1986, p. 78). Later he states that "I believe that a sense of deep personal conviction may be the key to achieving good results in the lab" and "In the course of my conversations with Blackmore I have come to suspect that she resists—at a deeply unconscious level—the idea that psychic phenomena exist" (Rogo, 1986, p. 80).

The view that ESP and related phenomena are "jealous" has been carried even further by other writers. It has been argued that skepticism can act backward in time to change the initially positive results of parapsychological experiments (Collins and Pinch, 1982). The argument runs that when good evidence for psi phenomena is found, it is written up and published. If, after publication, a lot of skeptics read the paper, their skepticism will act in the past to change the outcome of the experiment. It is a tribute to the lack of demonstrable psi phenomena that some proponents have had to resort to such explanations for their overwhelming failure to demonstrate the existence of the phenomena they believe in.

Early Research: J. B. Rhine and S. G. Soal

The work of J. B. Rhine and his wife Louisa at Duke University and S. G. Soal in England marks the beginning of modern experimental parapsychology. This line of research, and its recent descendants, claim to have provided evidence for the existence of ESP and related phenomena. Such claims, however, do not stand up to critical evaluations.

The basic card-guessing method used by the Rhines and others failed to provide evidence for ESP. The major problem was the failure of the early successes claimed by the Rhines to replicate. There have been many reasons for the failures to replicate. For example, the cards that first gave such seeming success were poorly printed—the designs were often stamped on the cards with such force that embossing resulted and the design could actually be seen from the back of the card (Randi, 1982; Zusne and Jones, 1982). Some of the cards were transparent enough that the designs could be seen through the cards (Zusne and Jones, 1982).

The methods the Rhines used to prevent subjects from gaining hints and clues as to the design on the cards were far from adequate. In many experiments, the cards were displayed face up, but hidden behind a small wooden shield. Several ways of obtaining information about the design on the card remain even in the presence of the shield. For instance, the subject may be able sometimes to see the design on the face-up card reflected in the agent's glasses. If the agent isn't wearing glasses it is possible to see the reflection in his cornea. Of course, this wouldn't be possible all the time, and certainly not every subject would take advantage of such information. But remember that the Rhines' results showed that only certain subjects were able to score above chance and then not a great deal above chance, although the difference was significant statistically. This is just what would be expected if a few subjects, some of the time, were able to make use of a slight advantage based on information from such sources.

Other sources of information not controlled in the Rhines' experiments were the facial expressions and tone of voice of the agent. Such clues can be valuable sources of information, even for nonhuman subjects. This is demonstrated by the famous case of the horse named Clever Hans (Pfungst, 1911/1956; Sebeok and Rosenthal, 1981). Hans was owned by a Herr von Osten in Berlin, Germany, in the early 1900s. Hans was able, or so it seemed, to perform arithmetical calculations and answer simple questions by tapping with one of his hooves. Thus, when asked for the square root of sixty-four, he would tap eight times. His performance amazed many, and it was concluded that he had the intelligence of an eight-year-old human. Herr von Osten swore he wasn't cuing Hans in any way and, in fact, never attempted to make any money from Hans's startling abilities.

One investigator, Oskar Pfungst, then a graduate student in psychology, was skeptical. In a series of experiments he demonstrated that if the person who asked the question didn't know the answer, Hans was unable to reply correctly.

Further, Hans didn't reply if he couldn't see the questioner. Pfungst discovered several subtle cues that started and stopped Hans's tapping behavior. The questioner's looking down at Hans's hooves started the tapping. Raising the head and certain facial expressions stopped the tapping, even if no question had been asked. It so happened that, after asking Hans a question, most people would look down at his hooves. Hans obligingly started tapping. When Hans got to the "right" number of taps, the questioner would look up and Hans would promptly stop tapping. If the "stop" cue wasn't given, Hans would tap right on past the correct answer. Hans was, then, no different from other horses; he had just learned, apparently by chance, a clever trick. The incident shows how even small cues can provide a considerable amount of information, even when people are not aware that they are giving the cues. Incidentally, J. B. Rhine's first (1929) publication in the field of parapsychology was a report of a horse named Lady Wonder who could answer all sorts of questions. Rhine believed the horse was telepathic, although it was later revealed that the owner was using subtle signals to control the horse's behavior.

Other nonparanormal sources of information existed about the design on the cards in Rhine's experiments. The small shield did not eliminate clues when the agent wrote down which card was presented on each trial. The sound of a pencil writing provides information about what is being written. Try this experiment: Have someone write the numeral two and then the numeral four behind you while you listen carefully. Now have the person write "lines" and "square," names of two of the Zener cards. In both cases, you can hear the difference. Observing the top of a moving pencil or pen also provides information about what is being written. Magicians use this technique in several tricks; with a bit of practice, one can become quite good at it. Obviously, since there are only five alternatives in the Rhine experiments, even a little information based on such sources would boost a subject's score above chance, with no paranormal powers needed to explain the results.

Other procedural flaws in the Rhine experiments have been detailed by Zusne and Jones (1982) and Hansel (1966, 1980). Zusne and Jones (1982) point out that "the keeping of records in Rhine's experiments was inadequate. Sometimes, the subject would help with the checking of his or her calls against the order of cards. In some long-distance telepathy experiments, the order of the cards passed through the hands of the percipient [subject] before it got from Rhine to the agent" (p. 375). In other words, the subject was given a list of the cards that he or she was later to attempt to guess. The opportunity for nonparanormal transfer of information in such situations is obvious. As early as 1939, Kennedy concluded that the vast majority of the seemingly positive experiments by Rhine were due to poor experimental control. Three studies that Kennedy did not fault on procedural grounds have since been questioned on the basis of opportunity for cheating or use of clues that Kennedy was not aware of (Hansel, 1966; Zusne and Jones, 1982).

The procedural errors in Rhine's experiments have been extremely damaging to his claims to have demonstrated the existence of ESP. Equally damaging has been the fact that the results have not replicated when the experiments have been conducted in other laboratories. In a very real sense, Rhine and ESP have been the Blondlot and N-rays of the middle part of this century. Crumbaugh's (1966) comments on his failure to repeat Rhine's findings, even after years of effort, have been noted previously;

other researchers fared little better when trying to repeat Rhine's work. By 1940, "six different researchers, using some 500 subjects in experiments totaling about half a million trials demonstrated nothing but chance scores" (Zusne and Jones, 1982, p. 375). See also Hansel (1966, 1980) for detailed accounts of the failures to replicate Rhine's findings.

Occasionally, of course, apparent replication would occur. It should be remembered, however, that replications were also reported of Blondlot's N-ray findings. As in the N-ray case, reports that seemed to support Rhine's work were few and could be attributed to some of the same procedural problems as found in the original work. In addition, it should be remembered that what is taken as evidence for ESP is above-chance performance on some sort of card-guessing task. If one tests enough subjects long enough, sooner or later one of them will score above chance at a statistically significant level, for at least some set of trials. Does this mean that, for this brief time, the subject possessed ESP? No, it simply means that chance is operating as expected. Let us assume that out of one hundred subjects, one scores significantly above chance at the .01 level. That is, the deviation from chance would be expected to occur once in one hundred times. This will impress no one who has any knowledge of statistics, since the fact that an event that is expected to occur by chance once in one hundred times does so when you give it one hundred opportunities to occur is not evidence of anything extraordinary.

Real-world analogues to the card-guessing experiments occur frequently. One can consider every spin of the roulette wheel, every throw of the dice, every draw of the card in gambling casinos the world over as a single trial in a worldwide ongoing study in parapsychology. At gambling casinos, the odds are in favor of the house by only a tiny margin (if the margin were greater, people would lose much more frequently and be much less willing to play). Nonetheless, this tiny margin is enough to produce huge amounts of money for the house. Over the billions of "trials" in this real-world "experiment," there has been no hint of any deviation from the strict laws of chance. State-run lotteries offer another opportunity to look for ESP in real-world situations. Billions of state lottery tickets have been sold since New Hampshire introduced the modern state lottery in 1964. Skolnick (1985, personal communication) has examined the data from the New York State Lottery for several years. He found that New Yorkers were not winning the lottery at a rate higher than chance. If ESP had been operating, even in only a minority of players, the rate of winning would have been higher than chance.

The argument is often made by proponents of paranormal claims that these powers cannot be used for profit, so when one tries to use ESP to foresee the outcome of a spin of a roulette wheel, a football game, or the movement of a company's stock on Wall Street, psi powers promptly vanish. However, not all parapsychologists agree with this position. Rhine himself contended that highly motivated subjects did better in ESP experiments (Rhine and Pratt, 1962). For most people, money is a strong motivating factor.

In England, S. G. Soal attempted to replicate Rhine's findings. At first Soal believed he had failed, stating, "I have delivered a stunning blow to Dr. Rhine's work by my repetition of his experiments in England . . . there is *no evidence* that individuals guessing cards can beat the laws of chance" (Thouless, 1974, quoted in Markwick, 1985, p. 287). Soal's studies included 160 subjects and a total of 68,350 trials. Later, however, Soal reanalyzed his data for what has been termed a *displacement effect*. That is, he compared the card guessed, not with the card actually present on that trial, but with either the card that had been present on the previous trial or with the card that had appeared on the succeeding trial. When this was done, two subjects out of 160 showed hit rates well above chance. The two subjects were Mrs. Gloria Stewart and Basil Shackleton.

Soal's further work with Shackleton lasted for forty sessions and totaled 12,000 trials. Cards with a picture of one of five animals were used instead of Zener cards with symbols. Each design was coded with a digit from one through five. Before a session, Soal reported, he would obtain a random list of the digits 1 through 5 from a book of logarithms. He described in detail the procedure he used to obtain these lists of digits. This was important, as it permitted other investigators, years later, to find the exact source of the random digits used and to attempt to duplicate the tests. The random digits were written in a "target" column on the score sheets for the session and were used to determine the order in which the five different designs would be presented. Thus, if the digit 1 was the code for the elephant design, when a 1 appeared in the target column on a trial, the elephant design would be used. Shackleton would make his guess by naming the animal, not naming a digit. His guess was also coded into the appropriate digit and that digit recorded on the score sheet. Thus, if he guessed "elephant," a 1 would be recorded in the "guess" column.

Soal's work with Shackleton (reported in Soal and Goldney, 1943) was extremely successful. It was long considered the best evidence for the existence of ESP by both proponents and skeptics. As might be expected, critics spent considerable time and effort attempting to refute the results. Frequently these attempts were unfair, distorted, or simply wrong (see Markwick, 1985, for a brief review). Then in 1960 it was revealed (Soal and Goldney, 1960) that in 1941 Soal had been charged with changing some of the 1's in the target column to 4's or 5's after a session. The accuser was a Mrs. Gretl Albert, who had taken part in the experiment as an "agent," the individual who attempted to send the identity of the card to Shackleton. Soal had originally denied the charge and had not permitted it to be published until 1960.

The publication of Mrs. Albert's charge heightened suspicion regarding the Shackleton studies. Medhurst (1971) examined a small portion of the data from Soal's sessions with Shackleton and found that there was an excess of hits when the target was a 4 or a 5. Scott and Haskell (1973, 1974) examined all the data, using a computer, and showed that not only were hits much more likely to occur than chance would predict when the target was a 4 or 5, but that there were far fewer 1's as target when a 4 or 5 was guessed than would be expected by chance. These results showed how Soal had been cheating. He filled the target digit sequence with extra 1's. When Shackleton guessed a 4 or 5 on a trial when the target was one of these supernumerary 1's, the target was changed to a 4 or 5, whichever was correct. This inflated the hit rate to above-chance levels. Markwick (1978, 1985) discovered that Soal (who died in 1975) had cheated in a second way. He had left blanks in the target column and had later filled in the digit corresponding to whatever design Shackleton guessed.

The discoveries of how Soal had faked his results destroyed the credibility of his work in the eyes of skeptics and most parapsychologists. One parapsychologist, J. G. Pratt, who had worked with the Rhines at Duke, proposed an astonishing defense of Soal. According to Pratt (1978), Soal had powers of precognition and had inserted the extra digits in the target columns guided by his precognition. The desire to believe knows no bounds.

The Uri Geller Episode

Rhine had pioneered the study of parapsychology using card-guessing experiments. As the years passed, many became dissatisfied with this approach. It was dull for all involved, including the readers of the final papers. Worst of all, it failed to produce convincing evidence for ESP or other paranormal abilities. By the 1970s, then, the stage was set for something new to burst upon the scene. This turned out to be an Israeli psychic named Uri Geller. Starting with his arrival in the United States, Geller quickly became the parapsychological sensation of the decade. Many parapsychologists became convinced that in Geller they finally had positive proof that psychic powers were real and that they could be demonstrated more or less on demand. Geller also became a darling of the media, appearing on talk show after talk show, where his powers were amply demonstrated and declared genuine. He convinced millions that he was at last the real thing.

Geller's alleged powers were truly amazing. He could bend solid metal objects with his mind alone. He could read minds. He could see inside sealed envelopes and boxes and tell what was in them. These powers were apparently verified when Geller was studied by physicists Russell Targ and Harold Puthoff at California's prestigious Stanford Research Institute. Targ and Puthoff (1974) published a paper in *Nature*, one of the world's leading scientific journals, in which they declared they had demonstrated that Geller's powers were real.

Unfortunately for Geller and his supporters, it soon became obvious that the truth about Geller was very different from his claims. Geller turned out to be nothing more than a fairly good magician using sleight of hand and considerable personal charm to fool his admirers. The tests at SRI turned out to have been run under conditions that can best be described as chaotic. Few limits were placed on Geller's behavior, and he was more or less in control of the procedures used to test him. Further, the results of the tests were incorrectly reported in Targ and Puthoff's *Nature* paper. For details the reader is referred to magician James Randi's *The Truth About Uri Geller* (1982), which is the definitive exposé of this modern psychic fraud. Marks and Kammann's (1980) *The Psychology of the Psychic* also contains excellent material on Geller.

Geller was caught blatantly using sleight of hand on many occasions (Randi, 1982; Marks and Kammann, 1980). In early 1973 *Time* magazine was considering doing a story on Geller, and he was invited to give a demonstration of his powers for members of *Time*'s staff. Unknown to Geller, magician Randi (The Amazing Randi) was present, posing as a *Time* employee. Strangely, for all Geller's professed powers, he failed to detect the presence of a trained professional magician and went on to give what Randi (1982, p. 93) terms "the saddest, most transparent act I've ever seen." Now Geller never performs if there is a trained magician watching. They give off "bad vibes" that make his powers go away, he says.

It will be of interest here to describe how Geller does a few of his better-known tricks. In his stage show, which convinced millions of paying customers that he was truly psychic, he does a simple mind-reading act. He asks members of the audience to think of one geometric figure inside another, often saying something like "don't think of a square—that's too easy for me." After a few moments, he says that he has received the mental impression of a circle inside a triangle, and asks how many in the audience were thinking of that design. Many amazed hands go up. He then typically says that he initially was going to say a triangle inside a circle, but changed his mind. How many in the audience were thinking of that combination? More hands go up in amazement until, perhaps, well over half the audience members have their hands up. Simple as it is, this can be an impressive gimmick in the excitement of a live performance. The trick is simple—after you've excluded the square, there really are only two "simple" geometric figures left, the circle and the triangle. There aren't going to be many geometric whizzes in the house who think of a dodecahedron inside a rhombus.

In another favorite trick of Geller's, the audience is asked to think of an odd two-digit number less than fifty, with the restriction that the two digits can't be the same. With much fanfare, Geller announces that he has received the number 37. Typically, about one-third of the audience will have picked this number. Geller may then say he first was going to say 35, but changed his mind. How many were thinking of 35? More hands go up. It has been shown that about 56 percent of a group of people will pick either 35 or 37 when given these instructions (Marks and Kammann, 1980). These response patterns are called *population stereotypes*, and the magician or phony psychic can make good use of them to convince people that their minds really are being read.

Geller's most famous trick was bending metal objects, supposedly by psychic energy. The bent objects were usually keys or spoons. Both are surprisingly easy to bend when you know how. Keys are easiest—all one needs to do is distract the audience for a moment and slip the key into some slot or press it on a solid surface and give it a good push. The audience, of course, won't have seen this since their attention has been distracted. Another way of bending a key is to use a second key that has a large enough hole in the top (figure 4) that the end of the key you want to bend can be inserted. You do so and, while the audience is distracted, apply pressure. Geller, always a master of distraction, would perform such simple tricks on various television shows and amaze his hosts. Randi (1982) reports that one could see him palm keys and bend them physically when one carefully viewed a videotape of the program later.

Bending spoons takes a bit more preparation, if the trick is to have maximum effect. One has to prepare the spoon beforehand. Let us assume that you are going to a party and wish to amaze those present with your psychic powers. When you arrive, go to the kitchen and borrow an all-metal spoon. (The trick doesn't work with plastic or nonmetal spoons.) Prepare the trick by bending the spoon back and forth at the point where the stem and bowl meet. At first, bend only a small bit, then gradually increase the angle of the bend. It's best to do this under running water, as the spoon becomes quite hot from the friction that occurs during the bending. You'll have to practice with many spoons before you'll be skilled enough to know when the spoon is just about ready to break at the junction between stem and bowl. There will be almost no visible sign on the top of the spoon that anything is amiss, although there will be a small crack on the underside. Now mark the spoon in some way so you can distinguish it from the others in the cutlery drawer (a small scratch will do fine) and return it to the drawer. Then, mention casually in conversation that you have psychic powers. Don't be too loud about it—act modest and perhaps a little embarrassed. Usually, someone will take the bait and ask you to demonstrate. At this point, hedge—say the powers come and go, you're not sure, and so forth. Finally, allow yourself to be talked into giving a performance.

As you start, emphasize one point: your powers aren't 100 percent reliable. They depend not only on you, but on those around you. Say something to the effect that everyone has such powers, and the audience has to help. That way, if you fail, whose fault is it? Not yours—the audience didn't help, or didn't believe. Geller very frequently used such a ploy.

Don't start off with the spoon-bending act. Instead, do a little mind reading, like the cold readings described in chapter two, to warm up the group and convince them there is really something to your claim. Then trot out the spoon trick. But—and the importance of this point can't be overemphasized—fail at it the first time you try. That may seem strange, but as Randi has frequently pointed out, it is very important for psychics to fail some of the times they attempt a trick. After all, if the psychic were a magician doing tricks, the trick would always work. Therefore, if the trick fails, the person must be a real psychic. This way, psychics get "credit" both when the trick works and when it doesn't. This psychological ploy was widely used by Geller and his supporters.

After the mind reading, say you're going to try something really difficult—bending a piece of silverware. Ask someone to bring the drawer with the silverware or, better yet, go into the kitchen yourself, ask where the drawer is (even though you already know), open it, and "randomly" select the spoon you've previously worked on and marked. Ask another person to hold the spoon at points 1 and 2 (figure 5). Tell the audience to concentrate on seeing the spoon bend. Have them chant "bend, bend, bend" if you think they'll go for it. Sweat will pop out on your forehead as you concentrate, focusing all your psychic powers on the spoon. Exclaim that you feel the spoon getting warm. Does the person holding it feel the same thing? (Of course it's getting warm, with one person holding it and you stroking it!) But, try as you will, the spoon doesn't bend; you've failed. Explain that your powers are weak tonight, or that the mind reading drained you, and say you'll try to bend the spoon again later. Then, carefully and in view of everyone, put the spoon in some prominent place and state that no one should touch the spoon until you try to bend it again. This is to forestall "any question of faking." Of course, you don't have to go near the spoon before your second attempt to bend it. The work has already been done. The audience doesn't know that, however, and it's an effective ploy.

When, about fifteen minutes later, you feel that your powers have recovered, it's time to try again to bend the spoon. Pick another person to hold the spoon at points 1 and 3 (figure 5). This tiny difference in your method will go entirely unnoticed, but it is crucial. Now, stroke the spoon as before, between points 1 and 2. At first put no pressure on the spoon stem. You don't want it to bend right away. Strain some, and have the group chant "bend, bend" again. After a half-minute or so, apply gentle pressure to the stem as you stroke it. The spoon will start to bend! It will continue to bend until, if you've worked it enough, the stem will fall off. The audience will be utterly amazed. Even people who already believe in psychic powers will be astonished at having seen such a powerful demonstration with their own eyes.

What makes this trick so very convincing is that the following three facts about what the audience sees are all true:

1. You failed to bend the spoon on the first attempt.

2. No one went near the spoon between the first and second attempts to bend it.

3. The spoon did bend on the second attempt.

The conclusion that almost everyone will draw is that your powers returned to full strength between the two attempts. Few will catch on to the trick. It's a simple trick, but Uri Geller used it to make tens of millions of dollars.

After your performance is over, you are ethically bound to tell people that what you did was just a trick. You are not, however, bound to tell them how it was done. Some will not believe that it was a trick. Randi, who has not only duplicated all of Geller's tricks, but performed tricks that are far beyond Geller's rather limited abilities as a magician, has from time to time been accused by Geller's supporters of being a real psychic himself. They claim that Randi is a powerful psychic trying to convince the world that such powers don't exist so he can take the lead role in the psychic world.

Geller's well-publicized feats made psychic metal bending a popular addition to the repertoire of the would-be psychic. Even psychic children got into the act. Mathematics professor John Taylor of Kings College, University of London, had been very impressed by one of Geller's performances and began investigating such psychic phenomena. He discovered that children have an amazing ability to bend metal psychically. It turned out, however, that children can't perform while anyone is watching them. But if you give one a spoon and turn away for a bit, when you look back, the spoon is bent. Taylor would even send pieces of silverware and other bits of metal home with the children, where they could use their psychic powers at their leisure. Oddly enough, objects sealed in containers were never bent. Taylor was later shocked to discover that his young subjects had been fooling him. Two other investigators placed some supposedly psychic children alone in a room with metal objects that were to be bent. Unknown to the children, they were being videotaped. They promptly proceeded to bend the objects with their hands or by placing them against the edges of tables (Randi, 1980).

At one point Kent State University metallurgist Wilbur Franklin stated that a scanning electron microscope analysis of a ring Geller had broken, allegedly paranormally, showed that the break had not occurred by any normal, physical means (Franklin, 1976). Later, Franklin (1977) reported that this was incorrect and that a more complete analysis showed evidence of metal fatigue of the type caused by repeated bending. In other words, Geller had simply "put in the work" on the ring.

Another of Geller's feats that was allegedly confirmed scientifically also involved bending metal. This time the metal in question was an alloy of titanium and nickel called nitinol. When heated, a wire of nitinol can be bent into a particular shape. When cool, the shape can be changed. When the wire is heated again, it assumes the previous shape. Eldon Byrd (1976) has claimed that Geller paranormally altered the structure of some nitinol wire. However, Gardner (1977/1981a) has revealed that the conditions under which these nitinol "experiments" with Geller were conducted had looser controls than would be suspected from reading the description in Byrd's (1976) paper. In fact, the experimental conditions were chaotic and allowed Geller ample opportunity to engage in sleight of hand. In one case, Geller was actually given some nitinol wire to take home with him; the wire came back altered.

It may seem hard to believe that so many people, including highly trained scientists, could be taken in by Geller's sleight of hand. Note, however, that very few people have been trained in the art of magic. If we go to a magic show, we usually have no idea how the tricks are being performed. We know they are tricks because the performer does not mislead us about it. But when someone claims to be psychic and does tricks that most people can't figure out, they assume that the individual really is psychic. Few people question the claim or consider the possibility that the person may be lying. The psychic helps this assumption along by using the techniques described above. Some parapsychologists, who may have impressive scientific credentials and a career of real distinction in those fields, seem to believe they can't be fooled. They fail to realize that a Ph.D. in physics, psychology, or chemistry does not confer expertise in detecting trickery. Thus, they are just as vulnerable, if not more so, to the magic tricks of a Geller, as are people who lack their scientific training. This was clearly demonstrated in the Geller case by Targ and Puthoff and one hundred years ago in the investigations of spiritualism described in chapter two.

The Geller episode makes one vital point: in any investigation of psychics or psi phenomena, a trained magician *must* be part of the investigating team. Only such a person has the skill and training needed to spot sleight of hand and similar trickery. One would have thought this simple point would have been learned following the Geller incident, but, as we will see, one major parapsychology laboratory ignored it, to its shame and embarrassment.

What happened to Geller once his trickery was exposed? P. T. Barnum is alleged to have said that there is a sucker born every minute, and Geller is living proof of that statement. After his widely publicized exposure in the mid-1970s, he faded from the scene, but never lacked for supporters. Some admitted, however reluctantly, that Geller did cheat and use sleight of hand—sometimes. Geller has recently popped up again, now claiming to be a consultant to oil and mining businesses, using his psychic powers to advise them on where to drill and dig or when to go ahead with a merger. An article that neglected to point out that Geller had been shown to be a fraud appeared in *Forbes* magazine in 1984 (Cook, 1984). More recently, it has become known that the Australian mining firm Zanex paid Geller 350,000 Australian dollars to advise them on where to find gold. This disclosure has touched off a battle for control of the company, with several large shareholders demanding that two of the firm's directors be replaced.

Recent ESP Research

Even more than spiritualistic fraud, the exposure of Uri Geller convinced parapsychologists of the need for a professional magician to be involved in psychic investigations. Some, however, still ignored this vital point, especially when their psychics refused to perform when a magician was present or when it was discovered that their psychic powers disappeared if they knew a magician was present. Thus, parapsychologists continued to be hoodwinked regularly by sleight-of-hand artists. To drive home this point, and to investigate just how much could be gotten away with by someone posing as a psychic at a major parapsychology laboratory, Randi set up his now-famous Project Alpha. His detailed reports can be found in Randi (1982-83c; 1983-84).

In Project Alpha, two young magicians, Steve Shaw and Michael Edwards, with Randi's advice, went to the McDonnell Laboratory for Psychical Research at Washington University in St. Louis, Missouri. The

McDonnell laboratory was probably the best-funded psychical research laboratory in the world; it had been created with a $500,000 grant from James McDonnell, chairman of the board of the McDonnell-Douglas Aircraft Corporation.

Shaw and Edwards easily convinced the research staff at the McDonnell Laboratory that they had genuine psychic powers. They were tested by the laboratory for a period of three years. They rarely failed to achieve "psychic" feats. Metal was bent "paranormally," minds were read, the contents of sealed envelopes were mysteriously divined, fuses sealed in protective containers burned out, and mysterious pictures appeared "psychically" on film inside cameras (like the "thought pictures" of Ted Serios, discussed in chapter two). Randi (1982-83c, 1983-84) reports in detail on the simple ways in which these deceptions were carried out.

Before Shaw and Edwards began to be tested at the McDonnell Laboratory, Randi wrote to the director, Dr. Peter Phillips, a physics professor at Washington University. Randi outlined the type of controls that the lab should use to guard against sleight of hand and other such trickery. He also offered to come to the lab, at his own expense and without public acknowledgement, to assist in the preparation of "trick-proof" experiments. Randi's offer was rejected and his advice ignored. The controls that were placed on Shaw and Edwards were totally inadequate to prevent their use of trickery. Even when videotapes of their feats showed fairly clearly, to anyone watching them carefully, how the trick had been done, the enthusiastic laboratory staff failed to catch on.

In the last twenty years a number of new procedures have been introduced in parapsychology laboratories to study ESP and related phenomena. Unlike earlier experiments, such as those of Rhine and Soal, or the quite recent tests of "psychics" Shaw and Edwards, the new procedures are used largely to test "normal" individuals claiming no particular psychic powers. The remainder of this section will review these new procedures and the results they have achieved.

Remote viewing

The remote viewing paradigm was developed by Russell Targ and Harold Puthoff (1977), the same investigators who were so thoroughly deceived by Uri Geller. Regarding their remote viewing paradigm, Targ and Puthoff have made a familiar claim: finally, they say, a method has been found that reliably provides strong evidence for psi phenomena.

The basic procedure in a remote viewing experiment is simple. A subject sits in the laboratory with an experimenter. Another experimenter and one or two other people, who constitute the "demarcation team," visit randomly selected geographic locations outside the laboratory, such as airports, bridges, parks, or specific buildings. The team attempts to send information about the location to the subject at a predetermined time. Thus, for example, the team might be scheduled to be at an airport at 10 A.M.. At 10 A.M. the subject, back in the laboratory, will give a description of the location based on any impressions he receives. Of course, neither the subject nor the experimenter with him or her back in the laboratory knows the locations the team will be visiting.

Following the completion of the experiment, which may include several different locations, the subjects' tape-recorded impressions are transcribed. These are then given to an independent judge who, in Targ and Puthoff's experiments, visits each of the actual locations and rates each of the subjects' descriptions on how well it describes each location. If there were no ESP operating, the independent judge should not be able to match the subjects' descriptions to the actual locations at a rate better than chance. If, however, the subject is really picking up information from the team through ESP, then the descriptions should contain enough information to permit the judge to reliably associate a particular description with a particular location. Targ and Puthoff claim they have conducted more than one hundred such experiments and that "most" of them have been successful (Targ and Puthoff, 1977, p. 10). Several of their experiments seem to have been spectacularly successful (Targ and Puthoff, 1977; Marks and Kammann, 1980). At least one subject, Targ and Puthoff reported, was able to demonstrate precognition in this procedure, describing the locations to be visited, not only before they were visited, but before they were even chosen.

Impressed with these seemingly powerful and consistent results, Marks and Kammann (1980) attempted to replicate Targ and Puthoff's remote viewing results. In a series of thirty-five studies, Marks and Kammann were unable to replicate the results. Their results always showed chance performance. Naturally feeling that they were doing something wrong, they searched for differences in procedure between their studies and those of Targ and Puthoff that might explain the difference in results. The crucial variable turned out to be unexpected. Targ and Puthoff provided their judges with unedited transcripts of the subjects' impressions, including the comments made by the experimenter who stayed with the subject. Marks and Kammann edited their transcripts to remove cues that would enable a judge to match the subjects' transcribed comments to the location. Such cues can provide a great deal of information.

Examination of the few actual transcripts published by Targ and Puthoff (1977; Wilhelm, 1976) show that just such clues were present. To find out if the unpublished transcripts contained cues, Marks and Kammann wrote to Targ and Puthoff requesting copies. It is almost unheard of for a scientist to refuse to provide his data for independent examination when asked, but Targ and Puthoff consistently refused to allow Marks and Kammann to see copies of the transcripts. Marks and Kammann were, however, able to obtain copies of the transcripts from the judge who used them. The transcripts were found to contain a wealth of cues. In addition, the judge had also been given a list of the locations visited *in the order in which they were visited*. A simplified example will demonstrate how this information could easily have been used to correctly match the transcripts to the locations, with no paranormal powers needed. Suppose you are a judge in a remote viewing experiment in which only three locations are visited by the demarcation team. You are given three transcripts, A, B, and C, which are in random order. You are also given—as was the judge in the Targ and Puthoff experiment—a list of the order in which the three target locations were visited: (1) university library; (2) supermarket; and (3) large bridge. Transcript A contains the phrase "Third time's the charm." Transcript C contains the phrase "Don't be nervous— you're just starting." You can now correctly assign each transcript to the correct location. Transcript A is the large bridge, B is the supermarket, and C is the library. You've achieved an accuracy of 100 percent without even reading any of the actual descriptions in the transcripts. It would be very difficult for a judge to ignore such cues, even if he or she were trying to do so.

Marks and Kammann (1980) showed, in a procedure they wryly called "remote judging," that subjects were able to match the transcripts to the correct locations using only the cues provided. When these cues were eliminated, but the description of the subjects' impressions remained intact, matching fell to a chance level.

In 1980 Charles Tart (Tart, Puthoff, and Targ, 1980) claimed that a rejudging of now-edited transcripts from one of Targ and Puthoff's earlier experiments still resulted in above-chance performance. However, Targ and Puthoff again refused to provide copies of the actual transcripts used in this study. They suppressed this vital evidence until July 1985, when it was made available. The transcripts still contained numerous cues, and Marks and Scott (1986, p. 444) concluded that "considering the importance for the remote viewing hypothesis of adequate cue removal, Tart's failure to perform this basic task seems beyond comprehension. As previously concluded, remote viewing has not been demonstrated in the experiments conducted by Puthoff and Targ, only the repeated failure of the investigators to remove sensory cues."

Another aspect of the remote viewing situation was noted by Marks and Kammann (1980) and deserves mention. Their attempts to replicate the results of Targ and Puthoff were, as noted, complete failures. But before the judging was done, the subjects were given feedback about what target location corresponded to which of their descriptions. They frequently became convinced that their descriptions had been extremely accurate. Marks and Kammann note that descriptions in remote viewing experiments are vague, mentioning trees, buildings, water, and sky. Given the vagueness of the descriptions, when subjects are told or shown the location, they will always be able to find some points of similarity between the location and the description. Thus, like cold readers becoming convinced that they can divine hidden knowledge from their clients, subjects in a remote viewing experiment become convinced that their descriptions are paranormally inspired.

The remote viewing controversy lasted more than a decade. It is a sobering example of how sloppy experiments and the conclusions based on them can be accepted as evidence in parapsychology. It further demonstrates the great amount of hard work it takes to put such erroneous conclusions to rest.

Ganzfeld studies

The German word *ganzfeld* means "blank field." The procedure in a ganzfeld study of psi powers is in some ways quite similar to the procedure in a remote viewing experiment. Both types of studies use a subject trying to pick up impressions telepathically, and a sender trying to send them. In the ganzfeld study, however, the sender is thinking about an object (tree, orange, dollar bill, whatever) rather than location. The subject is seated in the "blank field" trying to receive the sensory impressions. The blank field may be a large opaque white screen covering the subject's entire field of vision, or it may be simply a ping pong ball, cut in half and fixed over the subject's eyes. The idea is that the ganzfeld cuts out extraneous sensory inputs and permits the telepathic "message" to be read more clearly by the subject who, at the appointed time, gives his impressions of the object the sender is concentrating on.

The ganzfeld technique was developed in the 1970s, and proponents of psi phenomena contend that it represents a method that gives consistent and repeatable evidence for such phenomena. Sound familiar?

Hyman (1985b) has reviewed forty-two studies using the technique (essentially the entire corpus of published studies up to the time of the review) and concludes, "I believe that the ganzfeld psi data base, despite initial impressions, is inadequate either to support the contention of a repeatable study or to demonstrate the reality of psi. Whatever other value these studies may have for the parapsychological community, they have too many weaknesses to serve as the basis for confronting the rest of the scientific community" (Hyman, 1985b, p. 38).

Hyman (1985b) found several different flaws in the ganzfeld studies. There was inadequate randomization of the targets in a large percentage of the studies. Opportunities for information on the target to inadvertently reach the subject and breaches in security that might have permitted cheating were also present in many of the studies. Many studies were not described in sufficient detail to allow evaluation of what actually happened in the study. Statistical problems were also common. These included the use of incorrect statistical tests and procedures and "multiple testing" errors in which the subjects' responses were tested several times against chance, using different criteria for scoring the responses for different tests. This, like testing numerous astrological predictions or numerous predictions of any theory, increases the chance of spuriously obtaining a significant result. Further, the greater the number of flaws in a study, the more likely it was to find a significant effect. This is another example of the phenomenon noted earlier, that evidence for ESP and related phenomena disappears as the tightness of experimental controls is increased. On the basis of Hyman's (1985b) review, the ganzfeld studies cannot be said to provide evidence for ESP, as claimed by proponents.

Another type of ESP study is not usually considered along with the ganzfeld studies, but because there are great similarities between them, these studies will be discussed here. These are studies of ESP during dreams. The procedure is like that used in the ganzfeld study, except the subject is asleep in a laboratory. The subject's electroencephalogram, or EEG, is monitored. When he or she is in a dream period (indicated by the presence of rapid eye movements, or REM), the agent is signaled to begin concentrating on a target object or picture. When the subject's REM period ends, signaling an end of dreaming, he or she is awakened and reports any dreams. The content of the dreams is then compared to the object or picture the agent was "sending." The basic procedure can easily be altered to study precognition or clairvoyance (see Child, 1985, for a review). Such research is time-consuming and expensive, like any sleep research. For one thing, a well-equipped sleep laboratory is needed. Thus, not a great deal of parapsychological research has used this paradigm.

Initial studies at the Maimonides Medical Center in Brooklyn, New York in the 1960s and early 1970s seemed promising. Child (1985) correctly points out that these studies have sometimes been badly misdescribed by critics. Nonetheless, serious problems remain. Akers (1984, p. 129) has noted that there was a violation "of the experimental protocol" that "leaves doubts as to the rigor with which the experiment was conducted." Further, as Child (1985) has noted, three attempts at replication have failed (Belvedere and Foulkes, 1971; Foulkes et al., 1972; Globus et al., 1968). In addition, some of the Maimonides studies failed to obtain significant results, although Child (1985) reports that the series, taken as a whole, still yields statistical significance. In view of these problems, the Maimonides results cannot be taken as providing convincing evidence of psi phenomena.

Schmidt's random events studies

In recent years a series of studies by physicist Helmut Schmidt has attracted the attention of parapsychologists and the field's critics. Schmidt uses a random number generator to cause one of several lights to turn on. In his precognition studies, subjects are to press a button to predict which light will turn on. After the button is pressed, the random number generator determines the light that will turn on. In clairvoyance studies, the light that will turn on is determined before the subject's response. Schmidt's published reports (for a brief review see Hansel, 1980; Akers, 1984; Rush, 1982) claim that subjects are able to show better than chance responses in these situations.

Schmidt's work does face some problems, as has been pointed out by critics (Hansel, 1980; Hyman, 1980-81). For one thing, the details of the random number generator change frequently in Schmidt's work, often from one experiment to the next. Thus, one cannot gather "cumulative experience with one particular generator to fully understand its peculiarities and . . . properly 'debug' it" (Hyman, 1980–81, p. 37). Further, there are problems with the control trials that Schmidt uses. These are series of trials during which the random number generator is generating random numbers, but no subjects are making attempts to predict what its output will be. This is an absolutely necessary procedure but, as Hyman (1980–81) points out, the control trials that Schmidt uses are hundreds of times longer than the actual experimental series. Thus, the various generators Schmidt uses may show temporary deviations from randomness in the short run that are obscured by the very lengthy control runs. Thus, comparing short experimental runs to very lengthy control runs would spuriously give significant results. Subjects could become aware of these deviations and adjust their predictions accordingly. This would especially be a problem in the psychokinesis (PK) studies, where subjects are to attempt to influence the counter so that one of two events occurs more than 50 percent of the time. Here the crucial comparison is between the probability of the two events in the short experimental runs and vastly longer control runs. Any short-term deviations from randomness due to the generator would be likely to be interpreted as significant PK effects. Another problem with Schmidt's work is that the subjects are left largely unobserved and unsupervised during the experiment. Randall (1975, p. 131) has said of Schmidt's studies that they "provide us with the final proof of the reality of ESP." But almost the exact words have been used many times in the last one hundred years to describe the latest sure-fire demonstration of the existence of psi, which promptly fell to pieces upon close examination. In view of the problems with Schmidt's work, Randall is certainly premature in his evaluation.

Schmidt is not the first investigator to have used this sort of paradigm to investigate psi. As early as 1963 Smith, Dagle, Hill, and Mott-Smith (cited in Hansel, 1980), working for the U.S. Air Force, tried a similar experiment. It was a failure. Parapsychologist Charles Tart (1976) used a random number generator to study the possibility of training people to use psi. Subjects were given feedback on whether or not their responses were correct following each trial. In standard learning theory, such feedback is extremely important and enhances learning greatly (Welford, 1976). Positive results were initially found, as subjects came to be able to match their responses to the numbers generated by the machine. It turned out, however, that the sequence of targets generated by the random number generator was not random. This finding renders highly problematic the contention that the experiment demonstrated psi. Tart's response (see Akers [1984] for a brief review of this controversy) to the discovery of nonrandomness was to suggest that it was partly due to PK. Thus, a serious procedural flaw in an experiment has itself been claimed as evidence for psi, in yet another example of the use of a nonfalsifiable hypothesis.

More recently, my students and I have been using what should be a more sensitive method to examine claims for psi. This method uses reaction time as the major dependent variable, or measure. To date, the vast majority of studies of psi have used accuracy as their dependent measure, as can be seen from the studies described above or in any review of modern psi research (e.g., Akers, 1984; Morris, 1978, 1982; Palmer, 1978, 1982). In cognitive psychology, which is the experimental study of human learning, memory, and higher mental processes, accuracy is rarely used as the sole dependent measure. The dependent measure of choice is reaction time. This is because reaction time is a much more sensitive indicator of cognitive processes and processing than is accuracy. In other words, phenomena that are easily shown using a reaction time measure are not revealed by an accuracy measure.

An example will make the difference between the two measures clear. In a lexical decision task, subjects see, in each of several hundred trials, a string of letters. The string either is a real word—such as "QUEEN"—or is not a real word—such as "RARDEN." The subjects' task is simple: press one button if the letter string is a word, and another button if the letter string is not a word. Reaction time and accuracy are recorded. Consider the results in two situations. In the first, the subject sees the letter string "KIND" on one trial, makes a response, sees "QUEEN" on the next trial, and again responds. In the second situation, the letter string in the first trial is "KING" and in the next, "QUEEN." The reaction time to respond that "QUEEN" is a word is faster by about fifty to 100 milliseconds in the second situation (Shoben, 1982). Thus, having processed one word speeds up subsequent processing of words that are associated with it in meaning. This is a highly replicable result and has served as the basis for literally hundreds of published studies of reading, semantic memory effects of brain damage on cognition, and so forth. The important point here is that accuracy measures do not reveal the effect of having just processed an associated word (Shoben, 1982). This is a common result in studies of cognition—accuracy measures are not precise enough to demonstrate the often small, but very important, effects studied.

The implications of this analysis for psi should be obvious. Perhaps the repeated failure to find evidence for psi is due to the almost universal use of a dependent measure that is just too crude to find the looked-for effects. With this in mind, my students and I (Hines and Dennison, 1988; Hines, Lang, and Seroussi, 1987) have conducted a series of studies of psi using reaction time as a dependent measure.

One study (Hines and Dennison, 1988) followed naturally from Schmidt's work described above. On each trial a computer generated, randomly, a 0 or a 1. In the ESP condition, this digit was stored in the computer's memory. The computer then generated another random 0 or 1 and displayed that digit on a television monitor in front of the subject. The subject had to decide, as quickly as possible, if the digit on the screen was the same as the digit stored in the computer's memory or not. Reaction time, measured from the onset of the digit on the monitor to the time the subject responded, was recorded, as was the accuracy of the subject's responses.

Even if ESP is a real phenomenon, the accuracy measure would be unlikely to demonstrate it. Previous studies have failed to provide any adequate evidence for ESP when accuracy measures have been used. In line with this prediction, our subjects performed no better than chance when the accuracy measure was used. The real test, however, was the much more sensitive reaction time measure. If ESP exists, subjects should respond more quickly when they are correct than when they are incorrect. Whatever the source of the hypothesized extrasensory information, if it were getting to the brain, where it would have to be processed to have any effect at all on behavior, it would speed up the process of making a correct decision. However, we found no difference between correct and incorrect reaction times that even approached statistical significance. Nor did providing feedback to the subjects regarding their accuracy on each trial change these results. Reaction times of correct and incorrect responses remained the same.

We also examined a precognition condition, again with and without feedback to subjects on their accuracy. In the precognition condition, the computer generated a random 0 or 1 and displayed it on the monitor. The subject then had to decide if the digit the computer would generate *after* he or she responded would be the same as or different from the one on the screen. After the subject responded, the computer generated another 0 or 1. As in the clairvoyance condition, subjects were no more accurate than expected by chance. Nor were they any faster when their responses—predictions, in this condition—were correct than when they were incorrect. Again, the presence or absence of feedback to the subject did not alter this pattern.

In another study, Hines, Lang, and Seroussi (1987) adapted the lexical decision task described above to the study of ESP. There were two conditions. In both the control and the ESP conditions, a subject made a series of lexical decisions on letter strings presented on the right side of a television monitor controlled by a computer. In the control condition, the lone subject had no companion. In the ESP condition, there was a second subject who made decisions about letter strings presented on the left side of the television monitor. The two subjects sat on opposite sides of a divider that prevented either from seeing the other or the other side of the monitor. In the ESP condition the subject who sat on the left side of the divider—the agent or "sender"—saw a letter string, and 400 milliseconds later the receiver—the subject on the right side of the screen—saw a letter string. Both subjects had to make lexical decisions on the letter strings they saw. On some of the trials in the ESP condition, the letter string the agent saw was the same one the receiver saw, 400 milliseconds later. In the standard lexical decision task, if the same subject sees the same letter string twice in a row, reaction time on the second presentation is greatly reduced. This is due to the fact that the location in memory that stores the concept, if the string is a word, is activated by the first presentation and when the same word occurs again, that location is much more able or ready to be activated again. This activation decays after a few seconds. If, then, there is extrasensory communication between individuals, even of a very low level, it should show up in the reaction times of the receiver when the agent had just processed, 400 milliseconds previously, the same letter string that the receiver was processing. We found no hint of any such effect in our data.

Failure to find an effect is not conclusive evidence that the effect is not real. However, the fact that several of our studies using a highly sensitive reaction time measure have consistently failed to show any evidence for psi seems to be convincing prima facie evidence against the reality of the phenomena.

Psi phenomena of one sort or another have been systematically studied for more than one hundred years. This century of investigation shows a common, repeating pattern. A new phenomenon or method is found that "finally shows that psi is real," the skeptic is told. However, upon careful examination, the claim collapses. But by the time one claim has been carefully investigated and found faulty, another phenomenon or method has come along that, once and for all, shows psi to be real. And on it goes. First there was spiritualism, then card-guessing experiments, then individual psychics like Geller, then the ganzfeld studies, and now the random events studies of Schmidt and others.

It is important to realize that, in one hundred years of parapsychological investigations, there has never been a single adequate demonstration of the reality of any psi phenomenon. Why, then, does the field of parapsychology continue to exist? Why has it not withered away, like the study of N-rays and polywater? I think that there are two major, and not unrelated, reasons. First, especially since the early 1960s, parapsychology has acquired a following that is made up of people—most of them not active investigators and most with almost no scientific training—who accept the reality of psi not because of any empirical evidence, but simply because psi fits well with their view of what the world and reality ought to be like. This is a world where the spiritual dominates over the scientific and rational; a world where simply thinking good thoughts can make the world "right" again; a world where what one feels to be true is, automatically and without effort, true; a world where there is no need to carefully consider evidence to arrive at the truth. In the 1980s, I suspect that this group is quite large and helps to support the enormous number of uncritical books, television programs, and newspaper articles about psi and other aspects of the paranormal. Thus, these topics are kept in the public eye. This in turn fuels the interest of the general public and helps to support parapsychological research, both in terms of funding and in terms of the publicity that is so rewarding to researchers in any field.

The second reason for the persistence of parapsychology as a discipline has to do with the type of logical arguments permitted within the field. The use of the nonfalsifiable hypothesis is permitted in parapsychology to a degree unheard of in any scientific discipline. To the extent that investigators accept this type of hypothesis, they will be immune to having their belief in psi disproved. No matter how many experiments fail to provide evidence for psi and no matter how good those experiments are, the nonfalsifiable hypothesis will always protect the belief. The investigator will thus persist in conducting experiment after experiment, even when none of them produces positive results. The nonfalsifiable hypothesis always permits, almost requires, the attribution of the experiments' failures to something other than the nonexistence of psi. This attitude is epitomized in the quotation from Rogo (1986) earlier in this chapter regarding the reasons for Blackmore's decade-long failure to find any evidence of psi in her numerous experiments. Rogo doesn't even consider the possibility that psi doesn't exist. Rather he puts forth the totally untestable idea that Blackmore's failure to find evidence of psi is due to her deeply hidden, unconscious motives. In any other area of scientific research, it would be impossible for anyone to seriously propose such an "explanation" for the failure to find a hypothesized effect. The type of reasoning so frequently used in parapsychology, reasoning that is nearly invulnerable to empirical disproof, is much more characteristic of religion than of science. Alcock (1985) has persuasively argued that for many, but certainly not all, parapsychologists the search for psi has become an almost religious quest, a quest to dethrone materialistic science and re-establish the dominance of a spiritual approach to the world.

Psi Theory and Belief

Many theories have been proposed by parapsychologists to explain how psi takes place. To skeptics, such theory building seems premature, as the phenomena to be explained by the theories have yet to be demonstrated convincingly. The theories cover a wide range of proposed mechanisms (see Rao, 1978 for an excellent review). At one end of the spectrum, there are theories that implicitly accept the "transmission hypothesis" of psi, according to which information is actually transmitted during psi. Dobbs (1967, cited in Rao, 1978) proposes the existence of particles with "imaginary" mass and energy called *psitrons*, which are emitted in great numbers by the brain. Dobbs is one of several theorists to use quantum mechanics to support parapsychology. Gardner (1981b) has reviewed the use of quantum mechanics in parapsychology. He finds it is often used incorrectly or to hide, in complex terminology, old nonfalsifiable hypotheses. Thus, for example, the fact that psychics can't or won't perform their feats in front of skeptics is attributed to the fact that skeptics' "wills kept reducing wave packets the wrong way" (Gardner, 1981b, p. 69). This sort of conceptualization does not provide much substance for a theory of psi (Rae, 1986).

More recently, even more bizarre theories have been proposed and seem to be gaining popularity in parapsychology. These theories have to do with what is called *synchronicity*. This is a notion dreamed up by psychoanalyst Carl Jung in the 1950s (Jung and Pauli, 1955). The idea is straightforward, if naive. According to synchronicity, there is no such thing as a coincidence. All "coincidences" are meaningful. Palmer (1978, 1982) and others (Rao, 1978) have suggested that what they feel are adequate examples of psi may not be due to transmission of information, but may be examples of such "meaningful coincidences." The changes in theoretical views of psi may be a result of the criticisms of earlier views. As we will see in the case of UFOs, proponents of pseudoscientific claims, when faced with effective criticisms, frequently adopt even more extreme hypotheses. As the information transmission hypothesis of psi becomes less and less tenable, some in the field, while accepting the demise of one theory, are unwilling to move toward the skeptical view that allegedly positive psi results were and are due to subtle biases and experimental design flaws. Rather, they gravitate toward increasingly bizarre explanations for why the results occur.

Finally, it is important to address the issue of belief. Why is the existence of ESP and related phenomena so widely accepted by the public in spite of what is at best very poor evidence for its reality? One reason is that paranormal topics are constantly and uncritically discussed in the media, both print and electronic. Given the high visibility of paranormal topics in the media, it is natural for people to believe that there must be something to them. Another powerful factor influencing belief is the startling personal experiences that many people have. These convince them, on purely subjective grounds, that they have had an ESP experience and, therefore, that ESP is real. The constructive nature of memory and related cognitive illusions combine forces to convince people of the reality of ESP and related phenomena.

Greeley (1987) surveyed more than 1,400 American adults and found that 67 percent had "experienced ESP." What type of experiences occur in everyday life that are classified as being due to ESP? Very commonly, they are hunches or dreams that seem to come true. The cognitive illusions that operate to make this type of precognitive experience seem so real were discussed in chapter two. A similar experience more directly related to ESP is that of thinking of a friend that one has not heard from in some time. Shortly after one has thought about the individual, one receives a phone call, letter or some other form of communication from or about the person. As we have seen, this can be a striking experience. Such occurrences are, of course, coincidences. But most people are quite poor at estimating the probabilities of events and using probabilistic information in decision making (Kahneman, Slovic, and Tversky, 1982).

Gilovich, Vallone, and Tversky (1985) have demonstrated that people's poor intuitive grasp of probabilities underlies a common belief about sports.

This is the belief—held by players, coaches, and fans alike—in the "hot hand" or "streak shooting." Gilovich, Vallone, and Tversky (1985, pp. 295-96) define this as the "belief that the performance of a player during a particular period is significantly better than expected on the basis of the player's overall record." In fact, an analysis of field goal performance of the Philadelphia 76ers during forty-eight 1980–81 home games revealed no departure from chance. Gilovich, Vallone, and Tversky (1985) also conducted a shooting experiment with members of the Cornell University basketball team. Although there was no actual nonchance streak shooting in the shots taken for the experiment, observers of the shooting believed the effect was present.

Gilovich, Vallone, and Tversky's (1985) results show that the "hot hand" is a cognitive illusion brought about by the tendency to judge short sequences having runs—whether sequences of successful shots in basketball or sequences of heads or tails in coin flipping—as differing from chance when in fact such sequences do not violate the laws of chance. As predicted by this finding, when asked to generate random sequences, people include more alternations than would occur by chance alone and fewer runs than would occur by chance. Thus, when confronted with a truly random sequence, people will perceive it as nonrandom and feel a need to "explain" the perceived nonrandomness. Thus, the "hot hand" belief is used to explain the perceived nonrandomness in basketball shooting, just as ESP is used to explain the perceived nonrandomness in the outcome of hunches, dreams, thoughts about acquaintances, "predictions" of psychics, and so forth.

Blackmore (1985) found that believers in ESP are worse than nonbelievers at making judgments of probability. In a coin-flipping experiment, believers significantly underestimated the number of heads or tails that would occur due to chance alone. Nonbelievers made accurate estimates. Thus, when believers are faced with a sequence of random events, they, more than the nonbeliever, will perceive it as nonchance and seek some explanation for the perceived nonchance nature of the sequence of events. ESP, or other paranormal powers, provide a perfect "explanation."

Another study has shown that believers in ESP are less able to interpret and assimilate new information if the new information is contrary to their belief in ESP than if it confirms their belief in ESP. Russell and Jones (1980) gave believers and nonbelievers articles to read about ESP. The articles were either supportive of the reality of ESP or argued that ESP didn't exist. Believers remembered the articles that supported their position very well. Believers' memories about the article that argued against ESP, however, were quite inaccurate, and more than 15 percent actually remembered the article, incorrectly, as favorable to the existence of ESP.

Nonbelievers, on the other hand, showed excellent memory for both articles, regardless of whether the articles supported or argued against the nonbelievers' position.

The finding that believers are less willing or able than nonbelievers to deal with information that counters their preconceived belief is not limited to belief in ESP. It may be a general characteristic of believers. Glick and Snyder (1986) studied belief in astrology; their findings are highly relevant here as they take the results of the Russell and Jones (1980) study one step further, to ask what effects confirming or disconfirming information has on believers' and nonbelievers' beliefs. Glick and Snyder (1986) gave subjects, who were classified as believing or not believing in astrology, the opportunity to test a particular astrological prediction by asking an individual questions about his personality and habits. The "hypothesis" being tested was that this individual was, according to his horoscope, extroverted, friendly, and outgoing. Unknown to the subjects, the individual who was interviewed was a confederate of the experimenters and was instructed to provide responses of a particular type. If the question was such that it invited an "extroverted answer" (i.e., "Do you like to go to parties?"), the confederate gave an extroverted answer ("yes," in this case). If the question invited an introverted answer (i.e., "Do you like to stay at home alone and read?") the confederate gave an introverted answer ("yes," in this case).

Glick and Snyder (1986) found that both believers and nonbelievers asked more questions that would tend to confirm the "hypothesis." Thus, both believers and nonbelievers got the same information from their questioning of the confederate. However, for the believers the information confirmed their belief while, for the nonbelievers, it disconfirmed their prior attitude. What effect did this information have on the attitudes toward astrology of the believers and nonbelievers? Nonbelievers were more likely than believers to see the astrological prediction as confirmed. That is, they used the information to modify their prior attitude. Believers did not use the information obtained to modify their belief in astrology. Within the group of believers there was a variation in the number of confirmatory questions asked of the confederate and, therefore, variation in the amount of evidence the believers received that confirmed the astrological hypothesis. This made no difference in the believers' ratings of whether or not the hypothesis had been confirmed. No matter how much or how little confirming evidence they obtained, they saw the hypothesis as confirmed. The nonbelievers showed the opposite effect. The more confirming responses a nonbeliever received, the more he believed the hypothesis had been confirmed. In other words, nonbelievers were more willing than were believers to assimilate new information that countered their preexisting attitudes and to use that information to change their attitudes.

The pattern that emerges from these studies is one in which believers in paranormal phenomena are more rigid and unchanging in their beliefs than are skeptics, who are more willing and able to change their attitudes when presented with evidence that shows their beliefs to be incorrect. In other words, believers appear to be considerably more closed-minded than nonbelievers.

5

Psychoanalysis

Founded by Sigmund Freud in Vienna in the late 1800s, psychoanalysis has had enormous influence on Western culture. For most people, Freud and psychoanalysis are synonymous with psychology. Psychoanalytic approaches have been applied to such widely diverse fields as history and political science, literature, music, and the arts. Nonetheless, psychoanalysis is based in large part on pseudoscientific formulations that are inherently unfalsifiable. This unfalsifiability accounts for the popularity of psychoanalytic "explanations" in many fields. In some instances, psychoanalytic theory does make testable predictions; these predictions have usually been found to be incorrect. The next section will summarize the major components of Freud's theories.

Freudian Theory

One major aspect of Freud's theory was his division of the mind into three levels of consciousness. First, there was the conscious level; below this lay the preconscious, equivalent to a mental library and storing most of our memories. Freud believed these memories were available to consciousness, so the preconscious would thus correspond to what modern psychologists call long-term memory. Below the preconscious lay the unconscious. Freud believed this contained memories, desires, and feelings that had been repressed by the individual because they would be too traumatic or painful to face directly. For example, Freud believed that all children go through a period when they have sexual desires for the parent of the opposite sex. He termed this the Oedipus complex. Since these incestuous desires would be considered perverted by most societies, they were repressed. Castration anxiety, discussed below, also resulted in the repression of the Oedipal feelings. Highly traumatic events that took place in childhood or adulthood could also be repressed and relegated to the unconscious because memories of these events would be too painful to face directly. Material in the unconscious was not available to consciousness, but could still exert powerful influences on behavior. Thus, the repressed memory of some childhood trauma could result in severe psychological difficulties later in life, even though the patient would deny that the actual trauma had ever taken place.

Freud's theory also deals in great detail with the development of personality and specifically with the development of sexual behavior and sexual identity. Freud divided this development into four stages. In some of these stages there were specific "complexes" that had to be overcome if the developmental process was to proceed normally. The first of these is the oral stage, where the infant focuses on the pleasure received from oral stimulation. The second, the anal stage, appears when the child is about two. Here pleasure is said to be obtained largely by "withholding or expelling feces" (Hilgard, Atkinson, and Atkinson, 1979, p. 391). The next stage is the phallic stage (about age three to six), where pleasure is derived from the fondling of one's own genitals. Finally, as adolescence is reached, one enters the genital stage where sexual desires are directed to others.

Mature personality was a tripartite structure in Freud's view, with the *id*, the *ego*, and the *superego* each playing very different roles. The id was thought of as the "seed" of personality. The newborn has only an id and the other structures of the personality develop from it. The id is also the most animalistic part of the personality, seeking only to obtain pleasure and avoid pain. The ego develops as the child grows. It is reality-oriented and modifies or controls the desires of the id by taking into account the possible consequences of an action. Finally, the superego is the conscience of the individual. It judges whether an action is right or wrong, according to whatever set of moral standards the child has been taught. These three structures of personality interact in complicated ways, depending on the situation. "Sometimes the three components of personality are at odds: the ego postpones the gratification that the id wants right away, and the superego battles with both the id and the ego because behavior often falls short of the moral code it represents. But more often in the normal person, the three work as a team, producing integrated behavior" (Hilgard, Atkinson, and Atkinson, 1979, p. 390).

Symbolic interpretation

The repressed contents of the unconscious could result in psychological disorders. It was the task of the psychoanalytic therapist to discover the repressed, hidden contents of the patient's unconscious and to help the patient achieve insight into the psychological roots of his or her problems. According to psychoanalytic theory, once insight was achieved, the psychological problems would fade away because the insight eliminated the repressed cause of the problems. The problem for the therapist, of course, was how to get at the contents of the unconscious, since the patient did not have conscious access to this material. Symbolic interpretations of various forms of behavior, from dreams to accidents, became the primary method by which psychoanalysts attempted to delve into the unconscious. Freud tried hypnosis for a time, but abandoned it. He became especially enthusiastic about the method of free association and dream interpretation as roads to the contents of the unconscious. In free association, the patient simply says anything that comes to mind, often while reclining on the analyst's couch. Freud felt that such free associations would be uncensored by higher levels of consciousness and would thus reflect the contents of the unconscious. If these free associations were interpreted using the proper psychoanalytic symbology, they could give valuable information about the patient's hidden fears, anxieties, and desires. Another valuable source of such information was to be found in dreams. For Freud, a dream had two types of content, *manifest content* and *latent content*. Manifest content referred to the psychoanalytically uninteresting images of the dream itself. The latent content was the meaning hidden in those images. Latent content could be revealed only through the analyst's symbolic interpretation of the images in the dream. Thus, "all sharp and elongated weapons, knives, daggers, and pikes represent the male member. . . . Small boxes, chests, cupboards, and ovens correspond to the female [sex] organ; also cavities, ships, and all kinds of vessels. A room in a dream generally represents a woman" (Freud, 1913/1950, p. 242). The symbolism could be much more complex: "a woman's hat may often be interpreted with certainty as the male genitals. In the dreams of men one often finds the necktie as a symbol for the penis" (Freud, 1913/1950, p. 243). Everyday errors and slips of the tongue were also interpreted, symbolically, as reflecting hidden conflicts and motivations.

There is an extremely serious problem in symbolic interpretation, whether it is behavior or anything else that is being interpreted: such interpretations are inherently nonfalsifiable. This is especially true in psychoanalytic theory where the concept of repression can be used to further protect any interpretation, no matter how absurd, against falsification. Consider a hypothetical example in which a woman dreams that a man forces his way into her apartment through the front door. Doors and other entrances are said to be symbolic representations of the vagina. Since the "entry" in the dream was forced, the easy interpretation of this dream is that it symbolizes rape. Perhaps the dreamer has a great fear of rape or perhaps she has a hidden desire to be raped or otherwise sexually abused. Is there any way to disprove either of these symbolic interpretations? Absolutely not—if we ask the woman, and she protests that she is neither abnormally afraid of rape nor desirous of being raped, it merely shows that her fear or desire is deeply hidden. In fact, her denial is interpreted as further evidence that the interpretation is true. Thus, no matter whether she agrees with the interpretation or argues against it, her behavior will be seen by the psychoanalyst as supporting the interpretation.

The nonfalsifiability of symbolic interpretations of dreams is not limited to psychoanalytic interpretations. Rather, it applies to any type of symbolic interpretation. In nonpsychoanalytic symbolic schemes, where repression does not play such a large role in protecting an interpretation from falsification, another mechanism operates to make the interpretation seem more valid than it is. This mechanism is highly similar to the fallacy of personal validation that was discussed in chapter two. It will be recalled that this fallacy convinces people that the vague "predictions" of psychics are much more specific than they really are. Like psychic predictions, dreams are vague in the sense that a given dream can appear, after the fact, to be consistent with almost any outcome. This characteristic of dreams has already been discussed in the context of prophetic dreams, but it applies with equal force to the symbolic interpretation of dream content. A major study of the effects of stress on dreaming (Breger, Hunter, and Lane, 1971) illustrates this point.

Many nonpsychoanalytic psychologists reject the specific symbolic interpretations of psychoanalysis, but still believe that dream content is at least partially symbolic. A common view is that stressful situations the dreamer is experiencing, or is about to experience, will be symbolically represented in the dream, presumably allowing the dreamer to deal with the stress at less than its full intensity. Breger, Hunter, and Lane (1971) set out to test this view by examining the dreams of a number of individuals who were about to undergo the very stressful experience of major surgery. Their dreams were recorded during the nights before the surgery and were then analyzed to see if the content of the dreams symbolically reflected the impending surgery. The authors concluded that in fact the upcoming surgery was featured symbolically in the dreams of the patients.

The Breger, Hunter, and Lane (1971) study is an influential one, but the conclusions are seriously flawed because of both the way in which the data were collected and the way they were presented in the published report. The authors, who collected the dream reports from the patients and later interpreted them, were well aware of the particular type of surgery that each patient was facing. Thus, it was an easy matter, given the vagueness of dreams, to find symbolic relationships between dream content and the specific surgery that the authors knew patients were facing. In the published report, the reader is first presented with a medical case history for each dreamer; only then are descriptions of the actual dreams provided, followed by the authors' interpretations of the dreams. Given such a sequence, it is not at all surprising that the reader will agree with the authors' interpretations. But the seeming correctness of the interpretation is biased by the previous knowledge the reader was given. This knowledge acts like mental "blinders" to prevent the reader from thinking of alternative interpretations. The authors also had such previous knowledge before they interpreted the dream; it prevented them, as well, from seeing alternative interpretations.

The biasing effects of previous information about the dreamers' surgery can be most clearly seen when that information is absent. If there really is a relationship between the symbolic dream content and the nature of the surgery, it should be possible to determine what type of surgery the patient is going to have from the dream itself, without any previous knowledge. Unfortunately, Breger, Hunter, and Lane (1971) made no attempt to find out whether such determinations could be made. Nor did they bother to assess objectively whether it was possible to distinguish between the dreams of stressed and nonstressed individuals if one did not already know which group the dreamer fell into.

The importance of the biasing effect of information about the dreamer can be most clearly seen when such information is absent. As an example, read the following dream report from Breger, Hunter, and Lane (1971, p. 118-119), as edited by Antrobus (1978, p. 570-71), and try to determine the type of surgery this patient will undergo:

> We was working on a train . . . a work train . . . this Oregon crew came over on account of some washout or something . . . So we saw them come down to that last station and do some switching. We figures . . . also they came across the bridge up there someplace and hooked over onto our railroad. We was . . . looking at this other engine and . . . we lined the switch, it seemed like our switch . . . it was a funny thing. They had to come off this private [rail] road onto ours and them switches weren't a standard switch. We had to dig some rocks out of the ground . . . and throw this switch over. And I was doing that, I was helping . . . I can't tell you what a switch is, instead of them being flapped over and locked down to the padlock they was flapped over, the ends of two pipes together and there was a piece of this crooked zigzag piece of iron that was run first in one pipe and then the other so you couldn't lift the one out . . . and we was digging them things out of them pipes so we could throw the switch for them guys so they wouldn't have to stop . . . they hadn't used that switch it seemed like for years and naturally the sand and dust had blowed into these pipes and it was rusty. It took quite a while . . .

The salient features of the above dream, as far as its symbolic interpretation by Breger, Hunter, and Lane (1971) and Antrobus (1978) is concerned, are the train and train tracks, the switch, and the rocks and dust that seem to block the switch. Even knowing which "symbols" in the dream are considered important by those with knowledge of the dreamer's surgery does not constrain at all the possible interpretations if one does not have such knowledge. In fact, it is almost impossible to think of an operation that is not consistent, after the fact, with the dream if symbolic interpretation of the dream content is permitted.

Perhaps the dreamer will have a brain tumor removed. In that case, the rocks and dust would symbolically reflect the tumor mass. The train and its tracks would represent the normal flow of cognition that was interrupted by the tumor. The switch could further represent the ability to change ("switch") from one type of cognitive process to another, an ability lost in many types of brain damage. Or, perhaps, the fellow had a kidney stone. Here the train would symbolically represent the fluid in the kidney that is blocked by the kidney stones. The stones and dust in the switch would, of course, represent the kidney stone itself. The train tracks would no doubt be interpreted as symbolic representations of the actual nephrons of the kidney, the tubular structures through which fluid actually moves. In the case of a gallstone, interpretation is almost identical except that, if the gallstone was at the junction of the cystic duct, which originates in the gall bladder, and the common hepatic duct, which originates in the liver, the blocked switch would almost certainly be interpreted as an elegant symbolic representation of the dreamer's particular anatomical problem. The dream could also be symbolically interpreted to represent a tumor of the intestinal tract, blockage of one of the major arteries of the brain, a stroke in which a blood vessel in the brain had burst, or atherosclerosis, a build-up of fatty materials in the blood vessels that, when it occurs in the arteries of the heart, can lead to coronary bypass surgery.

All of the possibilities given above could be seen as symbolically represented in the dream. But the dreamer was suffering from none of those conditions. Instead, he suffered from "vascular blockages in his legs" (Breger, Hunter, and Lane, 1971, p. 106), and the surgery was to remove a portion of the blood vessel that was blocked. Naturally, Breger, Hunter, and Lane (1971) interpret this dream only in terms of the operation they know the patient is going to have, stating that the railroad tracks and switch represent the patient's "clogged blood vessels" (p. 122). Antrobus (1978, p. 571) gives an even more detailed symbolic interpretation, contending that "there is a double representation in this report of some features of the impending surgery. The veins are similar to the railroad track. Blood moving through the veins is similar to the train moving along the tracks."

Certainly one must agree that some of the images in the dream are "similar," in one way or another, to certain features of the patient's disease. But they are also "similar," given a little creative interpretation, to some features of almost any other conceivable type of surgery. In summary, symbolic interpretation of dreams, whether the intepretation is explicitly Freudian or not, meets one of the major criteria for being considered a pseudoscience: the interpretations are unfalsifiable.

It is appropriate to inquire here a bit further into the nature of the content of dreams. If the contents are not symbolic, what are they? Studies of the neurobiological basis of dreaming sleep have shown that the dreams contain semi-random collections of images, thoughts, and feelings thrown together in a hodgepodge that seems particularly bizarre and incoherent (Hobson and McCarley, 1977; Hobson, Lydic, and Baghdoyan, 1986). Dreams are generated only during certain phases of the sleep cycle when structures in the midbrain randomly activate groups of neurons in the cortex. Since most memories are stored in the cortex, this pattern of activation of cortical neuronal groups results in a bizarre, at least semirandom, sequence of images that are experienced as a dream. The dream content is not totally random because activities during the day can influence dream content. However, such influence is rather direct and not symbolic. Thus, one's dreams are likely to have rather different characteristics if one has just seen a Walt Disney film as opposed to a horror movie. Similarly, studies have shown that personal problems and anxieties do show up in dream content, but in a fairly straightforward way (Hobson and McCarley, 1977). Thus, if one is worried about an important exam, one might dream about being in the examination room but not being given a copy of the exam and being unable to attract the instructor's attention so as to obtain a copy. Similarly, if one has spent a good portion of the day working on one's stamp collection, a stamp-related theme is somewhat more likely to appear during the night's sleep. This is probably because those areas of the cortex corresponding to the activity engaged in during the day are somewhat more easily activated by lower brain center stimulation during dreaming sleep.

The process of dream generation, at least as far as content is concerned, can perhaps best be compared to taking one hundred feature-length films, cutting them all up into two-foot-long segments, and mixing all the tens of thousands of segments together. One would then draw out about fifteen or twenty minutes' worth of these segments and splice them together. When the result was shown, one would have a bizarre and incoherent set of images, most of which would still be recognizable to some degree. The film would, of course, have no "meaning" whatsoever, but this would certainly not prevent those inclined to find hidden, symbolic messages everywhere from interpreting the film symbolically in any way they wished.

Any such interpretation would have no validity, in spite of the fact that it might be highly creative.

Dreams were not the only aspect of behavior that Freud interpreted in symbolic fashion. His penchant—almost mania—for finding hidden, symbolic meanings nearly everywhere reveals the absurdity not only of his specific method of symbolic interpretation but also of the process in general. Freud was a very close friend of Wilhelm Fliess, inventor of biorhythms, who was a surgeon in Vienna in the late 1800s. Fliess was a man of many peculiar ideas, biorhythms being just one of them. He believed that many of his patients suffered from what he termed the *nasal reflex neurosis*. As Crews (1984) points out, this neurosis could manifest itself in any number of symptoms and Fliess was "rarely at a loss to discover that one of his patients had a nasal reflex neurosis" (Crews, 1984, p. 10). The treatment for this disorder? Application of cocaine to the inside of the nose. No doubt a popular treatment, at least if Fliess were practicing today. Unfortunately, if the local application of cocaine didn't cure the neurosis, more drastic measures had to be taken. Fliess would cauterize the spots in the nose upon which the sexual organs were represented (Fliess believed that the nose was a secondary sexual organ itself) and, if that unpleasant procedure failed, one of the small bones inside the nose would be surgically removed.

So it was with Emma Eckstein, who was unfortunate enough to be a patient of both Fliess and Freud. Surgical skills and procedures in the late 1800s were not all they are now. Nor, apparently, was Fliess what one might call a master surgeon. When he removed the bone from Emma Eckstein's nose, he left several feet of gauze in the wound. Not surprisingly, this resulted in nasal hemorrhages. Freud, who was also treating Emma at the time, came to an astonishing conclusion about the nature of these hemorrhages. They were, so Freud wrote to Fliess, symbolic representations of Emma's sexual "longing" for Freud and an attempt by her to seduce him (Crews, 1984; letter to Fliess originally published in Schur, 1966).

Crews (1984) describes another aspect of Freud's love of symbolic interpretation. Fliess believed, and apparently influenced Freud strongly in this regard, that all humans were inherently bisexual. Thus, all males had hidden, or "latent," homosexual tendencies. These tendencies, of course, had to be repressed if normal heterosexual activity was to take place and the species to perpetuate itself. But, in the distant past, males weren't so skilled at repressing their latent homosexual urges. Rather than actually having sexual intercourse with other males, they expressed their only partially repressed homosexual desires symbolically. How was this done? Crews (1984, p. 23) in his scathing essay, "The Freudian Way of Knowledge," summarizes Freud's view clearly: Our male ancestors "went around dousing fires with urine, thus experiencing a homosexual gratification in vanquishing the phallic flames." Civilization began to really develop, according to Freud, when fire was domesticated—when man "could sufficiently master his homosexuality to save and nurture a fire instead of obeying his drive to pee on it" (Crews, 1984, p. 23).

In addition to applying his psychoanalytic symbolism to understanding, if one can call it that, his own patients and the history of the development of civilization, Freud applied these techniques to the understanding of historical individuals. In doing so, he created the field of psychohistory. His most famous psychohistorical subject was Leonardo da Vinci (Freud, 1916). Stannard (1980) has critiqued Freud's psychohistory of da Vinci and found it based on little more than "contrived facts of Leonardo's childhood" (p. 14) and, of course, the usual symbolic interpretations. One of the "facts" that Freud symbolically interprets is the famous "vulture fantasy" that Leonardo allegedly had as a child. He dreamed, according to Freud, of a vulture that stuck its tail in his mouth. Freud felt that this fantasy was basic to the understanding of Leonardo's life (Stannard, 1980), but it had to be symbolically interpreted. For Freud, the tail of the vulture "cannot possibly signify anything other than a male genital, a penis" (quoted in Stannard, 1980, p. 7). Freud then goes on to base his thesis about Leonardo's creativity and genius on this basic symbolic interpretation of one dream. For various arcane reasons, mostly dealing with the vulture as a mother symbol through history, it is vital for Freud that the bird in Leonardo's dream be a vulture. But it wasn't—Freud read of the dream in a biography of da Vinci that contained a mistranslation into German. While Leonardo's notes refer to a "kite," a very different type of bird, the translation gave the German word for vulture. Thus, Freud built his entire psychohistory on an error. Interestingly, this does not seem to have bothered later psychohistorians who, in true pseudoscientific fashion, have not modified their views of da Vinci to take into account the new data.

Since Freud's psychoanalysis of da Vinci, numerous other historical figures have been subjected to psychohistorical analysis based on symbolic interpretations of their actions, childhoods, and relationships. The symbolic interpretations have not always been strictly Freudian, but such psychohistories are inherently pseudoscientific. Stannard (1980, p. xiii) cogently sums up the situation by saying that while "some works of psychohistory are vastly superior to others, little, if any, psychohistory is good history."

History is certainly not the only field in which symbolic interpretation, Freudian or other, has been applied. Such symbolic interpretation has been adopted with special vigor in the study of drama and literature. Probably everyone who has ever taken a high school or college English course has heard symbolic interpretations of stories or poems. Such interpretations vary in their degree of absurdity, but all are equally nonfalsifiable and invalid. My personal favorite came from an instructor in a college English course. We were reading James Joyce's set of short stories, *The Dubliners*. One question concerned the reason for the presence of snow in the stories. I suggested that this reflected the fact that it snows in Dublin, the setting of the stories, in the winter. To me, this seemed a logical response. I was informed, however, that my response revealed that I didn't understand the symbolic meaning of literature. Far from being a mere realistic representation of Dublin's climate, the instructor informed us, the snow was a psychosexual symbol. Snow is wet, white, and sticky; semen is also wet, white, and sticky. Therefore, snow is a symbol of semen, and from this one can deduce that Joyce had deep anxieties about his masculinity. I did not have the nerve then to point out that there is at least one major difference between snow and semen: one is cold, the other warm. However, I doubt that this would have presented any difficulty to the symbolic interpretation. In fact, I suspect that my instructor would have used the difference to support his symbolic interpretation, perhaps along the lines that Joyce's anxieties made him "cool" to sexual matters and the coolness of the snow symbolically represented this.

In summary, the use of symbolic interpretations of behavior suffers from the same problems found in the symbolic interpretations of psychic predictions, as discussed in chapter two. No matter what the prediction, or how the subject behaves, the symbolic interpretation will supply "evidence" that appears to validate the theory in question.

Theories of psychosexual development

As noted at the beginning of this chapter, Freud divided psychosexual development into four stages. One of the most important was the anal stage because it was during this stage that toilet training took place. As is well known, Freud believed that toilet training had great influence on the development of personality. Specifically, "the methods employed by the mother in training the child, and her attitudes about such matters as defecation, cleanliness, control, and responsibility, determine in large measure the exact nature of the influence that toilet training will have upon the personality and its development" (Hall, 1954, p. 107). If toilet training is strict, it may have one of two possible outcomes. First, the child may "get even with frustrating authority figures by being messy, irresponsible, disorderly, wasteful, and extravagant" (Hall, 1954, p. 108). Second, strict toilet training may result in "meticulous neatness, fastidiousness, compulsive orderliness, frugality, disgust, fear of dirt, strict budgeting of time and money, and other over-controlled behaviors" (Hall, 1954, p. 108). So, strict toilet training can result in either a slob or a neatness freak or, presumably, anything in between. Thus, the theory can "explain," post hoc, any degree of neatness or sloppiness as being due to strict toilet training.

The theory becomes doubly nonfalsifiable, if such a thing is possible, when one considers the effects of gentle toilet training—the effects of gentle toilet training are indistinguishable from those of strict training. On the one hand, if the training is such that the mother

> pleads with the child to have a bowel movement and praises him extravagantly when he does, the child will come to regard the product he has made as being of great value. Later in life he may be motivated to produce or create things to please others or to please himself as he once made feces to please his mother. Generosity, giving presents, charity, and philanthropy may all be outgrowths of this basic experience (Hall, 1954, p. 108).

Does this mean that gentle toilet training will always result in this sort of behavior? Not at all:

> If too much emphasis is placed on the value of feces, the child may feel that he has lost something valuable when he defecates. He will respond to the loss by feeling depressed, depleted, and anxious. He will try to prevent future loss by refusing to give up his feces. If this mode fixates and generalizes, the person will be thrifty, parsimonious, and economical (Hall, 1954, p. 108).

So, gentle toilet training can result in either a generous person or a tightwad. Again, both styles of personality can be "explained" after the fact, but neither can be predicted.

Further, note that strict toilet training can be used to explain the "strict budgeting of time and money," while gentle toilet training can result in someone who is "thrifty, parsimonious, and economical." Also, gentle training can result in "generosity, giving presents, charity, and philanthropy," while strict training can produce "extravagant" behavior. Thus, the same behavior can be "explained" by opposite types of toilet training and opposite types of behavior can be "explained" as being due to identical toilet training procedures.

Freud's fecal fascination does not end here. Hall (1954, p. 108) states that "the gentle pressure on the intestinal walls of the rectum is sensually satisfying" and "if a person gets fixated upon this form of erotic pleasure it may develop into a generalized interest in collecting, possessing, and retaining objects." But, if a reaction formation develops, the "person will feel impelled to give away his possessions and money in a heedless manner or lose them by making foolish investments or by reckless gambling. Having things makes such people so anxious that they will do almost anything to get rid of them." A *reaction formation* is a Freudian mechanism that permits a post hoc "explanation" of behavior that is the opposite of that "predicted" by some part of the theory. It is only possible to tell that a reaction formation has taken place after observing that the behavior in question did not occur as predicted.

In spite of the fearsome logical problems with Freud's formulation of the relationship between toilet-training procedures and personality, it is possible to ask whether there is any consistent relationship between these variables. The answer is no. Research in which the actual toilet-training procedures used by parents have been investigated has shown that there is no relationship between this variable and personality (Klein, 1968; Eysenck and Wilson, 1973).

Klein's (1968) study is of special interest here as it shows the type of research findings that are touted as "supporting" Freudian theory. Klein (1968) argued that investigations that examined the actual toilet-training procedures used were unreliable. He used a different, indirect method to assess the relationship between toilet training and personality. He gave subjects the "Blackie pictures." This is a set of eleven drawings showing a little black dog in various interactions with other dogs. These interactions are supposed to represent, symbolically, various stages and conflicts in human psychosexual development. One of the pictures shows Blackie defecating between two dog houses, one occupied by his mother, the other by his father. If a subject's response to this picture indicates that it upsets or disturbs him more than the other pictures in the set, this is taken as evidence that psychosexual development has fixated at the anal stage. Further, if the story the subject makes up about the picture contains themes related to revenge or aggression against the parents, this is taken as a sign of "anal expulsiveness." If the stories the subjects make up contain themes relating to cleanliness and concealing things from the parents, these are said to indicate "anal retentiveness."

Klein (1968) correlated subjects' Blackie responses with responses on several paper and pencil tests of obsessive-compulsive personality traits. He found several statistically significant positive correlations, from which it was concluded that "anal eroticism" is related to later obsessive-compulsive traits. The anal eroticism is presumably related to toilet training, so it is argued that the results support the existence of a relationship between toilet-training procedures and personality. This conclusion is invalid for several reasons. First, toilet-training procedures to which the subjects were exposed as children were never measured. It is simply assumed, in the absence of any supporting data, that anal eroticism is caused by toilet-training procedures. Second, the Blackie test is an example of a projective test. Such tests have very low reliability and validity, as will be discussed later in this chapter. Finally, as Eysenck and Wilson (1973) have cogently noted, there is a much simpler explanation for the positive correlations Klein (1968) found. The paper and pencil tests used appear to be reasonably good measures of obsessive-compulsive tendencies. People who are tidy are more compulsive than those who are not and are likely to be more disgusted and upset by defecation than are messy folk. In fact, one of the questions on one of the paper and pencil tests that Klein (1968) used was "Do you regard the keeping of household dogs as unhygienic?" Other questions concerned cleanliness and related topics. In view of this, the correlations Klein (1968) found aren't surprising. They simply demonstrate that tidy people are more put off by canine fecal matter than are less tidy and clean people. This is not exactly a finding that will set psychology on its ear, and it is certainly no warrant to infer support for vague Freudian hypotheses that have not been verified in earlier studies where the crucial variable—toilet-training procedure—was much more directly measured.

Another well-known aspect of Freud's theory of psychosexual development is the *Oedipus complex* and the castration anxiety that is said to result from this complex. Hall (1954, p. 109) describes the Oedipus complex as the state in which "the boy craves exclusive sexual possession of the mother." Considering that the complex is alleged to occur at about the age of five, the claim seems, at best, a bit far-fetched. At that age, hormonal processes related to normal adult sexual behavior are essentially nonexistent. In spite of this, Freud claimed that every five-year-old male wants to have an erection and have sexual intercourse with his mother. This lust is unconscious, of course. As if the basic Oedipus complex were not bizarre enough, Freud adds another touch. The boy's father naturally resents the son's lusting after his wife. The boy realizes this and fears that his father will do something to retaliate for the boy's sexual interest in his mother. What will the father do? Why, cut off the boy's penis, of course. This fear is the "castration anxiety" talked about at great length by Freudian psychologists. Apparently, castration anxiety develops spontaneously, but "the reality of castration is brought home to the boy when he sees the sexual anatomy of the girl, which is lacking the protruding genitals of the male. The girl appears castrated to the boy. 'If that could happen to her, it could also happen to me,' is what he thinks" (Hall, 1954, p. 109).

Several studies claim to have found experimental support for the reality of the Oedipus complex and castration anxiety. These have been critiqued by Eysenck and Wilson (1973). These studies demonstrate the strong tendency of Freudian psychologists to interpret even the most straightforward results symbolically as evidence for Freudian theories even though much simpler explanations of the findings are available. Hall (1963), in a study titled "Strangers in Dreams: An Empirical Confirmation of the Oedipus Complex," found that (1) more strangers in dreams were male than female; (2) this effect was greater for male than for female dreamers; (3) aggressive interactions in dreams were more common with male than female strangers in the dream; and (4) there were more aggressive events in the dreams of males than of females. None of these findings is surprising and none provides support for the reality of the Oedipus complex. All can be simply explained by noting that the dream content reflects everyday reality. Thus, males are more aggressive than females and the dreams' content merely reflected this fact. Ignoring this far simpler explanation, Hall (1963) bases his claim that the findings support the reality of the Oedipus complex on the further, unsupported claim that male strangers in dreams symbolically represent the father.

Schwartz (1956) similarly ignores simple explanations that do not support Freudian theory in his study of the responses of male homosexuals and heterosexuals to the Thematic Apperception Test. In this test, the subject sees photographs of people in ambiguous situations and has to make up a story about each photograph. The content of the stories is then scored. In Schwartz's (1956) study the heterosexual and homosexual males scored differently on measures of guilt, fear of punishment, "sexual inadequacy"—which, according to Schwartz (1956), includes "renunciation of heterosexuality"—and general anxiety. Schwartz (1956) claims that the first three of these measures indicate castration anxiety, and that thus homosexual males have greater castration anxiety than heterosexual males. However, as Eysenck and Wilson (1973) note, the study was done in 1956 when homosexuality was not only considered a serious disease by most psychiatrists, but was actually a crime and the subject of much more fear, disgust, and loathing than is now the case. Given these circumstances, it is not very surprising that homosexuals would show more fear and guilt than heterosexuals. Nor is it surprising that homosexuals showed more "renunciation of heterosexuality" than did the heterosexuals. In fact, it's about as surprising as finding that professional basketball players are taller than professional jockeys. And it offers just about as much support for the reality of castration anxiety.

The female equivalent of castration anxiety is penis envy. "The girl's love for her father is mixed with envy because he possesses something that she does not have. This is known as *penis envy*" (Hall, 1954, p. 111, emphasis in original). Hall and van de Castle (1965) performed what Eysenck and Wilson (1973, p. 166) term "the most celebrated of empirical 'verifications' of Freudian theory." It turns out to be an astonishingly bad study. Dreams of male and female college students were collected and their contents scored for themes that were assumed, in the absence of any supporting data, to symbolically represent castration anxiety and penis envy. The reader will not be surprised to hear that more castration anxiety themes were found in dreams of males and more penis envy themes were found in the dreams of females. But, as Eysenck and Wilson (1973) note, there was a fatal flaw in the study. Some of the critieria for scoring a dream for castration anxiety could only be applied to males. Examples are "inability or difficulty of the dreamer in using his penis" and "a male dreams that he is a woman or changes into a woman." Similarly, some of the criteria for penis envy could only occur in female dreams. An example is "a female dreams that she is a man or has acquired male secondary sex characteristics, or is wearing men's clothing or accessories." Thus, the study almost had to come out as it did. Even if this problem were not present, the unsupported symbolic interpretation of the dreams' contents would invalidate the authors' conclusions that the results support Freudian theory.

Hall and van de Castle (1965) also found that males had more dreams than females in which injuries occurred. Females had more dreams than males about babies. Rather than adopt the simple, straightforward explanation that these results reflect real-life differences between men and women, the authors relentlessly interpreted them symbolically as showing castration anxiety on the part of males and "displaced penis envy" on the part of females.

Repression and the unconscious

The concept of repression is obviously of great importance in Freudian theory, as the foregoing discussion has demonstrated. A defining feature of repression is that it is "motivated" forgetting. That is, it is an active process in which certain memories are blocked from reaching consciousness because of their emotionally negative content. Should such memories reach the conscious level, they could cause serious psychological disturbance.

One well-known phenomenon has long been used to argue for the reality of repression. This is *infant amnesia*, which refers to the fact that adults have very poor memories for the first few years of life. Freud proposed a characteristically creative explanation for this amnesia. The period of early childhood, according to psychoanalytic theory, is one during which the child is awash with strong sexual desires, most of them incestuous. Since these desires cannot be fulfilled, they result in considerable frustration. Further, in the case of the boy, his lust for his mother may, he fears, result in his castration. These factors lead to a repression of early childhood memories when the Oedipus complex is resolved. Why are all childhood memories repressed, and not just the ones dealing with the child's sexual desires? Because if any memory from this period came to consciousness, there would be risk that memories of the perverted (by adult standards) and frustrating sexual desires the individual had as an infant would also emerge into consciousness, perhaps causing serious psychological damage.

There is no question that infant amnesia is a real phenomenon. However, research on memory and the brain has shown that its causes are very different from those proposed in psychoanalytic theory. Spear (1979) and Coulter, Collier, and Campbell (1976) have shown that rats also show infant amnesia. Specifically, infant rats trained on simple learning tasks show considerable loss of memory for those tasks over a period of time. Older rats, trained on the same tasks to the same level of performance, show much better memory for the tasks after the same amount of time has passed. In addition to rats, monkeys also show infant amnesia (Mishkin and Appenzeller, 1987). It seems most unlikely that rat or monkey infant amnesia is due to the rats or monkeys repressing their incestuous desires for their parents.

The real reason for infant amnesia, in rats, monkeys, and humans, lies in the nature of the brain of the immature organism. The immature brain is both anatomically and physiologically different from the mature brain. Deep in each temporal lobe of the mammalian brain is a structure known as the hippocampus. Together, the two hippocampi (and, of course, other brain structures) are vital for normal memory function (Squire, 1986; Teyler and DiScenna, 1986; Mishkin and Appenzeller, 1987). The hippocampi in the human brain do not begin to undergo maturational changes until between four and five years of age (White and Pillemer, 1979). Significantly, it is at about this time that the earliest memories adults can recall are found (Waldfogel, 1948). Thus, it is the anatomical and physiological changes that take place in the brain, specifically in the hippocampi, that result in more lasting memories being formed by rats, monkeys, and humans who have passed the infant and very young child stages of development.

A second variable operates in the case of humans to make memories of events that took place during early childhood and infancy difficult to recall. This is the development of language. Infants and very young children have no, or at best very limited, language skills. As language develops, it becomes, among other things, a major way of storing information in memory. Adult human memory is language-oriented. Memories of events that took place before language developed must be stored in some nonlinguistic fashion, if they are stored at all. Since the human adult typically uses language processes to code and to retrieve memories, the mismatch between the type of coding of prelanguage (infant and early childhood) memories and postlanguage (later childhood and adult) memories will render the former difficult to retrieve. White and Pillemer (1979) have discussed this idea at length.

Many experimental studies have been conducted to validate the existence of repression. Holmes (1974) has reviewed this large literature. He concluded that "there is no consistent research evidence to support the hypothesis" that repression actually exists (Holmes, 1974, p. 649). He further commented that the failure of numerous studies to support the reality of repression was "especially notable in view of the wide variety of approaches which have been tried and the persistent effort which has been made during the last half century to find support" for repression (Holmes, 1974, p. 649).

More recent research on repression has been no more successful in turning up evidence in support of the concept, although claims to the contrary are sometimes made. For example, Davis and Schwartz (1987) argue that the results of their study, in which they asked college students to recall emotional memories from childhood, shows the existence of repression. These authors found that students they termed "repressors' recalled fewer negative emotional memories from childhood than did other students. However, they also found that these "repressors" recalled fewer emotional memories from childhood for which the associated emotion was positive. What Davis and Schwartz (1987) have demonstrated is that some people are better than others at recalling emotional experiences, positive or negative, from childhood. This is not repression.

The unconscious plays a large role in psychoanalytic theory. It includes "instinctual drives and infantile goals, hopes, wishes, and needs that have been repressed, or concealed from conscious awareness, because they cause internal conflict" (Bootzin, Bower, Zajonc, and Hall, 1986, p. 455). Thus, the Freudian unconscious is a seething cauldron of lusts, desires, and frustrations. Does such an unconscious actually exist? Modern research in cognitive psychology has revealed a great deal about the nature of conscious versus nonconscious cognitive processing. It is clear from this research (for reviews see Snodgrass, Levy-Berger, and Haydon, 1985; Posner, 1978; Lachman, Lachman, and Butterfield, 1979; or any recent cognitive psychology text) that a great deal of cognitive processing goes on outside conscious awareness. Further, such processing cannot be brought to consciousness even when an individual wishes to do so. However, the character of the "unconscious" processes that have been discovered by cognitive psychologists are different from the processes in the unconscious postulated by Freud. For example, it has been repeatedly shown that when a single word is presented visually, that presentation activates a stored representation of the word's meaning in the subject's long-term memory. In addition to activating the presented word's semantic representation, it also activates the semantic representations of words related in meaning to the presented word. Thus, the presentation of the word "KING" will also activate the internal representation corresponding to the word "QUEEN." This activation of the representations of both "KING" and "QUEEN" is automatic in the sense that it takes place without any conscious awareness on the part of the subject. Further, the subject cannot block such activation should he or she wish to do so. This activation process can be likened to a reflex. It simply happens once a word is presented. It takes place extremely rapidly, with some activation demonstrable as soon as forty milliseconds following word presentation. The activation is also short-lived, lasting no more than a second or so in most situations. So, here is an example of a cognitive process that is unconscious in the sense that the individual is not aware of it and, apparently, cannot become consciously aware of it. Nonetheless, it is a very different type of process than those postulated by Freud to be taking place in the unconscious.

Some psychologists have misinterpreted work in cognitive psychology and the closely related discipline of neuroscience, as supporting the existence of an unconscious of the type Freud proposed. Miller (1986, p. 60), for example, argues that such research "may be rallying to Freud's support." Some of the research Miller discusses in his article does, in fact, show the existence of an unconscious. None of it, however, supports an unconscious even remotely like that hypothesized by Freud. The argument is seriously flawed that states that because research in cognitive psychology and neuroscience has shown that some mental processes take place outside consciousness, Freud's specific postulations about the nature of the unconscious have been supported. Such an argument is equivalent to an astrologer pointing out, correctly, that both astrology and astronomy postulate the existence of stars, and then arguing that because modern research in astronomy and astrophysics verifies the existence of stars, that research also shows that astrology is valid.

Freud and neurobiology

Freud was a physician who had considerable training in neurology. This was to influence strongly the development of psychoanalytic theory. Basically, Freud felt that psychoanalysis was a biological or neurological theory of the mind and that the constructs found in psychoanalytic theory— such as repression, the unconscious, and all the rest—were neurologically real. Much of his theory was based on what was believed about the neurophysiology of the nerve cell (the neuron) at the time the theory was being developed, in the late 1800s. Unfortunately, as McCarley and Hobson (1977, p. 1213) point out, "many of Freud's ideas about the function of neurons were simply and fundamentally wrong." These fundamental errors became incorporated into psychoanalysis.

One of the greatest misconceptions about the nature of nerve cell function, which was widely accepted in the late 1800s, had to do with the concept of neural inhibition. It is now well known that one neuron can be excited (made more likely to generate a tiny electrical signal) or inhibited (made less likely to generate such a signal) by other neurons. In Freud's time, such neural inhibition was unknown, and it was believed that all processes in the nervous system were excitatory. It was further believed that the nerves were akin to high-tension lines, constantly bringing energy into the body. That energy had to be expended somehow. It is now known that nerves are much more like telegraph or telephone wires. They use tiny amounts of energy to transmit information. Thus, the problem of what to do with all the energy the nerves are bringing into the body is not a real problem. But in Freud's time, this was an important problem and one that influenced psychoanalytic theory deeply. It was to deal with this problem, in fact, that many of the basic constructs of psychoanalytic theory were developed (McCarley and Hobson, 1977). McCarley and Hobson (1977; Hobson and McCarley, 1977) show, for example, that much of Freud's view of the nature of dream content was based on his incorrect notions about the way neurons functioned.

Hobson and McCarley's (1977) theory of dream generation, based on knowledge of modern neurophysiology, has been described earlier in this chapter. What is of interest at this point is to note the response that this new physiological theory of dream generation received from psychoanalysis. In true pseudoscientific fashion, one major response was "it doesn't matter." Like Velikovsky (see chapter nine), who never revised his "theory" in the face of contradictory evidence, and other pseudoscientists who ignore data that conflict with their theories, the response of many psychoanalysts to the refutation of the basis of Freud's dream theory was to deny that the refutation mattered. One general approach (see LaBruzza, 1978, and Letters to the Editor, 1978) was to claim that mind and brain are different and that knowledge about the function of the brain cannot be used to constrain theories about the nature of cognitive processes. In fact, theories of cognition (of mind, if you will) must be constrained by what is known about the function of the brain. A theory of mind that is inconsistent with what is known about brain function must be wrong. Similarly, a theory of brain function that is inconsistent with what is known about cognitive function is also in need of serious revision. Returning directly to the issue of the validity of psychoanalysis, it is clear that psychoanalytic theory rests on incorrect notions of how the neurons in the brain operate. On those grounds alone, the theory can be rejected.

Clinical Applications of Psychoanalysis

Psychoanalysis was developed to be more than a theory of the mind: it was also developed as a method of treatment for numerous psychological disorders. This section will consider three issues related to the clinical applications of psychoanalysis. The first is the use of psychoanalysts' clinical experiences as evidence for the validity of psychoanalytic theory. The second is the use of projective tests, because the rationale for these tests rests largely in psychoanalytic theory. The third issue concerns the efficacy of psychoanalytic therapy.

Clinical experiences as proof for psychoanalytic theory

Psychoanalysts since Freud have argued that the strongest proof of the validity of psychoanalytic theory is to be found in the clinical experiences of actual psychoanalysts. This is the data on which their "science" is founded. These data consist of symbolic interpretations of dreams, free associations, and such that seem to confirm psychoanalytic theory. The data are taken as strong evidence for the theory. Thus, an analyst might have a male patient whom he believes has unresolved Oedipal feelings. That is, he still has some incestuous sexual desire for his mother. One night the patient dreams that he entered a cozy, familiar home through a window, Further, he was wearing an absurdly large tie at the time. Obviously, such a dream can be interpreted symbolically as a wish to have sexual intercourse with the mother, symbolized by the familiar house. The large tie is a symbolic representation of the erect penis. The serious problems with symbolic interpretations have been discussed earlier in this chapter. The important point here is that interpreting a patient's dream or free association in such a way that it appears to confirm one's diagnosis will help convince both the psychoanalyst and the patient that psychoanalytic theory "works." Numbers of such "correct" interpretations over the years of an analyst's experience will, understandably, result in a powerful belief that psychoanalytic theory is valid. It is clear, however, that the psychological processes that yield this strong belief in the validity of psychoanalytic theory are the same as the processes that engender strong, but incorrect, beliefs in the validity of the predictions made by psychics, as discussed in chapter two. The license to interpret symbolically ensures that it will be possible to interpret any dream or action of the patient in a way consistent with the psychoanalyst's diagnosis. Thus, like the vague psychic predictions that "come true" after the fact, the perceived validity of psychoanalytic theory, at least as far as it is based on data from the clinical situation, is based on the fallacy of personal validation and the P. T. Barnum effect.

Projective tests and illusory correlation

On most projective tests, test takers are confronted with some ambiguous stimulus that they must make up a story about or describe. Responses are interpreted, frequently symbolically, and are said to reflect the basic, stable personality characteristics of individuals. The responses can also be used to reveal hidden psychological problems, desires, and anxieties, even if these are lodged in the unconscious. Thus the term *projective*: the test taker is assumed to project information about personality and any psychological disturbances onto the ambiguous stimulus. The classic example of a projective test is the Rorschach Ink Blot Test (Rorschach, 1942), in which test takers are presented with a series of ink blots and asked to tell what each reminds them of. Another type of projective test is one in which test takers produce some nonverbal response. This type of projective test is typified by the Draw A Person test in which individuals are simply asked to draw a person. The drawings are then interpreted to reveal personality traits, anxieties, and so forth.

Projective tests are widely used by psychiatrists and psychologists. The important question is whether they actually provide useful information. That is, do they "work," in any objective sense? For a test to work in this sense, it must possess two basic characteristics: it must be both reliable and valid. Briefly, a test is reliable if it gives the same individual close to the same score on two different test administrations. A test is valid if it can be shown to measure what it is claimed to measure. There are numerous ways of measuring reliability and validity that are beyond the scope of this section, but they can be found in any text on psychological testing. Projective tests lack both reliability and validity (Anastasi, 1976). Specifically regarding the issue of validity, Anastasi (1988, p. 621) says, "The accumulation of published studies that have *failed* to demonstrate any validity for such projective techniques as the Rorschach and the D-A-P (Draw A Person Test) is truly impressive. Yet after five decades of negative results, the status of projective techniques remains substantially unchanged" (emphasis in original).

If projective techniques are so poor when measured objectively, why are they still so widely used, especially by psychoanalysts? One reason is that in many cases the test results are interpreted symbolically. For example, in an unpublished report it was noted that one test taker ". . . provided a Rorschach response of cells dividing, in the process of pulling apart, reflecting a lack of separateness and differentiation. Another subject's sense of incompletion and deficiency was illustrated in many anatomical responses, which indicate concerns over bodily integrity. . . ." The projective test essentially becomes the "gimmick" in a cold reading (see chapter two), replacing the astrological chart, tea leaves, or palm lines that the storefront cold reader uses. Thus, it will always be possible for projective test users to convince themselves that the test has revealed something about the test taker.

Another, somewhat more subtle, mechanism also works to increase the perceived validity of projective tests. Known as *illusory correlation,* this mechanism has been extensively studied by Chapman and Chapman (1967; 1969; Chapman, 1967). Illusory correlation simply means that the individuals perceive certain variables as co-occurring more frequently than they actually do. Chapman and Chapman (1967) demonstrated this in a series of studies using the projective Draw A Person (DAP) test. In these studies, college undergraduates with no knowledge of the DAP were presented with DAP drawings. Each drawing was paired with two statements which, the students were told, described the psychological symptoms of the man who had drawn each drawing. For example, a drawing would be accompanied with a statment like "The man who drew this (1) is suspicious of other people (2) is worried about how manly he is." Of course, the statements that were presented with each drawing had nothing to do with the actual symptoms, if any (some of the drawings were done by presumably normal graduate students), of the man who had produced the drawing. The drawings varied on a number of characteristics, several of which clinicians with experience using the DAP believe are signs of particular symptoms. For example, a drawing that has broad shoulders or is muscular or manly is said to be characteristic of a man who is worried about his masculinity. A man worried aobut his intelligence is said to draw a large or emphasized head. The actual set of drawings and symptom statements used by Chapman and Chapman (1967) was specifically constructed such that there was no correlation between any symptoms and any drawing characteristic. That is, the symptom "is worried about how manly he is" occurred equally often with drawings that were muscular and manly and with drawings that weren't.

After having examined the forty-five drawings and the pair of "symptoms" associated with each, subjects were asked to indicate which characteristics of the drawings went with each of the symptoms. In fact, there were no such relationships. Nonetheless, the subjects' responses showed that they had perceived in the drawings they had examined relationships between drawing characteristics and symptoms that were not really there. Thus, they reported that men who worried about their masculinity overwhelmingly draw figures with broad shoulders. Chapman and Chapman (1969) later showed that trained psychodiagnosticians showed similar illusory correlation effects. Additional research has shown that even explicit warnings about the illusory correlation effect fail to abolish it (Waller and Keeley, 1978; Kurtz and Garfield, 1978). As Kurtz and Garfield (1978, p. 1013) note, individuals, even trained clinicians, "try to find something in the clinical material presented." Even if the meaning isn't really there, it will be found.

Chapman and Chapman (1967; Chapman, 1967) have further found that the degree of the illusory correlation effect is due to what is termed the associative strength between variables that are perceived, incorrectly, to be correlated. Thus, the head and intelligence are logically associated. So are broad shoulders and masculinity. Based on these associations, people assume that a broad-shouldered drawing means that the individual worries about his masculinity and that people worried about their intelligence draw large-headed figures. Chapman (1967) showed the importance of associative strength in the genesis of illusory correlation in a study that used pairs of words. Subjects saw sets of word pairs, one pair at a time. Some of the pairs contained associated words (e.g., "lion tiger") and some pairs contained unassociated words (e.g., "lion notebook"). Although each word in the list of pairs that the subjects saw appeared equally often with each other word, subjects reported that words were paired with a strongly associated word much more frequently than was actually the case. Returning to the clinical situation with projective tests, these results show that the associative strength variable produces the illusory correlation. Selective memory is probably responsible for the continued acceptance of the correlations. When one finds an actual instance in which a man worried about his masculinity has drawn a broad-shouldered picture, that instance will stand out in memory much more than one in which a man worried about his masculinity doesn't draw a broad-shouldered picture. This will be recognized as the same process that maintains belief in psychic predictions, hunches, and prophetic dreams.

Illusory correlations, license to make symbolic interpretations, and selective memory all combine to produce a strong belief that unreliable and invalid projective tests are accurate ways of discovering psychologically relevant information about people.

Psychoanalytic therapy

Does psychoanalytic therapy work? The question of whether any type of psychotherapy works or not is much more difficult to investigate than

might be expected. One of the problems lies in the definition of "work."
If by "work" one means only that the therapy is better than doing nothing
at all, then nearly all types of psychotherapies "work." However, there
is a very large placebo effect in psychotherapy. Simply believing that one
is being treated can result in beneficial effects. A more rigorous definition
of "work," then, requires that the therapy in question be more effective
than a placebo therapy in which patients engage in some activity they
believe is therapeutic, rather than receiving the actual type of psychotherapy
being evaluated. Another problem in evaluating psychotherapeutic
effectiveness is spontaneous remission. Many of the problems about which
people consult psychotherapists will simply go away if left untreated. If
an individual is seeing a therapist during the period of time when the
problem would have disappeared on its own, it is quite natural for both
the therapist and the patient to attribute the elimination of the problem
to the therapy, not to the passage of time. Such processes result in strong
beliefs on the part of many psychotherapists, psychoanalytic as well as
nonpsychoanalytic, that their particular brand of therapy works. These
same processes also produce scores of testimonials for any type of psychotherapy one wishes to name.

The problems discussed above all operate to make it appear that various
types of psychotherapy are more effective than they really are. Actual
research on the effectiveness of psychotherapies in general has shown
that, as expected, so-called "talk therapies" are more effective than doing
nothing (Smith, Glass, and Miller, 1980). However, such psychotherapies
show almost no greater effectiveness than placebo therapies (Prioleau,
Murdock, and Brody, 1983). Although these conclusions may at first seem
surprising, they become more understandable after a bit of "demythol-
ogizing" of psychotherapy is done. Most people consult psychotherapists
not because they suffer from major psychoses—such as schizophrenia or
manic depressive psychosis—but because of smaller neurotic problems or
just because they are upset by the "slings and arrows of outrageous fortune"
that beset everyone from time to time. Gross (1978), in an excellent and
much overlooked book, has cogently argued that we are becoming a
"psychological society" in which we are led to define every little
disappointment, setback, and depression as something to be treated by
some mental health professional. Albert Ellis, founder of rational emotive
therapy, has pungently commented on this trend: "I find that increasingly
in our society much of what we call emotional disturbance is *whining*"
(quoted in Gross, 1978, p. 315, emphasis in original). The type of problems
that many people now consult a psychotherapist for, then, are frequently
minor in terms of true psychopathology. In past years, such problems
would have been talked over with a trusted friend, relative, or clergyman—

people who would have had no psychotherapeutic training. It is certainly true that talking about problems with someone else can be very beneficial. The other person may be able to propose solutions, may see the problem from a different perspective, or may simply provide moral support for a difficult and troubling course of action already decided upon. These are real and important benefits of what is generally termed "advice." Psychotherapists, no matter what particular type of therapy they practice, provide advice to their patients, in addition to the special ministrations their own brand of therapy calls for. It is this advice component of every psychotherapy that helps account for the general effectiveness of psychotherapy over doing nothing.

If psychotherapies in general are more effective than doing nothing because the therapist is providing advice to patients, one would expect that professional advice givers (i.e., trained professional psychotherapists) would not be much more effective than individuals lacking formal therapeutic training. This issue has been the focus of considerable research. Two reviews of the literature on this issue (Durlak, 1979; Hattie, Sharpley, and Rogers, 1984) have actually found that patients treated by trained professionals do worse than those treated by untrained "paraprofessionals." Berman and Norton (1985) have criticized the Hattie, Sharpley, and Rogers (1984) review on statistical grounds and reanalyzed the literature that Hattie *et al.* reviewed. In their reanalysis Berman and Norton (1985) find no difference in therapeutic effectiveness between trained professionals and untrained paraprofessionals.

Returning to the specific issue of the effectiveness of psychoanalytic therapies, what is true for psychotherapies in general is true for psychoanalytic therapies in particular. Over the past thirty-five years repeated reviews of the literature have failed to show any solid evidence that psychoanalytic therapy is superior to placebo therapy (Eysenck, 1952; Rachman, 1971; Rachman and Wilson, 1980; Erwin, 1980, 1986).

Does any type of psychotherapy provide a better result than placebo therapy? The answer is yes, and the type of therapy is behavior therapy and its close relative cognitive behavior therapy (Erwin, 1986). Developed as an alternative to the ineffective psychoanalytic treatments in the early 1960s, early behavior therapies concentrated on classical and instrumental conditioning as the explanation of disordered behavior. The idea was that such behavior was learned and could be eliminated using the techniques of reinforcement, punishment, and extinction drawn from work on conditioning animals. As the field of behavioral therapies has matured, it has become much more cognitive, admitting that patients' cognitions play an important role in disordered behavior and must be addressed by any therapy. Thus, Lazarus (1986, p. 251) notes that "terms such as 'expectancies,' 'encoding,' 'plans,' 'values,' and 'self-regulatory systems,' all operationally defined, have crept into the behavior literature."

The early behavior modifiers made the unfounded claim that all disordered behaviors were the result of learning or conditioning of one type or another. While this rather grandiose claim was wrong—for example, many behavioral disorders are biochemically caused—other disorders were properly thought to be due to learning factors. Behavior therapies were quite effective at treating these. Examples include phobias (Paul, 1969a, b), certain specific types of depression (Rehm, 1981) and other disorders ranging from obsessive-compulsive disorders to some sexual disorders (Bandura, 1969).

Interestingly, the advent of behavioral modification techniques that focus on the disordered behavior itself, rather than on hypothetical psychological causes such as unresolved Oedipal complexes and the like, provided an opportunity to test one strong prediction made by psychoanalytic theory. According to psychoanalytic theory, the overt disordered behavior a patient displays is merely a symptom of some hidden, deep psychological cause. According to psychoanalytic theory, it would not be sufficient to simply eliminate the symptom (i.e., the behavior), because the underlying cause of the disorder would still be there and would only cause some other problem behavior (i.e., symptom) in the future. This is known as the symptom substitution hypothesis. Studies of patients who have been treated behaviorally have shown no evidence of symptom substitution (Bandura, 1969; Franks, 1969).

Neurobiology and Mental Disorders

Although Freud believed that the constructs in psychoanalytic theory were biologically real, he also believed that the causes of psychological disorders, serious and minor, could be traced to experiences while growing up. The early years, during which psychosexual development was said to take place, were especially important. If the child was exposed to aberrant situations during this period, disorders of psychosexual development could occur that would appear in adulthood. Thus, for example, overt male homosexuality was thought to be due to the boy's failure to form a normal identification with his father. This could be due to a cold, unloving father or to a domineering mother. Mothers, it turns out in psychoanalytic thought, are often responsible for the psychological disturbances of their children. Depression is said to be caused when a loss during adulthood reactivates the represssed feelings of the traumatic loss during childhood of the mother's affection. Psychoanalytic psychologist Bruno Bettelheim (1967) has argued that the childhood disorder autism is caused by inept, unloving, and cold mothers.

Within the past decade great strides have been made in understanding the nature of many disorders. In a host of such disorders that were previously thought to be "psychological"—that is, caused by some abnormality in the interactions the individual had with his parents or peers, usually as a child—the actual causes have been determined to be physiological, usually involving abnormalities in the chemistry of the brain. Considerable evidence now exists to show that human homosexuality is caused, at least in large part, by hormonal influences that take place while the brain is developing in utero (Ellis and Ames, 1987; Goy and McEwen, 1980), although specific cultural influences are also at work (Green, 1987; Money, 1987). The important fact here is that modern research on the etiology of homosexuality fails to support the psychoanalytic view.

To take another example, there are several types of depression. One type, called reactive depression, is a reaction to some environmental event, such as the loss of a friend, lover, or parent, or even the loss of an environment, as in the homesickness one sometimes sees in first-year college students. Research on this type of depression shows no support for the psychoanalytic "explanation." More serious types of depression are biological in nature. So-called endogenous depression is caused by abnormalities in the levels of certain neurotransmitters, chemicals that allow neurons to transmit information to one another, in the brain (see Kalat, 1987 for a brief review). Endogenous depression is not linked to any objectively depressing event in the patient's environment and can be treated, although not perfectly, with medications designed to normalize the patient's brain chemistry. An even more serious type of depression is seen in manic-depressive psychosis, where the patient alternates between periods of deep depression and high-energy mania. Chemical treatment is available for this disorder, although it is sometimes necessary to use shock treatment. It was long thought that there was only one type of manic-depressive psychosis. Recent genetic studies, however, have revealed two separate chromosomal locations at which genes that can cause manic-depressive psychosis are found (Egeland et al., 1987; Hodgkinson et al., 1987), showing that there are two genetically distinct versions of the disorder. Such findings provide a far more profound understanding of depression than psychoanalytic cliches. Even suicidal behavior is now beginning to be understood in terms of an underlying neurochemical abnormality (Mann and Stanley, 1986) such that suicide-prone individuals may differ from others in levels of certain neurotransmitters in the brain.

Childhood or infantile autism is a serious developmental disorder in which the child's language develops more poorly, the child ignores his or her surroundings, and engages in stereotyped "self-stimulatory" behaviors such as waving the hands back and forth in front of the face for extended periods of time. The autistic child may engage in self-damaging behavior such as head banging and the chewing of his or her own flesh. It seems hard to imagine that such a severe disorder could be caused simply by cold, inept parents, as Bettelheim (1967) has contended. Kalat (1987) points out that these children are often insensitive to pain and suggests that the real problem is a faulty regulation of the mechanism that controls the level of the endorphins in the child's brain. (Endorphins help modulate the body's sensitivity to pain, among other functions.)

Other disorders often thought to be psychological are now known to be caused by neurochemical abnormalities. One of the best-known is schizophrenia, which Freud believed was related to narcissism or self-love. In fact, schizophrenia (there are probably at least two types) is now known to be a genetically determined neurochemical disorder in which environmental influences such as stress may play some, but not a major, role (Pincus and Tucker, 1985). Another disorder now linked to underlying biochemical abnormalities is anorexia nervosa, the "starving disease" that is seen mostly in young females (Pirke and Ploog, 1984). A final example is Tourette's Syndrome. This is a rare disorder in which the patient is afflicted with uncontrollable muscular movements (called "tics") and, at times, swears uncontrollably (Friedhoff and Chase, 1982). Psychoanalytic "explanations" for the syndrome run from "displaced unconscious muscular eroticism toward the father" to "masturbatory conflict" to "defense against auto-pleasurable thumb-sucking" (quoted in Garelik, 1986, pp. 79-80). Such "explanations" are, as might be expected, of little use in treating a patient who suffers from a neurochemical disease. Patients with Tourette's Syndrome were (and sometimes still are) believed to be possessed by the devil or evil spirits, as discussed in chapter two. It is important to note that the demonic and psychoanalytic "explanations" of the syndrome are essentially the same. Both hypothesize untestable internal entities whose existence is inferred from the patients' behavior. These same entities are then used, in totally circular fashion, to "explain" the same behavior. Whether the entity is labelled "Satan" or "masturbatory conflict" makes little difference. In fact, Freud's entire theoretical system for explaining disorders he thought were psychological is little more than medieval demonology dressed up in new terminology.

The Future of Psychoanalysis

If the problems with psychoanalytic theory and practice are so great, why is it still presented in so matter-of-fact and uncritical a way in almost all introductory psychology texts? One answer is that the seductive pseudoscientific and nonfalsifiable nature of major parts of psychoanalytic theory make it very easy to accept, even for trained psychologists. Another answer is more historical in nature. It holds, generally correctly, that Freud's ideas have had major influences on Western thought and that, within psychology, it was Freud who brought the important concept of an unconscious to the notice of the field. These two points provide weak support for the continued teaching of so faulty a theory as psychoanalysis. An analogy, first made by Dallenbach (1955), between psychoanalysis and phrenology is instructive in this regard. Phrenology was the nineteenth-century pseudoscience that held that an individual's personality could be determined by measuring the shape of his or her head. Phrenology was founded by Franz Joseph Gall, a well-known physician, in the last years of the eighteenth century. According to phrenology, each area of the brain was specialized for some particular function. This theory was in sharp contrast to the prevailing view that the brain was a mass of functionally homogeneous tissue. Gall further believed that if a particular "faculty" was well developed in an individual, the brain area that corresponded to that faculty would be enlarged. And, therefore, the skull over the brain area that controlled the faculty would bulge outward. All that remained, then, was to measure the skull, find where the bulges were and infer the individual's personality and abilities.

There were two great problems with phrenology. First, the faculties that the phrenologists believed were represented in specific brain areas were extremely vague, as can be seen from the phrenological "map" shown in figure 6. Second, even if the map had been organized as the phrenologists believed, measuring the skull would have revealed nothing about personality. This is because the gross shape of the brain is the same even in people with very different personalities and abilities. In spite of these fatal problems, phrenology had considerable, and often very positive, social influence (Davies, 1955). In the 1800s, phrenology was widely practiced all over the United States and Europe. Phrenological societies sprang up to work for needed reforms in education and treatment of prisoners, the mentally ill, and children. In the United States phrenology was a powerful enough movement to at least start many of these reforms. On the intellectual front, phrenology also had great influence. Neurologists began to consider that perhaps the brain wasn't homogeneous in function, but that different brain areas might control different functions. This view, known as localizationism, has been supported by more than one hundred years of experimentation. Unfortunately for phrenology, the functions that are actually localized in various areas of the brain bear no resemblance to those the phrenologists thought were localized. Specific aspects of sensory and motor function, as well as some cognitive functions, such as speech, language, and aspects of attention, can be localized in particular brain areas. Discussion of this can be found in any physiological psychology text (i.e., Kalat, 1987; Levinthal, 1983; Shepherd, 1987).

In spite of the fact that phrenology was a pseudoscience, it had an important effect on society and a large influence on the development of thought about brain function. However, today one does not find any treatment of phrenology, other than as historical curiosity, in texts on psychology or neurology. This seems to be an appropriate treatment and one which, in the future, psychoanalysis should be accorded more frequently.

This discussion of psychoanalysis has just scratched the surface of the critical literature on psychoanalysis. The books by Bandura (1969, especially chapters one and two), Sulloway (1979), Grunbaum (1984), and Crews (1986), and a paper by Cioffi (1970) provide much more detailed discussions.

The Psychology of Jung

Carl Gustav Jung was a devoted follower of Freud who later broke with strictly Freudian psychoanalysis over several theoretical issues. He merits special mention here because he was rather a mystic and two of his ideas have entered the mainstream of paranormal thinking. Jung was interested in astrology and actually conducted some astrological research. He was not particularly a believer in astrology, but felt that astrologers were occasionally accurate through what would now be called clairvoyance or ESP. Jung also had a life-long interest in coincidences that resulted in the development of his concept of *synchronicity* or *meaningful coincidences*. According to this view, some events that would be considered coincidences were actually meaningful, although they were not related through cause and effect. Von Franz (1964, p. 211) gives an example: "If I bought a blue frock and, by mistake, the shop delivered a black one on the day one of my near relatives died, this would be a meaningful coincidence. The two events are not causally related, but they are connected by the symbolic meaning that our society gives to the color black." The coincidental events are not causally related, but the meaning is, according to Jung, not just meaning imposed by the individual who experiences the coincidence. Jung believed that such coincidences did not occur at random. Rather, they tended to take place at psychologically important times in an individual's life. The coincidences were a manifestation of various *archetypes*, basic ideas or concepts stored in the *collective unconscious*, another Jungian concept. The collective unconscious was the storehouse of the accumulated memories and forms of behavior that date back to the dawn of the human species.

The archetypes could express themselves via meaningful coincidences. To continue with von Franz's (1964, p. 211) example: "To illustrate this in the case of the black frock: In such a case the person who receives the black frock might also have had a dream on the theme of death. It seems as if the underlying archetype is manifesting itself simultaneously in inner and external events. The common denominator is a symbolically expressed message—in this case a message about death." It is no trick at all to find "meaningful coincidences" if you look for them and, as always in this sort of theory, you are permitted to interpret the "meaning" of the event through symbolism. Thus, the concept that Jung felt was equal in importance to the notion of causality itself turns out to be yet another example of constructive and selective memory and perception.

A great lover of symbolic interpretation, although the nature of his symbols differed greatly from those of Freud, Jung found in the myths and legends of numerous cultures evidence for the various archetypes he believed to exist in the collective unconscious. Jung was fond of pointing out that myths and legends of cultures around the globe had symbols and meanings in common. This he interpreted as evidence for the collective unconscious. One need not, however, postulate a collective unconscious to explain the similarities of the myths and legends of different peoples. All human cultures have existed on the same planet and have faced the same basic problems, such as finding food and a mate, avoiding predators and enemies, obtaining protection from terrible weather and geologic phenomena, raising children, and so forth. Thus, it is inevitable that the myths and legends of all peoples will share common features (Barnard, 1966; Vitaliano, 1973). This will be true even if one looks only at the obvious (nonsymbolic) characteristics of myths and legends and does not further enhance the seeming number and psychological significance of the common features by using spurious symbolic interpretation, as Jung did.

Humanistic Psychology

Humanistic psychology, which became popular in the 1960s and 1970s, grew out of a dissatisfaction with both psychoanalytic and behavioral approaches, especially where therapy was concerned. Both psychoanalytic and behavioral approaches are deterministic in that both view human behavior as determined and controlled, either by ids, egos, and various complexes, in the case of psychoanalysis, or by reinforcers and punishers, in the case of behaviorism. Neither approach, the humanistic psychologies felt, gave any attention to human free will, which became a focal point for humanistic psychology and therapy. Humanistic therapy is said to be "client centered" or "nondirective." The therapist is supposed to give "unconditional positive regard, supporting the client regardless of what she or he says or does. Instead of interpreting or instructing, the therapist clarifies the client's feelings by restating what has been said" (Bootzin, Bower, Zajonc, and Hall, 1986, p. 590). If all this sounds vague, vagueness is one of the major characteristics of humanistic psychology. Out of this vagueness has grown most of the hollow and vacuous "psychobabble" (Rosen, 1977) that makes up current pop psychology. For example, one major concept in humanistic psychology is that of "self-actualization," a term coined by Maslow (1966). Stripped of its psychobabble, the term boils down to "be happy in your work and play, and be nice to others." It's hard to argue with that as a goal, but it is not very helpful in dealing with real problems of human beings.

Since its founding, humanistic psychology has spewed forth literally hundreds of different brands of "therapy," all couched in layers of vacuous psychobabble and containing considerable amounts of pseudoscience. The "human potential" movement, with its emphasis on self-actualization and "getting in touch with yourself" is an outgrowth of humanistic psychology. Rosen (1977) has critiqued several of the better-known therapies that have grown out of humanistic psychology. Janov's primal therapy, which involves screaming about your anger and frustration, is one example. Another is "rebirthing," which involves re-experiencing the birth process by means of tubs of warm water and shallow breathing. Also to be found are adherents of psychoanalyst Wilhelm Reich, now dead, who believed that an energy called "orgone energy" could cure mental and physical disease. Reich also believed that dowsing rods operated by orgone energy and that the energy was blue (Gardner, 1957). Happily for Reich, orgone energy could be accumulated in special phone booth-sized boxes in which the patient who wished to take the cure sat. Reich rented these for about $250 a month until the government put this particular fraud out of business in the mid-1950s (Janssen, 1980). One eminent current practitioner of psychobabblology and psychobabble therapy is Leo Buscaglia, who seems to believe that if we'd all just hug everyone, most of our own and the world's problems would go away (Buscaglia, 1983). Such a naive view exemplifies the intellectual sterility of humanistic psychology.

6

Astrology, the Lunar Effect, and Biorhythms

Ancient people must have learned well before the dawn of recorded history that observations of the stars and planets could predict the coming of the seasons, when to plant crops, when certain animals would give birth, and numerous other events vital to their survival. It seemed reasonable, then, that the positions of the heavenly bodies could predict, or even influence, human behavior. Thus, astrology, the oldest pseudoscience, was born.

Astrology's history goes back more than 4,000 years and testifies to people's unending fascination with the stars and attempts to predict the future. The first written records of astrology come from Mesopotamia, located between the Tigris and Euphrates Rivers in the area that is now Iraq and Syria (Culver and Ianna, 1984). The early astrology of the Mesopotamians was an "open" astrology and was much simpler than later astrology. Ancient people saw omens in everything, not just the stars. Almost anything that happened could be interpreted as an omen of something that was going to take place in the future. Examples of astrological omens from this period include:

> When Mars approaches the star Shu.gi there will be uprising in Amurru and hostility; one will kill another.

> When Venus stands high, there will be pleasure of copulation.

Nonastrological omens are of essentially the same character and are equally unlikely to have been based on empirical study, as the following examples indicate:

> If a woman gives birth to a pig, a woman will seize the throne.

> If a woman gives birth to an elephant, the land will be laid to waste.

If a ewe gives birth to a lion and it has two horns on the left, an enemy will take your fortress.

If a man goes on an errand and a falcon passes from his right to his left, he will achieve his goal.

The sources for these omens are Van der Waerden (1974) and Leichty (1975), both cited in Culver and Ianna (1984).

The horoscope is a much more recent development in astrology; the earliest known example dates from April 29, 410 B.C. (Culver and Ianna, 1984).

Modern astrologers claim their "science" is not based on magical associations, but the history of astrology shows this to be false. Astrology flourished in ancient Greece, where the magical influence is clear. The Greeks deified the planets, and each of their gods had certain characteristics. For example, Aphrodite (Venus) was the goddess of love and beauty, so the planet Venus was assumed to magically make one sensitive, emotional, and appreciative of beauty (Jerome, 1977). Similarly, Hermes (Mercury) was the messenger of the gods and was said to be "shrewd, swift, unpredictable" (Jerome 1977, p. 71) because the actual planet was hard to see and moved rapidly. By purely magical association, therefore, the planet Mercury was said to make someone difficult to predict, deceitful, and yet skillful. These associations were never based on empirical research, simply on ancient magical associations. They still form the basis for modern astrological predictions.

Even the grouping of stars into the constellations that make up the twelve signs of the zodiac is arbitrary. The stars are grouped together not because they are actually close together in space but because they appear to be close together when seen from earth. Further, different cultures group the stars in different ways and see different constellations in the sky. The only way these apparent groupings of stars called the constellations could have any special influence over human beings is through some unspecified sort of magic.

Ptolemy, the great astronomer and astrologer who lived in the second century A.D., also based his astrology on magical associations between the stars and planets and human behavior (Thorndike, 1923). During the Middle Ages in Europe, great emphasis was placed on the authority of previous writers. Ptolemy was considered to be the greatest astrologer of the ancient world, so his writings on astrology were accepted and passed down in this way (Thorndike, 1923, volume 1). Thus, modern astrologers' claims that their "science" is based on thousands of years of experimental and empirical observation are simply untrue; in fact, modern astrology rests largely on Ptolemy's writings.

Certainly, views about the exact nature of the hypothesized influences of specific stars and planets on human behavior have changed over the centuries, and differences of opinion did and do exist among astrologers. Speaking of the Renaissance period Shumaker (1972, p. 11) states: "There has never, perhaps, been a time when conflicting opinions [about how astrology should be practiced] were not held and practices were not being modified. If at first glance such tinkering might be thought to imply constant experimental rectification, no one who has read much [medieval or Renaissance] astrological literature is likely to believe this was the cause of the alterations." Shumaker (1972) has found no experimental studies of astrology. Instead, astrology was justified by appeal "regularly to authorities . . . or to abstract reason" (p. 11). It is only in the twentieth century that statistical tests of astrological predictions have been attempted. These are reviewed later in this chapter.

Astrology and Astronomy

Astrologers are fond of claiming that their craft is a science and that astronomy is merely an offshoot of astrology. As seen from the above, however, the basic structure of astrological hypotheses has changed hardly at all over the last 2,500 years. Greek astrologers believed, based on magical associations, that someone born under the influence of the planet Venus would love beauty and be a sensitive person. This type of lore, passed down through generations, is still accepted by modern astrologers, in spite of the fact that in the 4,000-year history of astrology, no astrologer has ever tried to see if the hypothesized relationships between heavenly bodies and human behavior really exist. Astrologers have never conducted research to support their claims. In chapter one it was pointed out that one of the chief characteristics of a pseudoscience is a refusal to change in the light of new evidence. Knowledge of astronomy and astrophysics has changed immensely since the Greeks looked up at the stars and saw their gods there. In spite of this, astrology has not changed at all—it is a static, stale pseudoscience.

On those few occasions when astrologers have made attempts to change astrological practice and theory, the nature of the attempts further reveals the pseudoscientific nature of astrology. In 1970, for example, astrologer Steven Schmidt argued that there are really fourteen signs of the zodiac, not twelve. According to Schmidt, the constellations Cetus and Ophiuchus should be added to the familiar set of twelve. From a purely astronomical point of view, there is much to recommend this change. The sun does, in fact, pass through these two constellations in addition to the signs of the zodiac. Schmidt's problem was to determine the character traits associated with these two "new" signs of the zodiac. Nowhere in his book does he present any data or suggest an adequate method of discovering what these traits might be. Rather, he simply "collected people" and "examined their character traits" (Schmidt, 1970, p. 18). The people he examined were hardly a representative or random sample, since they included movie stars, past presidents (dead and alive), famous politicians, and so forth. The method used is utterly worthless scientifically.

One of the best examples of astrology's refusal to change in the light of new knowledge is its failure to take into account the astronomical phenomenon of *precession*. The assignment of certain dates to certain signs of the zodiac (e.g., Aries ruling the period from March 21 to April 19) was made 2,000 years ago (Abell, 1981a) and has been followed by astrologers ever since. When it is said that the sun is "in" Aries between March 21 and April 19, this means that the sun, as seen from earth, is in the same part of the sky as is the constellation Aries. The correspondences between the twelve constellations of the zodiac and their assigned dates were correct 2,000 years ago—but not today. The earth "wobbles" slowly as it rotates and because of this the position of the sun relative to the constellations of the zodiac (as seen from the earth) changes over the centuries. By now, the difference is almost one complete sign so the sun is not in Aries from March 21 to April 19, but in Pisces for most of that period. Thus, if you are an Aries (born between March 21 and April 19), the sun was almost certainly not in Aries when you were born, but in Pisces! Most astrologers have been making predictions and casting horoscopes for the wrong signs for all these years. Many so-called "tropical" astrologers are aware of precession but choose to ignore it, arguing that somehow the "signs remember the influence of the constellations that corresponded to them two thousand years ago" (Abell, 1981a, p. 86). This does not explain "why those same signs do not also recall the influence of other constellations that corresponded with them in even earlier millennia" (Abell, 1981a, p. 86).

Astrologers claim that astrology is a science. When confronted with the fact that their "science" has hardly changed at all in the last 2,000 years, they respond that astrology was so well established twenty centuries ago that there has never been any need to change, in spite of the vast changes that have taken place in our knowledge of the universe over the same period of time. Linda Goodman, best-selling author of popular books on astrology, sums up the astrologers' position by saying, "Alone among the sciences, astrology has spanned the centuries and made the journey intact. We shouldn't be surprised that it remains with us, unchanged by time—because astrology is truth—and truth is eternal" (Goodman, 1971, p. 475).

Unfortunately for astrologers and their "ancient truths," these "truths" are not true. The best example is the ancient astrological teaching that there are only seven heavenly bodies, other than the earth, in the solar system—the sun, the moon, Mercury, Venus, Mars, Jupiter, and Saturn. All ancient astrological teachings, the same that have been handed down to the likes of Linda Goodman, had this as a basic tenet. Unfortunately, it is totally wrong. Three additional planets have been discovered since the eighteenth century—Uranus in 1781, Neptune in 1846, and Pluto in 1930. These planets, which can be seen only through telescopes or binoculars, were unknown to the ancient astrologers.

The ability to derive, test, and verify or falsify predictions is one of the most important characteristics of science. Astrologers never predicted the existence of the three outer planets, and never even had the slightest hint that the planets existed until astronomers discovered them. On the other hand, astronomers predicted the existence of Neptune twelve years before it was first identified through observation, and also predicted with great accuracy just where in the sky it could be found. It is in the discovery of Neptune that the contrast between the pseudoscience of astrology and the science of astronomy is most clearly seen. The exciting intellectual detective story of the discovery of Neptune is told in detail in Grosser's *The Discovery of Neptune* (1962) and will only be very briefly summarized here to further highlight the differences between astrology and astronomy.

The prediction of the existence of a planet beyond Uranus was based on observed irregularities in Uranus's orbit. Uranus was discovered in 1781, and astronomers noted almost at once that its orbit was irregular and could not be predicted with the same ease as the orbits of the other planets. In 1834 the British astronomer Thomas Hussey was the first to suggest that the perturbations of Uranus's orbit were caused by the gravitational influence of an as-yet-unknown planet (Grosser, 1962). In the early 1840s two young scientists, the English mathematician John Couch Adams and the French astronomer Urbain Jean Joseph Leverrier, independently began working on the problem of Uranus's orbit with the goal of finding the unknown planet that was responsible for the perturbations. Their predictions were tested in 1846, and the previously unknown planet was found to be almost exactly where Adams and Leverrier had said it would be found.

Today, astrologers claim to understand the astrological influences of the three new planets. The addition of the new planets didn't even cause much fuss among astrologers when they were discovered (Culver and Ianna, 1984). But for nearly 2,000 years, apparently not one astrologer ever noticed a planetary influence where there was no known planet or was able to predict the existence or location of additional planets. Again, the history of astrological practice is inconsistent with the astrologers' claims that astrology is a precise science. If, as astrologers claim, each planet has an influence on human behavior, even a small one, and if that influence varies according to where the planet is located, then predictions of at least the existence of the new planets should have been made long ago. But one will search the writings of Ptolemy and later astrologers in vain for any hint of such a prediction.

Astrologer Linda Goodman (1968) explains astrology's failure to note the influences of the three "new" planets before their discovery by saying that a planet doesn't have any astrological influence until it is discovered!

Astrologers are now claiming that there are more than nine planets in the solar system, apparently not wanting to be left out in the cold again should an additional planet be discovered. However, if there remain other unknown planets in the solar system, they are certainly not the ones the astrologers talk about. A favorite is a planet called Vulcan that is said to orbit the sun inside the orbit of Mercury. In 1968 Linda Goodman (p. 203) said of this planet, "It's important to mention here the still unseen planet Vulcan, the true ruler of Virgo, since its discovery is said to be imminent . . . Many astrologers feel that Vulcan, the planet of thunder, will become visible through telescopes in a few years." Well, a few years have passed, and no one has yet seen Vulcan.

Actually, the idea of Vulcan is an old one that astrologers latched onto long after it was abandoned by the astronomers who first proposed that such a planet might exist. Vulcan was proposed to account for deviations in the orbit of Mercury, using the same logic that led Adams and Leverrier to hypothesize the existence of Neptune. In fact, it was Leverrier who in 1859 published a prediction about where Vulcan would be found. In the next few years sightings of the planet were made, but these were due to "hoaxes or wishful thinking at the telescope" (Culver and Ianna, 1984, p. 164) and could not be confirmed. It is another important characteristic of science that incorrect predictions are recognized as such and dropped; astronomers wasted no further effort on Vulcan after it had been shown not to exist. (The deviations in Mercury's orbit turned out not to be due to the effects of a planet, but are explained by the General Theory of Relativity.)

Before moving on to a discussion of the studies that have examined the claims of astrologers, one additional theoretical problem of major proportions has to be discussed: the mechanism by which any alleged astrological influence would occur. In other words, how would the stars and planets make their influence felt? Several answers to this question have been proposed: gravity, tidal or electromagnetic forces, magnetic fields, or emission of some sort of particles.

Culver and Ianna (1984) have discussed the fatal weaknesses of all these hypothesized mechanisms for astrological influence. Basically, all the proposed forces or fields are far too weak to have *any* influence on human infants, let alone the massive influence that is required by astrology. The effects of gravity, for instance, decrease as the square of the distance between two objects. If planet A is twice as far from planet B as it is from planet C, the gravitational effect of A on B will be four times ($2^2 = 4$) less than the gravitational effect of A on C. The practical import of this is that the gravitational effects of the stars and planets on a newborn are essentially nonexistent. A mother holding her infant in her arms exerts a gravitational influence on the child that is twenty times greater than the gravitational influence of the planet Mars. Mars is much more massive than the mother, but it is also a great deal farther away from the child.

The case is even worse for tidal forces. These decrease as the cube of the distance between two objects. In the example above, the tidal forces of planet A on planet B are eight times less ($2^3 = 8$) than the tidal forces of A on C. This means that, when one takes into account the other factors that go into the equation used to calculate tidal forces, the mother's tidal influence on the child is 11 trillion times greater than that of the planet Mars.

Electromagnetic and magnetic forces are equally unlikely to be responsible for the influence astrology requires. Electromagnetic forces are well understood, and they are not responsible for astrological influence. Magnetic fields certainly exist, but some planets of great importance in astrology don't have any. For example, the moon, Venus, and Mars are devoid of such fields (Culver and Ianna, 1984). As for emitted particles, Culver and Ianna (1984) point out that in the solar system only the sun emits particles. The planets do not. Other stars also emit particles, but by the time they reach Earth they are so diffuse that they cannot influence individuals in the way that astrology requires.

Note also that astrology does not take into account any physical characteristics of the planets or stars. Their astrological influences are independent of size, mass, shape, temperature, age, composition, distance, and rotation. This disregard of physical characteristics is just what would be expected from a system based on magic, but not from a scientific system.

Testing Astrological Predictions

In spite of the historical, logical, and theoretical shortcomings of astrology, it is still important to ask the purely empirical question, "Does astrology work?" That is, can it make predictions about, for example, personality, personal destiny, mate selection, or sex life? Many studies aimed at answering this question have been conducted; they are summarized and described in detail in Culver and Ianna (1984), Jerome (1977), Gauquelin (1979), Dean (1977), and Eysenck and Nias (1982). The treatment in these sources is more thorough than is possible here. The Dean (1977) volume, for example, contains nearly 600 pages, all devoted to studies of astrological and related influences.

Before discussing studies of astrological predictions, it is necessary to review some elementary statistical concepts. This will be done in the context of an actual astrological prediction. This discussion will be vital not only in the present context but also in succeeding chapters where statistical tests are employed to evaluate pseudoscientific claims of various sorts.

According to astrologers, the most important astrological influence on personality is the *sun sign* (Dean, 1977), the sign of the zodiac in which the sun is located on the day of one's birth. Linda Goodman (1971, p. xvi) claims that "an individual's sun sign will be approximately 80 percent accurate" as a description of personality. There are hundreds of ways of classifying human personality, but one common method is to dichotomize personality types and then assign individuals to one or the other type. While this is a gross oversimplification, it is popular with many psychologists. One of the most popular ways of dichotomizing personality is into extroverts and introverts (Morris, 1979). The characteristic personality of the extrovert seems to be nicely defined by the typical description of Aries: bold, assertive, aggressive, self-confident, determined (Dean, 1977; Eysenck and Nias, 1982). An obvious astrological prediction, then, is that more extroverts than introverts should be born under Aries. If there are no astrological influences on personality, then the number of extroverts and introverts born under Aries should be about the same (that word *about* is the source of much trouble and the reason why statistical analyses are so necessary).

To find subjects for our study, we advertise in a campus newspaper for individuals born between March 21 and April 19; 32 respond, and each is given a reliable and valid test of introversion and extroversion. To test the astrological prediction made above, all we have to do is count up the number of each personality type born under Aries. What if we find that 16 extroverts and 16 introverts were born under Aries? Clearly, such a finding offers no support for astrological theory. What if we find that 32 extroverts but no introverts were born under Aries? This result would support astrological theory and one would not need to do fancy statistical analysis to know that. But what if we find that 17 extroverts and 15 introverts were born under Aries? The difference is in the direction predicted by astrology, but is very small. It would be reasonable to attribute the result to chance—that is, the effect is not really due to astrological influences, but just to random "noise" in the data. What if 20 extroverts and 12 introverts are found to be born under Aries? Is this difference due to chance or to some nonchance factor such as astrological influence? In this example it would be difficult to tell just by looking at the data. Some people might be willing to accept the results as indicative of astrological influence, while others might say it was due merely to chance factors. Without some objective way of quantifying the effect of chance, there is no way to settle the argument. Statistical analysis provides such quantification and allows a precise statement of how likely a particular result is to have occurred by chance as opposed to being the result of nonchance factors.

It is agreed upon in all the sciences that if a statistical analysis shows that a particular result would have occurred by chance fewer than 5 times out of 100 (less than 5 percent of the time, or 1 time in 20) the result is accepted as "statistically significant." This does not mean that the result could not possibly have occurred by chance, merely that it would have occurred by chance fewer than 5 times in 100. Investigators accept such a result as being due to some factor other than chance. Of course, as the results become more "statistically significant," the probability that they are due to chance decreases. A statistical test that reveals that a particular result would have occurred by chance only 1 time in 1,000 inspires greater confidence that the result is due to nonchance factors than a result that would have occurred by chance 5 times in 100. The numerous statistical tests, then, merely tell investigators how likely their results are to have occurred by chance.

Using the appropriate statistical test (called *chi square*), the details of which can be found in any statistics textbook, we can figure out the likelihood that the several hypothetical results of the extrovert-introvert experiment described above would occur by chance. This is shown in the table below.

Row	Number of extroverts born under Aries	Number of introverts born under Aries	Chi square (Yates correction used)	Probability that this result would occur by chance alone
1	17	15	.03	.65
2	20	12	1.53	.21
3	21	11	2.53	.11
4	22	10	3.78	.049
5	30	2	22.78	.001

The table can be interpreted as follows. If we conducted the experiment described above and obtained the results shown in row 1, there would be no basis for saying that astrological influence was at work. The difference here between the number of extroverts and introverts born under Aries is 2, and the statistics tell us that a difference of that size or less would occur purely by chance 65 percent of the time. Here, the statistics merely confirm our intuition that the result is unimpressive as evidence for astrology. Consider the results in row 5. Here again, the statistics confirm the obvious—these results are very unlikely to be due to chance alone. Such results would occur by chance alone only 1 time in 1,000. If our experiment actually yielded such results, we could be pretty confident that something was going on.

Statistical analyses are most valuable where it is not immediately obvious on inspection of the data whether the results are due to chance factors or not. Rows 2, 3, and 4 are examples. In all three rows, there are more extroverts than introverts born under Aries, but only the results in row 4 could convince the investigator that some nonchance factor, perhaps astrological influence, was involved. The difference in Row 2 is 8, but a difference of 8 or less would be obtained purely by chance fully 21 percent of the time in such an experiment. This is probably a somewhat higher figure that you might have guessed. In Row 3 the difference is 10, but this difference would be obtained 11 times out of 100 by chance and does not reach the standard criterion that a result must occur by chance 5 times or fewer in 100 to be considered as due to nonchance factors. In row 4, this criterion is met. The difference is 12, and such a difference would occur fewer than 5 times in 100 by chance. Here, as in row 5, we would be justified in attributing to some nonchance factor the differences in the number of introverts and extroverts born under Aries.

Statistical analyses can tell an investigator the likelihood that a set of given results is due to chance. However, while the statistics can indicate that a result is unlikely to be due to chance, they do not indicate what nonchance factors are responsible for the result. A nonparanormal example will illustrate this point. One semester I taught two sections of introductory psychology. One section met at 8 A.M., the other at 11 A.M. The textbook used in each section was the same; so, of course, was the instructor. I used the same sets of lecture notes for both classes and covered the same material in the same order. I gave equivalent tests to each section. These tests covered the same material to the same degree of difficulty, but used different questions. On the first test, the average score of the 8 A.M. section was 68 percent. The average score of the 11 A.M. section was 79 percent. This difference is highly significant statistically and would have occurred by chance only about two times in one hundred. The knowledge that this is a strong nonchance difference does not indicate the cause of the difference. A number of possibilities spring to mind. One is that students in the 8 A.M. section were dumber than those in the 11 A.M. section. Another possibility is that the 8 A.M. section was sleepier than the 11 A.M. section. Another possibility is that I am a better lecturer at 11 A.M. than at 8 A.M. Or perhaps a combination of these factors is responsible for the difference observed. Interestingly, the difference was maintained throughout the term. To determine what nonchance factor is responsible for the observed difference is an experimental question that cannot be answered just by pointing to the fact that the difference is statistically significant.

That is why, in the discussion above of the extrovert-introvert experiment, I kept referring to "nonchance factors," rather than directly attributing the differences in numbers of the two personality types born under Aries to astrological factors—even when the differences were clearly statistically significant. It is certainly possible, for example, to imagine obtaining the results in rows 4 or 5 even with no astrological influence operating at all. How? Remember that the subjects in our hypothetical experiment were recruited through advertisements in a campus paper. Extroverts are much more likely to respond to such an ad than are introverts, so we would end up with more extroverts in the sample of 32 subjects. The results are still statistically significant, but are obviously not due to astrological influence. It is not enough, then, to point to statistical significance as "proof" of anything. The experiment that generated the data that was subjected to statistical test must have been designed to eliminate the sort of artifactual finding of our hypothetical study.

Another important statistical point should be made here. As mentioned earlier, a "statistically significant" result is one that, according to statistical analyses, will occur by chance 5 times or fewer in 100. It could occur purely by chance, but such an occurrence would be rare. Rare events do occur, however, especially if you give them enough opportunities. In fact, rare events are almost certain to occur given sufficient opportunity. This is called the law of large numbers and is responsible for much acceptance of pseudoscientific beliefs.

What is the probability of flipping a fair coin 10 times and having it come up heads all 10 times? This obviously rare event would occur only once in 2^{10}, or 1,024, times. But what if you flipped the coin 100,000 times? You would expect that about 97 runs of 10 successive heads would occur in that run of 100,000 coin flips. The event, 10 heads in a row, is no rarer—you've just given it more opportunity to occur.

Now let us assume a universe where it is absolutely certain that there are no astrological influences whatsoever. We perform a well-designed study (as opposed to the poorly designed study described above) to test whether more extroverts than introverts are born under Aries. Since in this universe there are no astrological influences, it is unlikely that we will find more extroverts than introverts born under Aries if we conduct the experiment only once. But what if we repeat it 100 times, using a different sample of subjects each time? Out of that set of 100 different experiments, we would expect to find about 5 that yield "significant" results. Why? Because "significant" is defined as a result that occurs by chance alone five times or fewer in 100. Given 100 opportunities to occur, such "significant" results will be obtained about 5 times.

Think about it another way. If we tested 100 different astrological predictions in our nonastrological universe, would we expect to find that none of the 100 tests showed "significant" astrological effects? No—about 5 of the 100 tests would yield results that were "significant." Would this finding provide support for the existence of astrological influence? Certainly not—while the results are truly "significant" (that is, they are not due to poor experimental design and the like), they are not due to astrological influence. They are simply due to chance, since we would be giving these relatively rare events a large number of chances to happen. A problem appears, however, when one does numerous experiments to test, say, astrology, and reports only those that yield "significant" results, ignoring those that do not yield such results. This basically dishonest procedure is, unfortunately, all too common in the literature supporting pseudoscientific claims. Examples of these surprisingly common statistical errors will be pointed out frequently in the rest of this chapter and in succeeding chapters. Let us now return to the experimental literature on astrological predictions.

The hypothesis that there are astrological influences on extroversion and introversion has often been raised, although never in the exact fashion described above. Dean (1977) has reviewed these studies, which offer no support for any proposed astrological influence. For example, Forlano and Ehrlich (1941) examined the birth dates of 7,827 male college students and found no effect of any sun sign on extroversion and introversion. Lim (1975) used 163 subjects and found no correlation between extroversion and introversion and sun signs. Nor did Lim (1975) find any influence of moon signs on this personality variable. Mayo, White, and Eysenck (1978) reported a study of 2,324 individuals that seemed to give impressive support to the hypothesis of astrological influence on extroversion and introversion. In this study, subjects filled out a personality questionnaire; the results of that questionnaire were correlated with the subjects' birth dates. Later work by Eysenck, reported in Eysenck and Nias (1982), showed that the original result was artifactual. Specifically, the subjects had knowledge of their astrological sign and the type of personality that is supposed to correlate with each sign. In one study (Eysenck and Nias, 1982), 1,160 children, who were presumably unaware of astrological theory, were studied. There was no correlation between extroversion or introversion and astrological sign in these children. Another study reported by Eysenck and Nias (1982) was designed to test directly the prediction that subjects who had specific knowledge of the alleged astrological relationships between birth date and sign and personality would show greater correlation between sign and personality than those who didn't. One hundred twenty-two subjects were divided into three groups: those who were knowledgeable about astrological claims about personality, those who had a "borderline" knowledge, and those who had no knowledge about the alleged relationships. Both the "no knowledge" and "borderline" groups showed no correlation between astrological sign and extroversion or introversion. However, "the knowledgeable group . . . showed a marked tendency to assess themselves in accordance with astrological predictions" (Eysenck and Nias, 1982, p. 56). Thus, the original Mayo, White, and Eysenck (1978) results were due to the subjects' astrological knowledge, which was apparently extensive (Eysenck and Nias, 1982). This knowledge biased at least some subjects in the way they reported their personality on the questionnaire. If they knew, for instance, that people born under Aries are supposed to be extroverted and they knew that they had been born under Aries, they reported a more extroverted personality. An earlier study by Delaney and Woodward (1974) also demonstrated such behavior. In this study, fifty-five high-school students read personality descriptions based on their birth dates. Half received descriptions that were consistent with traditional astrological teachings ("Aries are extroverted," for example) and half received descriptions that were just the reverse (e.g., "Aries are introverted"). After reading the descriptions, they were asked to fill out a personality questionnaire. They were told that the purpose of the study was to "attempt to see if astrology has any real predictive value" and that the questionnaire was "concerned with your personality *not* the personality which was astrologically predicted" (Delaney and Woodward, 1974, p. 1214). The responses on the questionnaire were influenced by the descriptions of personality that had been read, whether or not those descriptions were those of classical astrology. That is, if a subject was an Aries and had read that Aries people are extroverted, the responses on the subject's personality questionnaire showed a more extroverted personality. If an Aries was told that Aries people are introverted, the subject's questionnaire responses showed a tendency toward introversion. In addition to showing that the original Mayo, White, and Eysenck (1978) results were not due to astrological influence, these studies further demonstrate how subtle uncontrolled experimental variables can produce results that look as if they support astrological influences. They further show the importance of conducting further studies to confirm the results and control previously uncontrolled variables.

Eysenck and Nias (1982) also failed to find any astrological influence on another major personality variable, emotionality versus stability, although subjects' knowledge at first resulted in spurious correlations between astrological sign and this personality variable as well.

Another common claim made by astrologers is that a couple's compatibility is determined, at least in large part, by their sun signs. That is, two people who have "compatible" sun signs will have a better chance of making a successful marriage than two people whose sun signs are "incompatible." Several studies have shown that in fact sun signs have no influence on marriage or divorce (Dean, 1977; Culver and Ianna, 1984). In these studies one obtains the birth dates for divorced and nondivorced couples. If sun signs have any influence, pairs with incompatible sun signs should be overrepresented among divorced couples and underrepresented among nondivorced couples. The studies reviewed in these two references reveal no influence of sun signs on marriage or divorce rates.

Culver and Ianna (1984) have further pointed out that astrologers disagree widely on which sun signs are compatible. Figure 7, taken from Culver and Ianna (1984, p. 132-33), shows the sun signs that Righter (1977), King (1973), Norvell (1975), and Omarr (1972) consider compatible and incompatible. Inspection of the figure shows the great degree of disagreement among these four popular astrologers, each of whom claims validity for his system, but not on the basis of any real data. The lack of agreement among astrologers should not be seen as reducing the importance of the research findings on sun signs and rates of marriage and divorce. These studies show that no combination of sun signs was associated with marriages or divorces. In other words, these studies examined all possible relationships between sun sign and compatibility and found that in no case was there any relationship. They did not simply test the few specific predictions made by astrologers.

Carlson (1985) has performed an extremely thorough and well-designed study of astrological predictions. This study is unique in that the help and cooperation of the astrological "profession" was sought and obtained. "So that the participating astrologers should be respected by the astrological community, we sought the advice of the National Council for Geocosmic Research" (Carlson, 1985, p. 420). Further, the astrologers involved agreed before the study was conducted that the procedures and design constituted a fair test of astrological predictions.

In the first part of the study, 177 subjects were recruited through newspaper ads. Based on their birth date, time, and place, their horoscopes were constructed and then interpreted by the astrologers associated with the study. Each subject was given an interpretation of three different horoscopes. One of the interpretations was of their own horoscope, while the other two were interpretations of horoscopes of two other randomly chosen participants in the study. If astrologers were able to divine personal information from a horoscope, then the subjects should have been able to choose the interpretation of their own horoscope over the interpretations of other individuals' horoscopes at a rate better than chance.

In the second part of the study, 116 subjects took the California Psychological Inventory (CPI), a widely used test of personality in normal (nonpathological) individuals (Megargie, 1972). The astrologers were then given one individual's horoscope and the CPI personality profile of three subjects. One of the CPI profiles was that of the same subject whose horoscope was given to the astrologer. The astrologers' task in this part of the study was to pick the CPI profile that matched the horoscope.

The results of both parts of the study provide no support for astrology. Subjects in the first part of the study were unable to pick the interpretation of their horoscope from the interpretation of two other individuals' horoscopes at a rate above chance. In the second part of the study, the astrologers were not able to match the horoscope of an individual to his or her CPI personality profile at a rate higher than chance. Given two opportunities to provide impressive empirical support for the reality of astrological claims, in a test that respected astrologers had agreed beforehand was fair, astrology failed.

Astrologers claim that numerous other personality traits—in addition to physical characteristics, occupation, and medical disorders—are influenced by one's sun sign. Culver and Ianna (1984) have summarized several studies that have examined these predictions. The predictions have been shown to be wrong. For example, of sixty different occupations studied, not one showed any influence of sun signs. That is, members of these sixty occupations were no more or less likely to be born under one sun sign than another. Among the occupations examined were those of actor, pilot, artist, astronomer, banker, baseball player, chemist, teacher, journalist, lawyer, doctor, opera singer, poet, politician, psychologist, and priest. Among the physical characteristics not related to sun sign were blood type, baldness, hair color, height, sex, handedness, and weight. Medical disorders found to be totally unrelated to sun sign included acne, allergies, diabetes, Down's Syndrome, heart attack, infant death, leukemia, lung cancer, multiple sclerosis, stillbirths, stroke, and muscular dystrophy. Age at death is also not related to sun sign. Finally, the following personality traits are not related to sun sign: aggression, ambition, creativity, feelings of inferiority, integrity, intelligence, leadership, self-expression, sociability, tough-mindedness, understanding, and wisdom. All these findings are in strong contrast to the empirically unsubstantiated claims of astrologers. Those claims can now be seen to be simply wrong.

There is more to astrology than sun signs, and the process of calculating a complete and accurate horoscope certainly takes considerable mathematical ability and training. Numerous variables in addition to the sun sign are said to influence the individual. Among these are planetary conjunctions, houses, ascendants, the relationship between the planets, and the planets' positions in the various signs. Culver and Ianna (1984) have calculated that there are some 10^{35} possible astrological predictions. This huge number compares with only 10^{27} grains of sand on the planet earth. Some of the predictions involving factors more complicated than sun signs have been tested (Dean, 1977; Culver and Ianna, 1984) but, again, these tests provide no support for astrological claims.

When confronted with the negative outcomes of numerous studies, astrologers sometimes argue that one cannot reject the theory until all, or at least a majority, of its predictions have been tested. This is an unsatisfactory defense of astrology for two reasons. First, because there is such a vast number of possible predictions, it would take forever to test even a small percentage of them. Thus, astrologers will always be able to claim that the theory has not been shown to be incorrect even if every future test of astrological predictions shows the predictions to be wrong. Second, as we have seen, it is unnecessary to test every prediction of a theory to show the theory to be incorrect. If the theory's major predictions are incorrect, the theory is rightly rejected by scientists and time is not spent testing endless minor detailed predictions. In the case of astrology, the theory's major prediction is that sun signs influence personality, occupational choice, and so forth. These predictions have repeatedly been shown to be dead wrong.

Moon Madness

The basic idea behind the lunar effect—or "moon madness" or the "Transylvania Hypothesis" as some more lyrical writers term it—is that the moon in its different phases exerts a strong influence on human behavior. It is especially held that the full moon accentuates or increases the probability of all sorts of odd and troublesome behavior. Suicides, admissions to mental hospitals, arrests for public drunkenness, and crimes of various sorts are all said to increase when the moon is full (Lieber, 1978). It is also widely believed, especially among maternity ward personnel, that more babies are born when the moon is full than during the other phases of the moon (Abell and Greenspan, 1979). The moon's gravitational influence is usually the mechanism used to explain the alleged effects of the full moon. After all, proponents say, the moon's gravity influences the oceans, which are largely water. Therefore, since the human body contains a great deal of water, the moon's gravity must also influence the human body. This in some unspecified way results in moon madness. But in fact the moon's gravitational influence on the human body is infinitesimal—equivalent to the weight of a single mosquito being added to the weight of a normal individual. Gravity is a weak force. As you hold this book, you are outpulling the entire planet Earth.

Campbell and Beets (1978), Abell (1981b), and Rotton and Kelly (1985) have reviewed the considerable number of studies that attempt to link the phases of the moon, especially the full moon, to human behavior. All three reviews conclude unequivocally that the phase of the moon does not influence human behavior. For example, Abell and Greenspan (1979) studied all the births that took place at the University of California Hospital, Los Angeles, from March 17, 1974, through April 30, 1978. During this period there were 11,691 live births, of which 8,142 were natural in that neither drugs nor caesarean section were used. There were 141 multiple births among the live births and 168 stillbirths. Analysis of this huge number of births showed no effect of phase of the moon in any of the four groups of births (all live births, natural births, multiple births, stillbirths).

Studies of other variables have also failed to find any effect of the full moon. Rotton and Kelly's (1985) paper reviews numerous published studies that showed the full moon did not influence (1) homicide rate; (2) other criminal offenses; (3) suicides; (4) psychiatric disturbances; or (5) psychiatric admissions to hospital.

Occasionally, of course, a study will report some sort of relation between the full moon and some variable. These studies require close examination. Under such examination, methodological or statistical flaws have appeared that invalidate the conclusions. Templer, Veleber, and Brooner (1982) found that highway accidents at night were more frequent when the moon was full. But their data showed no effect of the phase of the moon on daytime accidents. They devised a rather fanciful explanation of these results based on the effect of moonlight on the human pineal gland. However, as Rotton and Kelly (1985, p. 292) point out, "a disproportionate number of full-moon nights fell on weekends" during the period studied by Templer, Veleber, and Brooner (1982). Templer, Brooner, and Corgiat (1983) reanalyzed their data and, this time, took into account such variables as weekends, holidays, and such. They found that the supposed effect of the full moon on accidents disappeared. Thus, their original finding was due to the effect of weekends on accident rates, not to any effect of the full moon.

Arnold Lieber (1978) has been a strong proponent of the reality of lunar influence on human behavior. He claims to have found a relationship between homicide rates and the full moon in Dade County, Florida, and Cuyahoga County, Ohio, with more homicides taking place when the moon is full. However, Rotton and Kelly (1985) point out a fatal flaw in this data. In attempting to find an effect of the full moon, Lieber and Sherin (1972) conducted 96 different statistical tests on their data. They tested the effect of the moon on homicide rates by looking at these rates for, among others, "the three days before and after, the three days before, the three days after, two days before and after, two days before, two days after, one day before and after, one day before, one to two days after, and one to three days after full moons" (Rotton and Kelly, 1985, p. 293). Of the 96 analyses, 3 reached the accepted ".05" level of significance, meaning that such a result would be expected by chance only 1 time in 20, or 5 times out of 100. But, if one conducts 96 statistical tests, one would expect that 4.8 of them (96 × .05) would reach the .05 level by chance alone. Lieber and Sherin's (1978) data would provide evidence for the reality of lunar effects on homicide rates only if about 10 of their 96 different tests showed a significant result. Sanduleak (1984-85) analyzed all 3,370 homicides that took place in Cuyahoga County from 1971 through 1981. He found no lunar influences.

The data on the lunar effect, then, shows overwhelmingly that the moon's phase has no effect on human behavior. Why do so many people continue to believe that "moon madness" exists? A clue can be found in a study by Angus (1973). This study revealed that nurses who believed in the reality of the moon's influence on behavior made more notes of patients' "unusual" behavior when the moon was full than did nurses who did not believe the moon influenced behavior. Nurses who believed that the moon influenced behavior knew when the moon was full and at those times expected, looked for, and, not surprisingly, found more noteworthy behavior. Other nurses, who did not believe that the moon influences behavior, did not search for incidents to validate their belief.

Biorhythm Theory

According to biorhythm theory, three fixed and immutable rhythms, set at the moment of birth, cycle throughout human life and influence almost every facet of human behavior. There is a 23-day *physical rhythm*, a 28-day *emotional rhythm*, and a 33-day *intellectual rhythm*. The rhythms are usually depicted as changing over time in a sinusoidal fashion. Days when a given rhythm is above the baseline are referred to as "up" days and are supposed to be good days for engaging in behaviors related to the rhythm in question (Gittelson, 1982). On the other hand, days when a particular rhythm is below baseline are "down" days and are thought to be poor days for engaging in behavior related to the rhythm in question. For example, athletic performance would be expected to be better on days when the physical rhythm is above baseline and poorer on days when that rhythm is below baseline. Similarly, scores on examinations should, according to the theory, be higher on intellectual "up" days than on days when the intellectual rhythm is below baseline.

There is another aspect to biorhythm theory. This concerns the *critical day*, a day on which one of the rhythms is changing from the up to the down phase, or vice versa. These days, according to the theory, represent "our weakest and most vulnerable moments" and are when "we can expect ourselves to be in the most danger" since "at these points the rhythms that guide our lives become unstable" (Gittelson, 1982, p. 15). The worst of all possible days is the much-dreaded *triple critical day*, when all three rhythms are changing phase. On such days, biorhythmists will tell you, you should stay in bed. Critical days (including double and triple critical days) make up only a little more than 20 percent of all days.

The basics of biorhythm theory were developed around the turn of the century by Viennese physician Wilhelm Fliess, a friend of Sigmund Freud. By any standards, Fliess was a world-class crackpot. He believed that all humans were basically bisexual, that being left-handed meant that the other sex's characteristics determined, in large part, one's personality, and that the sexual organs were represented on certain areas of the membranes in the nose. Fliess' contribution to biorhythm theory was to invent the 23- and 28-day cycles that, in line with his theory of bisexuality, he termed the "male" and "female" cycles. The 33-day intellectual cycle was invented in the 1930s by Alfred Teltscher, an Austrian engineer (Wernli, 1961; Thommen, 1973). Martin Gardner (1966) has described the history of biorhythm theory in detail.

On the face of it, biorhythm theory is unlikely to be true. It requires an extremely precise type of biological timekeeping that does not exist. While it is certainly true that there are many biological rhythms—as distinct from "biorhythms"—known to affect human, animal, and even plant behavior (Moore-Ede, Sulzman, and Fuller, 1982), these rhythms all have a feature strikingly absent in the alleged biorhythms: variability. Real biological rhythms are variable; their period changes over time. Even the best-known human biological rhythm, the female menstrual cycle, varies greatly from one female to another and from one cycle to another within the same female (Matsumoto, Nogami, and Ohkuri, 1962). Further, the menstrual cycle has a very small effect on cognitive abilities and skilled performance (Sommer, 1973). Unlike known biological rhythms, however, biorhythms are said to be absolutely unvarying throughout a person's life. Changes in health, periods of illness, crisis, activity level, work schedule, and so forth, are said not to influence biorhythms.

It is largely this unvarying nature of the alleged biorhythms that makes them so easy to reckon. To calculate an individual's position on any of the three biorhythms on a given date, all one has to know is the person's birth date and the date for which the calculation is to be made. One then figures out how many days the person has lived until the day in question; that number is divided by 23, 28, or 33, depending on which biorhythm one is interested in. The remainder gives the person's position in the biorhythm cycle on the day in question.

The evidence put forth by biorhythm proponents for the existence of these rhythms offers some classic examples of pseudoscientific thinking. The commonest ploy is to present lists of terrible things (like dying) that happened to people when they were on the down side of one or more of the rhythms. Airline crashes are favored by biorhythm proponents, who take joy revealing that the pilot, copilot, navigator, or a flight attendant was on a critical day of one or more of the three rhythms, or low on one or more of the three rhythms, the day the plane crashed. Of course, there have been a fair number of plane crashes and other disasters over the past century, so it's not hard to find someone somehow associated with the disaster who was having a biorhythmically down or critical day at the time of the disaster. Similarly, lists of wonderful things (pitching a no-hitter, winning a boxing match, and so forth) that have happened to people when they were on the up phase of one or more of their biorhythms are presented as further proof of the validity of the theory.

Such lists are highly selective reporting and prove nothing. If one believed that, for example, accidents and disasters were more likely to occur on odd-numbered Thursdays that fell on even-numbered dates in years that end in odd numbers, one could probably come up with quite a list of accidents "proving" that danger lurks on such days. In fact, two minutes of looking through *The World Almanac* turned up two such accidents: The airship *Hindenburg* crashed on Thursday, May 6, 1937. May 6 was the first Thursday that month. On June 18, 1953, a U.S. Air Force C124 crashed near Tokyo, killing 129. June 18 was the third Thursday that month.

Further examination of the dates of disasters reveals many that took place on days other than Thursday, let alone a Thursday with the special characteristics noted above. But, if one were writing a book to convince people that certain types of Thursdays were dangerous, or trying to sell a consulting service based on that premise, one certainly wouldn't mention all the accidents that took place when the theory predicts that they shouldn't have. Similarly, you'll never read in books written by biorhythm proponents about the thousands of events, good and bad, that took place when biorhythm theory predicted they shouldn't. Many of these promoters have financial stakes in the theory's validity. For example, Bernard Gittelson is the author of the most popular book on biorhythm theory, first published in 1975 and, as of August, 1986, in its twenty-first printing. Gittelson also runs a biorhythm computer and consulting service in which he advises companies on how to schedule their employees according to their biorhythms. Another biorhythm author, Vincent Mallardi (1978), also ran a biorhythm consulting business.

The real question regarding the relationship between accidents (or other events) and critical days is whether more accidents occur on critical days than expected by chance. Since critical days make up 20 percent of all days (20.4 percent, to be exact), if biorhythms really exist and influence behavior, more than 20.4 percent of accidents will occur on critical than on noncritical days. That is, if biorhythm theory is false, about 20 percent of all accidents should occur on critical days. Hines (1979) reviewed thirteen published studies that examined 25,000 accidents of various types for biorhythm effects. In that vast number of automobile, aircraft, and industrial accidents, there was not even a hint of any biorhythm effect, even when those accidents not clearly due to human error were excluded from consideration. Many other variables have been examined for biorhythm effects. Hines (1979) has provided a detailed review of these studies so it will suffice to indicate here that studies of sports performance of various types, reaction times, intelligence test performance, fluctuation in human moods and emotions, days of death of large samples of individuals, days on which women give birth and the sex of their children, and classroom tests have all failed to reveal any biorhythmic effect.

Given these overwhelmingly negative results, which had emerged by the late 1970s, it is easy to see why interest in further testing of biorhythm theory has waned in recent years. However, a few studies not reviewed by Hines (1979) should be mentioned. One is particularly interesting in that it seems to give strong support to biorhythm theory. Latman (1977) studied 260 motor vehicle accidents and found that 37 percent of them occurred on critical days, a figure significantly higher than the 20 percent expected by chance. Since this study was well done and free of the common statistical errors found in some studies claiming to support biorhythm theory, it seemed to provide the first good evidence in favor of the theory. However, in a later study, Latman and Garriott (1980) reported that these initial positive findings had been the result of an unexpected source of error. Latman (1977) had used a "Biomate" brand biorhythm calculator to determine the biorhythmic position of the individuals involved in the traffic accidents. Further study showed that this brand of biorhythm calculator miscalculates biorhythms such that the number of critical days comes out as 37 percent instead of the correct 20 percent. When Latman and Garriott (1980) re-examined Latman's (1977) data using accurate methods for determining individuals' biorhythmic position, all signs of any biorhythm effect vanished.

Other studies done since Hines's (1979) review have been entirely negative in regard to biorhythm theory. Wood, Krider, and Fezer (1979) studied 700 accidents that brought their victims to the local emergency room, and found no biorhythmic effects. Dezelsky and Toohey (1978) found the date of suicides unrelated to the suicides' biorhythmic position. Hunter and Shane (1979) and Feinleib and Fabsitz (1978) found no biorhythm effect on the day of death. Englund and Naitoh (1980) found no effect on classroom quiz scores of college students or on the landing performance of experienced Navy pilots. Reilly, Young, and Seddon (1983) found no biorhythm effects on the "best performances in 610 top ranked European female track and field specialists over a single competitive season" (p. 215). James (1984) found no biorhythm effect on a major test of academic performance taken by 368 students or on a test of psychoneurotic tendencies given to 338 students. The results of more than thirty well-designed studies now in the literature are clear: biorhythms do not exist.

It is important to ask why biorhythm theory became so popular in the first place. What was the nature of the evidence that convinced so many people that there was something to the theory? As mentioned above, a major source of support was lists of events that seemed to confirm the theory. This type of useless data no doubt convinced many. However, proponents of biorhythm theory also allude to various scientific studies that are said to show either that using biorhythm theory reduces a company's accident rate or that about 60 percent of a firm's accidents take place on critical days. Thus, both Gittelson (1982) and Thommen (1973) mention several Japanese transportation firms that allegedly have used and studied biorhythm theory. Unfortunately, no references are given for the studies cited, and attempts to confirm that the studies were actually conducted or that the firms in question use biorhythm theory have always been fruitless. This sort of study can best be referred to as *phantom studies,* as they seem simply not to exist. This has not prevented biorhythm proponents from quoting them to increase sales of their books and services.

A second type of study said to support biorhythm theory turns out, upon inspection, to suffer from fatal statistical flaws, often because the author had little idea how to carry out a correct statistical analysis. One particular flaw is most common and concerns the method used to determine which day is critical. As mentioned earlier, critical days account for about

20 percent of all days. But it is not always clear, according to biorhythmists, exactly which day is critical for an individual. What if someone is born at 11:58 P.M.? Or 12:01 A.M.? Williamson (1975, p. 18) points out that "an individual born shortly following midnight is biorhythmically closer to the preceding day than an individual born at noon. Similarly, an individual born approaching midnight is closer to the coming day." To get around this problem, in his study of helicopter accidents, Williamson (1975) tallied as falling on a critical day any accident that fell on the calculated critical day, the day before, or the day after. Naturally, if you add in the days before and after the critical day, you are now defining 60 percent of all days as "critical" (20 percent × 3). With such a definition, one would need to find that significantly more than 60 percent of a sample of accidents fell on the critical day, plus and minus one. Williamson (1975) fails to realize this, however, and claims that his finding that 58 percent of the accidents in his sample fell on critical days (as he defined them) is strongly supportive of biorhythm theory, since 58 percent is clearly greater than 20 percent. Pittner and Owens (1975) make the same error in their study.

Another statistical error, occurring either in the authors' interpretation of their own data or in biorhythm proponents' interpretation of others' data, can be termed the "shotgun" approach. Thus, Knowles and Jones (1974) studied police-suspect altercations as a function of the biorhythmic position of both individuals. It is not clear from their paper, but they may have examined as many as 15,625 different biorhythm predictions, saying they examined "all relationships of patterns of days and periods . . . for each of the three cycles" (p. 54). Since there are two people involved— the policeman and the suspect—and three cycles; and since there are five possible positions for a biorhythm (up phase, ascending portion; up phase, descending; down phase, ascending; down phase, descending; critical), there are 5^6, or 15,625, possible patterns to be examined. Out of however many patterns the authors did examine, only four significant effects were found, and none of the major predictions of the theory regarding critical days was verified.

Biorhythm proponents also mix real science in with their pseudoscience. Such mixing is another common characteristic of a pseudoscience (Radner and Radner, 1982). Thus, Dale (1976) and Mallardi (1978) include in their discussion of biorhythms considerable material on the known and scientifically verified biological rhythms that are found in humans as well as other animals and plants. These authors appear to hope readers of their paperbacks won't be sophisticated enough in biology to spot the difference between the two types of rhythms. Biorhythm proponents also mislead their readers by failing even to acknowledge the existence of, let alone discuss, the numerous studies reviewed above that show biorhythm theory to be false. Thus, the 1984 edition of Gittelson's *Biorhythm: A Personal Science* mentions none of the dozens of such studies conducted during the last decade. Like a used car salesman knowingly selling a defective car, biorhythm proponents are more interested in fleecing their customers than in telling the truth.

Finally, blatant misrepresentation of results has sometimes been used to sell biorhythm theory. Most often misused in this fashion was the work of psychologist Rexford Hersey (1931, 1932, 1955), who studied cyclic changes in workers' moods and emotions. It is often claimed by biorhythmists (e.g., Dale, 1976; Holden, 1977) that Hersey's work supports the theory. It doesn't. Hersey did show that workers' moods and emotions vary cyclically, but his data clearly show that the cycles vary greatly within an individual, due to environmental and other factors, and that different individuals have different cycles. This is just the opposite of what biorhythm theory requires.

An additional factor led many to accept the validity of biorhythm theory as it applied to predicting events in their own lives. This factor, termed the *fallacy of personal validation*, helps explain the belief in numerous occult and pseudoscientific systems, such as astrology and psychic predictions. Here only its application to biorhythm theory will be discussed. The fallacy of personal validation hinges on the selective nature of human memory, as discussed earlier. Every day in our lives has its good and bad points, with most days being rather neutral—some bad things happen, but also some good things. Thus, if biorhythm theory predicted for an individual that a particular day was going to be "up" or "down," there would always be events occurring during that day that would seem to verify the prediction. Thus, the prediction will seem to be quite accurate. Randi (1980) makes the point nicely. He gave a woman a biorhythm chart that covered two months and told her it had been made up based on her birthdate. She was to record its accuracy and report back. At the end of the two months, she reported that it had been very accurate in predicting her personal ups and downs. But it wasn't her chart: To test the effect of belief on the perceived accuracy of the chart, Randi had sent her a chart based on his own birthday. He apologized and promised to send her the correct chart. She received it and, when she checked the new chart against the diary she had been keeping, "reported that this one was *even more accurate*" (Randi, 1980, p. 165 [emphasis in original]) than the previous chart. But the second chart wasn't hers either. It didn't matter what the chart "predicted"; as long as she believed it was hers, she perceived it as accurate. This is the heart of the fallacy of personal validation.

7

UFOs I: Close Encounters
of the First Kind

The belief that unidentified flying objects (UFOs) are some sort of extra-terrestrial spacecraft is certainly one of the most prevalent pseudoscientific beliefs in western culture. Dozens of movies have reinforced the view that "flying saucers," or UFOs, are alien craft. Massively popular modern films like *Close Encounters of the Third Kind* have kept the UFO theme in the public eye.

UFOs are almost exclusively a post-World War II phenomenon. There was a series of sightings of cigar-shaped UFOs in the United States from late 1896 to early 1897, but this was an isolated series (Cohen, 1981). During World War II both Allied and Axis pilots reported seeing "foo-fighters," strange lights that followed their aircraft, but these reports attracted little attention (Jacobs, 1975). The modern era for UFOs began on June 24, 1947, when private pilot Kenneth Arnold was flying near the Cascade Mountains in Washington and saw nine unidentified flying objects that he described flying "like a saucer skipping over water" (Jacobs, 1975, pp. 36-37). The term *flying saucer*, and the public's interest in the phenomenon, was born.

After Arnold's sighting was reported, the number of other sightings around the country and the world grew. There was a major wave, or "flap," of sightings in 1952. That year also saw the first reported contact between earthman and spaceman, or *close encounter of the third kind*. The first "contactee" was George Adamski, a handyman and failed mystic, who met a visitor from Venus in the California desert on November 20, 1952. Adamski was the first of a series of contactees during the 1950s. Jacobs (1975) has noted that contactee stories of this era contain several common elements. The lone earthman was given a ride in the UFO. The occupants explained their advanced culture to him and explained the workings of the craft. One contactee, Howard Menger, was lucky enough to have the aliens show him how to construct a "free-energy motor" (Menger, 1959), although this marvelous invention somehow failed to forestall the energy crisis of the 1970s. The aliens would also predict dire happenings on earth, such as atomic war, that would affect other planets. The contactee was usually given a mission to prevent this disaster and set the stage for final contact between the human and extraterrestrial civilizations. Somehow, the aliens always forgot to give their contacts any proof that they existed. They also must have been very bad psychologists, because the people they chose to carry their messages were almost invariably crackpots, lunatics, or charlatans. Thus, close encounters of the third kind were not taken seriously by many people until the 1970s when such reports cropped up again, in rather different form.

As the 1950s wore on, UFO reports continued, and the U.S. Air Force became concerned. After all, people were reporting strange things in the skies—often reporting them directly to the Air Force—and they might be some type of Russian device. Recall that this was the period of the McCarthy anticommunist paranoia. Thus, Project Blue Book was set up in 1952 by the Air Force to investigate UFO reports. However, the Air Force appears not to have taken the project too seriously; it had a small staff with little technical competence. Predictably, Project Blue Book was heavily criticized by those who felt there was really something to the UFO reports. In 1954 NICAP, the National Investigations Committee on Aerial Phenomena, was formed by retired Marine Corps Major Donald Keyhoe. It was the first private UFO research group and the most conservative. NICAP correctly dismissed as crackpots or frauds the various contactees of the 1950s, when other private UFO investigating organizations were often taking at least some of these stories seriously.

From about 1958 until 1965 came a period of constant controversy over UFOs. The several private UFO groups battled with each other over who was the best and with the Air Force, since they were convinced that the Air Force knew that UFOs were alien spacecraft but was keeping this truth from the American public. There were constant calls for congressional investigations of the UFO sightings, the Air Force, and the Air Force's handling of the UFO reports.

By 1966 the Air Force had concluded that there was nothing to UFO reports, either as a concern of national security or as extraterrestrial contact. Devoutly wishing to be rid of the entire matter, the Air Force contracted with a group of independent scientists to investigate all aspects of the UFO question. This group, headed by University of Colorado professor of physics Edward Condon, came to be known as the Condon Committee. Creation of the Condon Committee was greeted with optimism by all sides (Jacobs, 1975). However, pro-UFO groups quickly became dissatisfied with the committee's investigation. Factions within the committee fought over how to approach the problem. One group felt that the focus of the investigation should be the extraterrestrial hypothesis, while another faction "thought the extraterrestrial theory was nonsense and believed the solution to the UFO mystery was to be found in the psychological makeup of the witnesses" (Jacobs, 1975, p. 230). This dispute led to much internal dissension and fueled the private UFO groups' discontent with the committee.

The Condon Committee issued its report in 1969 and concluded that there was no evidence that UFOs were of extraterrestrial origin. In December 1969 the Air Force officially got out of the UFO business, closing down Project Blue Book for good.

The conclusions of the Condon Committee and the government's official withdrawal from UFO investigations have not ended public furor over UFOs. A 1973 Gallup poll showed that 11 percent of American adults believed that they had seen a UFO. Another Gallup poll conducted in 1978 showed that 57 percent of Americans believe that UFOs are "something real." Klass (1978-79) has rightly been critical of the wording of the UFO-related questions on the Gallup polls, pointing out that "something real" does not necessarily mean "something extraterrestrial" and that even skeptics would agree that UFOs represent *"something real."* Nonetheless, these figures testify to the high degree of belief and interest in UFOs on the part of the American public.

Since the issuance of the Condon Report several pro-UFO groups have continued to investigate UFO sightings and to claim that there is good evidence for their extraterrestrial origin. A major argument put forth for the reality of extraterrestrial UFOs is the large number of reports that continue to be made. Astronomer J. Allen Hynek, a former skeptic where UFOs were concerned, changed his mind and came to support the extraterrestrial hypothesis (he also coined the term *close encounters of the third kind* and was an adviser for the film of the same name) based on the large number of sightings (Hynek, 1972). Hynek, who died in 1986, frequently emphasized not only the large number of sightings, but the fact that they come "from all parts of the world and in many instances from remarkably competent witnesses" (Hynek, 1976-77, p. 77). This is a theme sounded over and over again in the UFO movement. The fact that many UFO witnesses are trained pilots, radar operators, or other professionals, and that they are not crazy, drunk, or on drugs leads UFO proponents to conclude that they must have seen just what they say they saw. This conclusion is, in fact, fundamentally wrong. The great failure of the pro-UFO movement has been its unwillingness to accept the fact that human perception and memory are not only unreliable under a variety of conditions (and these conditions are exactly those under which most UFOs are reported) but that perception and memory are also *constructive.*

That is, perception is a function not only of the actual sensory stimulus that is picked up by the eye or the ear but also a function of what we know and believe about the world, even if that knowledge and belief are wrong. The constructive nature of perception is greatest when the actual sensory input is weak, unclear, or ambiguous—just the type of sensory input present in most UFO sightings. Memory, too, is constructive. Experiments reviewed below show clearly that what we remember about an incident can actually be changed after the fact. When this happens, the witness truthfully testifies to remembering something that never happened.

The Constructive Nature of Human Perception

The fact that knowledge influences how we perceive the world, that it modifies the pure sensory input received from the sense organs, is of vital importance: it allows us to make sense of what would otherwise be a very confusing world. Perceptual psychologists have studied so-called *perceptual constancies* for more than 100 years. These constancies are among the best examples of the constructive nature of perception.

Consider color perception. A red apple will look red under a wide variety of lighting conditions. Under normal white light the apple looks red because the red wavelengths of light are reflected from the apple skin to the eye. By changing the light that falls on the apple, it is possible to change the composition of the light that is reflected from the apple skin to the eye. But, except for extreme cases, changes in reflected light do not result in a change in the perceived color of the apple. It is still perceived as red. This effect depends on the perceiver's knowledge that the object is a red apple. If that knowledge is removed, the color does not appear the same under different lighting conditions. This can be demonstrated by placing two identical red apples in two boxes. Each box has a small hole that permits the viewer to see only a small section of apple skin. This is not enough for the observer to figure out that the object is an apple. As far as the observer is concerned, all he is looking at is a section of color. If the light is different in the two boxes the color of the apple skin will appear very different to the observer. In this situation the observer doesn't know the color is that of a red apple, and with this knowledge eliminated, the perceived color is almost totally a function of the actual wavelengths of light reflected to the observer's eye. Hence, knowledge plays a major role in determining what color is perceived. It must be emphasized that this is not a conscious process on the part of the observer. Rather, the brain automatically takes into account what is known about the object and adjusts the perception accordingly.

Another form of constancy is called *size constancy*. What happens to your perception of a friend's size as he or she walks away from you? Nothing, of course—your friend's size stays perceptively constant. But the actual sensory information that your eye is sending your brain changes radically as your friend moves away from you. The image that your friend casts upon your retina decreases in size constantly as the distance between the two of you increases. The size of the retinal image when an object (your friend in this case) is ten feet away is half what it is when the object is five feet away. But you know that people and other objects don't shrink simply because you are farther away from them. In the real world they stay the same size. Their size is constant, and the brain's knowledge about this fact allows it to compensate for the change in retinal image size and produce a perception of size that is constant, just like the real object. Again, if that knowledge is lacking, size constancy is lacking. Certain tribes in the African jungles live in an environment where they never have the opportunity to develop size constancy because when something moves away from them, it is obscured by the jungle. When individuals from these tribes are exposed to an object far away from them, they badly misjudge its size, thinking that large objects far away are really small objects close to them. However, after a few days' experience, they develop normal size constancy (Turnbull, 1961).

Another impressive example of constructive perception also concerns color vision. People who have normal color vision perceive the entire visual field as colored. This is taken for granted. But in spite of this, the cells in the retina of the eye that enable us to see color are found only in the very center of the retina in an area called the *fovea*. If we depended only on retinal input for color perception, we would perceive a small central area of color, while the rest of the visual field would be black and white. This can easily be demonstrated. Have a friend look straight ahead, then slowly move some colored object (a colored pen or pencil is ideal) into his or her field of vision. There will be a point at which the person will be able to see something in peripheral vision and will be able even to identify it, but will not be able, if the object is unfamiliar, to say what color it is. If the object is unfamiliar, the person will not be able to identify its color until it is well inside the field of vision.

Another example may clarify this point. As I sit here writing this, there is an orange red door off to my left. I can just see the door out of the corner of my eye and I clearly perceive it as colored, in spite of the fact that the light being reflected off the door to my retina is falling on a part of the retina where there are no color receptors. Since I know what color the door is—it is very familiar to me—my brain constructs a perception of the color. How the brain manages this is not known (see

Boynton, 1979, for a full discussion of human color vision), but the phenomenon demonstrates the great importance of knowledge in even the simplest types of perception.

Color and size constancy are just two examples of many perceptual constancies. Others include *position constancy, shape constancy,* and *brightness constancy.* Details can be found in most introductory psychology texts and any textbook on perception. The important point about these constancies is that they demonstrate that even in such straightforward tasks as judging color or shape or size, knowledge plays an extremely important role in influencing the way in which an object is perceived. The brain takes into account what is known about the object and constructs a perception based both on the actual sensory input and on knowledge.

Other perceptual processes contribute to the constructive nature of perception. Look at the object in figure 8 and then close the book and make a copy of it from memory. Chances are very high that you did not include in your copy the small gap at one corner. If you had been asked to describe the figure to someone, you would almost certainly have left out that small gap. This is an example of *perceptual closure.* Along with several related processes, it tends to "clean up" a perception and make it into more of a unified object, even if the stimulus was not such an object in the first place.

An impressive example of constructive perception that is not well understood physiologically is that of *illusory contours* (Coren, 1972), seen in figure 9. The triangular shape that you see isn't really there; the brain constructs it.

The constructive nature of perception accounts for a famous astronomical illusion—the canals of Mars. These were first reported in 1877 by the Italian astronomer Schiaparelli. They were popularized in the early twentieth century by the American astronomer Percival Lowell. Figure 10 shows a map of the canals after Lowell's 1908 book *Mars as the Abode of Life.* In this book Lowell argued that the canals were constructed by an advanced Martian civilization. It turns out, however, that the canals of Mars don't exist. Sagan and Fox (1975) have compared the photos taken by Mariner 9, which photographed the entire Martian surface, with maps of the canals. When the actual Martian surface is examined, there are no canals and no other physical features that could account for what Schiaparelli and Lowell reported. So, where did the canals come from? Sagan and Fox (1975, p. 609) state that "the vast majority of the canals appear to be largely self-generated by the visual observers of the canal school, and stand as monuments to the imprecision of the human eye-brain-hand system under difficult observing conditions."

A number of well-known visual illusions play a role in what witnesses report in UFO sightings, especially those that take place at night. One is the *autokinetic effect*. This effect refers to the fact that, if one views a small source of light in a dark room, the light will appear to move, even though it is stationary and even though the observer's head is stationary. One theory is that the effect is due to tiny movements of the eyeball that are not under the conscious control of the observer. These tiny eye movements cause the image of the light to move across the retina. The brain incorrectly attributes this movement to the light source, since the head is steady and the brain itself receives no information from the eye regarding the tiny eye movements. The effect is eliminated if a clear frame of reference is provided so the brain can compare the position of the light source with that of a larger, clearly stationary object (Haber and Hershenson, 1973). Otani and Dixon (1976) have shown that social influence can affect the degree of the autokinetic effect—that is, one person saying he sees the light moving in a particular direction can induce others to make similar reports.

Another illusion is that of *apparent motion*. Consider two positions in a dark room, A and B. A small light is turned on at A, then turned off. Moments later, a second light is turned on at B. What does the observer perceive? The obvious answer would be that the perception is of one light going on and going off, followed by a second light in a different position going on and then off. But this is not what the observer sees at all. What is perceived is a *single* light appearing at point A, moving to point B, and then going off. The brain creates a perception of movement where none exists. It also creates a perception of light where none exists—between positions A and B.

These constructive phenomena are extremely important for our survival in the real world. The constancies and other mechanisms described evolved because they help organisms interact with the world. However, when the sensory input is minimal and only our knowledge and beliefs remain, our resultant perceptions can be very, very misleading. In these situations, we can perceive complex objects that are not there at all, and be absolutely convinced that they were there. In some sense, then, people who report seeing impressive flying saucers are not lying. They really perceive them, even though they weren't there: The objects were a construction of their brains and seem just as real as if they really had been there. Before moving on to the numerous UFO sightings that prove this point, it is important to discuss briefly the fallibility of human memory.

You don't need expertise in experimental psychology to know that human memory is fallible. Anyone who has ever taken an exam or tried unsuccessfully to remember someone's name or telephone number knows that human memory doesn't always work perfectly. The important insight about the fallibility of human memory to come from experimental psychology over the past twenty years is that memory is fallible in a very special way. It can be changed after the fact by new information, and the resultant memory may be very different from what actually took place. And yet, the person will swear that his or her memory is accurate. In some sense, it is. The witness is not lying in the usual sense of that word. The reported memory is really a memory, but due to the nature of memory, the reported memory differs greatly from what actually happened.

The best examples of this process come from the work of Elizabeth Loftus (1979). In one of her earlier experiments (Loftus and Palmer, 1974), Loftus showed students in her introductory psychology classes a film of a car accident. Afterwards, the students were given a questionnaire to fill out about the accident they had seen. There were two versions of the questionnaire, identical except for one word. One version of the questionnaire had as one of the ten questions, "About how fast were the cars going when they smashed into each other?" The other version of the questionnaire was identical except that "hit" was substituted for "smashed into." This slight change had two effects. First, students who got the "smashed into"question gave higher speed estimates than those who got the "hit" question. More important for the issue at hand, when asked one week later whether or not they had seen any broken glass in the film, students who had answered the "smashed into" question were more than twice as likely to report seeing broken glass as those who received the "hit" question (16 percent vs. 7 percent). There was no broken glass in the film. Thus, a leading question given *after the fact* can alter a memory, not only for the actual subject of the question—speed, in the present case—but also for related material.

Loftus demonstrated how powerful this effect can be in a later experiment (Loftus, Miller, and Burns, 1978). She again showed subjects a film of a car accident. After the film, subjects were given a questionnaire about the film. One of the questions was, "How fast was the red car going when it ran the stop sign and hit the green car?" In fact, there was no stop sign at the intersection in the film where the accident occurred. A week later subjects were shown two photographs. One showed the intersection as it had actually appeared in the film, without a stop sign. The other showed the same intersection, but with a stop sign. Subjects were asked which picture was from the film. They overwhelmingly picked the picture with the stop sign, even though there was no stop sign in the film. The question that presupposed the existence of a stop sign had implanted a stop sign in the subjects' memories, even though none had been there. As before, the subjects were not really lying—they really remembered seeing a stop sign, even though it had never been there.

Loftus's work has important implications for eyewitness testimony in court, and Loftus (1979) has addressed this issue. Her findings also have extremely important implications for UFO reports, as will be seen in the next section.

Close Encounters of the First Kind

The most common type of UFO report is the so-called *close encounter of the first kind* (CE I). It consists of a sighting of a UFO, but with no physical evidence of the object left behind. Nonetheless, a CE I can be quite impressive, especially when the witnesses are trained, reliable, stable individuals.

The earliest UFO sightings—the six-month wave of sightings of a "mysterious airship" between November 1896 and April 1897—fall into this category. In the UFO literature, the "airship" is amost always reported to have been a dark cigar-shaped object (Jacobs, 1975). In a careful investigation of this wave of sightings based on the newspaper reports of the day, Cohen (1981) has found that the popular descriptions of this wave of sightings are much exaggerated. In the best traditions of constructive perception, what was usually seen in the sky was not a dark cigar-shaped object, but merely a light. It was "simply assumed that the lights were attached to the mystery airship. People sometimes added that they thought they saw a dark shape above the light which they took to be the body of the airship, but most witnesses seemed to indicate that this dark body, if they saw it at all, was vague and indistinct" (Cohen, 1981, p. 186).

The light itself was probably the planet Venus. Venus is the brightest of all the planets in the night sky and is responsible for more UFO reports than any other single object (Hendry, 1979). Sheaffer (cited in Cohen, 1981) has calculated that Venus was at its brightest in March 1897. The "mysterious airship" sightings were most numerous just a few weeks later, in April 1897.

Hoaxes also played a major role in the airship mystery. Cohen (1981, pp. 189-90) notes that "the papers contain scores of reports of airship sightings stimulated by jokers who released balloons with some sort of flaming material attached, or flew lighted kites." Some of these hoax reports may themselves have been hoaxes, but many were certainly real. There were even crash hoaxes in which bits of mechanical apparatus would be scattered about and it would be claimed that these were the remains of the crashed ship. Hoaxing by railroad telegraph operators, who reported an inordinate number of sightings, was also a factor. The *Des Moines Leader* editorialized on April 11, 1897, that the airship reports amounted to the "most successful fakes in an era of such successes" due to the false reports of railroad telegraph operators (Cohen, 1981, p. 192).

As noted above, one of the major arguments put forward by proponents of the view that UFOs are extraterrestrial in origin is the large number of impressive reports by reliable witnesses. However, such witnesses are just as liable as anyone else to the processes of constructive perception and thus to the attendant misidentification of known objects as UFOs. Klass (1981) has described several instructive cases. For example, who better to correctly identify objects in the sky than an experienced astronomer? One Arizona astronomer with "thousands of hours of experience in observing the night sky" (p. 312) saw, on the night of October 5, 1973, a most "striking and unusual" UFO. He wrote a description of what he had seen and, being unable to identify it immediately, attempted to discover what it might have been. His investigation revealed that he had seen "the rocket-engine plume from a large air-force Titan 2 intercontinental ballistic missile being launched from Vandenberg Air Force Base, California; *more than five hundred miles away*" (Klass, 1981, p. 312). Not only had this experienced astronomer failed to recognize what he was seeing, he also found that his written report contained "several inaccuracies and inconsistencies" due to "the usual difficulties of perceiving and remembering an unusual, rapidly changing phenomenon. This report . . . is perhaps typical of the reliability of a UFO observation by a trained observer" (Klass, 1981, p. 312).

Another case reported by Klass (1981) is extremely impressive. There were multiple independent witnesses, several UFOs appeared, and, in one instance, the presence of the UFOs seemed to terrify the dog of one of the witnesses. These strange events occurred on the night of March 3, 1968. In Columbus, Ohio that night a science teacher walking her dog saw three small UFOs, which she observed through binoculars. They were flying in formation, she reported, and seemed to be "under intelligent control." Her dog appeared to be "frightened to death" and lay on the ground whimpering. On the same night three witnesses in Nashville, Tennessee, reported seeing a huge metal saucer with many square windows glowing from the inside. The estimated altitude was about 1,000 feet. The third report for this active evening came from Indiana, where a cigar-shaped UFO was seen that had a rocket-type exhaust and windows.

These reports seem to indicate an impressive phenomenon. What was going on in the sky that night? Klass (1981, p. 314) reports that on that night a Russian Zond 4 launch rocket reentered the atmosphere. It "reentered on a southwest-to-northeast trajectory that took it across Tennessee, Ohio, Pennsylvania, and southwestern New York State. As the rocket reentered it broke up into many luminous fragments as it traversed the atmosphere at very high speed." Many other people saw this spectacular reentry that night. It is important to note that the UFO witnesses did not see the reentry in addition to the UFOs. In this case we see the power of constructive perception. The witnesses reported windows, an exhaust, and a huge saucer—all details that weren't there. These additions and embellishments were purely the creation of the witnesses' minds: not because they were crazy, drunk, or stupid, but because that is the way the human brain works. It can be said that these witnesses did perceive what they said they did. This doesn't mean, however, that what they perceived was the same as what was really there. Note, too, how inaccurate was the estimate of the object's altitude made by the witness from Nashville, Tennessee. The witness estimated about 1,000 feet while, in fact, the reentering rocket was miles high and scores of miles away. This type of gross inaccuracy frequently occurs when one sees a light in the sky with no background, as is the case at night. Under these circumstances, the many cues the brain uses to judge distance are not present, so no accurate basis for the judgment exists.

But what about the science teacher's dog, whimpering on the ground? This witness certainly attributed the dog's behavior to the three UFOs she saw through her binoculars. But if the objects she really saw were miles away, how can one explain the dog's behavior? Actually, it can be explained very simply: It was a cold night and, as the witness stated later, her dog hated the cold. Given the extra time no doubt taken by the witness to watch the UFOs, the dog was most probably cold and simply wanted to go home. UFO witnesses commonly attribute to the UFO almost anything that happens while they are observing the UFO, ignoring more prosaic explanations.

Pilots are often thought to be among the most reliable witnesses when it comes to reporting things seen in the skies. On June 5, 1969, near St. Louis, Missouri, a UFO sighting occurred that involved pilot witnesses in three separate aircraft. A "squadron" of UFOs was reported, and two UFOs were seen on radar at the same time. A Federal Aviation Administration observer in one of the commercial aircraft involved estimated that the group of UFOs was only several hundred feet away from his aircraft and that they were going to strike the aircraft. He reported that the UFOs were colored like "burnished aluminum." They were said to be shaped like a "hydroplane." After this alarming incident was over, it was reported to the tower at St. Louis airport. The tower reported that there were two "unidentified targets" on radar. These targets were to the west of the first aircraft; the UFOs had been heading west. At this point a second commercial aircraft called to report that the UFOs had passed the aircraft moments previously and were still headed west. According to the pilot, the squadron of UFOs had "nearly collided with the aircraft," but avoided disaster at the last second by maneuvers that suggested they were "under intelligent control."

Can any nonextraordinary occurrence account for these simultaneous visual and radar reports? Klass (1981) demonstrates that the visual reports were due to a meteor and associated fireball "with a long, luminous tail of electrified air, followed by a smaller flaming fragment, also with a long tail, flying in trail behind" (p. 315). The fireball was moving from east to west and was the source of a large number of reports from all over the Iowa-Illinois-Missouri area. Thus, the actual object was more than one hundred miles north of the reporting aircraft. Yet pilots in all three aircraft mistakenly perceived the object as extremely near—in two cases only hundreds of feet away.

But what about the radar report of two unidentified targets? Amusingly, it turns out that the targets were two of the aircraft that reported the UFOs in the first place. In 1969 airport radar did not automatically identify planes that appeared on the screen. The operator had to place a written note next to the screen identifying each "blip." Aircraft that were passing over rather than landing at a particular airport were not honored with such a written identification. None of the three aircraft that reported the UFOs was landing at St. Louis. Thus, when the first aircraft reported seeing the UFOs, the tower at St. Louis correctly reported that there were two "unidentified" targets in the area. There were—the two other aircraft that moments later also reported the UFOs. Modern airport radars now automatically identify all aircraft in their area by picking up a special signal from each aircraft's transponder. Klass (1984-85) has noted that, as radars have become more sophisticated at correctly identifying aircraft and filtering out sources of error, the number of radar UFO reports has dropped almost to zero. Of course, if UFOs were real, one would expect the increased sophistication and sensitivity of modern radar to *increase* the number of UFOs seen on radar.

A most frightening CE I took place on April 17, 1966. Two policemen chased a UFO at high speed for about sixty-five miles from eastern Ohio into western Pennsylvania, between 5 A.M. and 6 A.M. (Sheaffer, 1981, chapter 19). This case is a classic demonstration of how a commonplace object, such as Venus in the dawn sky, can be misidentified as a UFO and endowed with the ability to move under intelligent control, creating the belief on the part of trained observers that they are witnessing something outside the realm of normal explanation. The most astonishing thing about this UFO, from the police officers' point of view, was that it appeared to be "teasing" them. When they first saw the object, it was stationary in the sky. When they got into their cruiser and slowly moved toward it, it slowly moved away. When they increased their speed, the UFO increased its speed. When they slowed down, it slowed down, always keeping a constant distance from them. This is exactly the type of behavior that can convince UFO witnesses that the object is "under intelligent control"—it seems to be pacing them and responding to their own movements in a purposeful manner. This type of behavior is also characteristic of celestial bodies. The moon, for example, seems to pace a car as the car drives along a road at night. This happens because the moon is so far away that the movement of the car produces no change in the perceived position of the moon. It is obvious to adult observers that the moon is not really following the car, although children are often fooled by this illusion. The situation is much the same for an object like the planet Venus. Venus is much too far away to change its position perceptibly as an automobile moves. However, Venus lacks the obvious visual features that make the moon so easy to identify. Venus is little more than a very bright steady light in the sky. Further, the lack of visual features on Venus—such as the patterns of craters that exist on the moon—means an observer has no way to correctly judge the size of the object. Such size judgments are especially difficult at dawn when the stars are no longer visible. Venus may then be the only object visible in the sky. This situation provides none of the usual cues that permit the brain to calculate how large and how far away an object is. The object could be something the size of an aircraft less than a mile away, or it could be something very large, but farther away. When the apparent motion of the object following the car is added, the illusion that it is an object the size of an aircraft and that it is deliberately "following" the observer is frequently very powerful.

This is exactly what happened in the case of the two policemen. During the entire hour-long chase, although the officers' attention was riveted to the sky and the UFO they were chasing, they never once saw Venus. Further, the position of the UFO that they reported is the same as the position Venus occupied that morning. As dawn came on, Venus rose higher in the sky, and the UFO was reported to do the same. Finally, as the sun brightened, Venus faded from view—as did the UFO. A few moments later, the UFO was reported to reappear, but to have dropped about ten degrees in altitude. It then rose slowly. Sheaffer (1981) identifies this second object as a research balloon because the object's behavior as reported by the officers is just what one would expect of such a balloon.

As the chase progressed, a second police car joined. Now, if two police cars really were chasing a large UFO only hundreds of feet above the road, one might reasonably expect that other independent witnesses would have seen the same object. In fact, the chase was twice slowed by early morning traffic. Yet none of the hundreds of people who saw the speeding police cars reported seeing the UFO they were chasing.

Although it might initially seem ridiculous to claim that an object like Venus could be mistaken for a large spacecraft that chased an automobile, this case clearly shows that such gross misidentification is possible. It also shows that people can and will attribute apparent movement to "intelligent control" when no such control exists.

Hendry (1979) has provided even more examples of the unreliability of witnesses' reports—witnesses who are sane, sober individuals who have no reason to lie about what they saw—or, to be more precise, what they think they saw. Another source of false, but very impressive, UFO reports is advertising aircraft. These are small, usually single-engine, aircraft that carry underneath an array of small lights that can spell out an advertising, message. For obvious reasons, these aircraft fly only after dusk and at night. If one sees such an aircraft from any vantage point other than directly underneath, it may be very difficult to read the message. On a dark night it may be almost impossible to see the aircraft itself. One is left with an ambiguous visual stimulus—a bunch of disembodied lights in the sky—that is virtually guaranteed to result in UFO reports. Shown in figure 11 are drawings made by people who reported seeing UFOs. All these UFOs have been positively identified as advertising aircraft, yet look at the additions the witnesses have made to the known stimulus of a more or less random set of lights in the sky. All the objects are more or less saucer-shaped, all have some sort of windows, many have some sort of device on top (propellers in one case!). In all cases the perception is vastly more elaborate and detailed than was the actual stimulus. Again, it must be emphasized that these witnesses were not consciously "making up" their reports. Rather, the knowledge they had about what a UFO, or "flying saucer," ought to look like greatly influenced the way their brains interpreted the ambiguous stimulus of lights seen in the night sky.

Hendry (1979, p. 85) reports another impressive example of the power of constructive perception. The actual stimulus was the planet Venus. The woman who reported the UFO

> described it as a "star," only much brighter. It was positioned low in the southwest sky, starting around seven o'clock in the evening on January 30, 1976 — exactly where Venus was located at that time. She did not see Venus in addition to this "object." She then watched the light descend gradually to the horizon during an hour's period of time, which is exactly what Venus would do. This setting motion was perceived by her as being "jerky"; her husband thought that it was only a star, but she encouraged him to perceive the "jerky" descent, too, which got him excited. After staring at it for a sufficiently long time, the woman became convinced that she was looking at the illuminated window of a UFO and that she could see the round heads of the occupants inside, heads with silvery-

colored faces. She then proceeded to see this apparition in the same place every night for successive nights. Yes, I told her that it was Venus. Her reply: "You are talking to a woman fifty-four years old. I know what stars look like."

People's conviction that they have seen a real flying saucer, when in fact they've seen nothing of the kind, can be very convincing to others. No one is so likely to be believed as someone who truly believes what he is saying. Such belief sometimes pushes believers to absurd lengths to maintain their beliefs. This effect is seen in the series of UFO sightings in Westchester County, New York, from early 1983 through late 1984. The sighting reports were impressive, as is often the case. People who were pillars of the local communities reported seeing UFOs the size of a football field with multicolored lights. These UFOs could not have been aircraft since, according to the reports of numerous witnesses, they were too big, made no sound, hovered for minutes at a time in one spot, made perfect right-angle turns in the air, and winked in and out of existence—appearing here, then disappearing, only to reappear suddenly, moments later, somewhere else. The late J. Allen Hynek, who was director of the Center for UFO Studies, said in the center's publication *International UFO Reporter* that these sightings were among the most impressive in the history of UFO reports. He felt there was no possible way to "explain away" these sightings by scores of witnesses. But, in fact, the reports had a prosaic explanation: they were all a hoax. A group of private pilots flying from a small airport in Stormville, New York, had been flying in formation at night. They would fly along with all their lights out and then, on cue, turn on both the red and green wing lights and the bright white landing light. They flew in a boomerang formation, and many of the witnesses reported that the UFO had a boomerang shape. The appearing-disappearing trick was easy to pull off too. When all the lights were turned out at once, the UFO vanished. Thirty seconds later, after the planes had flown about one mile, the lights were all turned back on at once, so the UFO appeared to have moved from one spot to another in the twinkle of an eye.

The reports of the UFO hovering motionless for minutes were based, as the reader might by now expect, on the lack of cues available to the witnesses to tell them how far away the planes were. All they saw were lights in the night sky. In the absence of any other cues, the brain uses the size of the actual retinal image to judge distance. Small lights on aircraft don't significantly change retinal image size as the plane moves toward or away from the eye. Thus, the perception is of unchanged distance, even though the planes are moving. As far as the lack of noise is concerned, many modern private aircraft are quiet and are only heard when directly overhead. They may not be heard even when overhead if they are above 1000 feet, depending on the wind conditions and the presence of other noises on the ground.

The pilots at Stormville Airport had a good time with their hoax. It was revealed, however, by the local paper (Walzer, 1984) and in a long investigative article in the November 1984 issue of *Discover* magazine (Garelik, 1984). The response of several of the local UFO buffs has been surprising. Not willing to admit they were fooled they devised a bizarre and astonishingly elaborate conspiracy theory to explain what happened: the night-flying pilots were put up to their tricks by the *real UFOs* who wanted the hoax to cover up the existence of their activities and to obscure the *real* sightings!

One final example will show, in an elegant controlled experiment, the unreliability of eyewitness testimony in UFO reports. Simpson (1979-80) describes a controlled UFO hoax set up to determine just how distorted witnesses' reports of a UFO can become. The hoax was carried out on Cradle Hill in Warminster, England, on the night of March 28, 1970. Simpson (1979-80, p. 33) describes the stimulus for the hoax:

> At 11 P.M. a 12-volt high-intensity purple spotlamp was directed from a neighboring hill toward a group of about 30 sky-watchers on Cradle Hill, three-quarters of a mile away. The lamp was switched on for 5, and then 25, seconds, with a 5-second pause between. During the second "on" period, a bogus magnetic field sensor, operated among the sky-watchers by a colleague, sounded its alarm buzzer, apparently indicating the presence of a strong magnetic field. (UFO folklore states that strong magnetic fields are a characteristic of UFOs, so this sensor was not an unusual sight.) In practice, the alarm was simply synchronized to sound while the distant spotlamp was on. The "strangeness" of the purple light was thereby enhanced.

Another important aspect of this hoax was the production of fake photographs of the UFO. Four exposures were produced, but two had been taken months previously and doctored to show UFOs that did not look at all like the "UFO" produced by the purple lamp. The UFO in these two photos was much more saucer-shaped. It was in a different position in each of the two photos, indicating movement. In one photo it was above the hill, in the other below it. Another important point about the first two photos is that, because they were taken months before the actual hoax, they showed an incorrect pattern of street lights along a road running at the base of the hill. Due to repairs on some of the lights, that pattern changed between the time these photos were taken and the night of the

Figure 1. One of the Cottingley fairy photographs. See page 4.

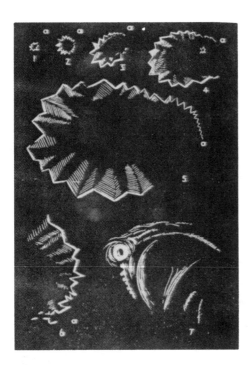

Figure 2. Typical fortification illusions of migraine. See page 58. (From Sacks [1985].)

Figure 3. Examples of the illusions of the eleventh-century mystic Hildegard showing their similarity to migraine fortification illusions. See page 59. (From Sacks [1985].)

Figure 4. A simple way to bend a key when your audience is distracted—but certainly not the *only* way. See page 89. (Photo by Mike Ackerbauer.)

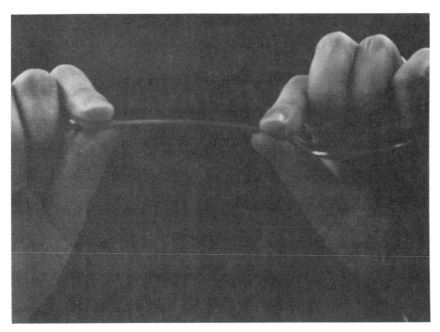

Figure 5A. A spoon held at points 1 and 2.

Figure 5B. A spoon held at points 1 and 3. See page 91. (Photos by Mike Ackerbauer.)

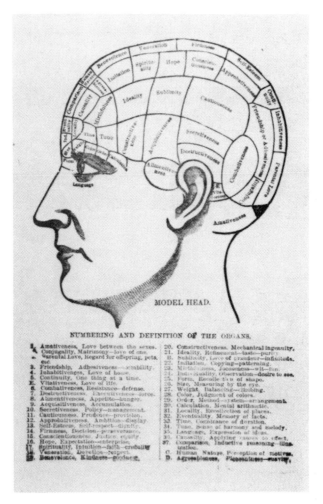

MODEL HEAD.

NUMBERING AND DEFINITION OF THE ORGANS.

1. Amativeness, Love between the sexes.
A. Conjugality, Matrimony—love of one.
2. Parental Love, Regard for offspring, pets, etc.
3. Friendship, Adhesiveness—sociability.
4. Inhabitiveness, Love of home.
5. Continuity, One thing at a time.
E. Vitativeness, Love of life.
6. Combativeness, Resistance—defense.
7. Destructiveness, Executiveness—force.
8. Alimentiveness, Appetite—hunger.
9. Acquisitiveness, Accumulation.
10. Secretiveness, Policy—management.
11. Cautiousness, Prudence—provision.
12. Approbativeness, Ambition—display.
13. Self-Esteem, Self-respect—dignity.
14. Firmness, Decision—perseverance.
15. Conscientiousness, Justice, equity.
16. Hope, Expectation—enterprise.
17. Spirituality, Intuition—faith—credulity.
18. Veneration, Devotion—respect.
19. Benevolence, Kindness—goodness.

20. Constructiveness, Mechanical ingenuity.
21. Ideality, Refinement—taste—purity.
B. Sublimity, Love of grandeur—infinitude.
22. Imitation, Copying—patterning.
23. Mirthfulness, Jocoseness—wit—fun.
24. Individuality, Observation—desire to see.
25. Form, Recollection of shape.
26. Size, Measuring by the eye.
27. Weight, Balancing—climbing.
28. Color, Judgment of colors.
29. Order, Method—system—arrangement.
30. Calculation, Mental arithmetic.
31. Locality, Recollection of places.
32. Eventuality, Memory of facts.
33. Time, Cognizance of duration.
34. Tune, Sense of harmony and melody.
35. Language, Expression of ideas.
36. Causality, Applying causes to effect.
37. Comparison, Inductive reasoning—illustration.
C. Human Nature, Perception of motives.
D. Agreeableness, Pleasantness—suavity.

Figure 6. A typical phrenological map of the brain. See page 137. (Author's collection.)

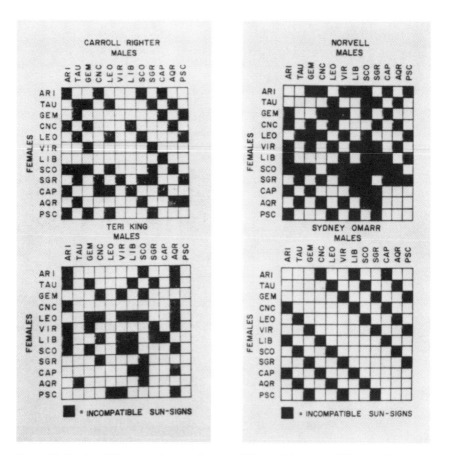

Figure 7. Vastly different patterns of compatible and incompatible sun signs used by four leading astrologers. See page 154. (From Culver and Ianna [1984].)

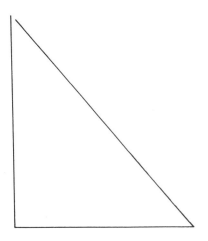

Figure 8. What is this figure?

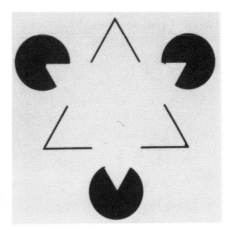

Figure 9. Illusory contours. The brain creates the contours of a white triangle that isn't really there.

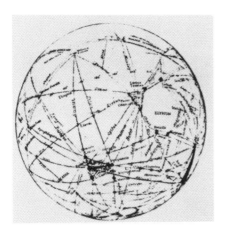

Figure 10. Lowell's illusory Martian canals. See page 170. (From Lowell [1908].)

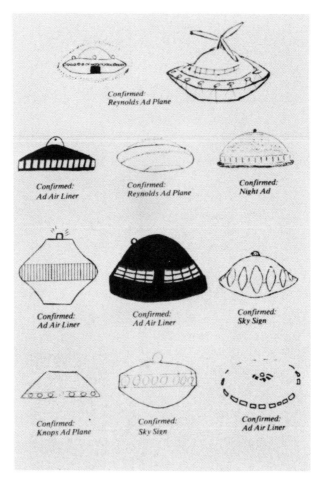

Figure 11. Drawings of UFOs by witnesses. All these sightings were actually due to misperceptions of advertising aircraft. See page 178. (From Hendry [1979].)

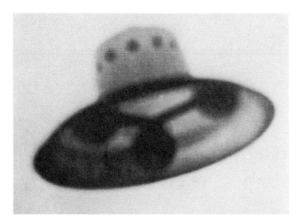

Figure 12. Impressive looking, but faked, UFO photos. See page 184. (From Sheaffer [1981].)

NICAP · 3

Figure 13. The fake Brazil UFO photo. See page 185.

Figure 14. One of the fake Heflin UFO photos. See page 185.

Figure 15. One of the fake Trent UFO photos. See page 185.

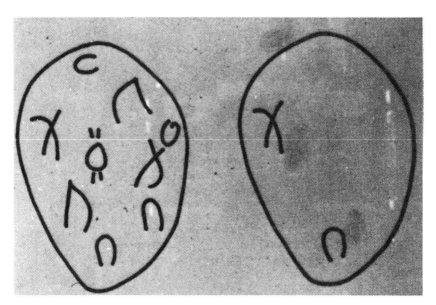

Figure 16. The Dogon's actual representation of the Sirius system (left) contains numerous unseen objects not verified by modern astronomy. Temple (1976) presents a censored version (right) of the actual Dogon view of Sirius. See page 218. (From Randi [1980].)

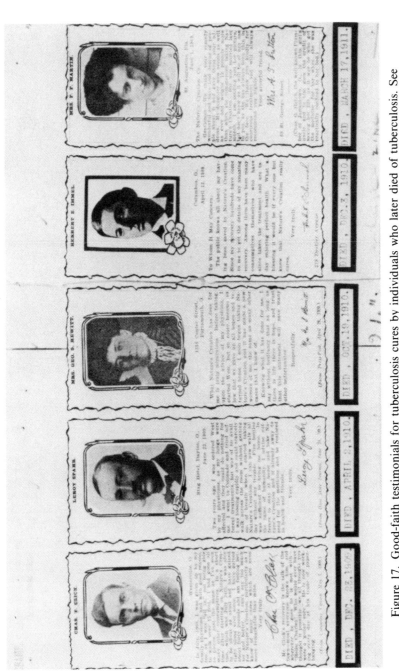

Figure 17. Good-faith testimonials for tuberculosis cures by individuals who later died of tuberculosis. See page 237. (Photo of early American Medical Association poster, courtesy of the AMA Library and Archives.)

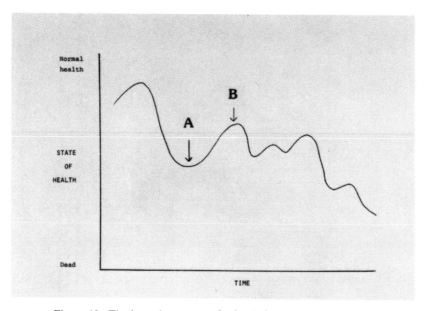

Figure 18. The irregular course of a fatal disease. See page 237.

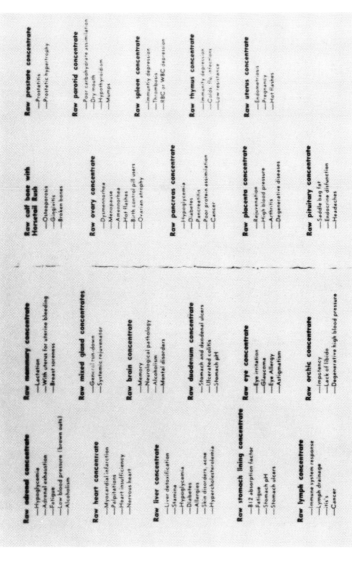

Figure 19. Various raw organ concentrates and the conditions they are said to cure. See page 258. (From Pepper [1984].)

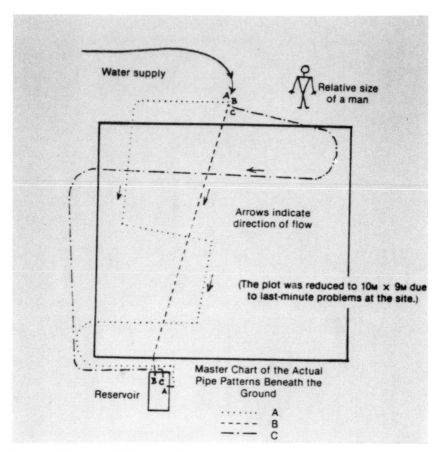

Figure 20. Layout of the water pipes used by Randi to test the claims of several dowsers. See page 291. (From Randi [1979-80].)

hoax. Two additional photographs were taken on the night of the hoax, after the sighting. They did not show any UFO, but they did show the current pattern of street lights. This difference in the pattern of the street lights is an obvious clue to the fake nature of the photographs. The important question was whether anyone would spot it.

The film was given to *Flying Saucer Review*, a major international UFO magazine. *Flying Saucer Review* stated that the negatives had proven "genuine beyond all doubt" (Simpson, 1979-80, p. 34). The photographs were submitted to several experts, who declared them genuine. Consider the opinion of Pierre Guerin, director of research at the Astrophysical Institute of the French National Center for Scientific Research: "In my opinion there is no question of the object photographed being in any possible way the result of faking." (Guerin, 1970, p. 6). Guerin did spend some effort to explain why the UFO in the photographs was so different in appearance from the UFO that was seen. Impressive scientific jargon abounds in his statement: "The object photographed was emitting ultra-violet light, which the eye does not see. Around the object, however, a ruby-red halo, probably of monochromatic colour and doubtless due to some phenomenon of air ionisation, was visible only to the eye and in actual fact made no impression on the film." (Guerin, 1970, p. 6). Now, if someone with the title of director of research at an astrophysical institute told you something in an area seemingly related to astrophysics, you would tend to believe him. But in this case an expert was misled by a rather obvious hoax. He failed to spot the clues in the photographs and went on to a grandiose pseudoscientific explanation of a phenomenon that never really existed in the first place. This sort of carelessness is, it turns out, a hallmark of investigations by UFO proponents, a point we will return to later.

The photographs contained yet another clue to the fact that they were faked. The first two photos were shot at a 10 percent greater magnification than the second two. And yet, a land surveyor who attempted to determine the position of the UFO in the photos failed to notice this large discrepancy (Simpson, 1979-80).

How do the witnesses' reports of the UFO that was seen compare to the actual stimulus? As would be expected, great differences show up between what actually took place and what the witnesses reported. These differences cover almost every aspect of the situation. The actual light was stationed on top of the nearby hill. The witnesses' reports had the light twenty degrees above the hill, in the air. The actual light was purple, but reports said it was purple and crimson. The light was stationary, but reports indicated that it moved slowly to the right and lost altitude. The light was said to dim considerably during the movement, a dimming which lasted twenty to thirty seconds. When it stopped moving, it increased in intensity. Ten to twenty seconds later, the UFO disappeared. According to the witnesses, the total duration of the sighting was one to one-and-a-half minutes. In actuality, the time from the first onset of the light to its final disappearance was thirty-five seconds. In addition, the witnesses failed to note that the light went out for five seconds. They only reported that it "dimmed."

Aside from the partially correct report of the light's color, nothing else in the witnesses' reports was accurate. This is especially important when one recalls that these were not random witnesses taken by surprise. They were UFO buffs expecting—and prepared for—a UFO sighting.

The several cases described above are only a fraction of the numerous cases in which careful investigation has resulted in straightforward natural explanations for even very impressive-sounding UFO reports. Details of additional cases can be found in Hendry (1979), Klass (1974, 1983), Sheaffer (1981), Oberg (1982), and Menzel and Taves (1977). All these cases make clear the nearly total unreliability of eyewitness reports. In almost every case, the witnesses' reports differed substantially from the actual stimulus, but in only a very few cases were the witnesses wilfully lying. Their knowledge about what UFOs "ought" to look like influenced their reports, along with the effects of visual illusions.

Another point emerges from a study of these explained cases: UFO organizations do a terrible job of investigating UFO reports. They are likely to naively accept witnesses' reports at face value and to fail to look carefully for possible natural explanations. The prevailing attitude assumes that the witness is telling the truth, so there is no need to look for an explanation other than that of an extraterrestrial spacecraft. Thus, time and time again impressive-sounding UFO reports are "investigated" by one or more of the major UFO organizations, declared to be genuine and verified, and highly touted in UFO publications and the popular press. Then, on careful investigation, the case is shown to have been due to some natural phenomenon or is revealed as a hoax. The results of the careful investigation almost never appear in the papers that printed the sensational false claims when the sighting was first stated to be "genuine."

Proponents of extraterrestrial UFOs reply to this sort of criticism by claiming that although many, even a great majority, of UFO sightings are due to some type of natural or manmade phenomenon, there is an "irreducible minimum" number of sightings that skeptics cannot explain away. This is quite true—and a totally unconvincing argument. There will always be sightings that can never be attributed with certainty to any particular natural or manmade phenomenon, simply because the information needed to find the correct explanation is no longer available.

Hendry provides an excellent example here. As editor of the *International UFO Reporter*, published by the Center for UFO Studies, he reported a case that took place in Nevada in 1977. In trying to track down an explanation he was "by sheer luck . . . put in touch with the EPA [Environmental Protection Agency]" (Hendry, 1979, p. 8). The EPA had sent aloft a balloon that was the source of the sighting. Had Hendry not had the good fortune to make contact with the EPA, that particular sighting would probably never have been explained. It would have become one of the "irreducible minimum" that the supporters of the extraterrestrial hypothesis claim proves their position.

As we have seen, eyewitness reports of UFOs are inadequate as support for the extraterrestrial hypothesis. But what about cases involving photographs or physical traces (close encounters of the second kind), or cases where witnesses saw the craft's occupants or where humans were abducted by UFOs (close encounters of the third kind)? These types of cases will be discussed in the next chapter.

8

UFOs II: Photographs, Physical Evidence, and Abductions

If eyewitness reports are unconvincing evidence for the reality of UFOs as extraterrestrial visitors, some sort of physical evidence could certainly settle the case. If, as UFO proponents claim, the Earth is being visited so frequently by extraterrestrials, physical evidence in some form or another should exist. This chapter examines the status of the claims that such physical evidence has been found. Also examined are UFO photos and reports of humans being abducted by UFO occupants.

Photographic Evidence

Authenticated clear photographs of a UFO would be excellent evidence for UFOs as something other than hoaxes and perceptual constructions. UFO photographs certainly abound; the question is whether the extant photos are genuine. UFO photographs are extraordinarily easy to fake: a double exposure, a little trick photography, and you have a very nice-looking UFO photo or film. Several simple but impressive fake UFO photos produced by Robert Sheaffer (Sheaffer, 1981) are shown in figure 12. Sheaffer (1981) has pointed out that most people don't realize how simple trick photography is and will accept photos such as those in figure 16 as convincing evidence. As was noted in the case of the controlled UFO hoax described in chapter seven, UFO organizations are notoriously poor at spotting hoaxes, being inclined to accept statements that photos are genuine with little further investigation. Like the highly publicized UFO sightings that turn out to be explainable upon careful investigation, we will see in this section that highly publicized UFO photos said to prove the reality of the phenomenon turn out to be fakes when examined with a little care.

Most UFO photos show nothing more than indistinct blobs of light. Many such blobs appear only when the film is developed, although the photographer didn't see any UFOs when the pictures were taken. Such blobs are defects in the film, lens flares, or byproducts of film development. The numerous UFO pictures of "strange lights in the sky" that show nothing but vague blobs are photos of aircraft, seagulls, or balloons. Under certain viewing conditions, such familiar objects can lose their distinctive and familiar features and appear "mysterious," often resulting in a UFO report and photographs. Night photos of blobs of light can easily be attributed to aircraft, the planet Venus, and other such causes (Sheaffer, 1981; Menzel and Taves, 1977). To be of value, a UFO picture should show at least some structure in the UFO and should have enough background to permit one to judge the relative size of the UFO, its distance from other objects in the picture, and—especially if successive photos are obtained—its speed and direction. Only a tiny minority of UFO photos contain such information. They are the best photographic evidence for the reality of UFOs.

One of the most famous UFO photos is reproduced in figure 13. It is widely cited by pro-UFO groups as excellent evidence for UFOs. It would be—if it were genuine. But this photograph is a fake. The photo was allegedly taken on board a Brazilian naval training ship in January 1958. The photographed UFO was said to be seen by many of the vessel's crew. The photographer was one Almiro Barauna who, by an amazing coincidence, was a trick photographer who had previously made fake UFO photos to illustrate an article titled "A Flying Saucer Haunted Me at Home" (Sheaffer, 1981). Sheaffer also points out that the crew of the vessel, upon investigation, said they had not seen the photographed object. Much is made of the fact that the film was developed on board ship and under supervision, but this would not have prevented a double exposure in which the UFO was photographed before boarding the ship, the film rewound, and the terrain photographed from the ship.

A famous set of UFO photos was taken in August 1965 by Rex Heflin in Santa Ana, California. One is shown in figure 14. The photos were allegedly taken through the window of Heflin's truck. At first, he reported shooting only three photos, but several weeks later a fourth turned up. His explanation was that three photos were "enough for one day" (Sheaffer, 1981, p. 57). This is very suspicious behavior and should be considered as a strong hint of a possible hoax. After all, if four photos were taken originally, there would be no reason not to show them all when making the report. Other aspects of this case are also most suspicious. The photos were taken with a Polaroid camera, but the original prints have disappeared. Heflin claims that they were taken away by men from NORAD (North American Air Defense Command) two days after he reported the sighting. NORAD denies sending any investigators to take the photographs, and Heflin did not ask for a receipt for photographs that, if genuine, would be among the most important in the history of science. Further, the road with cars on it seen in the photograph is the Santa Ana Freeway—hardly a deserted stretch. Yet, no one else reported seeing this UFO, which, if the photographs are genuine, was flying and hovering in plain view almost directly over the road.

One UFO organization, Ground Saucer Watch (GSW), has branded the Heflin photos a deliberate hoax, based on computer enhancement of the photos (Sheaffer, 1981). The enhancement on a set of excellent duplicate prints reveals that "in the first of the three UFO photos, which shows the object at its minimum distance from the camera, the object is not in focus, as it is in the other two. Distant objects, however, are in focus in all three. This strongly suggests that the object was small and extremely close to the camera" (Sheaffer, 1981, p. 57). The enhancement also showed similar findings for two other photos. Finally, and most damningly, the enhancement showed traces of a very thin string from which the UFO is hanging. Once again, careful investigation has shown that what once was accepted as a genuine UFO photograph is a fake. This case shows the importance of considering all available evidence before reaching a decision about the genuineness of alleged UFO photos. The suspicious behavior of the photographer and the lack of confirming sightings—which should have been present in abundance if the UFO were really there— both point to a hoax.

Perhaps the single most famous and, according to UFO proponents, best piece of photographic evidence for UFOs is the set of photographs taken in McMinnville, Oregon, on May 11, 1950. One of the two photos is shown in figure 15. Hall (1984, p. 88) calls the Trent photos "two of the clearest UFO photographs on record." Before considering the photographs themselves, the behavior of the Trents in regard to the photos is enough to arouse considerable suspicion. The roll of film with the two UFO photographs was not developed immediately. Rather, the Trents waited to develop the roll until the few remaining exposures had been used up. In addition, Sheaffer (1981) reports that the precious negatives were left lying around and that one interviewer found them "on the floor under the davenport where the Trent children had been playing with them" (p. 60). Sheaffer (1981, p. 59–61) has pointed out other inconsistencies in the Trents' story of how the photos were taken. He has also pointed out that the Trents are *repeaters*—people who claim to have sighted UFOs on several occasions. Mrs. Trent in particular claims to have seen UFOs several times before the photos were taken and several times since. Even UFO proponents are generally suspicious of photos taken by such repeaters and NICAP usually refused to accept any such photos as genuine.

On behavioral grounds alone, the Trent photos must be viewed as a probable hoax. An analysis of the photos themselves clinches the case as a hoax. According to the Trents' story, the photos were taken around 8 P.M. The pattern of light and shadow in the photographs shows they were really taken at about 7:30 A.M. Further, the UFO is under the same spot in the telephone wires at the top of both pictures, in spite of the fact that the camera has moved from one picture to the next. As the camera moved away from these wires, the wires and the UFO shrank in size by about the same amount. This is just the result one would obtain if one took a photograph of a small model hung from the wires.

I would agree that the Trent photos are about the "clearest" available, and that they are thus about the best photographic evidence for UFOs. This merely shows, however, the extremely poor quality of the photographic evidence. After more than thirty-five years and thousands of sightings, the best photographic evidence consists of a few grainy shots taken by trick photographers or people who claim to have had repeated experiences with UFOs. That's not very impressive evidence, to say the least.

It should be remembered at this point that excellent photographs exist of rare events. The photos of the airline crashes in Chicago in 1979 and San Diego in 1978 come to mind. Both clearly show airliners falling from the sky—an extremely rare event, but the photos are sharp and clear and show every horrible detail. Such photos exist because Americans carry their cameras everywhere and are almost always ready to take a picture. But in spite of this, there is no UFO photo that can be considered genuine showing anything other than vague shapes or blobs of light.

To the skeptic this total lack of photographic evidence points to one conclusion—UFOs don't exist. UFO proponents, however, interpret the situation differently. Admitting that the lack of photographic evidence is most odd, Hynek and Vallee (1975) go on to conclude that UFOs are a "jealous phenomenon" that doesn't *want* to be photographed. Further, UFOs somehow know when someone has a camera and selectively appear only to those who have left their Nikons at home. It should be noted that this is yet another example of an irrefutable hypothesis.

UFO films

If UFO photos are rare, films are still rarer. One film received a great deal of media coverage when it was shown on the nationally syndicated television program "PM Magazine" in February 1983. The film was allegedly made near Woonsocket, Rhode Island, during September 1968. The photographer was Harold Trudel, who had taken numerous UFO photos during the 1960s. These photographs have apparently not been taken seriously even by UFO proponents. Interestingly, the 1968 film, which shows a tube-shaped object below a tree branch, wasn't made public until 1982 because of little public interest in UFOs. Emery (1982–83) reports that the negative for the film is missing and that only about twenty-five feet of film exist, even though the film was part of a fifty-foot reel. Trudel says he doesn't know what happened to the rest of the film. It's clear that the film is a fake made by hanging some type of tube, probably a cardboard tube from a roll of paper towels, from the overhanging tree branch and then filming it. The object bobs up and down in the film as well as back and forth. Computer enhancement shows it to be very small and very close to the camera (Emery, 1982–83). Much of this information was made available to "PM Magazine" by Emery, who was asked to comment on the film before it aired. Yet the claim was made on the air that "this is no hoax," and an interview with Emery in which he put forth the simple explanation was not used. In this instance "PM Magazine" wilfully deceived its audience. As will be seen later, this is but one example of the often unethical behavior of the media where UFO claims are concerned.

Another set of UFO films was taken late in December 1978 off New Zealand. This was during a flap of UFO sightings in New Zealand in late 1978 and early 1979. The films are unclear; one sees bright blobs of light jumping about with seemingly random jumps and bounces. They were shot at night from an aircraft with no background available to provide a frame of reference for the objects. Sheaffer (1981, chapter 21) has discussed these films and the New Zealand flap in detail. The sightings can best be attributed to squid fishing fleets, which use extremely bright lights at night to attract squid to their nets. These lights are visible from great altitude. Venus also played a role in the sightings, and one film shows nothing more than that planet. The several films were sold at high prices to CBS, for the "CBS Evening News"; ABC, for "Good Morning America"; and the BBC. The films that are not of Venus simply show a jumpy, fuzzy image of the reflection of the lights of the squid fishing fleet over which the aircraft was flying. Sheaffer (1981, chapter 21) and Klass (1983, chapters 25–27) have provided detailed analyses of the New Zealand sightings and films. The reader is referred to these sources for further information.

Astronaut UFO sightings and photos

It is difficult to think of a more highly trained and credible potential UFO witness than an astronaut. UFOs seen in space would be even more impressive than ground sightings since several possible sources of misidentification are not found in space (i.e., aircraft and weather balloons).

The UFO literature is replete with alleged astronaut UFO sightings and alleged pictures of UFOs taken by astronauts. Nowhere in the UFO literature, however, does one find such a high level of outright fraud and deception, not on the astronauts' part, but on the part of those who have knowingly distorted astronauts' reports and doctored official pictures. Oberg (1977b, 1978–79a, 1982) has conducted extensive research on the astronaut UFO sightings and pictures and has concluded that ". . . the compelling conclusion of the first serious analysis of all the astronaut UFO reports is that every one of them is false. Those that originated from the astronauts themselves were distorted in the UFO press, even as ordinary explanations became obvious" (Oberg, 1977a, p. 7). Several representative astronaut sightings and photos will be described here. The interested reader should consult Oberg's work for further details and explanations for the other sightings.

Hynek and Vallee (1975, p. 64) reprint a list of astronaut UFO sightings compiled by UFO researcher Jim Fawcett. The following report is of a sighting said to have taken place during the Gemini 12 mission in November 1966. "Jim Lovell and Edwin Aldrin saw four UFOs linked in a row. Both spacemen said the objects were not stars." The objects certainly weren't stars, but that doesn't mean they were UFOs or flying saucers. Oberg (1977a) has traced this alleged sighting and found the original debriefing document that gives the entire report of this event. The following quotation is from the document titled *GT-12 Astronaut Debriefing* and occurs on pages K/3, 4: "During the last EVA we discarded, in addition to the ELSE [life support system], three bags. About 2, maybe 3 or possibly 4 orbits later at sunrise condition, we looked out again and saw 4 objects lined up in a row and they weren't stars I know. They must have been these same things we tossed overboard." By selectively eliminating the astronauts' own explanation for what they saw, Fawcett, as well as Hynek and Vallee, have misled their readers into thinking that the sighting is more mysterious than it was.

Oberg (1977a, p. 23) gives another example of Fawcett's unreliability and therefore of the general unreliability of those who manufacture astronaut UFO sightings. This sighting is said to have taken place during the Mercury 7 mission of May, 1962 and to have resulted in a photograph. "Scott Carpenter reported that he had what looked like a good shot of a saucer," we are told, and the photograph was "of a classical saucer-shaped UFO with a dome that followed his capsule." Oberg (1977a, p. 23) comments, "In fact, the photographs show an entirely ordinary object: a space balloon ejected from the capsule for tracking practice. The balloon did not inflate but spun in a limp oblong sack. The flight schedule and the voice transmissions confirm this unexciting explanation." Again, the sensational reports of astronaut UFO sightings and photos turn out to be the product of deliberate deceit on the part of some UFO proponents.

Usually such deceit is limited to small-circulation UFO magazines and books published by UFO enthusiasts who don't bother to check their facts. However, one forged astronaut UFO photo made its way into a major American science magazine. The magazine is *Science Digest*, now defunct, published by Hearst Corporation. The phony photograph appeared in an article alleging a massive UFO cover-up by the government (Berliner, 1977). As a photograph, it doesn't show much—just a view of the northern hemisphere, taken from Apollo 11 during its July 1969 mission. At the top of the picture, above the planet, is a small white blob which is described as an "unidentified object." The picture is said to have been obtained from the National Aeronautics and Space Administration (NASA). The object is said to be evidence of an official UFO cover-up because current prints of the same shot obtained from NASA do not show the white blob. They do show a piece of insulation debris in another location, but this piece of insulation does not appear in the *Science Digest* photo. *Science Digest* editor Daniel Button believed the article caused NASA to retouch the photos. He said, "My suspicion is right now that NASA has changed its story and altered its negatives and prints" (Oberg and Sheaffer, 1977–78, p. 44). There is one major problem with this theory: NASA prints of this shot obtained well *before* the *Science Digest* article don't show the white blob either. They do show the piece of debris. Has NASA somehow been able to locate and change every print of this shot ever released? What an effective cover-up!

Physical Evidence

Even better than photographs as evidence for the reality of UFOs as spacecraft would be a chunk of metal from one, preferably inscribed in some unknown writing, "Planet #5, Alpha Centauri." As the reader might expect by now, claims have been made that pieces of UFOs have been found. The reader will not be surprised to learn that these claims are unfounded. Sheaffer (1981, p. 25–26) describes a piece of magnesium that was said to come from a UFO seen in Brazil in 1957. The Aerial Phenomena Research Organization (APRO) had the metal tested, and stated it was so pure that it could not possibly have been of human or earthly manufacture. The Condon Committee tested the metal later and found that, in fact, it was much less pure than magnesium that could be produced by technology available in 1940. This fact has not prevented UFO proponents from continuing to claim the metal as evidence for the extraterrestrial hypothesis. Sheaffer (1981, p. 26) reports that APRO's research director claims that "we can say it is an authentic fragment, beyond any reasonable doubt, of a UFO" because the sample contains no mercury and a 1940 sample of industrial magnesium did. Where did the sample come from in the first place? It was sent anonymously to the society columnist of a Rio de Janeiro paper with a note describing the explosion of a UFO over a nearby beach.

Other physical evidence is sometimes said to accompany UFO sightings. "Angel hair," a soft, wispy, diaphanous material made up of extremely fine strands, is one such piece of evidence that is reported from time to time. It turns out to be masses of spider web used by some species of spider to allow their eggs to travel on the wind over great distances (Menzel, 1972). The size of these webs can often be quite large—then the webs themselves are responsible for both a UFO sighting and the so-called physical evidence (Menzel, 1972).

Physical effects, as well as hard evidence, have been attributed to UFOs by witnesses. The stalled car is one of the most common. The usual scenario is that a UFO appears and the witness reports that the car he or she was driving stalled at about the same time. UFO proponents explain that, somehow, the strong magnetic field that powers the UFO interferes with the car's electrical system, causing the stall. It is possible to test such an explanation. Any magnetic field strong enough to cause such a disruption of an automobile's electrical system would leave clear traces in the metal of the engine. The Condon Committee (Condon, 1969) studied two cars that allegedly stalled because of proximity to UFOs. In neither case could any change in the magnetic characteristics of the metal of the engine be found. Had the automobiles actually been exposed to magnetic fields strong enough to cause electrical system failure, such changes would have been clear and easy to detect.

What causes these seemingly UFO-related stalls? Most likely the excitement of the witness. Emotional arousal leads to poorer performance of many manual tasks (Welford, 1976). Under the conditions of extreme emotional arousal experienced by many UFO witnesses, people become much less able to engage in manual tasks such as shifting gears properly. Improper shifting can result in a stall.

Another explanation for the stalls is that witnesses incorrectly attribute normal engine failures to the UFO. Perhaps the car stalls every other day or so. When no UFO is present, the stall isn't thought to be anything other than an annoyance. But when the stall coincidentally happens when a UFO is seen, then the stall is suddenly transformed into something mysterious, and is attributed to the UFO. Similar incorrect attributions of engine failures were noted in England during World War II in areas where radar was being used. Radar was then top secret, and residents near radar towers had no idea what the towers were for. They began complaining that the towers were causing their cars to stall, although it is impossible for radar to cause engine failure. When the true purpose of the radar towers was revealed, the reports of mysterious stalling promptly stopped (Condon, 1969).

The Tunguska Event

An interstellar ship develops engine trouble. It drops out of hyperspace and the captain finds himself (herself? itself?) near a planet. A quick scan shows that the planet is inhabited by intelligent beings who have not yet learned the secret of space flight. Nonetheless, the situation is desperate, so the decision is made to land in a relatively uninhabited area to make repairs. Just as the ship is entering the planet's atmosphere, a catastrophe occurs, and the ship explodes with the force of many nuclear bombs. The few primitive inhabitants in the area look up in wonder. Years later, scientific expeditions to the site reveal to the natives of the planet clear evidence of the spaceship's explosion and, thereby, of the existence of extraterrestrial space-traveling beings.

UFO enthusiasts claim this story is not science fiction but a true description of what happened over Siberia on June 30, 1908. (Some authors give the date as June 22, which was the Russian date. In 1908 Russia had not yet converted to the Gregorian calendar.)

Something clearly happened in Siberia that day in 1908. When the first scientific expedition arrived in the area in the late 1920s, much devastation was found—even after nearly 20 years. Trees had been blown down for miles around "ground zero." But those who argue that the Tunguska event was caused by an exploding UFO fabricate evidence to support their explanation and selectively omit evidence that argues against the UFO explanation.

If a nuclear-powered UFO were the cause of the Tunguska event, one would expect to find abnormally high levels of radioactivity in the area. In their 1976 book *The Fire Came By*, television drama critics Thomas Atkins and John Baxter state that high levels of radioactivity consistent with the exploding-UFO hypothesis have been found at the site. Erich von Däniken (1970) says the explosion "must have been a nuclear one" (p. 147). Oberg (1978-79b) and Story (1976, chapter 10) have both reviewed the evidence on this point. In fact, their reviews show that no abnormal radioactivity is present at the Tunguska site. Reports of high levels of radioactivity are due to Russian physicist Aleksey Zolotov who has "organized several college expeditions to the Tunguska site and made a series of announcements of 'abnormal radioactivity', followed by embarrassed retractions" (Oberg, 1978-79b, p. 52).

The usual scientific explanation of the Tunguska explosion is that a meteorite entered the Earth's atmosphere and exploded before striking the ground. This explanation would demand that a crater be found, and UFO proponents point out that no crater was ever found. That's true. But a group of ten craters was found, all at the center of the blast area, with sizes ranging from 30 to 160 feet across and an average depth of 10 feet (Story, 1976). This is just what would be expected from the explosion of a large meteorite that produced smaller chunks that then struck the ground.

UFO proponents also claim that no trace of a meteorite has ever been found. But meteorites are generally composed of nickel and iron, and a high concentration of tiny nickel-iron fragments about 5 millimeters in size has been found at the center of the blast zone (Story, 1976). Larger fragments are probably buried beneath the wet, swampy surface of the marshy area that makes up the Tunguska site.

Close Encounters of the Third Kind

UFO reports in which the witnesses either see the occupants of the UFO or are actually abducted by a UFO are certainly the most dramatic. In the 1950s such individuals were referred to as "contactees" and their stories were not taken seriously even by most UFO organizations. Things changed in the early 1960s with what is still the most famous CE III—Betty and Barney Hill's alleged abduction by UFO occupants. This case was brought to the public's attention by John Fuller's (1966) *The Interrupted Journey* and his sensational series of articles in *Look* magazine.

The standard version of what has become almost a legend in UFO circles has the Hills driving back to their home in Exeter, New Hampshire, from Montreal on the night of September 19, 1961. While driving through New Hampshire's White Mountains, they spot a UFO. It begins to follow their car. Barney Hill stops the car to get a better look at the UFO and sees windows in the object. Through the windows he sees the faces of the occupants. Frightened, he climbs back in the car and drives home, fearing capture. The Hills arrive home two hours later than normal and cannot account for the missing two hours. A week or so later Betty Hill begins to dream about being abducted and physically examined by UFO occupants. Several years later the Hills consult a psychiatrist because of marital problems. Under hypnosis, both the Hills tell separate, but mutually confirming, stories of being abducted and examined by the occupants of the UFO that had chased them several years previously. This period of examination accounts for the lost two hours. Betty is able to draw a "star map" that shows the major trade routes through the stars used by the civilization that built the UFO that abducted them. The map is said to be almost identical to a group of stars that Betty could not have known. Finally, the legend goes, government records show that the UFO was tracked on several different radars that night. Betty Hill has claimed that seven separate radar confirmations of the UFO are known (Sheaffer, 1981, p. 38).

This report is indeed impressive, if true. But, as is so often the case with UFO reports, the description presented to the public by credulous writers and investigators is very different from that which emerges after careful investigation.

The first question one can ask about this report concerns the identity of the object Betty first saw and later concluded was a UFO following the car. Sheaffer (1981) shows quite convincingly that it was the planet Jupiter. He points out that on the night of September 19, 1961, there were three bright objects visible in the night sky in northern New Hampshire. One was the moon; the other two were the planets Saturn and Jupiter. In her report Betty Hill says that she saw the moon, one bright "star" and the UFO. She does not report seeing two bright "stars." This is a crucial point. If a real UFO had been present that night, she would have seen *four* objects in the sky—the moon, the two "stars," and the UFO. But she saw only three objects.

What about the "lost" two hours that later take on so much importance as the time during which the abduction took place? An examination of the Hills' reports regarding their time of arrival home in the months and years following the incident shows them to be extremely inconsistent (Sheaffer, 1981; Klass, 1974). The fact that two hours were allegedly missing from their lives was not even noticed by the Hills until a few weeks after the incident and after extensive questioning by pro-UFO investigators (Sheaffer, 1981).

How does one account for the Hills' reports of the abduction that were revealed under hypnosis? It is commonly believed that hypnosis allows lost memories to be retrieved. Actual research on hypnosis shows a far different picture: Memories retrieved under hypnosis are even more unreliable than normal memories. Hilgard (1980-81) reports that he "implanted in a subject a false memory of an experience connected with a bank robbery that never occurred, and the person found the experience so vivid that he was able to select from a series of photographs a picture of the man he thought had robbed the bank" (p. 25). Similar fictitious memories can be created in hypnotized subjects simply by asking leading questions that presume that an event occurred, even if it didn't (Laurence and Perry, 1983). Claims that hypnosis enhances memory in real-world situations, such as crime reports, also turn out to be incorrect (Smith,

1983). Hypnosis is used in crime situations only after several nonhypnotic sessions have been conducted with the witness to try to retrieve more details from memory. Such repeated attempts at recall themselves enhance memory, and hypnosis adds nothing to this enhancement (Dywan and Bowers, 1983; Nogrady, McConkey, and Perry, 1985). Consider two groups of individuals who are asked to recall a particular incident. Both groups are quizzed three times without hypnosis. On the fourth attempt at recall, one group is hypnotized, the other isn't. In this sort of study, recall on the fourth attempt is better than on the first for the hypnotized group—but it is equally improved for the nonhypnotized group. It is the repeated recall attempts, not the hypnosis, that are responsible for the improved recall (Smith, 1983). What hypnosis does do—and this is especially relevant to the UFO cases—is to greatly increase hypnotized subjects' confidence that their hypnotically induced memories are true. This increase in confidence occurs for both correct and incorrect memories (Nogrady, McConkey, and Perry, 1985). Thus, hypnosis can create false memories, but the individual will be especially convinced that those memories are true. People repeating such false memories will seem credible because they really believe their false memories are true. Their belief, of course, does not indicate whether the memory is actually true or false. Hilgard (1980-81, p. 25) has concluded that "the use of hypnotic recall as evidence in UFO abduction cases is an abuse of hypnosis" because "abundant evidence exists that fabrication can take place under hypnosis." Klass (1980-81) has noted examples of such fabrication in several abduction stories.

The psychiatrist who hypnotized the Hills was asked whether he believed that their abduction and examination stories were true. He replied, "Absolutely not!" (Klass, 1974, p. 253). The psychiatrist had told John Fuller the same thing, but Fuller somehow failed to include this relevant expert opinion in his book or articles

The reports elicited under hypnosis were very likely simply the retelling of the dreams that Betty had had and which she had described to Barney in some detail. Betty had also read some sensational UFO literature after the incident, and the reports therein could easily have formed the basis for her "memories" related under hypnosis.

Betty Hill's claim of multiple radar confirmations of the UFO also disappear, when examined closely. The documents that she says prove her claim have mysteriously disappeared. Only one radar report of an unknown target took place that night. This was at Pease Air Force Base in Portsmouth, New Hampshire, on the coast miles from the place where the Hills saw the UFO. The one unidentified contact that night at Pease was on the base's Precision Approach Radar, which looks directly down a runway and is used to guide planes landing on the runway. The object was four miles out and was described as a "weak" target. Sheaffer (1981) points out that this type of radar is so sensitive that it sometimes detects birds. More importantly, the base Airport Surveillance Radar, which scans the entire area, showed no unidentified target that night.

Betty Hill's "star map" is often claimed to be the best evidence for the reality of the Hills' close encounter. How could Betty possibly have drawn such an accurate map of stars that she didn't even know existed unless, as she claimed, she saw the map when she was aboard the UFO? The map consists of twenty-six dots representing stars, some of which are connected by lines representing trade routes between the stars. Several attempts have been made to match the pattern of dots on the map to patterns of actual stars. Great success has been claimed for these attempts but, as usual, the claims fall short on examination.

Saunders (1975) reports that one attempt to match the map to a pattern of actual stars is so accurate that such a match would be expected to occur by chance only once in one thousand times. What Saunders fails to mention to his readers is that the seemingly impressive match uses only fifteen (57 percent) of the twenty-six stars. Eleven (43 percent) of the stars on the original map are simply ignored, apparently because they don't fit. Errors occur in this match as well (Sheaffer, 1981). There is an incorrect orientation between the supposed "home star" of the UFO occupants and a nearby star in the match. That is, the orientation in the match turns out to be quite different from that on Betty Hill's original map. Soter and Sagan (1976) have noted a further problem with the match proposed by Saunders. If one removes the drawn-in lines on both the match and the original map, the resemblance disappears. The lines impose an illusory similarity which is not present when considering the actual stars alone.

The Milky Way Galaxy consists of approximately 100 billion stars. Out of that number, there will be, by pure chance alone, many sets of twenty-six stars that match the pattern on Betty Hill's map with impressive accuracy. If enough time were spent, one could probably find thousands of such matches. They would, of course, prove nothing, as the same number of matches could be made to a random pattern of twenty-six dots on paper. The much-discussed "star map" appears, after close inspection, to be nothing more than just such a random pattern produced by Betty Hill's fertile imagination.

In the 23 years since her close encounter (her husband Barney died in 1969), Betty Hill has become a guru of the UFO movement. Her close encounters have continued, multiplied, and are described in a short item in the Fall 1978 issue of the *Skeptical Inquirer* (p. 14):

Now that Mrs. Hill is retired, she divides her time between giving UFO lectures and watching UFOs land at the semi-secret "landing spot" she claims to have discovered in New Hampshire. Mrs. Hill's recent claims are straining even the almost boundless credulity of the UFO groups, Mrs. Hill claims that the UFOs come in to land several times a week; they have become such a familiar sight that she is now calling them by name. Sometimes the aliens get out and do calisthenics before taking off again, she asserts. One UFO reportedly zapped a beam at her that was so powerful that it "blistered the paint on my car." Mrs. Hill also reports that window-peeping flying saucers sometimes fly from house to house late at night in New England, shine lights in the windows, and then move on when the occupants wake up and turn on the lights.

The same item reports that when at her secret UFO landing site, Mrs. Hill is unable to distinguish street lights from UFOs.

On October 20, 1975, NBC-TV broadcast a made-for-television movie based on the Hills' close encounter. It was called *The UFO Incident.* In the months following this broadcast, numerous similar close encounters were reported (Sheaffer, 1981). They contained the same major elements as those found in the Hill story and in the movie: abduction and medical examination by aliens. (I've always wondered why the aliens were so interested in and ignorant of human anatomy and physiology. A species capable of sending ships across the galaxy certainly ought to be able to obtain a few basic anatomy and physiology texts without kidnapping innocent earthlings.) The cases also featured missing periods of time, just as in the Hill case. Sheaffer (1981, chapter 5) described several of these cases. It is difficult to take them seriously, but they are taken very seriously by the UFO groups. In their book *Abducted* James and Coral Lorenzen, founders of APRO, worry that too many teenagers are spending too much time in deserted areas. This is dangerous because it is from just such areas that most UFO abductions occur. "Each and every inhabitant of this earth is a potential victim" (Lorenzen and Lorenzen, 1970, p. 210), we are told.

Reports of UFO abductions continue to be made. One of the most productive "finders" of abducted individuals is Dr. Leo Sprinkle, a psychologist at the University of Wyoming. He hypnotizes witnesses who have seen UFOs and finds, in a surprisingly high number of cases, that the witnesses were abducted. Strangely, the witnesses usually are unaware of having been abducted until Dr. Sprinkle, who is apparently unaware of the problems with hypnosis noted above, has hypnotized them.

The Psychology of Abduction Stories

In the past year or so there has been a radical shift of focus among UFO proponents. New sightings are no longer of much interest. Rather, graphic reports of close encounters of the third kind, up to and including sexual relations between humans and UFO occupants, have captured the movement's attention. An early, and generally little-noticed, item along these lines was a book by Ruth Montgomery, whose earlier works had described the psychic wonders of Jeane Dixon (Montgomery, 1965). In *Aliens Among Us*, Montgomery (1985) contended, based on numerous personal reports she had received, that the "space brothers" had already arrived and were living here on earth among us, disguised as humans. Montgomery's aliens were beneficent beings, here to help humanity through troubled times.

The aliens reported in two very recent books (Strieber, 1987a; Hopkins, 1987) are anything but friendly space brothers. Whitley Strieber is an author of horror fiction whose best-known book, until his *Communion* hit the best-seller lists, was *Wolfen* (1978), made into a movie in 1980. *Communion* is the "true story" of Strieber's encounters with and abduction by some type of alien beings. During his terrifying experience, which began in December 1986, Strieber had a needle inserted into his head and an instrument of some sort had been inserted into his anus.

Both Klass (1988) and Swords (1987) have critiqued Strieber's accounts of his experience. Klass' (1988) book is especially valuable as it covers the entire subject of UFO abductions. Both critiques note that Strieber's life has been filled with highly unusual and bizarre occurrences. When he was twelve, for example, he was assaulted by a skeleton on a motorcycle; earlier, he had had a threatening encounter with Mr. Peanut. In the early 1970s, he awoke in the night and saw a tiny humanoid figure run by him holding a red light. In 1985 he was awakened while staying at his cabin in the Catskills and found the place surrounded by a strange blue light glowing in the fog. In all, Swords (1987) lists thirty-three separate highly unusual experiences of this sort reported as fact in *Communion* and finds no independent confirmation for fully thirty of them. For three experiences, the "confirmations" confirm only the most mundane aspects of the event. For example, Strieber reported that in 1982 he had a series of encounters with a mysterious white figure. A babysitter confirmed seeing a youngster in a white sheet outside a window. Strieber's wife Anne "clearly says that she didn't see anyone or anything, just was poked while asleep; and that W.S. first started talking about little white things. All her subsequent 'description' of a being was in response to imagining what it *might* look like" (Swords, 1987, p. 5). Strieber uses as further confirmation of some of the events he claims to have experienced the testimony of his son, born in 1979 and seven years old in 1986. Swords (1987, p. 5) properly excludes the child's comments from the class of confirming evidence "because of the powerful potential for idea suggestibility which exists" between father and son.

Strieber is clearly obsessed with intruders, an obsession that apparently began long before he had his encounter with the aliens in 1986. He admits that late at night he often searches for possible intruders by "opening closets and looking under beds" and "especially [in] corners and crannies. I always looked down low in the closets, seeking something small" (Strieber, 1987a, p. 101). He also has elaborate burglar alarms in both his New York City apartment and the cabin in the mountains.

Klass (1988) shows that Strieber has a history of telling stories he claims to be true but which turn out to be false. In an interview published in Winter's (1985) book of interviews with famous horror fiction writers, Strieber described in graphic detail being present and nearly shot in 1966 when Charles Whitman killed many people in his sniper attack from the Texas Tower on the campus of the University of Texas in Austin. In *Communion,* however, Strieber admits that he was not present at the tragedy. Sprinkled throughout the book are other recantations of stories Strieber previously held out as true.

From reading *Communion* and hearing Strieber on several television and radio talk shows, I believe that he really believes that the encounters he says he had with the aliens were real. He is, however, not at all sure that the creatures are "only" members of an advanced civilization. He thinks they represent something even stranger, perhaps "mankind's first encounter with a quantum reality in the new macrocosm" (Strieber, 1987b, p. 8). He also feels that "the abduction experience is *primarily* a mystical experience" and that following the experience "spiritual and paranormal life events" become more common (p. 7).

Strieber's book is the report of only his own abduction experience. Bud Hopkins, a New York artist, argues in his *Intruders* (1987) that many other people have been abducted by aliens as part of an alien plan to cross-breed with humans. The abduction victims whether male or female, are commonly sexually abused. Hopkins argues that many people who have been abducted do not remember the event consciously, so hypnosis is necessary to bring their terrible experience to consciousness. Hopkins makes wide use of hypnosis, even hypnotizing alleged abduction victims himself, although he has no professional training in psychology, psychiatry, or hypnosis. This being the case, it is not surprising that he either is unaware of or chooses to ignore the fact that testimony induced by hypnosis is extremely unreliable and that hypnotized individuals are highly suggestible. In fact, he frequently uses leading questions in his questioning of hypnotized abduction victims. The often colorful and creative stories that Hopkins hears when his subjects are thus hypnotized are, therefore, worthless as evidence for the reality of the events recounted.

Other factors further detract from the credibility of Hopkins's book. Hopkins says he is a skeptic, but then defines the term in a most unusual way. For him, a skeptic is one who cannot "deny the possibility of anything" (p. xiii). He naively accepts at face value almost anything an alleged abduction victim says, without bothering to check on those claims that might be able to be verified. In some cases, he goes beyond what the victim says to find evidence of an abduction, even when the victim doesn't claim to have been abducted. Klass (1987-88) highlights two such cases of Hopkins's highly uncritical attitude toward his evidence. These are the cases of a woman named "Andrea" and Kathie Davis, the latter being the case that Hopkins feels is the strongest one in the book.

When Andrea was thirteen years old, she had never had sex with a man. She did dream of having sex with an odd-looking bald fellow with strange eyes. Later, she told Hopkins, she discovered she was pregnant. She had an abortion and, before the abortion, the doctor examined her and confirmed that she was still a virgin. Hopkins reports no attempt to locate the doctor in question to verify this story.

Kathie Davis's story also involves a mysterious pregnancy. Two months after she discovered she was pregnant, she suddenly was no longer pregnant, although she had not miscarried. Later she had a dream in which she saw many "little grey guys" and a beautiful female baby-like "elf." She came to believe that she had a daughter, but one to whom she had not given birth. Under repeated hypnosis, Hopkins extracted further details, including an incident in which the aliens had abducted Kathie and removed her fetus from her, thus explaining her disappearing pregnancy. Kathie and some other individuals who Hopkins believes have been abducted refer to their experiences as "dreams." Given the nature of the experiences, this is certainly a most reasonable view. But it is one that Hopkins does not accept. He argues that saying the experiences were dreams is just a way for the individuals to protect themselves from the true terror of their experiences. This should at once be recognized for the nonfalsifiable hypothesis that it is. There is no way to prove that these experiences were just dreams. Even if a squadron of flying saucers landed tomorrow at noon on the White House lawn and the occupants denied that they had ever abducted any humans, it could, and probably would, be argued that they were engaged in a cover-up.

What is one to make of the stories told by the people Hopkins has found who report being abducted by aliens and then having various sexual and medical indignities performed upon them against their will? It seems clear that they are not just lying to achieve publicity or money. Those few I have seen on various television talk shows appeared to believe what they were saying. This included one woman who told of being abducted when she was a child. At that time the aliens implanted some sort of metal device high up in her nose. Years later, when she was an adolescent, she was re-abducted and the metal device removed. Unfortunately, during the years the device was in her nose no one, including doctors, noticed it, and she didn't mention it to anyone. Such stories are simply unbelievable. But why do seemingly normal people tell these tales? A common misconception about the nature of sanity and insanity holds that a person is either crazy or sane, with little ground in between the two conditions. That stories so unbelievable are told by individuals who appear to be quite rational understandably adds to their credibility. In fact, psychological disturbances come in numerous shades and varieties. This point is vital in understanding the psychology of those who report being abducted.

The real question is whether those who report being abducted show any psychological abnormalities that can account for their reports, especially when other factors are taken into account. It has not been possible to test all those who make such reports. However, the Fund for UFO Research has provided an extremely valuable service by having nine individuals who reported being abducted studied by a professional psychologist. The nine were given a battery of psychological tests by Dr. Elizabeth Slater who, at the time she gave and interpreted the test results, was unaware that the nine all claimed to have been abducted. Thus, her findings were not biased by any preconceived notions she might have had about the psychological health of individuals who make such reports.

Slater's (1985a) findings indicated that the nine individuals were certainly not generally crazy or psychotic. But they weren't normal, either. She said "in lay terms, several individuals involved in this project might be labeled downright 'eccentric' or 'odd'" (Slater, 1985a, p. 19). They also had low self-esteem and were found to have "considerable sensitivity . . . to fantasy" (p. 20). Stress brought out even more disordered behavior: "When under stress, all nine subjects are predisposed for impulsivity either in the form of acting out behaviors or for intense and disorganizing emotional storms. Moreover, under stressful conditions, at least six of the nine show a potential for more or less *transient psychotic experiences involving a loss of reality testing* along with confused and disordered thinking that can be bizarre" (Slater, 1985a, p. 21, emphasis added). In other words, at times these individuals have great difficulty in distinguishing reality from fantasy.

After Slater had written her final report on the subjects she tested, she was informed of their abduction reports and wrote an addendum to her original report (Slater, 1985b). In this addendum she argues that an individual would have to be very seriously disturbed (i.e., be schizophrenic or suffering from multiple personality) if the disturbance was going to be able to account for the reported abductions. Since these individuals were not that seriously disturbed, Slater argues that the degree of disturbance she did find cannot account for the abduction reports. Unfortunately, although Slater is a professional psychologist, she is here adopting the naive view that an individual must be totally insane to be able to evidence, on occasion, highly bizarre behaviors and beliefs. Her own findings—that six of the individuals she tested could at times show transient psychotic episodes in which they found it difficult if not impossible to distinguish reality from fantasy—argue against this position. She also seems to accept, in the first part of the addendum, a strict dichotomy between normalcy and multiple personality. This is simply wrong: there is a continuum from normalcy to multiple personality that passes through more mild states of multiple personality known as *dissociative states* or *dissociative phenomena*. Such dissociative states explain a variety of bizarre reports from otherwise seemingly sane individuals. A case in point is that of medium Helene Smith (see chapter three) who claimed that, while in a trance, she was controlled by the ghost of a dead Martian. She even drew pictures of Martian landscapes. Slater herself, later in her addendum, seems to acknowledge both the existence of such mild dissociative states and their importance in understanding the abduction reports when she says, correctly, "one would want to know more about the potential for dissociative phenomena in these subjects" (Slater, 1985b, p. 39).

In and of itself, then, the results of Slater's testing provide a sufficient picture of psychopathology to account for the abduction reports. Other factors further strengthen the argument that these experiences are not real but are the result of psychological processes such as dreams, fantasies, and psychotic thinking that the individuals, at least part of the time, are not able to distinguish from external reality. (Remember, however, that at least part of the time they can make this vital distinction, as when Kathie Davis speaks of her dreams. Hopkins, however, doesn't accept this aspect of what his informants tell him.) The individuals who report being abducted are, as previously noted, hypnotized by Hopkins, who is untrained in hypnosis, uses leading questions, and deeply believes in the reality of the reported abductions. And what sort of people are being hypnotized? If the set of nine individuals studied by Slater form a representative sample of abduction reporters, and I believe they do, they are likely to be low in self-esteem and to have difficulty telling reality from fantasy. This is precisely the type of person who will be highly susceptible to the suggestive aspect of leading questions under hypnosis and to the suggestions, rewards, and pressures to produce detailed abduction stories that are certainly present when interacting with a committed believer such as Hopkins. Stories generated by leading questions under hypnosis can come to be seen as real by the hypnotized individual. It is thus easy to understand how, for example, a frightening dream about being abducted by a UFO can come to seem real to an individual who is repeatedly hypnotized to recall further details of the experience and is explicitly told by the hypnotist that the experience is real. If the individual already has difficulty telling reality from fantasy, the process of becoming convinced that the dream or fantasy was real will occur more rapidly. It is no rare event for someone to have a dream that, at least briefly, may seem to have really happened. In fact, almost everyone has had dreams that, upon awakening, were so vivid that it was not possible, for a while at least, to decide whether they really happened or not. Some such dreams are bland, some pleasurable, and some frightening. Most people, however, can sort out the dream and the reality after a few moments.

In his introduction to the report on Slater's testing of the nine alleged abduction victims, Westrum (1985) comments on the fact that some individuals do not report abductions under hypnosis. He believes this is fatal to any theory that suggests that the abduction reports are due to psychological aberrations combined with the effects of suggestion, and are not reports of actual events. This is nonsense. The fact that hypnosis did not elicit such stories in some people is certainly not evidence that it wasn't responsible in other cases. To use a medical analogy, if one gave identical injections of a mild flu virus to one hundred people, some would actually come down with the flu and some wouldn't. It would be absurd to argue that the fact that some people didn't get the flu following the injection meant that the illness in those who did get it wasn't caused by the injection, but by some other mysterious factor.

Westrum (1985, p. 4) also claims that "many of these cases display the symptoms of Post-Traumatic Stress Syndrome so common with Vietnam veterans" and that this shows the terrifying experiences must have been real. In her report Slater (1985a) does note that all nine individuals suffer from high levels of anxiety. However, nowhere does she suggest that it is the result of any traumatic event in their lives. If a psychologist evaluated individuals who actually suffered from post-traumatic stress syndrome, due to service in Vietnam or to actual rape, it is very likely that the symptoms would be obvious enough for direct comment.

Nonetheless, the subjects were anxious, and their anxiety was, at times, sufficient to impair their ability to deal with "practical reality" (Slater, 1985a, p. 21). Where did this anxiety come from? Part is probably due to the basic psychological makeup of this type of individual. Hopkins, however, must share the blame for increasing anxiety in those individuals he has managed to convince that they suffered real abductions. A terrifying dream or fantasy is real only for a short time, but if a misguided believer convinces an already-unstable person—especially through hypnosis—that the dream or fantasy was a real event, the terror may last a lifetime.

The Hollow Earth

Insiders in the UFO business these days are often heard to say that the belief that UFOs are extraterrestrial craft is silly. There is insufficient evidence to justify such a belief. Further, the logistics of space travel from some distant star are too difficult. (In this they agree, surprisingly, with Carl Sagan [1972] when he points out the difficulties in overcoming such obstacles to space travel as the speed of light and the amount of fuel needed.) Do these "avant garde" UFOlogists conclude from all this that UFOs exist only as perceptual constructions, misidentifications, and hoaxes? Not at all. Instead, a host of bizarre new hypotheses has sprung up to save the dedicated UFOlogist from having to admit that there is no foundation to all the reports. One UFO group based in Toronto, Ontario, called "Samisdat" believes that UFOs are really secret Nazi aircraft. Supposedly, just as World War II ended in May 1945 Hitler and all the other missing leaders of the Third Reich were whisked away by UFO to a secret Nazi hideout in the Antarctic, where they reside today, plotting the rise of the Fourth Reich. This same group also markets Nazi propaganda.

Some fundamentalist Christian groups believe that UFOs are really angels and foretell the Second Coming or Judgment Day. Of course, only those who truly believe in the UFOs will be saved when the world ends. Actually, this type of group has a longer history than might be suspected. Even in the 1950s there were groups who believed that UFOs were harbingers of the end of the world, sent to save believers. One such group was infiltrated and studied by several social psychologists who wrote a classic book on the dynamics of such a group and the group's response when the end of the world did not come as predicted (Festinger, Riecken and Schachter, 1956). As you might expect, the failure of the world to end on schedule did not suggest to several members of the group that their belief was wrong. Instead, they rationalized events to convince themselves that they had simply miscalculated. That particular group is no longer in existence, but another group that suffered several failed end-of-the-world predictions is still around: the Seventh-Day Adventist Church. This sect was founded in the 1840s when one William Miller predicted that the world would end in the year following March 21, 1843. It didn't, so Miller promptly recalculated that the end would come on October 22, 1844 (Randi, 1980). It didn't. Nonetheless, the Church is still in business.

They now contend that the end of the world is near, although they are wise enough to avoid making specific predictions about the date.

Occasionally these "end of the world" movements are financially motivated, at least in part. In the West in the late 1970s two people, variously called "Bo and Peep" or "The Two," convinced several hundred people that the world would soon end. They told their followers that they would be saved by UFOs, that to purify themselves they should give up all their worldly goods (by transferring them to Bo and Peep), and that they should follow "The Two" into the Montana wilderness.

My own favorite way-out theory of UFOs is that they come from an advanced civilization not somewhere in space but right here on earth. Where might such a civilization be hiding? Where else but inside the earth. The earth is hollow, this theory maintains, and an advanced civilization is hiding there, complete with UFOs. This hollow-earth theory is the creation of the late Ray Palmer, a science fiction writer who believed not only that the earth is hollow but also that it has a hole at the north pole through which the flying saucers come and go. And how has this hole and the hollowness of the earth escaped the notice of geologists, explorers, airline pilots, and governments? Palmer maintained that they all know about it and are involved in a giant cover-up to hide this important knowledge from the rest of the world's people. Only those few who have managed to penetrate the curtain of silence and who are trying to bring this momentous news to the public can be trusted. Gardner (1987b) describes the origin of the hollow-earth theory in some detail.

The Great UFO Cover-up

The existence of absurd beliefs like the hollow-earth theory and the fact that some people strongly believe them raise interesting questions about the distinction between charming eccentricity and certifiable craziness. Presumably, no sane individual would take seriously the ideas of Ray Palmer and his followers. But just such charges of a massive government conspiracy to hide the truth about UFOs from the American people have been made for decades by UFO proponents, all without a shred of evidence to support the charges.

The basic idea is that the government has conclusive evidence that UFOs are real extraterrestrial spacecraft and that it has had this evidence since shortly after the first modern UFOs were seen in 1947. Further, the government is hiding this evidence from the American public. Only a few dedicated UFOlogists have managed to penetrate the cloak of government secrecy to find the truth, often at considerable risk, and bring it to the attention of the public. The Central Intelligence Agency (CIA) is said to be heavily involved, along with the military and almost every other branch of government.

Before considering the evidence put forth to support this conspiracy theory, let us examine it on purely logical grounds. Logically, the conspiracy theory is absurd. Over the past several decades the government has shown its inability to keep even extremely important secrets. The Pentagon papers were leaked to the press. The power of the presidency was not enough to keep the secret of Watergate. The secret bombings in Cambodia at the end of the Vietnam war weren't secret for long. More recently, the Iran-Contra arms-for-hostages deal was revealed. And yet, over a thirty-five year period, what would be the biggest news story of the century—the discovery that we are being visited by beings from another planet—has somehow been successfully kept from thousands of military personnel and untold numbers of federal bureaucrats. If the cover-up idea were not so widely held, it could be dismissed as the paranoid fantasy that it is.

However, since it is so widely believed and used by UFO groups to explain the lack of good evidence for the existence of UFOs, the cover-up story calls for detailed examination. The alleged cover-up started in the 1950s. Those individuals lucky enough to get a good look at a UFO or to learn the "truth" about UFOs were often visited by the dreaded Men in Black (MIBs in the UFOlogical literature). At first it was felt that MIBs were agents of some secret U.S. government agency. They certainly were frightening fellows, according to UFO proponent Gray Barker (1956, p. 92). Those visited by MIBs were so frightened by them that they "turned pale and got awfully sick" and "couldn't get anything to stay on [their] stomach for three long days." The 1976 UFO Annual (p. 16) says: "This much is known about those mysterious Men in Black who show up after almost every important saucer sighting or landing; they do not represent any *known* government; their basic purpose is to discredit or terrorize eyewitnesses; and they have seized or obliterated all UFO evidence for more than 27 years!" Efficient fellows, these—and what a nifty excuse for the otherwise totally unimpressive evidence for the reality of UFOs. Obviously, this is yet another irrefutable hypothesis.

Throughout the 1950s and 1960s the UFO movement repeatedly charged that the U.S. Air Force was hiding secret files and documents that proved that UFOs were "real," that is, extraterrestrial. Later the CIA became the alleged repository for the secret files. The most far-fetched claim is that the Air Force has an entire crashed flying saucer, complete with frozen (or embalmed) remains of the occupants, hidden at Wright-Patterson Air Force Base in Ohio. Just how the UFOlogists managed to discover this secret, in spite of the MIBs and government secrecy, and why the government permits them to "blow the cover" on the most sensational secret of the century is never made clear.

In 1977, Ground Saucer Watch filed a Freedom of Information Act suit against the CIA in an attempt to force the agency to reveal all its secret UFO files. This resulted in the release of nearly 1,000 pages of materials from CIA files related to UFOs. The genesis of CIA interest in the UFO issue in the 1950s, as Klass (1983, chapter 2), points out, was the fear that Russia, "with its growing fleet of long-range bombers and its newly acquired atomic bomb, could conceivably exploit UFO-mania within the U.S. to stage a surprise attack." Not a very realistic fear, perhaps, but it certainly indicates that the CIA never took seriously the idea that UFOs are extraterrestrial.

Klass (1983) obtained copies of all the released documents. The 997 pages of documents covered a thirty-year period, from 1949 to 1979. This works out to about three pages of material per month on the topic accumulated by the CIA. Of the total material, Klass reports that about 350 pages had been classified. This means that the CIA generated "an average of only one page of classified UFO-related material per month" (p. 14). If the CIA were really involved in some sort of massive cover-up, the amount of material generated would be much greater.

The actual contents of the released documents further destroy any claims of a government cover-up. The documents included letters to and from the CIA regarding UFOs, among them letters from people inquiring about the CIA's role in the UFO cover-up and the replies. Also included were miscellaneous newspaper clippings relating to UFOs, a Russian bibliography on parapsychology, and inter-office memos on the topic.

More revealing were several secret briefings for high-level CIA officials on the topic of UFOs. One such briefing took place in August 1952 and covered several theories about the nature of UFOs. The following quotation is relevant:

> The third theory is the man from Mars—space ships—interplanetary travellers. Even though we might admit that intelligent life may exist elsewhere and that space travel is possible, there is no shred of evidence to support this theory at present. . . .
>
> The fourth theory is that now held by the Air Force, that the sightings, given adequate data, can be explained either on the basis of misinterpretation of known objects, or of as yet little understood natural phenomena.

Remember that this was a secret briefing for high-level CIA officials. As Klass puts it, it is "inconceivable" that the Air Force could have knowledge of a crashed flying saucer and still convince the CIA that they believed sightings were the result of misidentifications and such. Another declassified secret briefing paper from August 1952 states that "no debris or material evidence has ever been recovered" from a UFO sighting (Klass, 1983, p. 18).

It is true that certain items were censored by the CIA before the documents were released. But this is hardly evidence for a cover-up; what was censored were the names of individuals making UFO reports and individual employees in the government whose names appeared on the released documents. This censoring was done in conformation with Privacy Act requirements simply to protect the privacy of individuals who had communicated with the CIA on the topic.

An examination of the secret CIA papers and documents on UFOs reveals an agency mildly interested in the phenomenon but skeptical of the extraterrestrial hypothesis. These documents also clearly contradict the silly claims that the Air Force (or the CIA, the National Security Agency, or the Boy Scouts) have a flying saucer hidden somewhere. They also contradict the oft-repeated claims of a government cover-up of the "truth" about UFOs.

The Role of the Media

The fact that the released CIA documents relating to UFOs clearly showed that the claim of a government cover-up was nonsense didn't stop Ground Saucer Watch from issuing a press release stating just the opposite. A profound lack of respect for the facts is nothing new among UFO groups—especially when the facts don't fit the belief that UFOs are extraterrestrial—so GSW's "big lie" technique is not all that surprising. What is both surprising and very disturbing is that several major newspapers around the country carried GSW's press release essentially verbatim and made no attempt to check whether the astonishing statements made therein were true. The *New York Times* ran the release on January 14, 1979, under the headline "C.I.A. Papers Detail U.F.O. Surveillance." According to the story, the released CIA papers showed that "the Government has been lying to us all these years." GSW Director William Spaulding also made the absurd claim that "he has sworn statements from retired Air Force colonels that at least two U.F.O.s have crashed and been recovered by the Air Force. One crash, he said, was in Mexico in 1948 and the other was near Kingman, Ariz., in 1953. He said the retired officers claimed they got a glimpse of dead aliens who were in both cases about four feet tall with silverish complexions and wearing silver outfits that 'seemed fused to the body from the heat.'" This, then, was reported by the *New York Times* as serious news. It's obvious that the *Times* never believed a word of it; otherwise, it would have launched the biggest journalistic investigation in the history of the paper to come up with the story of the century. Where UFOs are concerned, it is almost impossible to distinguish the editorial policies and ethics of the *New York Times* or the *Washington Post* from those of the *National Enquirer* or the *Midnight Star*. The most absurd UFO reports are accepted at face value and published as news stories. Attempts are seldom made to verify the truth of the report or to seek comment from skeptical investigators.

The Committee for the Scientific Investigation of Claims of the Paranormal (CSICOP) sent out its own press release refuting the claims of GSW. Neither the *Times* nor any other paper saw fit to print it. Sheaffer (1981, p. 141) correctly sums up the situation as follows: "Wild and unfounded claims of massive UFO cover-ups are news, it seems. Reasoned refutations of such claims are not."

An excellent example of such shoddy journalism comes from the *Washington Post*, the paper that broke the Watergate story and is world-renowned for its excellent staff of investigative journalists. In its April 30, 1977, issue it ran on the front page a story on a UFO sighting by President Jimmy Carter that had occurred in Georgia in 1973. Sheaffer (1981, p. 140) pointed out to a *Washington Post* reporter who contacted him about the story that it "was not news" as the story of the sighting had appeared in several other papers, including the *National Enquirer*. Nonetheless, the story appeared on the front page and contained nothing but rehashed old news. A few days later Sheaffer, who had been working on the Carter sighting for months, positively identified the UFO that Carter had seen as the planet Venus. Sheaffer reported this to the *Washington Post*, which reported his identification in a tiny item in the gossip column in the May 9, 1977, issue. The front-page story reporting the sighting received ten times more space, while the report of the solution to the mystery was given minimal treatment.

Whatever the reasons for the perverse editorial policy of not checking UFO stories (a check would certainly be made on any major story on nonpseudoscientific or nonparanormal topics), the result is to badly mislead readers. One reason why so many people think that there is "something to" the extraterrestrial explanation for UFOs is that they "hear so much about it." By reporting as factual news stories wild, unsubstantiated, and false claims, many newspapers shirk their responsibility to correctly inform their readers.

The print media are certainly not alone in their irresponsibility where UFO stories are concerned. The electronic media are, if anything, even more irresponsible in presenting unverified and clearly false material as fact to their listeners and viewers. William Spaulding, the Ground Saucer Watch director whose incorrect claims about the released CIA documents made the *New York Times*, appeared on Tom Snyder's "Tomorrow" television show on February 2, 1979. He continued to spread his fantasies about a government cover-up and to distort the facts. NBC-TV made no attempt to have a responsible critic dispute these unfounded claims.

As noted above, the New Zealand UFO films showing nothing more than the planet Venus or the Japanese squid fishing fleet were shown on American network television. Both NBC and CBS presented such films as "real" UFO films during their evening news broadcasts. Neither made any attempt to contact responsible critics or to check whether the films showed what they purported to show.

In May 1984 a symposium titled "Edges of Science" was held at the annual meeting of the American Association for the Advancement of Science. This symposium featured UFOs among other topics. Speakers were J. Allen Hynek, James Oberg, Arthur C. Clarke, and Isaac Asimov. The symposium received considerable media coverage. Hynek appeared on ABC's "Good Morning America," but no one was invited to challenge his specious claims. United Press International (UPI) distributed two stories on the symposium over its wires. One contained twelve paragraphs, all devoted to the view that UFOs are extraterrestrial. No hint was given the reader that any other viewpoint existed. The second UPI story consisted of ten paragraphs touting the extraterrestrial hypothesis and three sentences noting that some disagree with this hypothesis. MacDougall (1983, chapter 27) has further documented that where UFOs or other pseudoscientific or paranormal topics are concerned, even otherwise respectable newspapers, television programs, and the like, sink to the lowest levels of sensationalism. Meyer (1986) makes the same point in the prestigious *Columbia Journalism Review*.

This and the preceding chapter have shown that the evidence for UFOs as extraterrestrial spacecraft "rests entirely on . . . uncorroborated human testimony" (Sheaffer, 1978-79, p. 67), the most unreliable type of evidence to be found. In nearly forty years of investigation, not one authentic photo of a UFO has been taken and not one piece of genuine debris or other physical evidence has been found. Impressive-sounding sightings are reported year after year and, year after year, when carefully examined, they disappear into the mists of misperceptions, misidentifications, and hoaxes. This has no effect on true believers; there is always another case to be sloppily investigated and trumpeted in the media as—finally—the conclusive proof that UFOs are "real." Upon investigation, this new case joins the multitude of others that were caused by misidentification of Venus, advertising aircraft, or hoaxes. Soon, however, there is *another* case that proves beyond a doubt. . . .

9

Ancient Astronauts, Cosmic Collisions, and the Bermuda Triangle

This chapter covers three pseudoscientific theories that share a number of similarities. All three emerged suddenly and rapidly became very popular with readers who, otherwise well educated, had little background in the specific fields the theories are concerned with. All three theories were developed by articulate but scientifically untrained individuals who had little knowledge of how scientific theories are really validated. Finally, even after thorough refutations, all three theories still command dedicated bands of followers whose belief in them has an almost religious fervor.

Ancient Astronauts

The "ancient astronaut" theory of Erich von Däniken was amazingly popular during the 1970s. Von Däniken proposed that the Earth was repeatedly visited in the historic past by intelligent beings from other worlds. The "ancient astronauts" gave ancient cultures the knowledge and skills that enabled them to create some of the great wonders of the ancient world such as the great pyramid, the statues on Easter Island, and the huge markings on Peru's Nazca desert. Von Däniken claimed that there is clear evidence of these ancient astronauts (whom primitive humans viewed as gods) in the drawings, carvings, myths, and legends of ancient peoples and that the ancient astronaut theory solves many archeological mysteries.

Von Däniken is not the first promoter of this theory (Krupp, 1981; Story, 1976), but he is certainly the most successful. He has made tens of millions of dollars from his numerous books, movies, television shows, and lectures. Von Däniken is a master of that popular technique among proponents of pseudoscience, looking for mysteries where none exist (Radner and Radner, 1982). He searches the archeological literature to find unexplained reports, objects, and phenomena and then attributes them to the ancient astronauts. His style of writing is such as to direct readers' thoughts away from other possible explanations for the phenomena in question. "How could such and such have been produced," he asks rhetorically, "if not by ancient astronauts?" The reader, whose knowledge of archeology is limited, doesn't know how the object was actually produced and so accepts the ancient astronauts explanation. Von Däniken has developed this technique further: he may fabricate a mystery where one never existed in the first place. His comments about the Piri Re'is map, a map dated to 1513 showing the Mediterranean area, illustrate this technique. Von Däniken claims that the map is "absolutely accurate" and that "the coasts of North and South America and even the contours of the Antarctic were also perfectly delineated" (von Däniken, 1970, p. 30). What is the explanation for this great accuracy? "Comparisons with modern photographs of our globe taken from satellites showed that the original of the Piri Re'is maps [sic] must have been aerial photographs taken from a very great height. How can that be explained? A spaceship hovers high above Cairo and points its camera straight down" (von Däniken, 1970, p. 31).

Even if the reader of the above scenario doesn't immediately accept von Däniken's explanation for the great accuracy of the Piri Re'is map (in spite of von Däniken's frequent use of the plural, there is only one map), the mystery of the map's great accuracy will certainly stay in mind. But there is no mystery that needs explaining in the first place. The Piri Re'is map is a very good map—but only in comparison with other maps of its day (Story, 1976). Hapgood (1966) has pointed out numerous inaccuracies in the map, such as leaving off half of the island of Cuba. This would hardly be expected from the advanced civilization that von Däniken proposes. In this instance, as in so many others, von Däniken lies to his readers. He fabricates evidence and distorts the facts with the sole purpose of supporting his theories. Readers unaware of the detailed archeological research on the various pseudo-mysteries that von Däniken makes up are tricked into thinking that the evidence for the ancient astronaut theory is much stronger than it really is. Another nonmystery concerns the island in the Nile called Elephantine. Von Däniken (1970, p. 84) says it is called Elephantine "even in the oldest texts" because the island is shaped "like an elephant." But how, he asks, "did the ancient Egyptians know that? This shape can be recognized only from an airplane at a great height." In fact, the island is not shaped like an elephant. A glance at a map reveals it to be rather long and pointed at one end. The island bears the name it does because there may have been elephants on it at one time and because it was the site of ivory trading (Story, 1976). Again, von Däniken has lied to his readers.

Von Däniken is at his most creative when he discusses the alleged mysteries of ancient Egypt. The Pyramids of Egypt fascinate him, as do the mummies. More than anything else, von Däniken's distorted and inaccurate writings on ancient Egypt were responsible for the belief in "pyramid power," the idea that the shape of the pyramid is itself magical and possesses preservative powers. Belief in pyramid power became popular in the 1970s. This will be discussed further in chapter twelve.

Von Däniken tells us that the primitive Egyptians couldn't possibly have built the pyramids by themselves. The entire culture of ancient Egypt "appears suddenly and without transition with a fantastic ready made civilization" (von Däniken, 1970, p. 95). Certainly the Egyptians couldn't have evolved such an advanced culture so rapidly; it must have been due to infusions of advanced knowledge from extraterrestrial visitors. As usual, von Däniken's facts are simply wrong, as any text on Egyptian history shows (see, for example, Mertz, 1978). The evolution of Egyptian culture is well known from the time of the region's unification, about 3100 B.C., through the Old Kingdom, about 2680 to 2180 B.C., to the New Kingdom, about 1600 to 1085 B.C. The New Kingdom was the period of the great pyramids.

Contrary to von Däniken's claims, the pyramids did not simply spring up out of the desert with no history of development. The history of the pyramids can be traced from their predecessors, called *mastabas*, which were small brick tombs. One famous pyramid shows that the pyramid builders occasionally made errors. This pyramid, at Meidum, was originally built with its walls too steep to support its own weight. The top part of the structure collapsed into the rubble now found at the base of the pyramid. This is hardly the kind of accuracy one would expect from superadvanced space-traveling beings. The Egyptian engineers, like any intelligent humans, learned from their mistakes, and later pyramids were built with less steep sides.

Von Däniken (1970) makes other claims about the pyramids that simply aren't true. He asks, "Is it really a coincidence that the height of the pyramid of Cheops multiplied by a thousand million—98,000,000 miles—corresponds approximately to the distance between the earth and sun?" (Von Däniken, 1970, p. 98). The answer is clearly yes. And Von Däniken even manages to get the distance between the earth and the sun wrong: 93 million, not 98 million miles. An error of 6 percent is hardly the accuracy to be expected from interstellar navigators. Such a numbers game is easy to play, even if one takes the effort to get one's numbers right. As was pointed out on National Educational Television's "Nova" program "The Case of the Ancient Astronauts," which was first broadcast in 1978, the height of the Washington Monument multiplied by forty gives the distance in light years to the second nearest star, Proxima Centauri. About the year 5330, will some Von Däniken-like charlatan claim that ancient Americans were much too dumb to have built such a magnificent monument themselves and must, therefore, have had help from space travelers from a planet in the Proxima Centauri system?

Von Däniken also claims that the building of the pyramids was impossible for the Egyptians because they lacked the necessary technology. He says (von Däniken, 1970) that the method of building the pyramids remains unknown and that conventional methods could not have been used since the Egyptians didn't have rope or trees to make rollers to move the stones. All this, as the reader might expect, is false. The methods of building the pyramids are recorded in the pyramids themselves. Rope, for example, was available in great quantity, and examples are preserved in many museums. Logs for rollers were widely used. The methods of quarrying the stone and transporting it by barge from the quarries to the site of the pyramids are also known (Story, 1976).

If pyramids baffle von Däniken, mummies pose even more of a puzzle for him. Their existence suggests to him that the Egyptians were given the secret of immortality by their extraterrestrial visitors. Further, the extraterrestrials will be able to bring the mummies back to life when they return. In an interview broadcast with the "Nova" program mentioned above, von Däniken said the extraterrestrials might have told pharaoh, "Listen, we come back let's say in 5,000 years, we are able to reconstruct your body, if you only take care that we find at least a few living cells of your body, but be careful, take your brain away into a separate pot because if we want to construct also the same memory as you had, we need your brain separately." In his 1970 book he says that mummies are "incomprehensible" (p. 101) and that the techniques of mummification remain a mystery to modern science. This is all totally false.

Like the techniques used to build the pyramids, the techniques used in mummification developed gradually during the history of Egypt. Harris and Weeks (1973) describe this development briefly and then discuss in more detail the thirteen separate steps involved in mummification during the New Kingdom. Examination of the steps shows the ridiculous nature of von Däniken's claims regarding the purpose of mummification. Advanced as they were, the ancient Egyptians had little knowledge of the brain's function. They viewed the brain as an organ of little importance (the understanding that the brain is the organ of the mind is a very modern one, dating only from the seventeenth and eighteenth centuries in western thought). Thus, when the body was mummified, the brain was pulled out bit by bit through the nose, using long tweezers, and thrown away. Unlike the other internal organs, it was not saved in separate jars. So much for bringing back pharaoh, complete with his memories.

Von Däniken (1970) claims that the Egyptians mummified their leaders and important individuals so they could return from the dead and suggests they got the idea of immortality from the ancient astronauts. He says that mummification was intended to help preserve the body for later restoration. In fact, the elaborate mummification ritual was designed to aid the trip to the other world. The internal organs (except the brain) were preserved because the dead would need them in the other world, just as in this one. Pets and servants were often killed and mummified so they could accompany the deceased to the other world. The Egyptians clearly did not believe that people came back from the dead. This is shown in the lovely "Song of the Harpers," found inscribed on the walls of several tombs from the Middle Kingdom period (Harris and Weeks, 1973, p. 117):

What has been done with them?
What are their places (now)?
Their walls have crumbled and their places are not
As if they had never been
No one has (ever) come back from (the dead)
That he might describe their condition,
And relate their needs;
That he might calm our hearts
Until we (too) pass into that place where they have gone
(Let us) make holiday and never tire of it!
(For) behold, no man can take his property with him,
No man who has gone can return again.

In his later writings, von Däniken (1984) has suggested that the famous curse on King Tutankhamen's tomb may have been the result of some sort of extraterrestrial protection given the tomb. According to the usual legend, many of the individuals who opened Tut's tomb when it first was found in 1922 died shortly thereafter under mysterious circumstances. The deaths are attributed to the curse allegedly placed on anyone who defiled the tomb. This curse was said to be inscribed on the door of the tomb when it was found. Randi (1978) analyzed the deaths supposedly due to the curse and found that the death rate was just what would be expected, given that many of the members of the expedition were quite elderly and that they were living in a country where modern sanitary facilities and health measures were lacking.

It has recently been revealed (Frazier, 1980-81) that the curse was a hoax in the first place. The security officer for the expedition, Richard Adamson, stated in 1980 that the curse story was dreamed up to keep would-be robbers away from the opened tomb. The news that the Curse of Tut had been a hoax did not stop an enterprising San Francisco policeman from suing the city for disability payments when he suffered a stroke while guarding the King Tut museum exhibit while it was in San Francisco in 1979. He claimed that Tut's spirit "lashed out at him," causing the stroke. The suit was dismissed (Frazier, 1981–82, p. 12).

Another favorite von Däniken pseudomystery is the set of large designs found in the Nazca desert of Peru. Intricate patterns of lines, pictures of giant birds, monkeys, spiders, and other animals, cover an area sixty by ten miles. Von Däniken suggests that the lines are the remains of an ancient "spaceport" and landing field. He further doubts that primitive peoples could have produced the lines and figures without some extraterrestrial help through "instructions from an aircraft" (von Däniken, 1970, p. 33).

In reality, the lines in the Nazca plain represent a complex astronomical calendar and observatory, testifying to the astronomical sophistication of the peoples who created them (Story, 1976; Kosok and Reiche, 1949; Krupp, 1978; Hadingham, 1987). Von Däniken's contempt for "primitive" peoples is shown when he belittles their ability to create such large figures on their own. How, he asks, could they have created the nearly perfect circles found in some of the figures? Simple—dig a hole and place a stake in it. Tie a rope of a certain length to the top of the stake. Stretch the rope to its full length and then walk in a circular pattern. The stake, moving freely around in the unfilled hole, will turn and the rope, maintaining its length, will allow one to trace out a nearly perfect circle. Certainly the people who created the Nazca designs thought of this simple method. Nickell (1982–83) has shown that it is possible to produce a full-size duplicate of a Nazca drawing 440 feet long using only "sticks and cord such as the Nazcas might have employed" (p. 42). It took six people about a day and a half to complete the figure.

In his other six major books, von Däniken creates hundreds of other pseudomysteries. The books are masterpieces of distortion, evasion, and deceptive writing, all in support of his half-baked ideas. Like a true proponent of pseudoscience, von Däniken does not revise his theories or claims in light of new evidence. For example, in *Chariots of the Gods?* (1970) a picture appears with the legend, "This is very reminiscent of the aircraft parking bays on a modern airport." The picture shows part of the wing, with individual feathers, of one of the giant Nazca plain bird designs. What the reader is not told and cannot judge from the photograph is that the whole photo shows an area only twenty feet across—hardly enough to contain extraterrestrial aircraft. In his "Nova" interview, von Däniken acknowledged this, saying, "I fully admit that this explanation of being a parking place is simply ridiculous." But while the book has gone through numerous printings, the error has never been corrected.

The Case of the Dogon

A somewhat more sophisticated and specific ancient astronaut claim has been proposed by Robert Temple in his 1976 book *The Sirius Mystery*. According to Temple, the Dogon, a tribe living in Mali 190 miles south of the famous city of Timbuktu, were visited 1,000 years ago by amphibious creatures from the Sirius star system. The evidence for this is, first, that the star Sirius plays an extremely important role in Dogon belief and legend. Second, the Dogon are said to possess advanced astronomical knowledge of the Sirius sytem, knowledge that has been part of their legends for thousands of years and that they could only have obtained from extraterrestrial visitors. Temple says that the Dogon know there is a second star in the Sirius sytem, a white dwarf called Sirius B that is both the smallest and the heaviest star in the heavens. Further, according to Temple, Dogon legends tell of an "ark" which came from the sky bearing the Nomno, the founders of Dogon civilization. These are the ancient astronauts, says Temple. Since modern astronomy discovered a white dwarf star, invisible to the naked eye, in the Sirius system only in 1862 and since the Dogon legends telling of such a star date back much further, Temple argues that the only possible source of this sophisticated knowledge of the Sirius system is ancient extraterrestrial visitors.

There is apparently nothing in Dogon legend to indicate that the Nomno were amphibious in nature. Temple (1976) assumes they were because Sirius is a very hot star, so a watery environment would be needed to keep any inhabitants of a planet near the star cool. Ridpath (1978–79) has pointed out, however, that astronomical observations have shown that the environment of the Sirius system is not compatible with life-supporting planets. For example, Sirius B is a source of soft x-rays. The part of the system where water would be found in liquid form is constantly changing due to unstable orbits.

Both Ridpath (1978–79) and Story (1976, chapter 12) have examined Temple's claims in detail and found them to be unsubstantiated. At some points Temple gets his facts wrong. The Dogon were the subject of intense anthropological investigation during the 1940s, and our knowledge of their culture comes from the work of these investigators (Griaule and Dieterlen, 1954). Temple says that Dogon legend tells of an "ark" that comes from the sky, presumably a spaceship. But in fact Dogon legend tells of the Nomno coming on an "arch" or bridge from the heavens (Griaule and Dieterlen, 1954), which carries a different meaning, not consistent with an extraterrestrial interpretation. Nor are such legends unique to the Dogon; they are found rather frequently in Africa (Ridpath, 1978–79).

Another problem with the evidence used by Temple to support his theory is that much of it comes from literal interpretations of Dogon legends. Further, only those bits of legend that seem to support the theory are described. Temple does not inform his readers that Dogon legend is rich and complex and that it includes other elements that are inconsistent with his views.

The Dogon picture the Sirius system as shown in figure 16. According to Dogon legend, there are *nine* objects in the system, including Sirius A, and *two* (not one, as Temple says) invisible companion stars. In fact, there is only one invisible star in the Sirius system, so on this vital point of astronomical knowledge the Dogon legend is wrong.

It is still a puzzle that the Dogon do seem to know something about Sirius B—that it exists, for example, and that it is made of very dense matter. It's one thing to shoot down Temple's ancient astronaut explanation, which doesn't hold water on close examination, but skeptics should be able to provide at least a reasonable alternative explanation. It turns out that what the Dogon say about Sirius B corresponds very well to what astronomers thought about the star in the 1920s. At that time it was thought to be made up of the densest matter in the galaxy, just as Dogon legend says it is. It is now known that much denser matter is found, for instance, in neutron stars so this aspect of the Dogon legend is also incorrect. The error suggests that the Dogon obtained their knowledge of Sirius B not from space travelers, but from contact with westerners during the 1920s or later. Their legendary views about Sirius and its *twin* companions can be attributed to the great importance of Sirius itself in their religion and of "twinness"in their culture. This would lead the Dogon to the natural conclusion that any object as important as Sirius would have twin companions. If they couldn't be seen, they must still be there, but invisible. When westerners in the early twentieth century learned of the Dogon's interest in Sirius, they told them of Sirius B and that information was incorporated into the legends.

Is it reasonable to think that such contact took place? Yes—as Ridpath (1978-79) points out, the Dogon have had considerable contact with western culture since the early part of the twentieth century. There were French schools in the area as early as 1907, and missionaries visited the tribe in the 1920s and thereafter. The tribe is settled in an area near a trade route and the Niger River and has been in contact with Europeans since at least the late 1800s. There has been ample opportunity for them to acquire their knowledge of Sirius B.

Ridpath (1978-79) recounts an amusing story that demonstrates how quickly modern knowledge can become part of legend and folklore. A member of a primitive tribe in New Guinea astonished a physician by explaining that a particular disease was caused by invisible spirits that got into the body through the skin and made the victim sick. The native then drew in the sand and described verbally a picture that corresponded almost exactly to the view of germs through a microscope. Temple and von Däniken would no doubt have concluded that this knowledge had beeb obtained from extraterrestrial sources. How else could one explain this advanced medical knowledge on the part of so primitive a tribe? Happily, the story was told by the physician Arleton Gajdusek, who won the Nobel Prize in medicine in 1976 for his work on the New Guinea disease kuru. It turned out that Gajdusek had shown members of the tribe a view of germs through a microscope while he was doing field work in the area. The natives had remembered the explanation and incorporated it into their own world view, with a few changes.

The weaknesses and inconsistencies in Temple's (1976) extraterrestrial hypothesis for the Dogon's knowledge of Sirius B and the demonstration of contact between Europeans and the Dogon since the late 1800s add up to a convincing argument that there was never any contact between the Dogon and amphibious visitors from the Sirius system.

I will not spend the time or space to refute the hundreds of false claims, evasions of the truth, and deceptions perpetrated by von Däniken and his imitators. That has been ably done by several other authors. The interested reader is referred to the references cited above as well as to Stienbing, 1984; Krupp, 1981; Omohundro, 1976-77; Story, 1977-78; and Loftin, 1980-81. Krupp (1978) has edited an excellent book on the true astronomical abilities of ancient peoples.

The Bermuda Triangle

As popular as von Däniken's ancient astronaut theory was in the 1970s, by the 1980s it has largely faded away. Another modern myth fabricated in the 1970s, however, is alive and well: the Bermuda Triangle, where ships and planes allegedly disappear under the most mysterious of circumstances.

Stories of mysterious disappearances in the Bermuda triangle area are alleged to date back to the 1800s. For years they appeared in books of miscellaneous "mysterious" events, such as Frank Edwards's *Stranger Than Science* (1959) and *Strangest of All* (1956). It was Charles Berlitz's 1974 *The Bermuda Triangle Mystery* that really brought to the public's attention the idea that strange events were taking place in the area. The book became a bestseller and, like von Däniken's books, spawned a series of films, television programs, and imitators. Berlitz, like von Däniken, made a fortune from royalties and the lecture circuit.

The Bermuda Triangle is a manufactured mystery from start to finish. The numerous articles and books touting the "mystery" are inaccurate, misleading, and often wilfully deceptive in their descriptions of the alleged mysterious happenings in the triangle. Kusche (1981, p. 297) accurately characterizes the triangle mystery as "the epitome of false reporting; deletion of pertinent information; twisted values among writers, publishers and the media; mangling of scientific principles; and the often deliberate deception of a trusting public." For example, ships that are said to have vanished under mysterious and unexplainable circumstances turn out upon investigation to have sunk during hurricanes. Other reported disappearances never happened at all. In some cases ships said to have disappeared never existed in the first place. Other sinkings and disappearances attributed to the triangle took place thousands of miles away.

As was the case for von Däniken's claims, there is not enough space in the present volume to detail what really happened to each of the ships and planes that, according to the myth makers, vanished mysteriously in the triangle. I will describe several representative cases found in the sensational literature and contrast these fantasies with the results of careful investigations of the actual occurrences. These investigations were carried out by Kusche and are reported in his book *The Bermuda Triangle Mystery—Solved* (1975), to which the reader is referred for further details. Other critical discussions of the Bermuda Triangle can be found in Kusche (1977-78a) and Dennett (1981-82).

Berlitz's (1974) best-selling *The Bermuda Triangle Mystery* describes the strange case of the *Marine Sulphur Queen*. She carried a cargo of 15,000 tons of molten sulphur and sailed from Beaumont, Texas, on February 2, 1963. According to Berlitz (1974, p. 56), "the weather was good" and "the large vessel disappeared in good weather" (caption on fourth page of plates). Berlitz further states that two life jackets were the only remains of the ship ever found and that the Coast Guard investigation offered "neither solution nor theory concerning this disaster" (p. 57).

These statements are simply false. The weather may have been good on February 2, 1963, when the ship left harbor, but it certainly wasn't good when she sank. A routine radio message from the ship was sent at about 1:30 A.M. on February 4. This was the last radio contact. About twelve hours previously, according to the Coast Guard Board of Investigation report that Kusche (1975) has examined, another ship in the area reported that there were "very rough seas and her decks were awash" (Kusche, 1975, p. 186). Winds gusted to just below hurricane strength, and the waves were more than thirty-five feet high. This is hardly the calm, peaceful ocean scene painted by Berlitz.

The claim that only two life jackets were ever found adds to the picture of a ship simply vanishing without a trace. The Coast Guard Board of Investigation report shows that the true story is quite different. A foghorn from the ship was found, and over the second phase of the search "additional debris were recovered and identified as coming from the *Marine Sulphur Queen*" (Kusche, 1975, p. 188).

Contrary to Berlitz's claim, the Coast Guard did propose several theories and possible solutions for the sinking. Among these was the suggestion that the ship may have broken in two. During its conversion to a molten sulphur carrier, bulkheads that strengthened the hull had been removed. Another possible solution mentioned by the Coast Guard is that the ship capsized in the rough seas known to be running at the time. Also mentioned was the possibility of an explosion, either from steam or from the fumes of the sulphur. The latter theory is given credence by the fact that tons of molten sulphur were known to have leaked into the ship's bilges during previous voyages.

The loss of the *Marine Sulphur Queen* was certainly tragic, and the exact cause of the sinking will probably never be known. However, it is far from a mysterious occurrence. The weather was very bad and the ship suffered from at least two serious structural flaws (the removal of the bulkheads and the leaking of molten sulphur) that could have been responsible. The promoters of the triangle mystery, in their eagerness to sell sensational books, have failed to mention these facts.

Gaddis (1965), another triangle mystery proponent, described the loss of the *Sandra*, a freighter "350 feet in length," in June 1950: "she disappeared as completely as if she had never existed—in the tropic dusk, in peaceful weather—just off the Florida coast" (p. 202). In fact, the length given is nearly double the ship's actual size. The weather was not peaceful. The ship left harbor on April 5, 1950, and the *Miami Herald* reported (April 8, 1950, p. 1) that "a storm growing from the low pressure areas which caused thundershowers and strong winds in Florida during the past three days approached hurricane force and buffeted Atlantic shipping lanes Friday. . . . [Winds] reached a speed of 73 miles an hour off the Virginia Capes" (Kusche, 1975, p. 163). The "Friday" mentioned was April 7, two days after the *Sandra* left port in Savannah, Georgia. Once again, the "calm sea" picture is false—there is no mystery about this disappearance.

Berlitz (1974, p. 50) even manages to place one ship in the wrong ocean. He reports the case of the *Freya*, which he says was found abandoned "in the Triangle area . . . sailing from Manzanillo, Cuba, to ports in Chile." In fact, the *Freya* was found partially dismasted and floating on her side in the Pacific Ocean off the western coast of Mexico. In reporting the incident, the British science magazine *Nature* reported that severe earthquakes had occurred in western Mexico for two or three days after the ship's departure from a western Mexican port. Such quakes can cause tidal waves that "probably caused the damage to the *Freya* which led to its abandonment" (*Nature*, April 25, 1907, p. 610; cited in Kusche, 1975, p. 48).

Kusche (1981) has analyzed in detail the alleged mystery of the *Ellen Austin*. This is an excellent example of an incident that almost certainly never occurred. Kusche's analysis shows how reports of triangle mysteries grow as they are copied and embellished by one careless writer after another. The end product is a tale full of such specific detail that most readers will accept it as fact.

The basic story of the *Ellen Austin* is best given in the first version of the story that Kusche (1981) could find. The following passage is from that version, which appeared in Gould (1944).

> Last, and queerest of all, comes the case of the abandoned derelict, in seaworthy condition, which the British ship *Ellen Austin* encountered, in mid-Atlantic, in the year 1881. She put a small prize-crew aboard the stranger, with instructions to make for St. John's, Newfoundland, where she was bound herself. The two ships parted company in foggy weather but a few days later they met again. And the strange derelict was once more deserted. Like their predecessors, the prize crew had vanished forever.

Even after extensive research, Kusche (1975, 1981) was never able to find any evidence that the alleged incident had ever occurred. Gould— as is typical of "mysterious events" writers—gave no source for his information on the *Ellen Austin*. Kusche (1975, 1981) checked the indexes of the *New York Times* and the London *Times*. They contained no references to stories describing such an occurrence. The *Boston Globe*, the *Boston Herald-American* and the *Boston Evening Transcript* were also devoid of stories on the incident. The ship was said to be bound for St. John's, Newfoundland. The public library there could find no references to such an event in its files. The two St. John's newspapers of the day, the *Evening Telegram* and *The Newfoundlander*, were also empty of any reports relevant to either the incident or the ship *Ellen Austin*. If such a strikingly unusual occurrence had taken place, it is inconceivable that it would not have been reported in at least one of the papers Kusche searched. That no such story even appeared strongly suggests that Gould made up the whole thing in the first place.

Gould's original report contained eighty-six words. The word count grows over the years as the story is copied from one Bermuda Triangle author to another, none ever bothering to check whether the event really occurred as described. Vincent Gaddis's (1965, p. 131) version of the story contains 188 words and is marked by much detail that was not present in Gould's (1944) original report. Thus, for example, when the *Ellen Austin's* captain saw the derelict for the second time, it was "pursuing an erratic course. He ordered the helmsman to approach the derelict. When there was no response a boarding party was sent over. To a man the frightened remaining sailors refused to join another prize crew."

Where did these additional details come from? Gaddis references only Gould's original (1944) report, but since these details are not in Gould, Gaddis must simply have made them up to make the story sound better.

Sanderson (1970) reports the incident in 429 words and much new detail emerges. He mentions a temporary log kept by the prize crew, for example. Sanderson's version is an embellishment of Gaddis's version, which in turn is an embellishment of Gould's version.

In his 1974 *The Bermuda Triangle Mystery* Berlitz described the *Ellen Austin* mystery in a spare 172 words. But an amazing thing happened between 1970 (Sanderson's version) and 1974. In Berlitz's version, a second prize crew is persuaded to go aboard, and they vanish along with the derelict. Berlitz cites as sources both Sanderson (1970) and Gaddis (1965). Obviously, the story of the second prize crew is pure fiction made up by Berlitz to enhance the mystery.

Ships are not the only things at risk in the Bermuda Triangle. Aircraft of all sorts, we are told by the mythmongers, run the risk of mysteriously winking out of existence if they dare fly in or near the triangle. The reports of aircraft disappearances in the triangle are of the same low reliability as reports of disappearing ships. Relevant facts are withheld from readers and fictional details are added. It is largely because of such fictional additions that one of the missing aircraft stories has become the most famous of all the Bermuda Triangle legends. This is the case of Flight 19.

Flight 19 consisted of five U.S. Army Air Corps Avenger aircraft. These were designed as carrier-based torpedo planes and carried a crew of three. The flight was under the command of Lieutenant Charles C. Taylor. It left Fort Lauderdale, Florida, Naval Air Station on December 5, 1945, at about 2 P.M. The flight plan called for a course eastward, then a turn to the north, followed about seventy miles later by a turn to the southwest to bring the flight back to base.

The version of the Flight 19 story presented to the public by such unreliable writers as Gaddis and Berlitz has it that the pilots and crew were all "experienced airmen" (Berlitz, 1974, p. 13). As the flight progressed, these experienced flyers became mysteriously lost, in spite of the "ideal flight conditions" (Gaddis, 1965, p. 191). Radio communications between the pilots and the base revealed something strange going on: "Everything is wrong . . . strange. Even the ocean doesn't look as it should," Gaddis

(1965, p. 191) and Berlitz (1974, p. 14) quote one of the pilots as reporting. Gaddis (1965, p. 192) adds, "Apparently not only the sea looked strange, but *the sun was invisible*" (emphasis added). No trace was ever found of the planes or any of the crew. This too, we are told, is a great mystery. How could five such aircraft vanish so completely, especially in the face of the massive search that was conducted? Berlitz (1974, p. 18) suggests a shocking answer: The planes, crews and all, were kidnapped by UFOs. He says, "A mother of one of the lost pilots who attended the naval hearing stated at the time that she had received the impression that her son 'was still alive somewhere in space'." He also quotes approvingly the view of a local "scientist" that "they are still here, but in a different dimension of a magnetic phenomenon that could have been set up by a UFO" (p. 18). (Incidentally, the sharp-eyed movie viewer may recall that Flight 19 played a minor part in *Close Encounters of the Third Kind*. When the UFO finally lands at the secret government installation at Devil's Tower, who pops out of the UFO but the crew of Flight 19, all decked out in their original flight gear and not having aged a bit.)

As before, investigation of what actually happened to Flight 19 explodes the fictionalized stories that are foisted on the reading public as nonfiction. Kusche has devoted an entire book, *The Disappearance of Flight 19* (1980), to telling what really happened to this flight. The following information is taken from that book.

Flight 19, it turns out, was not manned by group of experienced aviators. It was a navigational training flight. With the exception of Lt. Taylor, the leader, the other pilots were not experienced, they were students. The "excellent flight conditions" are another fiction. For one thing, Lt. Taylor's two compasses malfunctioned after he was airborne. The weather was only "'average to undesirable' for a training flight" (Kusche, 1980, p. 7) with gusty winds up to thirty-one knots and a moderate to rough sea. The forecast called for scattered showers until about 6 P.M. On December 5, 1945, the sun set at 5:29 P.M. It is important to understand that aircraft in 1945 had none of the sophisticated navigational gear that is now carried even by some light private aircraft. The pilots of Flight 19 were navigating with compasses and air speed indicators. To make matters worse, air speed is not equal to ground speed. It can be greater than, equal to, or less than ground speed, depending on the strength and direction of the wind. Further, the compasses of the only experienced pilot in the flight were broken, so he couldn't navigate. He had to depend on the students for correct navigation. The flight was over water, which obviously has very few landmarks. These factors alone would lead any experienced pilot to predict trouble of some sort, but another factor is important. Lt. Taylor had been flying out of Fort Lauderdale for only two weeks. His previous flying assignment in Florida, after transferring stateside from the Pacific Theater, had consisted of eight months of flying from a base in Miami. Thus, when he led Flight 19 he was unfamiliar with the area into which he was flying. In particular, if he were flying out of Miami, he would be nearer to the Florida Keys than when flying from Fort Lauderdale.

As could be predicted on the basis of the poor conditions—meteorological, instrumentational, and experiential—about one hour and twenty minutes after takeoff, Lt. Taylor was unsure of his location. The Naval Board of Investigation quoted him as asking for directions and saying, "I'm sure I'm in the Keys" (Kusche, 1980, p. 4). As the afternoon wore on, the flight became more lost and confused. Radio messages among the five pilots that were monitored on shore and printed in the transcript of the Naval Board of Investigation or associated documents, reveal considerable confusion as to their location. Taylor ordered several changes of direction during the next few hours, including 180-degree changes. Importantly, the statements attributed to the flight that appear in the Gaddis and Berlitz volumes, and that were noted above, do not appear in the official record. They, like so much else in this manufactured mystery, were made up after the fact to spice the story.

By the time the sun set at 5:29 P.M., Flight 19 had been flying around lost for about two hours. Being lost, especially over the ocean with no landmarks (and no airports!), is a terrifying experience for any pilot, especially a student pilot. Fear does not lead to clearheaded, rational behavior, and even experienced individuals' decision-making abilities are severely impaired in stressful situations. This fear probably contributed to the several unhelpful course changes ordered by Taylor.

All during this time, radio communication between the planes and shore bases had been weak. Taylor did not switch from the static-filled training frequency to another frequency, perhaps, Kusche (1980) speculates, out of fear that switching radio frequency would put the five planes out of radio contact if it were not carried out correctly by all the students. As sunset approached, and as the planes flew farther and farther away from Fort Lauderdale, communication became even worse.

Where were the planes going? Contrary to the usual report of the incident, an approximate position for the lost flight was calculated from different directional bearings. These bearings revealed that the flight was much farther north than had been suspected, about 300 miles north of Fort Lauderdale and about 200 miles east of the Florida coast. At 6:04 P.M., thirty-five minutes after sundown, when the flight was flying in the dark, Taylor was heard to order the flight, "Holding west course. Didn't go far enough east. Turn around again. We may just as well turn around and go east" (Kusche, 1980, p. 36). Of course, flying east would take them away from land, not toward it. Taylor was obviously very confused about his position. At 6:06 P.M. Taylor ordered, "Turn around and fly east until we run out of gas" (Kusche, 1980, p. 36). Unfortunately, the flight's position as calculated by the radio bearings was never radioed to the flight due to failure of the teletype communication system used and radio problems.

The flight had fuel to last until about 7:00 P.M. Then they would have to ditch their aircraft in the sea. While Taylor had ditched twice before in the Pacific, the conditions there were quite different from those he now faced. His previous two ditches had been in daylight with rescue ships standing by. Now he had to ditch at night in rough seas. Of course, none of the students had ever ditched before. Landing an aircraft on the water is never an easy task, even in the best of conditions. When an Avenger ditched, it usually hit the water at about eighty miles an hour. Such an impact can produce everything from a dazed state to unconsciousness. The best "ditch" is one where the plane's tail hits the water first and pulls the rest of the plane down. Flying headfirst into the water will cause much greater injury to the crew. To be able to land tail down in the water, one needs first to be able to see the water, which is difficult at night, and second, experience, which only Lt. Taylor had. Rough seas, like those running that night, make ditching even more dangerous.

Contrary to the usual version of the story, the Avenger is a very unseaworthy craft. It sinks like a "lead banana" (Kusche, 1980, p. 28) within thirty seconds to a minute and a half. Nor is it easy to climb out of the aircraft and get out the emergency life raft. The pilot and the two crew members must get out of the plane, stand on the wing (in this case at night in rough seas), pull out and inflate the life raft, and get in it. On top of this, many of the crew were probably stunned and relatively helpless due to the impact of the crash. All this had to be accomplished by frightened men who had never had any such experience before. And it had to be done in the rolling seas in the dark in the ninety seconds before the planes sank.

Tragically, the task was not accomplished. That no bodies and no trace of life rafts or the aircraft themselves were ever found shows that no one was successful in freeing the rafts from the planes. Perhaps a few crew members got out of the planes and in panic jumped into the sea and drowned. In that vast expanse of ocean there would be almost no chance of finding a body. Probably most of the fourteen crew members, stunned by the impact and unsure of what to do, drowned when their planes sank. Their deaths, although tragic and unnecessary, are not mysterious.

The legend of Flight 19 is enhanced by the fact that one of the planes sent to search for the five Avengers also was lost. The plane, a Mariner, took off about 7:30 P.M. and not, as is often claimed, during the late afternoon. Mariners were called "flying gas tanks" by flight crews "because of the fumes that were often present, and a crewman sneaking a cigarette, or a spark from any source could have caused [an] explosion" (Kusche, 1980, p. 119). An explosion was seen in the air just where the Mariner would have been about twenty minutes after takeoff. Clearly, the Mariner had blown up. Another tragic, but not mysterious, loss of life.

The loss of Flight 19 turns out to be no less a manufactured mystery than any of the other nonmysteries described by the likes of Berlitz and Gaddis.

It is amusing and instructive to examine the explanations that Berlitz puts forward for the nonevents he has made up for his book. The Bermuda Triangle is a popular topic with UFO proponents, the idea being that the triangle is some type of prime hunting ground for the saucer people. As noted above, Berlitz describes the UFO kidnapping hypothesis as a reasonable one. In fact, over half of *The Bermuda Triangle Mystery* is devoted to UFOs, ancient astronauts, and even the tale of Atlantis. Berlitz, it turns out, has found out about a well-known structure called the Bimini Road or Wall. Of it he says, "Shape and placement of these monoliths, right-angled corners, and pillars underneath some of the stones are conclusive, although not yet universally accepted, proof that they are man made" (Berlitz, 1974, figure caption following p. 134). He goes on to speculate that the builders were the Atlanteans, who had an advanced civilization.

The "columns" Berlitz refers to are actually a mile or so from the "road" and are of recent origin—they are cement that was stored in barrels and tossed into the sea. The barrels rotted away, leaving the "columns." The actual rocks in the Bimini Road are known to be natural formations. They are just a little over 2,000 years old (Shinn, 1978). As Randi (1980) has noted, this is a little young for true Atlantean artifacts.

More recently Berlitz (1977) has claimed in *Without a Trace* that he has found a giant pyramid, like the ones in Egypt, in the triangle and that somehow it is responsible for all the disappearances in the triangle. No one else, including the U.S. Navy, has been able to locate this giant object, and the book contains Berlitz's usual false statements, errors, and deceptions (Kusche, 1977-78b; Klass, 1977-78).

Even more recently, Berlitz (Moore and Berlitz, 1979) has turned his attention away from the Bermuda Triangle and toward a most amazing Navy experiment. It seems that in the 1950s the Navy managed to make an entire battleship invisible and transport it instantly from Newport News, Virginia, to a Navy yard on the West Coast. Of course only Berlitz has managed to ferret out the truth about this. It's interesting that the Navy seems utterly unconcerned about having the most spectacular defense secret of the century revealed.

In the end, the Bermuda Triangle mystery turns out to be one of the longest-running hoaxes of the twentieth century. Yet many people are surprised to hear this. They have "heard so much about it" that they assume "there must be something to it." There isn't, but the continued existence of the triangle hoax is another example of the power of irresponsible writers and the media to deceive the public.

Immanuel Velikovsky and Cosmic Collisions

The late Immanuel Velikovsky was a psychiatrist who, in the early 1950s, created a huge scientific controversy, which continues to some extent today. Velikovsky, who died in 1979, put forth a view of the origin of the solar system radically different from that accepted by astronomers. His goal was to explain several biblical stories, which he believed were literally true, in terms of actual astronomical events. He believed the biblical stories were not reports of supernatural events but instead reflected actual physical happenings. Velikovsky's several books (*Worlds in Collision*, 1950; *Earth in Upheaval*, 1955; *Ages in Chaos*, 1952; *Oedipus and Akhnaton: Myth and History*, 1960; and *Peoples of the Sea*, 1977) present his ideas in detail. His views will be summarized in the next few pages, followed by a discussion of the difficulties.

According to Velikovsky, in about 1500 B.C. a comet was ejected from the planet Jupiter. This comet became the planet Venus. To get from Jupiter to the present orbit of Venus, the comet approached the earth and the earth passed through the tail of the comet. This caused a range of effects on earth, including a fall of red meteoric dust. The rivers turned blood-red. Petroleum fell from the sky in great quantities, creating the oil fields of the Middle East. Fires raged everywhere, started by meteorites from the comet. As the earth passed deeper and deeper into the comet's tail, the sun disappeared and earth was plunged into a darkness that lasted for days. Due to the gravitational influence of Venus, the earth's rotation slowed and earthquakes took place. New mountain ranges were born. Hurricane-strength winds and enormous tidal waves left some areas dry. This is the explanation of the Red Sea parting when Moses led the Israelites out of the land of Pharaoh.

So much heat was caused by the change in the earth's rotation that rocks melted, lava flowed from a host of volcanoes, and the seas boiled. As the earth left the comet's tail, the heat caused various "vermin" such as rats and frogs to reproduce at a great rate. A plague resulted. Eggs and larvae of extraterrestrial species of insects were in the comet's tail, and they dropped on the earth and reproduced. That's where flies come from.

The "manna from heaven" described in the Bible was produced when dust clouds, water vapor, and carbon and hydrogen—the latter two elements being found in the comet's tail—combined and reacted to form carbohydrates, which promptly fell from the sky to feed the Israelites.

The comet receded from earth, but about fifty years later it came very close again. This time the earth's rotation was halted by the comet, and Joshua and the Israelites defeated their enemies while the sun stood still in the sky, as recounted in the Bible. Then the earth began rotating again. Again meteorites fell in great abundance, and the earth was torn by more earthquakes, tidal waves, volcanoes, and other phenomena. For about 600 years, from 1400 B.C. to 800 B.C., all was well. Then Venus and Mars passed near each other, and Mars moved from its old orbit into a new one. Mars came near the earth four times before both planets adopted their present orbits.

According to Velikovsky, these dramatic events happened well within the period of recorded history. So why is there no written record of any of these events? The events were so traumatic that they resulted in worldwide amnesia. This prevented any clear statement of what happened from being written down. The events are, however, to be found recorded in symbolic form in myths and legends.

A bit of reflection on the ideas outlined above will suggest to the reader that Velikovsky was one of the greatest crackpots of the twentieth century. When I teach a course on pseudoscience at Pace University, the common response is, "Why bother with this? No one could ever really have taken such nonsense seriously." But Velikovsky's ideas were taken seriously—very seriously—by many people when his books were first published. The ideas still have a small band of dedicated followers.

Why did such patently absurd beliefs achieve such acceptance? One clue comes from an examination of where Velikovsky's ideas found initial support. *Worlds in Collision* received surprisingly favorable reviews in *Harper's* magazine and other literary magazines. These were magazines written for intelligent readers, but readers who had no scientific background. The magazine reviewers were apparently impressed with the symbolic interpretation of myths and legends that was one of Velikovsky's strengths. They were largely unaware that symbolic interpretations of anything—literature, dreams, myths, or legends—are almost entirely subjective and do not constitute acceptable evidence for anything. The readers of these magazines were also largely ignorant of scientific matters. They were impressed by Velikovsky's scientific jargon, but couldn't spot it for the gibberish that it was. It should be remembered in this regard that in the early 1950s general scientific education in the schools was much more primitive than in the 1960s during the post-Sputnik era. Finally, there was little popular interest in space and astronomical topics then, as opposed to the period since the development of the space program. Thus, the public in general was less well-informed in areas that would enable people to see through Velikovsky's claims.

The response of the scientific community to Velikovsky was, as might be expected, one of scorn and hostility. *Worlds in Collision* was first published by Macmillan, a company that also published many science textbooks. College professors threatened to stop using Macmillan textbooks if the publisher continued to print Velikovsky's book. The pressure was so great that Macmillan sold the book to another publisher. This enabled Velikovsky to paint himself as a martyr whose ideas the scientific establishment had tried to suppress. This further endeared him to the literati, who were probably already somewhat hostile to the scientific community, which was becoming a more dominant and controlling force in society.

Velikovsky's ideas and the evidence he and his followers say supports those ideas have been examined in detail elsewhere (Sagan, 1981; Goldsmith, 1977; Stiebing, 1984), and the interested reader is referred to these sources for further discussion. The following pages will briefly analyze Velikovsky's ideas and point out some of the major flaws, incorrect statements, and misinterpretations to be found.

Velikovsky says Venus is a recent addition to the solar system and that it appeared first about 1500 B.C. If this is true, then there should be no written records of the planet before that time. Huber (1977) has examined ancient records and found that Venus was mentioned as the morning and evening star by at least 1900 B.C. Sumerian tablets speak of a goddess or star Inanna as the morning and evening star. Venus was observed and worshipped in Babylon in the sixteenth century B.C. and, as Huber notes, the observations show that it was in its present orbital position at that time and that it stayed in that position. There is no mention of any wandering about, as Velikovsky claims.

Of course, records of such wandering about might be missing due to Velikovsky's hypothesized worldwide amnesia. This is obviously an irrefutable hypothesis and, in any case, does not explain why we find records of Venus before Velikovsky says it existed.

Sagan (1981) has discussed in detail the astrophysical problems with Velikovsky's theories. His outline will be followed here. Velikovsky says that Venus was ejected as a comet by Jupiter. How? What was the power source? None is ever specified by Velikovsky. The event just "happened." But, if it happened, Venus would have had to be moving fast enough to escape from Jupiter's massive gravitational pull. In other words, Venus would have had to reach escape velocity. But Venus is very massive, and the amount of energy needed for it to reach escape velocity is huge—

so huge that any rocky comet would have been melted before it could escape. So Venus's escape from Jupiter is impossible. Even if it were somehow possible, the escape velocity for Jupiter is sixty kilometers per second and escape velocity for the solar system is sixty-three kilometers per second (Sagan, 1981). Thus, there is an extremely narrow velocity range that would allow Venus to escape from Jupiter, yet stay in the solar system.

Further, Velikovsky never specifies any real mechanism for the earth stopping and starting as Venus passes by. The stops and starts must have taken place in only a few hours. If that were so, why wasn't everything on the planet tossed off into space? After all, the speed of the earth's rotation is just over a thousand miles per hour. If that speed were reduced sharply over a short period of time, almost everything on the planet other than mountains would fly off into space as a result of inertia.

According to Velikovsky, at least a considerable portion of the craters on the moon were created in historical times while Venus was whizzing about the solar system. Studies have shown, however, that the craters on the moon are millions of years older than Velikovsky claims. And if the cosmic events of which Velikovsky speaks caused craters on the moon, they should also have made craters on the earth. Such recent craters simply do not exist on earth. Sagan (1981) discusses other points of lunar geology that show Velikovsky's theories to be wrong.

If Venus were born of Jupiter, the composition of these two planets should be very similar. In reality, the compositions of Venus and Jupiter are extremely different. Jupiter is made up largely of hydrogen and helium gases. Venus is a solid planet, about five times denser than Jupiter, with a nickel and iron composition like that of earth. Nor is the atmosphere of Venus like that of Jupiter. Venus's atmosphere is a combination of carbon dioxide with some clouds that contain about 80 percent sulfuric acid.

Velikovsky's lack of scientific expertise is shown by his interchangeable use of the words *hydrocarbons* and *carbohydrates*. Thus, Velikovsky says that the manna that fell from heaven and fed the Israelites came from the tail of the comet Venus. It seems that comets' tails have been shown to contain hydrocarbon fragments. Hydrocarbons are organic compounds containing only carbon and hydrogen (acetylene is an example). Carbohydrates are organic compounds such as sugars and starches. They are good to eat, but they are not found in comets. Not knowing the difference between the two, Velikovsky assumed they were the same.

Velikovsky and his followers often claim that his theory made several correct predictions about the nature and characteristics of the planets. One such prediction concerns the temperature of Venus and Mars. Velikovsky said in *Worlds in Collision* (1950) that Venus was hot. Although his precise meaning is unclear, he apparently meant that Venus was giving off more heat to space than it was receiving from the sun (Sagan, 1981). This additional heat was said to have come from Venus's cometary travels when it passed close to the sun. Velikovsky also said that Mars gives off more heat than it receives from the sun, heat received when it encountered Venus in its travels. Neither Venus nor Mars radiates more heat than it receives from the sun. In this sense, then, both of Velikovsky's predictions were wrong. When it was discovered in the early 1970s that the surface temperature of Venus was high, about 850 degrees Fahrenheit, Velikovsky and his followers changed the nature of the prediction after the fact and claimed that it was correct. They conveniently forgot the prediction about Mars, which is wrong no matter how one interprets it. As Sagan (1981, p. 245) says, there is a "planetary double standard at work."

From start to finish, Velikovsky's ideas are the work of an erudite crackpot with a great ability to convince the scientifically untrained (himself included) that there was a great deal of validity in his ideas that establishment scientists were trying to suppress. As noted above, the initial response of the scientific community to Velikovsky was undisguised contempt and scorn. In the 1970s, as scientists began to see the importance of examining even very unusual theories and communicating the results of these investigations to the public, considerable effort has been directed toward a careful examination of Velikovsky's ideas. A symposium on the topic was held at the 1974 annual meeting of the American Association for the Advancement of Science. This conference is the major annual meeting for American scientists from all disciplines. A symposium at such a conference certainly belies the charge of closed-mindedness so frequently made by Velikovsky and his followers. The proceedings of the symposium were later published (Goldsmith, 1977).

In chapter one it was noted that one characteristic of a pseudoscience is an unwillingness to change the theory to take into account new knowledge. In a speech at Harvard University delivered in 1972 Velikovsky correctly stated that science textbooks from the 1950s were now "antiquated." He went on to say that his theories were just as valid in 1972 as in 1950. In other words, the vast advances in knowledge of astronomy, astrophysics, planetary geology, and related fields that had occurred in that twenty-two-year span were irrelevant to the validity of his theories. Velikovsky's attitude can be contrasted with those of establishment scientists faced with revolutionary advances in knowledge.

In the past few years a major change has taken place in astronomers' views of how the moon was formed. The view now widely held is that the moon was formed 4.5 billion years ago by a collision between the then-cooling earth and another, smaller planet about the size of Mars

(Gleick, 1986; Taylor, 1987). A typical response to the theory is that of Dr. H. J. Melosh of the University of Arizona, who was a "typical skeptic" regarding the theory. Quoted in Gleick (1986, p. C3), he said:

> I was sort of an expert on impact cratering, and people hadn't really looked at what happens during impact. So I decided to do it and get rid of this insane idea [that the moon resulted from planetary impact] once and for all. Instead, what I found within weeks is that the physics of what happened during an impact event agrees extremely well [with the impact theory]. The more I looked the more I thought that the giant impact theory was the only one that could explain what we saw.

Here is a typical example of a scientist who completely changes his mind in the space of a few weeks because he is confronted with evidence that his previous ideas were wrong. Gleick (1986) and Taylor (1987) describe in some detail the other evidence that has convinced so many astronomers that the impact theory is correct.

Why was this impact theory accepted, while those of Velikovsky were rejected? Velikovsky presented no evidence to support his ideas. He merely surrounded them with a forest of abstruse citations, many of which were inaccurate. Even more important, the impact theory of lunar formation makes predictions that are found to be correct when tested. Whenever a testable hypothesis could be wrung from Velikovsky's theory, it was found to be wrong.

10

Faith Healing

You are at a "Miracle Service" given by famed faith healer Kathryn Kuhlman. There are thousands of people in the audience. You have seen several seemingly amazing cures, but the most dramatic is about to occur. Kuhlman shouts out, "Someone here is being cured of cancer!" Then you see a fifty-year-old woman, a Mrs. Helen Sullivan [not her real name], arise from a wheelchair and hobble painfully up onto the stage. She has stomach cancer that has metastasized to her liver and the bones of her spinal column, making walking extremely painful. She can walk, but only with the aid of a back brace. William A. Nolen, MD, in his book *Healing: A Doctor in Search of a Miracle* (1974, p. 87) describes what happened next:

> Mrs. Sullivan had, at Kathryn Kuhlman's suggestion, taken off her back brace and run back and forth across the stage several times. Finally, she walked back down the aisle to her wheelchair, waving her brace as she went, while the audience applauded and Kathryn Kuhlman gave thanks to the Lord.

The effect of this miracle cure on the audience must have been immense. How could anyone, no matter how skeptical, doubt what they had seen with their own eyes: a woman devoured by cancer (and she really did have cancer—she was not a shill or a plant) had been cured by God. Now she could not only walk but run without assistance of any sort.

The above example is just one of tens of thousands of miracle cures claimed by faith healers worldwide. Faith healers, whether called that, or witch doctors or shamans, have been around since earliest times. In the twentieth century, at least among western cultures, belief in faith healing rapidly declined until the last few years. With the rise of religious fundamentalism in the 1980s, faith healing has again become extremely popular. It is practiced not only by traveling healers, who move from town to town, but also by many "prime-time preachers" such as W. V. Grant, Peter Popoff, Oral Roberts, Ernest Angley, and Pat Robertson, to name but a few.

Several factors are extremely powerful in convincing people that faith healers are actually able to cure the sick. One is actually witnessing a "cure" such as the one described above, or seeing it on television, or hearing about it from someone who saw it.

How can one explain a cure such as that described above? In fact, no cure took place. Nolen followed up the case and interviewed Mrs. Sullivan two months after her miracle cure. She had gone to the "Miracle Service" expecting a cure, she said.

> At the service, as soon as she [Kathryn Kuhlman] said, "Someone with cancer is being cured," I knew she meant me. I could just feel this burning sensation all over my body and I was convinced the Holy Spirit was at work. I went right up on the stage and when she asked me about the brace I just took it right off, though I hadn't had it off for over four months, I had so much back pain. I was sure I was cured. That night I said a prayer of thanksgiving to the Lord and Kathryn Kuhlman and went to bed, happier than I'd been in a long time. At four o'clock the next morning I woke up with a horrible pain in my back. It was so bad I broke out in a cold sweat. I didn't dare move. (Nolen, 1974, pp. 98-99)

X-rays revealed that one of the bones in her spinal column, a vertebra, weakened already by the cancer, had collapsed. It had collapsed due to the strain that had been put on it when she had run back and forth across the stage. She died two months later, of the cancer that Kathryn Kuhlman had "cured" her of before an audience of thousands.

Skeptics still must explain Mrs. Sullivan's surprising freedom from pain during and immediately after the service. It has been recognized in the past decade that the body has its own physiological and biochemical systems for dealing with pain (Watkins and Mayer, 1986). Several of these systems control pain by causing the release of endogenous substances that are naturally occurring analogues of drugs like morphine and its stronger biochemical relative, heroin. These endogenous substances, termed *endorphins*, are now known to be released at times of stress (Henry, 1982; Kelly, 1986). A high level of excitement, such as that clearly felt by Mrs. Sullivan, is a stressful event, in the physiological sense. Thus, her pain was temporarily eliminated, not because of any miracle cure, but because the excitement brought on by the environment caused a release of endorphins. A few hours later, when these endorphins were no longer present, her pain returned, much magnified by the new damage to her spinal column.

But, of course, Kathryn Kuhlman didn't see Mrs. Sullivan as she lay in her bed crippled and dying. Nor did the thousands of people who "saw with their own eyes" that Mrs. Sullivan had been blessed with what appeared to be a miraculous cure. Since faith healers almost never follow up on the cases they claim to have cured, it is easy to understand why both members of the audience and the healers themselves can become convinced that their cures are real. Psychologically, the situation is little different from that of cold readers convinced they can foretell the future (see chapter two). Their failures don't return, so they see only their successes.

Nolen (1974) followed up many cases of "cures" by faith healers and found no miracles. This has been the universal result when faith healers' "cures" are carefully investigated. Many people, if asked during or immediately after a healing session, will report that their pain has gone away or at least lessened. But, when asked about it again later, they will admit their pain has returned. This temporary reduction of pain that is so commonly reported is due to excitement-induced release of endorphins.

Testimonials are a second, related factor that falsely convinces people of the reality of faith healing—or of the effectiveness of any number of quack remedies and cures. People who genuinely believe that they have been cured by a faith healer, or a quack, are most effective at convincing others. The situation is similar to that of eyewitness testimony for UFOs. As was noted in chapters seven and eight, the one piece of "evidence" that proponents of the extraterrestrial origin of UFOs find most convincing is the testimony of eyewitnesses. As was also seen in those chapters, such eyewitness testimony is highly unreliable. The same applies to testimonials about cures. One can find testimonials attesting to the effectiveness of almost anything. In the early part of this century, before government regulation of advertising claims for medicines, it was common for manufacturers to claim that their particular brand of "snake oil" would cure "consumption," as tuberculosis was known then. They would provide genuine and sincere testimonials from people who had actually used their medicine and felt themselves to be cured. These people would later die of tuberculosis, because the remedies were in fact worthless (Young, 1967). This is illustrated by the poster shown in figure 17.

My own favorite testimonial touts a cure for cancer and cataracts so bizarre that it's difficult to believe it's not a joke. *Time* magazine, in its October 24, 1977, issue (p. 58) reported that then Indian Prime Minister Morarji Desai attributed his vigor at age eighty-one to drinking a cup of his own urine each morning. He said "it was a cure for cancer and cataracts; he claimed to have cured his own brother of tuberculosis" with urine. This item promptly brought another testimonial to the effectiveness of "urine therapy," which was published in *Time's* "Letters" column in the November 14, 1977, issue (p. 10). One Harish Jirmoun of New Bern, North Carolina, reported that he had adopted the custom of drinking his own urine and "have faithfully maintained it for the past twelve years, gaining a sense of vigor that few of my contemporaries (I am 74) can match." It is safe to say that if testimonials play a major part in the "come on" for a cure or therapy, the cure or therapy is almost certainly worthless. If the promoters of the therapy had actual evidence for its effectiveness, they would cite it and not have to rely on testimonials.

The Nature of Disease

The question still remains, however, as to why people give testimonials for worthless cures and treatments. One might expect them to be better able to tell whether they have been cured than to identify the real nature of a UFO they have sighted. But the issue is not so much the ability to determine whether one's condition has improved, but to what cause one attributes the improvement. People often mistake the cause of their improvement because they do not understand simple facts about disease. One such fact that plays into the hands of faith healers and quacks is that most diseases, even serious or terminal illnesses, show variability over time in how ill the patient feels and the severity of his symptoms. The patient with a terminal illness is ultimately going to die. But from day to day, week to week, and month to month, there can be large and irregular changes in how the patient feels and the severity of the symptoms. Sometimes the patient will feel better, other times worse, even though the overall course is downward. This is shown diagrammatically in figure 18.

Why is this variability so important? It means that, even though the overall course of a terminal illness is downward, it is possible to find two points in time, marked A and B in figure 18, between which the patient will think he has improved—he will feel better, for various reasons, even though the disease is still present and has not been cured. If the patient were to go to a faith healer at point A, he would very likely attribute his subjective improvement to the healer and give a glowing testimonial. A further point needs to be made here. When is an individual most likely to seek out some type of unorthodox treatment or cure? Unorthodox treatment is much more likely to be sought when the patient is feeling especially poor. Thus, the chances are great that, because of the variable nature of most diseases, the patient will perceive some improvement in the days following the unorthodox treatment. This has nothing to do with the treatment, but is simply due to the nature of the disease process itself. Nonetheless, the individual is quite likely to attribute the perceived improvement to the faith healer or quack. (Readers with some statistical training will recognize this effect as a type of regression to the mean.)

Two serious diseases that are extremely variable over time in the severity of their symptoms are multiple sclerosis and arthritis. Faith healers and quacks frequently claim to be able to cure these. McKhann (1982, p 232), in a review of the literature on multiple sclerosis, comments that "a striking feature of multiple sclerosis, particularly early in the course of the disease, is the degree of recovery patients can achieve during remissions." These remissions can last for months or years before symptoms reappear. Arthritis, a disease that often causes severe pain in a person's joints, also shows great variation in the degree of pain the patient is suffering. For years, copper bracelets have been a favorite quack cure for arthritis. In spite of the fact that the bracelets had absolutely no effect on the disease, testimonials abounded, along with pseudoscientific double talk used to promote the bracelets. Why did the patients provide the testimonials? Sufferers were much more likely to buy a bracelet when their pain was especially severe, so that ordinary measures, such as aspirin, would not be helpful. Thus, there was an excellent chance that, due to the temporally variable nature of arthritis pain, the pain would be less in the period following purchase of the bracelet. This would be incorrectly attributed to the bracelet, not to the nature of the disease.

Another important factor operates to convince people of the effectiveness of faith healing and quack cures, especially when the "cure" involves the removal or lessening of pain. This is known as the *placebo effect*. For decades it has been known that if a patient believes that a treatment is going to be effective at reducing pain, in about one-third of patients the treatment will actually cause a pain reduction. This occurs even though the pain is due to some actual organic process and the treatment consists of administering a totally inert substance, or placebo, such as sugar water (Melzack, 1973).

As far as pain reduction is concerned, the placebo effect is now understood to be due to the release of endorphins, the same substances responsible for pain reduction caused by the physiological stress of excitement. The placebo effect for pain can be eliminated by giving subjects an injection of the drug naloxone (Gracely *et al.*, 1983; Fields and Levine, 1984). Naloxone blocks the analgesic effects of the endorphins (Watkins and Mayer, 1982, 1986). It has also been shown that the release of endorphins in the placebo situation is a classically conditioned response that can be taught to rats (Watkins and Mayer, 1982, 1986). This research demonstrates that the placebo effect is due to endorphin release. The placebo effect and the temporal variability of pain in any painful disease work together to produce a powerful illusion that a faith healer or a quack has effected a "cure."

In addition to the temporary remissions and easing of symptoms seen in many diseases, in rare situations a disease may spontaneously disappear. This happens even in some types of cancer. Everson and Cole (1966) surveyed the world medical literature and found 170 well-documented cases of *spontaneous regression* or *remission* of cancer. Twenty-nine of the cases were of neuroblastoma, a malignant brain tumor, and nineteen were of malignant melanoma, a particularly lethal type of skin cancer.

Another factor that occasionally results in a seemingly miraculous cure of cancer is what is termed *cure by biopsy* (Rose, 1968). In a typical case the patient is suspected of having cancer on the basis of clinical tests and a biopsy is then taken to determine the exact type of cancer. When the clinical tests are later performed again, signs of the cancer are gone—the cancerous cells were totally removed by the biopsy procedure. This may sound unlikely, since the common image of a cancerous tumor is of a large lump. In reality, cancerous tumors start as tiny collections of cells. Nonetheless, these minute tumors are frequently detectable by various biochemical tests and can be totally removed during biopsy. Rose (1968) reports one case of a patient cured by biopsy who attributed his cure to a faith healer he had consulted following the initial diagnosis of cancer, which was based on the biopsy.

Most people who consult faith healers and quacks, as well as doctors, are not victims of terminal or chronic diseases. Instead, they have disorders of numerous types, from the flu to measles, that will disappear on their own, once the disease has run its course. The disease can either be sped on its way, or the unpleasant symptoms ameliorated, by proper treatment. But, even if the doctor did nothing, about 75 percent of patients would get better on their own. Thus, most people with nonchronic and nonterminal diseases who go to faith healers and quacks will get better after their visit. This has nothing to do with the healer or quack, but is due to the time-limited nature of most diseases and the body's own curative processes. The improvement, however, is often credited to the healer or quack.

Faith Healers' Techniques

Outright fraud and trickery are other tools of the faith healer. The last few years have seen a rise in the number of popular healers who use a variety of tricks to con their audiences into believing that miracle cures are taking place right before the audience's eyes and that the healer is in direct contact with God or Jesus.

Two notorious practitioners of this cruel con game are the Reverend W. V. Grant and the Reverend Peter Popoff. Both have recently been exposed as frauds (see Randi, 1986a, b, c; and Kurtz, 1986, for details). Randi's (1987) book *The Faith Healers* is highly recommended for a detailed treatment of all aspects of faith healing.

Both Grant and Popoff, and other such healers, make use of a combination of cold reading, sleight of hand, and fraud in their performances. In May of 1986 I played a small part in an investigation of faith healer W. V. Grant, spearheaded by magician James Randi. Grant gave a "service" at the Brooklyn Academy of Music in New York City and I, along with several others, went to see what we could find out. Randi had suggested that I volunteer when the call was made for volunteer ushers from the audience. I did so and, as an usher, had access to the backstage area and was able to wander about with considerable freedom during the performance.

We arrived at the Brooklyn Academy of Music well before the service was scheduled to start. During the healing portion of his services, Grant typically walks up to people in the audience, asks them to stand, if they're able, and announces their name, perhaps the name of their doctor, and what they are suffering from. How does Grant get this information? Our investigation confirmed what Randi (1986b) had reported earlier. Before the service starts, members of Grant's staff walk through the hall and chat with those who have arrived early. These people are actually being pumped for information, which is then reported to Grant. We saw, as did investigators at other Grant performances, that those who chatted with staff before the service started were quite likely to be called on to be "cured" later, during the service. When Grant is curing someone, he makes a point of asking whether the person has ever spoken to him or to the individuals who assist him during this part of the service. The person quite truthfully replies no. The response, although truthful, is misleading, as Grant knows, since the members of Grant's staff that the person talked with are different from the assistants on stage with Grant when he does his healing. Randi (1986b), after attending one of Grant's services in Florida, found crib sheets listing information about people who were "cured" in the trash. It was also noticed that one of Grant's staff was using hand signals to let the reverend know what part of his victim's body was "afflicted."

Peter Popoff uses a much more sophisticated method for obtaining information about people in his audience. His staff pump people for information before the show; that information is relayed to him during the show by radio. He has a tiny radio receiver in his ear through which he receives messages from a transmitter in a truck outside the hall where the service is being held. Alec Jason, a communications specialist working with Randi, managed to pick up and record these broadcasts to Popoff during a California service in 1986 (see Randi, 1986c, 1987, for details). Popoff's wife was feeding him the information via the transmitter, while Popoff was claiming to be receiving knowledge from God. Popoff's use of fraud was dramatically revealed on Johnny Carson's "Tonight Show" when Randi showed videotapes of Popoff performing a healing and simultaneously played a tape of the messages from Popoff's wife. Popoff's reaction was to deny everything and ask his followers to pray for him. His ministry then charged that NBC had hired an actress to imitate his wife's voice and that the videotape shown on the program had been faked. Finally, Popoff admitted that he "occasionally" was given names over the radio. Randi (1986a, c) notes, however, that during the service when the radio messages to Popoff were recorded, the names of all the people he called out were passed to him via radio.

At the Grant service I attended I was surprised to see how unsophisticated the healings were. Grant would frequently approach older people and announce that they had "the arthritis." Since many of the older people had canes, this was not a bad guess—and even if it was wrong, Grant didn't give people a chance to correct him. In one particularly sad case, Grant asked an old man with a cane to hobble out to the aisle. Grant then performed his usual healing routine—to the cheers of the audience—grabbed the man's cane, broke it in two, and tossed it down onto the stage. A great cheer rose up. Another miracle had taken place— the old man no longer needed his cane. Immediately Grant dashed off to another part of the theater, with all eyes following him. Except mine— I watched as the old man, now without his cane, hobbled back to his seat, walking no better than he had before.

For another cure, a man in a back brace was brought to the stage. He walked onto the stage perfectly normally. Grant asked the rather overweight fellow how long it had been since he had been able to touch his toes. "Years," came the reply. Grant then directed the fellow to bend over and touch his toes. He promptly squatted down and did so. This was no miracle, since there was nothing wrong with this man's *knees*, but the audience let out another cheer and praised the Lord again for showing another miracle.

For another cure, an old man in a wheelchair at the front of the hall was made to walk again—or so it seemed to the audience. Other members of our group had noticed that this man had walked into the hall before the performance and had been seated in the wheelchair by Grant's staff. I doubt if anyone else noticed this. So, when Grant had the man stand up and walk, the natural, if incorrect, assumption the audience made was that he had been miraculously cured. This is an example of a common trick used by Grant, Popoff, and other faith healers. Wheelchairs are rented and placed at the front of the theater. Before the service, when frail-looking older people enter, they are escorted to the wheelchairs. Then, when they stand up and walk during the service, the healer takes credit for a miracle.

Grant can be fast on his feet when the occasion demands. He approached one woman and asked how long she had been blind. She replied, "Partially," into the microphone, but Grant ignored her and asked the audience if they believed that Jesus could cure her. "Yes," they shouted. With that, Grant held up several fingers and asked the woman, "How many?" She promptly gave the correct answer—not surprisingly, since she was only partially blind. But Grant was given credit for yet another miraculous cure.

The final "cure" before the "offering," when money is collected, was obviously designed to impress the audience. Grant announced that one of the volunteer ushers had one leg shorter than the other and that this affliction would be cured. When this "volunteer usher" was brought onto the stage, he turned out to be a member of Grant's staff whom I had seen backstage when I first went there for my instructions on what to do as an usher. After a laying on of hands, Grant made a great show of removing the man's orthopedic shoes and tossing them to the corner of the theater, as if to say, "You're healed, no need for these anymore." Another huge cheer went up, and Grant's latest miracle cure walked, without limping, offstage. Of course, he hadn't limped when he came onstage, but I suspect this was not widely noticed. He also walked offstage barefoot, but that was quickly remedied as another Grant staff member scurried around, collected his shoes, and returned them to him. It appears that Grant does not always use a shill when he does this leg-lengthening trick. Randi (1986b) has described how, by pulling a person's shoes and making his or her leg move slightly, Grant can make it appear to the audience that the person's leg is being lengthened by an inch or so.

At this point the reader may be wondering how the audience could have fallen for what was, to me at least, such obvious trickery. This is an important question, and there are a number of factors involved. First, I did not go expecting to see miracles. I went prepared and knowing what sort of tricks to look for. The audience, unprepared and expecting miracles, was easily taken in. Second, before the healing portion of the service started, there had been about an hour of preaching and singing, which had roused the audience's emotions. At least one woman fainted. When people are in such a state, their critical faculties are impaired. The combination of the audience's high level of emotional arousal and their initial uncritical acceptance of the claim that miracle cures would happen was all Grant needed to allow him to succeed in what was, to those of us who were there to investigate him, such obvious trickery.

This is not to say—and this is a vital point—that the members of the audience were in any way "dumb" or less intelligent than the investigators. This was clearly not the case. Like the great majority of Americans, they simply didn't have the background information necessary to prepare them to spot Grant's tricks. Thus, they were taken in.

After the leg lengthening, it was time for the offering. Grant spent about fifteen minutes reiterating that no one was obligated to give (admission had been free), but he also spent time detailing the great expenses of his church's good works. He said his television program was seen in more than 300 cities. (In fact, he was then on television in only about 90 cities [Randi, 1986b].) He told of the great expense of his missions in Haiti. He also said that if people gave money, Jesus would return it to them one hundred times over by the end of the year.

Then it was time for the actual offering, and one of the jobs of the ushers was to pass the collection buckets. I was dumbfounded at the amount of money we collected. I had been assigned to a rather small part of the theater, yet I estimated that I collected at least $6,000 in my bucket. The donations were almost wholly in cash—$20, $50, $100 bills. There were at least twelve ushers to start with, although a few more appeared in time for the offering, so a conservative estimate of the amount of money collected during the offering alone was $72,000. But Grant had other ways to relieve people of their money. Earlier in the program there had been an opportunity for anyone who wished to do so to make a personal offering to Grant. The offering was to be placed in an envelope and handed to Grant, who stood on stage taking the envelopes one by one. You were supposed to write on a form that went with the envelope what your problem was and what you wanted healed. Those who made a personal offering were carefully instructed not to speak to Grant as they passed him their envelope, presumably so that no one could later claim they had given him personal information. But Randi (1986b) has found that Grant uses this period to commit to memory the faces of at least some of the people who make a personal offering so they can later be picked out of the audience and "cured." In any event, between 400 and 500 people stood in line to give Grant their personal offering. There is no way to know how much money was in the envelopes, but since it was implied that those who gave personal offerings would receive special healing, it seems safe to assume that these were larger than the average contribution given during the later offering.

Grant also had books, pamphlets, tape-recorded Bible study courses, and similar merchandise for sale. I would conservatively estimate that he took in $100,000 cash that night. If he stages this sort of show five days a week, forty weeks a year, his income would be $20 million a year. This does not count income from his huge direct-mail solicitations and money he receives in response to appeals made on his television program. Further, note that since Grant is running a "religious charity," he pays no taxes on any of this money. He doesn't even have to file an informational tax return (IRS Form 990). Grant and his fellow faith healers have literally found a license to steal. And they steal from those who can least afford it—the poor, the old, the sick, and the hopeless.

The saddest aspect of Grant's "service" was the truly lame and seriously ill people who were carefully herded by Grant's staff to the rear of the theater. There were several children with cerebral palsy, or some other crippling disease. There was an old woman, strapped into a wheelchair, who would thrash around, moan, and call out. She must have been a stroke victim. A handkerchief had to be placed in her mouth to keep her quiet. These people, and their parents or guardians, had come to Grant hoping for a miracle cure. They gave donations, like nearly everyone else. They would go home disappointed. And what was Grant's explanation to those who weren't cured? (He claimed that 90 percent of the people present would be cured). He said that Jesus would only heal those who were pure in heart and without bitterness. If anyone wasn't cured, his or her heart still had some bitterness. It might not be much, it might be unconscious, but still it was there and prevented the cure. So people who weren't cured would have only themselves to blame.

Pat Robertson, moderator of the popular "700 Club" television program broadcast nationwide by his Christian Broadcasting Network, does faith healing during the program. He makes use of the "multiple out" (described in chapter two) to make it appear that his cures are real. He typically "sees" some disease or problem and, after describing it, announces that it is being cured. For example, he might say, "I see a man with a hip problem. The Lord is curing you. There is a woman with a kidney illness. Jesus will cure you." Days, weeks, or months later, a woman may write and report that, after she watched the broadcast, her kidney infection cleared up. A man may write to say that his sprained hip was much less painful after he had seen the program. These reports are then taken as evidence of specific, predicted cures.

It's easy to see what is really going on here. The initial cure predictions are extremely vague. Robertson's audience is huge, and there will certainly be many in it with problems resembling the type he vaguely describes. Like most illnesses, most of these problems will go away, either spontaneously or under medical treatment. However, Robertson may be given credit for the "cure," even if the cured person was under a doctor's care. If the problem disappears spontaneously, it is even more likely that the "cure" will be attributed to Robertson and not to the body's natural, and considerable, ability to heal itself. Further, there is no medical verification that people claiming cures really had what they say they had. Further, people with kidney or hip problems who listened to the program but weren't cured are hardly likely to write in and say so. Thus, Robertson and his staff are selectively exposed to reports of cures and—like cold readers who become convinced of their power to foretell the future because their victims keep telling them they can—become convinced that true cures are taking place.

Another popular faith healer is Sister Grace, also known as "Amazing Grace." She makes impressive claims about the people she has cured and the miracles God has wrought through her. However, when actual evidence is requested to back up these claims, there is total silence. I had an interesting interaction with Grace on WCBS-TV in New York City in the spring of 1984. We briefly debated the issue of faith healing. Grace brought with her a man who claimed that she had cured him of lung cancer and of emphysema. He produced X-rays and a medical record to support the claim. These were shown with great flourish on the air. I have no doubt that they impressed the viewing audience. After the debate, I asked if I could obtain a copy of the medical record and the X-rays for further study and verification. Not only was the request flatly refused but also the name of the doctor who treated the patient was kept secret.

At her services, Grace claims that God tells her the names of audience members and what diseases they have. She then does the laying on of hands and "cures" the disease. In one particularly interesting case, Grace "cured" a man of a disease he didn't have (Steiner, 1986-87). Steiner (1986-87) had planted a "stinger" in Grace's audience at one performance; she not only "cured" him of a disease he didn't have but also called him by the pseudonym he had used to get into the performance, not his real name. Steiner (1986-87, p. 31) comments, "This is not religion. This is a con game."

Psychic Surgery

Psychic surgery, most popular from the mid-1960s through the mid-1970s, is one brand of faith healing where sleight of hand is relied on exclusively to achieve the "miracle." Psychic surgeons claim to be able to insert their hands inside the patient's body without making an incision and to remove dead and diseased tissue. As the psychic surgeon performs "surgery," his hand is seen to disappear into the patient's belly and a pool of blood appears. After groping around, apparently inside the body cavity, the psychic surgeon dramatically pulls his hand "out" of the body, clutching what is said to be the tumor or diseased tissue that was causing the patient's problem. The offending tissue is promptly tossed in a handy nearby fire to be purified. When the patient's belly is wiped clean of the blood, no incision is found.

Testimonials to and eyewitness reports of such miracle operations were common when psychic surgery was popular and still turn up from time to time. For example, in 1974 John Fuller wrote a glowing, credulous book on Brazilian psychic surgeon Arigo titled *Arigo: Surgeon of the Rusty Knife*. (This is the same author who wrote the "true" account of Betty and Barney Hill's abduction by a UFO discussed in chapter eight.) More recently, actor Andy Kaufman, who played in the television series "Taxi," visited a psychic surgeon in the Philippines in hopes of curing his terminal cancer. Kaufman's girlfriend was convinced that sleight of hand was not used (Gardner, 1984, p. 8) because she stood "not a foot away." Kaufman died of his cancer after his "cure." The Philippines was home for most of the psychic surgeons during the time of their great popularity, and tens of thousands of often desperately ill Americans and Europeans trekked there in hopes of a miracle cure.

Both Nolen (1974) and Randi (1980) have exposed the methods the psychic surgeons used; Nolen actually went to the Philippines and was "operated on" by one. The "operation" starts as the hand appears to enter the patient's belly. This is accomplished by creating an impression in the belly by pushing down and flexing the fingers slowly into a fist—the fingers thus appear to be moving into the belly, but are really simply hidden behind the hand. The blood that further disguises the true movement of the fingers and adds drama to the proceedings can come from two sources. One is a fake thumb, worn over the real thumb and filled with a red liquid. Such a fake thumb is a common magician's implement. Blood can also be passed to the surgeon in red balloons hidden in cotton the psychic surgeon is using, the cotton and its hidden contents being passed to him by an "assistant." The bits of "tumor" can also be passed to the psychic surgeon this way, or hidden in the false thumb. What is the "tumor" that is "removed" from the body, and what is the blood? Psychic surgeons are unwilling to give up samples of either material for analysis. When samples have been obtained—usually by grabbing the material before the surgeon can destroy it—the "tumor" material turns out to be chicken intestines and similar animal remains. The blood is either animal blood or red dye.

As if psychic surgery weren't enough, there is even at least one psychic dentist—Willard Fuller, who has been helping God fill teeth and reshape maloccluded jaws for nearly twenty years. In spite of the usual testimonials, Fuller is nothing more than a practitioner of sleight of hand. One dentist examined twenty-eight people before they were "healed" by Fuller. Those claiming to be healed were re-examined after the healing. In one case "gold fillings miraculously bestowed turned out instead to be tobacco stains" (Radke, quoted in Hegstad, 1974, p. 252). In another case, a woman reported a new silver filling where only a cavity had existed before the healing service. Dentist Radke had taken pictures of this woman's teeth before the service and found, on re-examining those pictures, that the filling was indeed there when the pictures were taken. The woman then "readily admitted that she had forgotten that the filling was there" (Radke, quoted in Hegstad, 1974, p. 253). In May 1986 Fuller went on a tour through Australia, where he was arrested, tried, and found guilty of practicing dentistry without a license and of fraud (Plummer, 1986). This did not in any way impede a coast-to-coast tour of the United States upon his return from Australia.

The Dangers of Faith Healing

One point about faith healers cannot be overemphasized: *they kill people.* Convinced that they are cured when they are not, patients may be dissuaded from seeking legitimate medical help that could save their lives. For example, many kinds of cancer are now treatable, if treatment begins early enough. However, the diagnosis of cancer still carries enormous emotional power and has driven many people to seek out faith healers. Since cancer of many types can now be detected very early, well before patients suffer any serious symptoms, it is likely that they will come back from the faith healer relieved and "feeling better" since they have received the assurance that they are cured. Since the cancer has been "cured," there is no need to go back to the physician—until the cancer, unaffected by the blandishments of the faith healer, continues to grow and reaches a point where it can no longer be ignored. A return to the doctor at this point will frequently bring a diagnosis of a now-untreatable cancer that could have been cured if treatment had been begun when the initial diagnosis was made. In an especially callous display of showmanship, faith healer Peter Popoff at the end of some of his services urges the audience to throw away their medicines because they have been cured by "Doctor Jesus." A shower of prescription and nonprescription bottles follows. How many of the largely elderly and poor members of Popoff's audience will go home to great pain, or even to die, because they have thrown away the medicine that is really treating their health problems?

Devout members of one well-known religious sect, the Christian Scientists, depend entirely on faith healers within the church, called *practitioners,* for treatment of their illnesses. The practitioners' training consists of a few weeks of religious instruction. The church teaches that disease and pain are "illusions" that are *caused* by medical diagnosis (Swan, 1983). The practitioner is not permitted to engage in any sort of assistance to patients, other than praying for them. Thus, the use of drugs, thermometers, and "even the simplest human measures for relieving suffering or discomfort, such as hot packs, ice packs, enemas, and back rubs" (Swan, 1983, p. 1640) are forbidden. The practitioner's praying may even be done over the telephone. Further, practitioners charge for their "services," and the Internal Revenue Service has been persuaded that such charges can be deducted as medical expenses. Even more astonishingly, Blue Cross-Blue Shield in many states will reimburse such expenses.

The bizarre practices of the Church of Christ, Scientist are also applied to children. Parents are forbidden to take their children, no matter how sick, to legitimate physicians, but must let them be treated solely by Christian Scientist practitioners. As might be expected, this has resulted in the deaths of Christian Scientist children from diseases that could have been treated, and the child's life saved, had medical attention been provided. The Christian Science church, along with many other fundamentalist sects and cults that believe in faith healing, argues that it is parents' right to withhold legitimate medical treatment from their children and that they should not be prosecuted for child abuse when children die from the lack of such treatment (Swan, 1983). In many states laws covering child abuse and neglect contain specific religious exemptions. These permit a parent to withhold medical treatment from a child if the parent is a member of a religious group that believes in the power of faith healing or in the power of prayer to heal. Such exemptions have resulted in the death of many children whose lives could have been saved by legitimate medical tratment. The Church of Christ, Scientist lobbies vigorously when attempts are made to eliminate such exemptions.

Responding to the serious issues raised by Swan (1983)—who was a Christian Scientist herself until one of her children died of a treatable meningitis at the hands of a Christian Science practitioner—Nathan Talbot, a church official, attempted to justify the church's reliance on prayer. He stated that "the most important body of evidence concerning Christian Science healing is the ongoing published testimonies of healing in the denomination's periodicals . . ." (Talbot, 1983, p. 1642). Talbot (1983) claims that a few of these cures have been medically verified, but cites no specific examples.

The Role of Shrines

Not only people but places have been alleged to produce miracle cures. The most famous is probably the shrine at Lourdes, France, where according to popular legend thousands of cures have taken place since 1858, when a teenage girl had a vision of the Virgin Mary at the site of the present shrine. Alleged miracle cures at Lourdes are now investigated by the Lourdes Medical Bureau. If the case warrants, it is then taken up by the International Medical Committee of Lourdes (IMCL), composed of Catholic doctors from each of the European countries that sends large numbers of pilgrims to Lourdes. If the IMCL decides that the case is medically inexplicable, it is up to the Roman Catholic Church to make the final judgment as to whether a miracle has taken place (Bernstein, 1982; Dowling, 1984). Out of the estimated 2 million sick who have traveled to Lourdes since 1858, the church has accepted sixty-four cures as miraculous. Nearly 6,000 other cases, in which individuals claimed to have been miraculously cured, have been rejected. Since 1954, when the IMCL came into existence, thirteen cures have been accepted as miraculous (Dowling, 1984).

A careful examination of the most recent cases certified by the church in 1978 as miracle cures suggests that the medical evaluations of even the certified miracles leave much to be desired (Bernstein, 1982). Serge Perrin was diagnosed as suffering from "recurring organic hemiplegia with ocular lesions, due to cerebral circulatory defects." Bernstein (1982, p. 134) concludes that "U.S. specialists agreed that if there were an organic illness at all, multiple sclerosis was a more likely possibility." Perrin's symptoms were also consistent with a hysterical disorder, in which seemingly physical symptoms are due to psychological problems. Such disorders are frequently "cured" when the patient believes a treatment will be effective. The belief is the key; it does not matter whether the treatment is a real one or a placebo.

That Perrin may have multiple sclerosis is an important point. Three other post-1954 certified miracle cures have been of multiple sclerosis. Dowling (1984, p. 635) says that one of the criteria for acceptance of a case by the IMCL for further study, even before it has been decided whether to recommend the case to the church for final judgment, is "that the natural history of the disease precludes the possibility of spontaneous remission." But it has long been known that multiple sclerosis shows just such remissions. In his review of the literature on the disease McKhann (1982, p. 232) states that "some patients have a . . . disease with inexorable progression. More common is the pattern of exacerbations and remissions followed by a decrease in exacerbations and the appearance of slow progression. Finally, some patients may have one or two episodes and then be symptom-free for many years." A follow-up study (Kurtzke, 1968, cited in McKhann, 1982, p. 232) of multiple sclerosis patients showed that "75 percent of the patients were alive 25 years after the onset of the disease. Of these survivors, 55 percent are without significant disability."

In 1963 a young woman was certified as having had a miraculous cure of Budd-Chiari syndrome in which the veins of the liver become blocked. In 1970 she died of Budd-Chiari syndrome. According to Dowling (1984, p. 637) the IMCL "concluded that when they reached their decision [that the woman had had a miracle cure] they were insufficiently aware of the natural history of Budd-Chiari syndrome and the possibility of natural remission." This shows admirable candor on the committee's part, but this case, as well as that of Perrin and the other three "miraculous" multiple sclerosis cures, points to very poor investigations.

A major source of the fame of Lourdes is not the certified miracle cures but the thousands of personal reports of people who went there and "got better." The shrine is lined with the discarded canes and crutches of those who could walk without them after their visit. However, the trip to Lourdes and the ceremonies performed there serve to build great excitement and hope in the pilgrims. Bernstein (1982, p. 146) describes the "electricity in the air as the huge crowd [of pilgrims] moves from the bank of the river to the grand upper basilica, singing in unison." This is just the type of exciting and physiologically stressful stimulus that causes release of pain-reducing endorphins, as described earlier. Those who come to Lourdes finding it difficult but not impossible to walk with crutches or a cane will thus experience a reduction in their level of pain, perhaps enough to allow them to walk unaided, at least for awhile. When the pain returns, at least the period of relative freedom from pain will be accepted as a miracle. After all, the biochemistry of pain reduction via endorphin release is far from common knowledge. The pain's return will be explained as due to failure to pray enough, or to some other mystical cause. The French writer Anatole France made a telling and pungent comment upon visiting Lourdes in the late nineteenth century and seeing all the abandoned crutches and canes: "What, what, no wooden legs???"

There is apparently a brisk market in the United States for water from Lourdes. It is imported by the Lourdes Center in Boston. The center's newsletter is filled with testimonials to the wonderful curative powers of the water: "For the past six years I was handicapped with a sore toe-nail; each spring I was obliged to have it lanced by the doctors. . . . I applied Lourdes water constantly [and] I now have a normal white nail and no infection" or "My mother was delivered from cancer pain" (quoted in Bernstein, 1982, p. 141). One need only remember the urine drinkers' testimonials to marvel at the miraculous power of belief to make people see miracles where there are none.

Along with the increased popularity of faith healing has come an increased interest—especially among the nursing profession and "holistic" medicine movement—in what has come to be known as the *therapeutic touch*. This is simply the laying on of hands to the patient's body. It is said to facilitate healing through the extremely vague mechanism of transfer of personal "energy" (Krieger, Peper, and Ancoli, 1979). The effect is not attributed to faith, the action of God, or the placebo effect. Clark and Clark (1984) have reviewed the research that has been conducted on therapeutic touch. They find that, due to poorly designed experiments, "current practice of therapeutic touch is empirically little more than practice of placebo" (p. 37). As was the case in the study of psychic phenomena such as ESP, poorly controlled and designed studies supported the effectiveness of therapeutic touch. Well-designed studies failed to find any effect. An example of the latter is a study by Randolph (1984) in which therapeutic touch had no effect on subjects' physiological responses to stressful events.

11

Health and Nutrition Quackery

Health and nutrition quackery is a major medical problem facing today's society. Ironically, this occurs in spite of a vast increase in scientific knowledge about the fundamental nature of diseases, their treatment, and cure, and about the scientific basis of good nutrition. The modern health quack fits naturally into the category of pseudoscience because his claims are couched in impressive sounding scientific or medical jargon. Impressive sounding unless one knows enough about the topic to see through the verbal smoke screen. A report by Congressman Claude Pepper, chairman of the House Select Committee on Aging, estimates that health quackery—defined as "the promotion and sale of useless remedies promising relief from chronic and critical health conditions" (Pepper, 1984, p. v)—costs the American public at least $10 billion a year.

It must be realized that the cost of health and nutrition quackery is more than the simple sum of the money wasted on useless cures and fad diets. There is also a great cost in needless suffering and death. Like those who believe in the faith healer's assurance that they have been cured, many people who consult quacks shun legitimate medical treatment that could either cure them or really ease their suffering.

The subject of health quackery is much too vast to be fully treated here, and this section will barely scratch the surface. For more detailed discussions, the reader should consult the following references: Barrett (1980a), Pepper (1984), Stalker and Glymour (1985), Consumer Reports (1980), Bender (1985), Whelan and Stare (1976, 1983), and Fried (1984). Historical perspective on quackery and nutrition nonsense is provided by Young (1967) and Deutsch (1977).

Fad Diets

Hardly a month goes by without the appearance of yet another quack diet book heavily promoted by its author and publisher as a surefire way to lose weight, stay fit, and cure what ails you. Such diets range from the merely useless to the deadly. Nor is the fact that the author is a medical doctor any guarantee that the diet is effective or even safe. For example, one of the most dangerous diets in recent years, the liquid protein diet, was promoted by Robert Linn, MD, in his 1976 *Last Chance Diet*. Since the mid-1970s, more than fifty people have died from liquid protein diets. The diet can also cause damage to the heart, liver, and kidneys, as well as "side effects like hair loss, muscle weakness, nausea, headaches, dizziness, bad breath, skin dryness, serious potassium imbalance, decreased sex drive, difficulty in keeping warm, menstrual irregularities, constipation, and nervous disorders" (Whelan and Stare, 1983, p. 78). What evidence did Dr. Linn provide his readers for the effectiveness of his diet? Testimonials.

Another dangerous and especially bizarre diet is the *No Aging Diet* of Benjamin Frank, MD (1976). This one claims to make you young again, or at least slow the aging process. The major constituent of this diet is sardines—lots of them, nearly every day. Why sardines? Because sardines have a high DNA and RNA content: Dr. Frank believes that aging is caused by a breakdown of DNA or RNA in the body. There may be some truth to this; at least one theory of the cellular basis of aging is a slow degradation of DNA (see Schneider and Reed, 1985 for a review). However, even if this theory of. aging is correct, to claim that eating lots of DNA in the form of sardines will somehow repair the damaged DNA is utter nonsense.

To prove the effectiveness of his diet, Dr. Frank presents before-and-after pictures of several people. The pictures taken after they have been on the diet do look better. Their faces are fuller, facial lines are smoothed, and their cheeks rosier. The reason for this change is fundamentally linked to the dangers of this diet. Sardines are high in salt (sodium chloride) as well as DNA and RNA. Sodium and chloride have a number of physiological effects but two are most important here. They increase water retention and increase blood pressure. Thus, lines in faces seem to smooth out, due to increased water retention, after a period of time on the diet and the cheeks look rosier due to high blood pressure. One need hardly point out, however, that high blood pressure is not healthy, especially in older individuals.

One of the country's best-known diet doctors is Robert Atkins, MD. His first book, *Dr. Atkins' Diet Revolution* (1972), was heavily criticized as dangerous nonsense (Whelan and Stare, 1983). His several later books, as Whelan and Stare (1983) show, fall into the same category. One, *Dr. Atkins' Nutrition Breakthrough* (1982), even claims that diet alone can be a safe treatment for various medical disorders and that medication can be dispensed with. Whelan and Stare (1983) also comment critically on the diets of Herman Tarnower, MD (Tarnower and Baker, 1981) and Irwin

Stillman, MD (Stillman and Barker, 1983). Medical doctors are capable of writing such nonsense because they generally receive very little training in nutrition.

Publishing diet books is extremely profitable, and publishers almost never check authors' claims with reputable scientific authorities. This reprehensible and irresponsible policy has undoubtedly cost lives. Had the publishers of Linn's deadly liquid diet checked Linn's regimen with experts they would, one hopes, have refused to publish it.

The credentials of diet book authors, and those who write glowing blurbs and reviews of these books, are also rarely checked by the publisher. As of this writing, the most popular quack diet book currently is Harvey and Marilyn Diamond's (1985) Fit for Life, published by Warner Books, which has been on the best-seller lists for months. The diet's major premise is that you can only eat certain types of foods at certain times of the day because the body processes of digestion, absorption, and elimination go on only at certain times of the day. This is utter nonsense. Harvey Diamond claims to have a Ph.D. in nutrition; in fact, his degree is from an unaccredited school that was never authorized to grant degrees. For the right amount of money, anyone can buy exactly the same degrees.

One dead giveaway of a quack diet is the claim that the diet rids the body of "impurities" or "toxins" of one sort or another. Exactly what these dread "toxins" are is never specified, but the typical quack diet claims that the diet somehow "cleanses" the body. The Diamonds' book fits directly into this category: one whole chapter is devoted to a pseudo-scientific "theory of detoxification."

Another sure sign of a quack diet is the claim that the foods eaten while on the diet require more calories to digest than they contain, so that one can "eat oneself thin." Such claims are baseless. Another sign of a quack diet, one that is also a general sign of a quack treatment of any type, is the use of testimonials as evidence for the diet's effectiveness. As has been noted earlier, testimonials alone are worthless. For example, in the case of diets or weight reduction devices, a person may actually lose a certain amount of weight, give a testimonial for the product, and then, later, regain the lost weight.

The best advice that can be given is to avoid diet books altogether. Body weight is in part under genetic control (Stunkard et al., 1986) and attempts to change it dramatically are probably doomed to failure. Further, dieting may actually make it more difficult to lose weight. Even when significant amounts of weight are lost through dieting, the fat cells do not die, they merely shrink (Kolata, 1986). Thus, they are still present, ready to absorb more fat when the dieter goes off the diet. As far as the fat cells and the rest of the body's physiology are concerned, a diet is actually a period of starvation. How can the body best cope with periods of starvation? By making sure that when the next one occurs, more fat is retained in the fat cells. Thus, it is commonly reported that it is relatively easy to lose a certain number of pounds the first time one diets. But, if one goes off the diet and regains the weight, it is harder to lose the same amount of weight the second time one tries. And it is even harder to lose the weight the third time around. This is due to a complicated interactive feedback system that involves the fat cells themselves and those parts of the brain that control eating behavior (Kolata 1985, 1986; Brody, 1987).

Vitamins and Health Foods

Food quackery is not limited to the subject of weight control. Claims abound that certain dietary substances, namely vitamins, can cure a variety of diseases. A vitamin is simply "an organic substance required to promote one or more essential biochemical reactions within living cells. Unlike foods, vitamins are needed only in tiny amounts and are not a source of energy [calories]" (*Consumer Reports*, 1986, p. 170). There are two categories of vitamins, the water-soluble (B complex and C) and nonwater-soluble (A, D, E, and K). The health food and vitamin industries spend milllions of dollars annually to convince the public that they need to add vitamin supplements to their diet in order to obtain a sufficient, healthy supply of vitamins. This is simply wrong. The vast majority of Americans get all the vitamins needed in their regular diet (*Consumer Reports*, 1986; Fried, 1975; Whelan and Stare, 1983), even if they eat fast foods frequently. Vitamin supplements, which are often quite expensive, are thus a waste of money. Bender (1985, p. 137) has commented that "Americans have the most expensive urine in the world" because excesses of the water-soluble vitamins, which the body does not store, simply pass out through the urine. "Treating the toilet" is another phrase that accurately describes attempts to increase levels of the water-soluble vitamins in people who already have normal levels. Supplemental doses of the nonwater-soluble vitamins are stored in the body, largely in the fat tissues.

Many people mistakenly believe that if a tiny amount of a vitamin is good, a huge amount must be even better. This attitude, actively encouraged by the health food industry, has led to the all-too-common practice of taking not only a daily vitamin supplement, but megadoses of assorted vitamins. Not only is such a practice a waste of money, it can be medically dangerous and even deadly. This is true even for the water-soluble vitamins (B and C), the excesses of which are excreted by the body in the urine. Megadoses of B_6, for example, have been shown to cause nerve damage that resulted in sensory and motor impairments in humans (Schaumburg, et al., 1983). Huge amounts of vitamin C, such as are recommended to cure various disorders by the health food industry and vitamin promoters, can cause breakdown of kidney function, kidney stones, and impairment of the immune system (Bender, 1985).

Megadoses of the nonwater-soluble vitamins can also be dangerous because the excess of these vitamins is stored in the body. It should be emphasized that the serious side effects of vitamin overdoses (see Herbert, 1980, for details of these effects) are never seen in people taking a simple daily vitamin supplement. However, the dangers of vitamin overdose are very real because so many people accept the quack recommendations of the health food industry and intentionally give themselves huge overdoses of vitamins. At such levels, vitamins are poisonous.

The late Adele Davis was one promoter of megadoses of vitamins and other nutrition nonsense who needs to be discussed in some detail because her dangerous views are still being propagated by several of her books that are still in print. Unlike most health food proponents, Davis had some real training: as an undergraduate at the University of California, Berkeley, she took courses in nutrition. She later, in 1938, received a master's degree in biochemistry from the University of Southern California, Los Angeles. However, her early training did not prevent her from writing several of the most dangerous and misleading quack books on nutrition ever published. Her *Let's Eat Right to Keep Fit* (1954), *Let's Get Well* (1965) and *Let's Have Healthy Children* (1959) became best sellers.

Like the works of Velikovsky discussed in chapter nine, some of Davis's books contain impressive-looking lists of references that seem to document the research that backs up her beliefs and recommendations. However, the references are often irrelevant to the topic she is discussing. For example, in *Let's Get Well*, a "reference given in her discussion of 'lip problems' and vitamins turns out to be an article about influenza, apoplexy and aviation, with mention of neither lips nor vitamins" (Knight, 1980, p. 162). This is far from an isolated incident. The irrelevant references must have been provided to give a false impression of erudition and scholarly support for Davis's claims.

The books are full of errors, some minor and some that have caused injury and even death to those who followed Davis's advice. There is, on the average, one error on every page of *Let's Eat Right to Keep Fit*, Davis's best-selling book (Knight, 1980). Like other nutrition quacks, Davis recommended massive doses of vitamins. In one case the mother of a four-year-old girl followed Davis's advice and gave her daughter huge doses of vitamins A and D, plus another recommended substance, calcium lactate. When the child was taken to the hospital, she "appeared pale and chronically ill. She had been having diarrhea, vomiting, fever and loss of hair. Her liver and spleen were enlarged and other physical signs suggested she had a brain tumor (Knight, 1980, p. 161). The symptoms were due to the vitamins and calcium lactate and went away when these "healthy" supplements were no longer given.

In another case, also reported by Knight (1980), a child was given large doses of vitamin A, following the recommendation in Davis's *Let's Have Healthy Children*. The result was that the child's growth was stunted. A suit was brought against Davis and her publisher, which was settled out of court in 1976 for $160,000. In a more tragic case (Knight, 1980), a four-month-old girl died when her parents followed Davis's advice, again from *Let's Have Healthy Children*, and gave her potassium chloride for colic.

Numerous claims have been made that above-normal levels of various vitamins can cure specific diseases. The best-known such claim is that by Nobel Prize winner Linus Pauling that vitamin C can prevent the common cold. While vitamin C may have a mild effect on some cold symptoms, like runny noses, the effect is small and can be obtained by taking much less vitamin C than the large doses recommended by Pauling. Pauling (1980) has also claimed that vitamin C is a useful treatment of cancer. This claim was tested in a rigorous study by Moertel *et al.* (1985) in which 100 cancer patients were given either a placebo or high doses of vitamin C. Neither the patients nor the physicians who evaluated their disease knew whether an individual was receiving vitamin C or a placebo. The results showed that vitamin C had no effect at all on either the progression of the disease or the survival rate of the patients in the two groups. Fried (1984), Whelan and Stare (1983), and Bender (1985) discuss numerous other claims that megadoses of vitamins are cures for various disorders. The claims are false.

It has recently been shown that there is a relationship between vitamins A and E and some types of cancer. Menkes *et al.* (1986) studied the blood serum of 25,802 individuals. The serum had been collected in 1974. In the next eleven years, 99 of these people developed lung cancer. The serum levels of vitamin E in the lung cancer patients was found to be significantly lower than in individuals who did not develop lung cancer. Earlier studies on serum vitamin E levels have given conflicting results, but this is probably due to the fact that these studies examined many fewer patients and were, therefore, less reliable. Menkes *et al.* (1986) found no difference in vitamin A levels in the serum of the lung cancer patients and noncancerous subjects. This finding confirms a similar finding (Friedman, *et al.*, 1986) in which no difference in serum vitamin A levels was found between 151 patients with cancer and a group of control subjects.

Animal studies have shown that vitamin E and beta carotene, a precursor of vitamin A, reduce the carcinogenic effects of some chemicals and cause tumor development to slow (Menke *et al.*, 1986). Given these results, investigations of whether dietary supplementation with vitamin E and beta carotene will reduce cancer incidence in humans are currently in progress (Hennekens, 1986).

The chemical 13-cis-retionic acid, a close chemical relative of vitamin A, has been shown to improve the condition of patients suffering from oral lesions that often become cancerous (Hong *et al.*, 1986). The Hong *et al.* (1986) study was conducted double blind, so placebo effects were controlled. After administration of the drug was discontinued, however, the condition relapsed in two to three months. Similar inhibition, but not eradication, of cancerous tumors has been shown in animals given retinoids (Hong *et al.*, 1986).

These results and similar studies (Meyskens and Prasad, 1986) do suggest that some vitamins play some role in the prevention and treatment of some types of cancer. It is important to realize, however, that studies of this sort do *not* show that self-administered megadoses of vitamins are either beneficial or benign. Megadoses of vitamins still have the effects noted above. In fact, the doses of 13-*cis*-retionic acid used in the Hong *et al.* (1986) study produced toxic side effects in many of the patients. Which vitamins have beneficial effects on which types of cancer and in which doses can only be determined by careful well-controlled studies in animals and humans. On the other hand, Herbert (1986a, 1986b) has briefly summarized evidence that indicates that excessive doses of vitamin A and C can actually promote cancer.

Health food promoters commonly make a distinction between *natural* and *artificial* vitamins, the former being taken from fruits and vegetables, the latter made in the laboratory. The natural variety costs more. In fact, the two cannot be distinguished.

Vitamins are far from the only products pushed by the health food industry. "Natural" foods and nonvitamin dietary supplements of all kinds are promoted, accompanied by claims for their effectiveness against diseases of every sort. Shown in figure 19 is an example of the types of claims made. This is a brochure from a company doing business as "nutrition consultants." An examination of figure 19 shows how simplistic are the claims and recommendations. The brain has something to do with memory, so eating raw brain concentrate is recommended for better memory, mental disorders, and the like. Raw orchic concentrate (ground-up animal testicles) is likewise recommended for sexual disorders. Such claims are groundless.

Recently, calcium has been heavily promoted as an important nutritional supplement with the claim that taking daily oral doses of calcium can prevent osteoporosis, a disorder in which bones lose calcium, becoming thin and brittle and liable to breakage. This condition is most evident in postmenopausal women; an estrogen deficiency found in such women is one of the major causes. Calcium is clearly an important item in the daily diet, and a daily intake of between 1,000 and 1,500 milligrams is recommended (Culliton, 1987). However, the evidence that calcium supplementation is effective in the prevention of osteoporosis is at best weak. Out of eight studies on the effects of calcium supplementation, a small slowing of bone loss was found in four and no effect in the other four (Culliton, 1987). In one study (Riis, Thomsen, and Christiansen, 1987) a two-year program of 2,000 milligrams of oral calcium daily resulted in only a minor slowing of bone loss in postmenopausal women. An additional problem with oral calcium supplements is that the calcium they contain may not be *bioavailable*—that is, the body would not be able to use it even if calcium could prevent osteoporosis. Calcium in spinach and some products sold in health food stores, for example, has extremely low bioavailability (Culliton, 1987). Finally, with all the attention that calcium and osteoporosis have been receiving, it is not surprising that some doctors have set up osteoporosis testing laboratories and clinics, some in rented storefronts. The claim here is that mass screening of women of all ages for osteoporosis is medically useful. Mass screening of women of all ages for osteoporosis is not medically justified (Culliton, 1987; Hall, Davis, and Baran, 1987) because the tests are frequently conducted with inferior equipment, producing worthless "diagnoses," and because finding lowered bone mass in a premenopausal woman has no treatment implications. As one physician put it, "If I screened a healthy 35-year-old woman and found low bone mass, I wouldn't tell her anything that I wouldn't advise her to do anyway, consume calcium and get exercise" (Johnston, quoted in Culliton, 1987, p. 834).

   Consumer Reports magazine in its May 1985 issue did an excellent exposé of quackery in the health food industry, highlighting the useless, but sometimes expensive, dietary supplements, cancer cures, and other nostrums that are sold through the mail, in health food shops, or door to door. One of the firms that *Consumer Reports* investigated was Herbalife, a highly successful health food firm that sells diets, supplements, and cures of all sorts. According to Herbalife, their products contain "herbs that cleanse the system so that you can more easily absorb nutrients" (quoted in *Newsweek*, April 8, 1985, p. 89). In fact, as the *Newsweek* article pointed out, what really happens is that those who follow the diet get diarrhea since it contains laxatives. *Newsweek* also noted that a month's supply of Herbalife products can cost over $300.

   Natural is the single favorite adjective of the health food industry.

Anything natural is assumed to be good, wholesome, and healthy, while other foods—those with artificial additives, flavors, colors, or preservatives—are alleged to be linked to cancer or otherwise poisonous. Much of the panic about the health risks of food additives grew from studies in which animals, usually white rats, were exposed to massive doses of some particular additive and were later found to have developed some sort of health problem. The most famous such study was one conducted in Canada, in which rats were fed huge doses of saccharine (Howe, Birch, and Miller, 1977). The rats fed saccharine developed bladder cancer at a higher rate than control rats that were not fed saccharine. In spite of the fact that the data from human studies shows no relation between bladder cancer and saccharine (Whelan, 1980), this study caused a furor. The media publicized the reported danger, leading to a "chemical phobia" that has not yet abated.

In 1958, an amendment to the Food, Drug and Cosmetic Act was passed that required the Food and Drug Administration (FDA) to ban saccharine from all foods intended for human consumption. The amendment is known as the Delaney Clause after the congressman who introduced it. It requires that any additive be removed from food if that additive is shown to cause cancer in animals or humans. On the surface, that sounds like a good idea. But the Delaney Clause makes no distinctions based on the type or adequacy of the evidence linking an additive to cancer. Thus, even though almost all reputable medical or nutritional authorities felt that the results of the Howe *et al.* (1977) study indicated that saccharine posed no hazard to humans, the FDA was compelled by law to ban it. It took a special act of Congress to overturn the proposed ban and permit the continued use of saccharine.

Another serious problem with the Delaney Clause is that it does not permit the FDA to utilize any calculations of the relative risks of banning or not banning a substance that has been shown to be even mildly carcinogenic in animal studies. This was an important issue in the saccharine case. Even if the results of the Howe *et al.* (1977) study could be directly extrapolated from rats to humans—and it's not at all clear that it would be valid to do so—the real risks to humans are small. Cohen (1978) has calculated that, given the Howe *et al.* (1977) data, a twelve-ounce can of a saccharine-sweetened soft drink would cut nine seconds off the drinker's life. Put another way, there would be an extra 1,200 cases of bladder cancer each year if every single person in the United States drank twelve ounces of a saccharine-sweetened soft drink every day for the rest of their lives. On an individual basis, a human would have to drink about ten gallons of a saccharine-sweetened soft drink every day to match the level of exposure of the rats in the Howe *et al.* (1977)

study. The real risk of saccharine is tiny, even if Howe *et al.* (1977) are correct. However, there are health benefits to be gained from saccharine, especially for obese individuals who want to cut down their sugar intake to lose weight and for people with diabetes, who must limit their sugar intake. In addition, there are benefits to nonobese individuals who are prudently watching their weight. The benefits of saccharine far outweigh any risks.

There is yet another problem with the Delaney Clause. The analytical techniques now available can detect substances in almost vanishingly small quantities. It is possible, for example, to detect many substances in the part-per-trillion range. Thus, substances can be detected at levels so small that they could never have any deleterious effect on human health, even if in much larger doses they are carcinogenic or otherwise harmful. One excellent example is selenium, a nonmetallic element in the sulfur group. In very small amounts it is essential for the normal biochemical function of the human body. In larger amounts, however, it is extremely poisonous. Another example is the compound DES, diethylstilbestrol. It was found in 1971 that, in very large doses, DES could in rare cases cause vaginal cancer in the daughters of women who had taken it as a medication while pregnant. DES, a synthetic hormone, had long been used to stimulate growth in cattle. In 1972 DES was found in small amounts in the liver, and no place else, in fewer than three out of every one hundred animals tested. Senator Edward Kennedy held hearings on the issue "because DES, a known cancer-causing agent, is appearing on thousands of American dinner tables" (quoted in Whelan and Stare, 1976, p. 166). Whelan (1980) has calculated that one would have to eat 100,000 pounds of beef liver to receive the same dose of DES that caused rare cases of vaginal cancer. Nonetheless, DES was banned by the FDA in 1979.

Artificial food colors and flavors have been charged with causing hyperactivity in children, and one physician, Benjamin Feingold (1975), has claimed that a diet free of these additives will treat or prevent hyperactivity. Controlled studies of the Feingold diet show that it provides no benefit for hyperactive children (Barrett, 1980a).

Nonetheless, many parents of hyperactive children believe the diet works. Why? There is a large component of the placebo effect involved, along with an understandably desperate desire to find something that helps one's child. Further, the diet is a complex one, so parents must attend more to what their children eat. Thus they undoubtedly attend more to their hyperactive children when they are using the diet than they did previously. Even for hyperactive children, attention is a wonderful thing and can have beneficial effects. These factors combined with testimonials from other parents produce a zealous belief in this ineffective diet.

Refined sugar has been labeled a "toxin" that, according to a common nutritional myth, increases aggressiveness and hyperactive behavior in children. Dietary treatments for hyperactivity thus attempt to eliminate sugar from the diet. Behavioral studies have found that sugar does not increase undesirable behaviors in either normal children (Milich, Wolraich, and Lindgren, 1986; Milich and Pelham, 1986; Rapoport, 1986; Spring, Chiodo, and Bowen, 1987) or in children with psychiatric disorders (Behar et al., 1984).

Modern "chemical phobia" identifies preservatives as the most harmful of all the additives found in food products. In all the hysteria about preservatives, their real function is usually forgotten: they keep food from rotting. Eating rotten food is most assuredly not healthy. Two widely used preservatives, BHA and BHT, were said to cause brain damage and other problems in rats, based on studies in which the usual massive doses were used. Later, it appeared that in much smaller does these substances actually had a slight anticancer effect (Whelan and Stare, 1976).

Consider the following substance: It is widely used in numerous industrial processes, including tanning leather. It is an excellent paint thinner for certain kinds of paints. When injected into the womb of pregnant rats, it produces horrible birth defects—such as rat pups born without limbs. Would you want this obviously poisonous substance in your diet? Of course you would—it's water.

The above example makes it clear that the hysteria-mongering approach to reporting research on food additives that characterizes both health food proponents and much of the popular media gives the public an extremely poor basis on which to judge the safety of any additive. What is generally not realized is that before a substance can be added to food, it must have passed a number of tests for safety. In spite of all the self-serving hysteria whipped up by health food proponents, food additives are generally safe (Effron, 1984).

The example also shows that what is natural is not always safe. Herbalife, the high-pressure, door-to-door health food firm mentioned previously, initially sold a diet preparation that contained mandrake root and pokeroot among the ingredients. Both are poisonous—and 100 percent natural. They were removed from the Herbalife preparation after the FDA took action.

Laetrile is another harmful but natural substance. It is best known as the quack cancer cure that received so much publicity in the late 1970s. It has no anti-cancer effect; what it does have is hydrogen cyanide, a deadly poison. The cyanide levels of laetrile can be as much as 6 percent of the drug by weight (Schmidt et al., 1978). In a study of the effects of laetrile in dogs, Schmidt et al. (1978) gave dogs various doses of laetrile, ranging from the equivalent of that given to humans, to a level five times greater than the usual human dose. Even doses of laetrile equivalent to the "normal" human dose produced signs of cyanide poisoning in the experimental animals. Doses above this "normal" human level produced severe symptoms, up to and including death. It should be remembered that the highest dose in this study was only five times the "normal" dose, and it is quite likely that some patients, believing laetrile to be a harmless and healthy substance, will administer levels well above normal. The fact that laetrile was and continues to be marketed as a "vitamin," spuriously numbered B17, enhances the danger of overdose. Further, laetrile is often taken along with a quack anti-cancer health food diet featuring nuts and beans that contain even more cyanide.

Based on their results, Schmidt *et al.* (1978) predicted that there would be an increasing number of deaths due to laetrile poisoning. Their prediction was verified, and there are now several reports of deaths of humans due to dosing with laetrile. One of the most tragic cases was that of a little boy, Chad Green, who was being treated for leukemia by his parents with laetrile. The parents refused to allow Chad to have appropriate chemotherapy, and he died of his leukemia in 1979.

Chiropractic

According to chiropractors, a major cause of human disease and even mental disorder is something called a *subluxation* of the spine. This supposedly occurs when the spinal nerves that travel through openings between the bony vertebrae of the spinal column are compressed. Chiropractors believe the way to treat the subluxation is to manipulate the spinal column so that the subluxation is removed. It's important to note that subluxation is different from a disorder like a slipped disk, where the vertebral disk is rubbing on the spinal cord or nerves.

How do subluxations cause disease? Chiropractic theory holds that when a spinal nerve going to, say, the liver is subject to a subluxation, this will cause liver disease. Thus, if a patient has liver disease, it has been caused by the subluxation of a particular nerve. The chiropractor then treats that nerve. It is certainly true that bone, or spinal disk, pressing on the spinal column or on spinal nerves can be extremely painful. It is also true that massage can be helpful in treating muscle pulls, sprains, and similar conditions. However, it is untrue to say that pressure on a particular spinal nerve will cause, say, a tumor in a particular organ. Many chiropractors claim to be able to treat infections, tumors, and other organic diseases. Such claims are not only without support, they are dangerous because the person being treated by the chiropractor may be told that no other treatment is necessary. Cases have been reported where people have been treated by chiropractors for diseases that could have been cured by legitimate medical treatment. By the time the condition was treated properly, death or serious injury had resulted (Barrett, 1980c).

A study by Crelin (1973, 1985) showed that subluxation, the fundamental concept in chiropractic, does not exist. Crelin subjected dissected human spinal columns to mechanical stress. He found that no amount of stress, no matter how it was applied to the spinal column, resulted in a pinching of the spinal nerves. The spinal column broke first. The chiropractors' only response to this devastating study was to charge that it wasn't valid because it was done on dead tissue. In fact, the physical characteristics of a freshly dissected spinal column are identical to those of a column still fully attached to its owner.

Brain Therapies

This section will discuss two questionable treatment approaches that claim to cure various manifestations of brain damage; failure of the brain to develop normally; and disorders of speech, reading, and writing that may or may not be caused by neurological damage. Interestingly, both these treatment procedures are promoted by physicians, showing that possession of an MD degree is no guarantee against quackery.

Glenn Doman, Carl Delacato (EdD), and Robert Doman (MD) at the Institutes for the Achievement of Human Potential in Philadelphia, Pennsylvania, have developed a therapy they call *patterning*, which they claim can overcome, or more accurately bypass, the effects of brain damage in children. They view the development of the brain as progressing through consecutive stages and the adult brain as divided into different areas corresponding to these stages. According to their view, brain damage in a child "blocks" development at one stage and thus, even if higher stages are not damaged, development cannot proceed until the "block" is either removed or worked around. This is where patterning comes in. The idea is a simple one: to overcome or circumvent the blockage, one identifies a stage that is undamaged. One then has the child practice behaviors characteristic of that stage over and over, day after day, week after week, month after month. Supposedly, this continuous practice will in some unspecified way have the effect of "breaking through any barrier to function . . . at the next higher level" (Doman, 1974, p. 151). An example will help clarify the ideas behind this type of therapy. Consider the case of Mary, a ten-month-old child described in Doman (1974, pp. 157-160). Mary is "for all practical purposes deaf." She does, however, show the normal startle reflex to loud, unexpected noises. This means that she's not really deaf. Since Mary does have a normal startle reflex and since in the Doman-Delacato system this means that there is a "blockage" at the next higher level of neurological organization, the treatment is to startle Mary repeatedly. Specifically, "Mother will stimulate her auditorily every waking half hour. . . . Mother will do so by unexpectedly banging two blocks of wood just behind Mary's head. She does so ten times at three-second intervals in each of twenty-four sessions" (Doman, 1974, p. 159).

The case of Sean provides another example of this type of therapy in action. Sean, six years old, has difficulty at the third stage of "tactile competence," which in the Doman-Delacato system means he has difficulty discriminating warm and cool. He is perfect, however, at the second stage of tactile competence, which is concerned with the perception of hot and cold. Since he is "blocked" at the third stage, he cannot perform at the fourth stage at all. This stage involves "tactile understanding of the third dimension in objects which appear to be flat" (Doman, 1974, p. 161). The therapy? "Mother will give Sean tactile stimulation" (Doman, 1974, p. 162). Sean's hands are alternately immersed in pans of warm and cool water, while mother explains to him that one feels warm, the other cool. After every ten immersions, Sean's hands are massaged while mother explains that this feels pleasant. Sean receives a total of 600 immersions and 30 messages every day.

On the face of it, these sorts of therapies certainly seem bizarre and unlikely to be effective. Doman (1974) never addresses the issue of how these extraordinary levels of stimulation are supposed to achieve their therapeutic effects and how they remove, or circumvent, the alleged "blockage." In fact, no evidence is ever presented to show that the children have brain damage, as opposed to some sort of psychological problem. Further, the "Doman-Delacato Developmental Profile" from which the entire therapy program is derived is based on a fundamentally incorrect understanding of brain organization. The Developmental Profile divides brain development into seven different stages that progress consecutively. Each stage is tied to a specific part of the brain. The first stage is linked to the medulla and spinal cord, the second to an area just above the medulla called the pons, the third to the midbrain, and the fourth through seventh to, respectively, the "initial," "early," "primitive," and "sophisticated" cortex. There are also six areas of "competence," including visual, auditory, tactile, manual, language, and mobility competence. Specific behaviors in each area of competence are assigned to each of the stages of brain development. Thus, in Mary's case, the startle reflex is assigned to the first stage of auditory competence and is said to be controlled by the medulla and spinal cord.

The Developmental Profile contains such a crop of fundamental errors in its concept of brain development and brain organization that it is impossible to describe them all here. Since this book lacks space for a complete discussion, a few of the more egregious errors only will be mentioned. First, the brain and spinal cord do not, as Doman (1974) claims, develop sequentially. Rather, the entire brain-spinal cord combination develops in parallel (Jacobson, 1978). The cortex, for example, does not have to wait for the spinal cord to be fully formed before it begins to develop. Secondly, the division of the cortex into the four different types listed above ignores the vast amount of information on how the cortex, the most advanced part of the brain, is actually divided. Doman's (1974) division of the cortex is contradicted by what has been known for nearly 100 years about the organization of the cortex. (See Kalat, 1987, for a review of this material).

Sean's case, described above, exemplifies the type of error so common in Doman and Delacato's thinking about the brain. In order to get Sean to appreciate "tactile understanding of the third dimension in objects which appear to be flat," Sean is given practice with warm and cool water. However, the areas of brain and spinal cord that underlie perception of temperature are anatomically and functionally separate from those areas that underlie the sensations of touch and feel. It is the latter that are necessary for tactile appreciation of the three-dimensional nature of objects. So, even if repeated practice could overcome damage in those areas where temperature sensation is mediated, this would have no effect on those other parts of the brain where touch sensation is mediated.

One would expect that anyone who develops a therapy for brain-damaged children would have studied fundamental neuroanatomy. This appears not to be the case as far as Doman and Delacato are concerned. Their Developmental Profile contains numerous errors even in basic neuroanatomy. For example, "outline perception" is said to be localized in a lower brain structure called the pons. In fact, the pons has no visual function. Outline perception is known to be a function of the visual cortex (Kalat, 1987). This is not a new finding, it has been known since at least the late 1950s. Staying in the area of visual competence, "appreciation of detail within a configuration" (Doman, 1974, p. 156) is said to be a function of the midbrain. Again, the midbrain has no such visual function and the processing of visual detail is also done by the visual cortex. The midbrain is further credited with "appreciation of meaningful sounds" when in fact it plays no role in the perception of such auditory stimuli. That too is a function of the cortex, this time the auditory cortex.

Doman (1974) says that hundreds of parents of children brought to the Institutes for the Achievement of Human Potential report that the therapy of repeated sensory stimulation really works and improves their children's condition. How can this be explained? In the first place, it is unclear whether all the children that Doman (1974) says are brain-damaged really are brain-damaged. Some probably have various emotional, psychological, and behavioral problems. Such problems often clear up on their own. If this spontaneous remission of the problem occurs while the parents are engaged in a vigorous therapeutic program, it is quite natural to attribute the behavior change to the program, even if the program actually had nothing to do with the behavior change. Second, in some cases, the development of various brain areas is simply delayed, but ultimately reaches normal levels. Normal levels of function would be reached in such cases without any therapeutic intervention but, again, if such a program is being undertaken by the parents, they will be strongly inclined to attribute any changes to the program.

One of the sure signs of health quackery is the claim that one therapy can cure a host of different disorders. With this in mind it is of interest to note the full title of Doman's (1974) book: *What to Do about Your Brain-injured Child, or Your Brain-damaged, Mentally Retarded, Mentally Deficient, Cerebral-palsied, Spastic, Flaccid, Rigid, Epileptic, Autistic, Athetoid, Hyperactive Child.* Finally, it is also of interest to note that the "recommended readings" at the end of the book contain two books "on human nutrition" by Adele Davis, including *Let's Have Healthy Children,* which, it will be recalled, contained advice that led to the death of at least one child.

In fact, even legitimate therapies for rehabilitation of brain-damaged adults, such as speech and physical therapy, appear to be at best of limited effectiveness. A review of the effects of such therapies on adult stroke patients (Lind, 1982), concluded that "functional gains experienced by stroke patients are primarily attributable to spontaneous recovery" (p. 133). Dombovy, Sandok, and Basford (1986) have pointed to the serious methodological problems that flaw studies that claim to show greater improvement for patients who receive, as opposed to those who do not receive, rehabilitation following a stroke. Rehabilitation therapies are believed to be effective by therapists, patients, and others because therapy is most likely to be given in the first few months following a stroke—and that is precisely when the most dramatic spontaneous recovery is taking place. It is therefore natural to attribute patients' improvement to the therapy and not to spontaneous recovery. This tendency to attribute recovery to a therapy and not to spontaneous recovery is even greater in cases of brain damage in childhood. The child's brain is much better able than the adult's to recover from damage, and the behavioral consequences of brain damage are therefore much less in children than in adults (Satz and Bullard-Bates, 1981). This well-known phenomenon helps to account for those highly touted "miraculous" recoveries claimed by proponents like Doman of quack brain therapies for children.

In recent years Doman's Institutes for the Achievement of Human Potential has turned its attention from "therapy" of brain-damaged children to accelerating cognitive development in normal children by exposing them early to reading, muscle stimuli, and the like. Doman (1984) described this work in *How to Multiply Your Baby's Intelligence*. Although the book is still filled with basic neuroanatomical errors (e.g., saying that the back half of the brain and spinal cord is "made up entirely of the five incoming sensory pathways" and the front half is made up of the outgoing sensory pathways), its basic premise that early exposure to different types of stimuli may facilitate children's intellectual development is not far-fetched. However, the dramatic enhancements that Doman (1984) reports are due more to wishful thinking and constructive perception on the part of parents and the Institutes' staff members than to actual quantum leaps in the children's abilities.

Another physician who has widely promoted an incorrect theory about the brain is psychiatrist Harold Levinson, who believes (Levinson, 1980) that dyslexia is caused by a dysfunction of the cerebellum and the vestibular system in the brain. These two structures work together in the brain to regulate and coordinate body movements, including movements of the eyes (Ghez and Fahn, 1985).

Levinson's misconceptions about the nature of cerebellar and vestibular function are enormous and hardly give one much confidence in his theories about dyslexia. For example, in his 1980 book he suggests, and then uses as a foundation of his theory, the idea that the "vestibular compass is as dependent on the reception of electromagnetic and gravitational signals as are the guided-missile compass systems" (p. 44). It is true that the vestibular system does respond to gravitational information. But it does not respond to "electromagnetic" information. Further, the concept of a "vestibular compass" is seriously flawed. Human spatial orientation is controlled by a multitude of factors and inputs from almost all sensory systems, not just the vestibular system, and numerous brain areas other than the cerebellum are involved (Howard and Templeton, 1966). In his 1984 book, Levinson states that "the inner ear is a pacemaker imparting timing and rhythm to various motor skills" (p. 124). This is simply wrong: the inner ear does contain the sensory portion of the vestibular system, but this has nothing to do with the timing and rhythmic aspects of behavior. Those aspects of behavior are controlled by a complicated set of neural structures throughout the brain (Kalat, 1987).

Since the cerebellum and vestibular system are involved in the control of eye movements, and since it is very difficult to read well if you can't control the movements of your eyes, Levinson's idea seems reasonable at first. However, it has several fatal flaws. First, actual damage to the cerebellum—such as tumors or strokes—does not produce dyslexia, although it does produce other kinds of reading disturbances (Adams and Victor, 1985). Second, dyslexic readers do not have trouble controlling their eye movements during reading in a way that would be expected if dyslexia were caused by cerebellar and vestibular disorders (see Ellis, 1984, for a brief review). Brown *et al.* (1983) specifically examined vestibular responses in dyslexic children and found them to be normal.

To get around these major problems, Levinson (1980, p. 108) proposes some more subtle sort of cerebellar dysfunction in dyslexics that "scrambled the temporal-spatial sequence of the visual input at the retinal site." This requires that the hypothesized cerebellar-vestibular dysfunction somehow interfere with visual inputs as they travel from the retina up to the cerebral cortex where printed words are finally decoded in the brain. The pathways from the eye to the cortex are well known, and there is no place along those pathways where cerebellar or vestibular inputs could have the interfering effects required by Levinson's theory. It is certainly true that the cerebellum and the vestibular system receive inputs from the visual system, but these travel over different pathways.

Another problem for Levinson's (1980) theory is his contention that the widely held view that dyslexia is due to some type of damage to the cortex is wrong. He cavalierly reinterprets (and misinterprets) symptoms long thought to be due to cortical problems in dyslexics (such as speech disturbances) as being due to cerebellar dysfunction. A recent report on the brains of five dyslexic children that were studied in detail at autopsy (Kemper, 1984) showed definite pathology in the cortex, not in the cerebellum.

Levinson's (1980) belief that dyslexia is caused by cerebellar and vestibular problems has led him to treat dyslexics with anti-motion-sickness drugs, such as dramamine. In his book he reports the positive results of this treatment. However, his findings are worthless because, as he admits, he has never conducted a placebo study to see whether: (1) the improvements that he believes he sees are really there, and (2) the reported improvement really takes place, whether due to the drugs or to other factors. It is unethical to continue to promote any kind of therapy without first having conducted careful, well-controlled placebo studies to ensure that the treatment is really effective.

Placebo studies are important because it is so easy for a physician, or anyone committed to the belief that a therapy is effective, to see improvement where none really exists. This is another case of constructive perception, as discussed in chapter seven. The physician who believes that a drug is an effective treatment for a certain condition will see, and will report in all good faith, that when the drug is given to someone with that condition improvement takes place—even if the drug is in fact worthless as a treatment for that condition. The history of medicine is littered with the remains of worthless therapies that were once believed, often by almost the entire profession, to be effective. Once correctly designed placebo studies were done, however, it became clear that these treatments were not effective at all.

Placebo studies are also important because the enthusiasm of the physician, the patient and those around him or her can cause an improvement all by themselves. The improvement may be real, but may have nothing to do with the drug or treatment in question. In the case of Levinson's dyslexic patients, it is highly likely that those receiving the anti-motion-sickness medication are excited about this new treatment that is promised to be a cure for their debilitating disorder. The excitement, in the patient and the parents, leads to greater attention to the child and more time spent with the child during reading. Naturally, such attention and encouragement may result in at least a temporary improvement. The physician (Levinson, in this case), the parents, and even the dyslexics are very likely to attribute the improvement to the drug and, hence, to become convinced that the drug is effective.

The only way to settle the issue is to conduct what is termed a *double-blind placebo study*. In such a study a number of dyslexic children would be divided into two groups. The children in one group would receive the actual drug, while the children in the other group would receive a placebo, usually a sugar pill, known to have absolutely no effect on behavior. Further, and most important, neither the children, nor their parents, nor the individuals who evaluated the children for any improvement in their dyslexia would know which group the child was in. Thus, improvement could be evaluated completely unbiased by preconceived notions of whether the drug will or will not work. Levinson's refusal to run appropriate placebo studies of his therapy raises serious ethical issues about his treatment.

Since 1980 Levinson (1984; Levinson and Carter, 1986) has announced another class of disorders that he says are due to cerebellar-vestibular dysfunction and can be cured with anti-motion-sickness drugs: phobias. Levinson bases this claim on his "observation" that many of the dyslexic patients he sees have phobias and on his further "observations" that anti-motion-sickness drugs seem to alleviate the phobias. The latter observations are, again, based on unreliable, subjective evaluations of the changes in the patients' phobias and not on placebo studies or studies that use careful evaluations of the severity of the patients' phobias.

Stress and Imagery

In the past few years it has become clear that psychological factors such as emotions, moods, and perhaps even personality play a role in physical health. The existence of *psychosomatic disorders,* in which psychological stress leads to physical problems such as ulcers, has been known for years. However, the effects of psychological factors on health and disease go well beyond those included in the traditional study of psychosomatic medicine. Even stress is now known to have greater effects on health than just the creation of psychosomatic conditions. For example, studies of elderly people forced to relocate from home to an institution or from a familiar to an unfamiliar institution, have shown that poor psychological adjustment to the new location is associated with higher rates of health problems and death (Botwinick, 1984). Uncontrollable aversive stimulation, such as very loud noise or painful electric shock, has been shown to increase the growth rate of cancerous tumors in several species (Sklar and Anisman, 1981; Bammer and Newberry, 1981). The important word here is *uncontrollable,* because if the same aversive stimuli can be controlled and terminated by the animals, tumor growth is not speeded (Sklar and Anisman, 1981). Thus, a basic psychological factor—the degree of control one has over a stressful event—has an important effect on a physiological process, the rate of tumor growth.

There is also some evidence that stress is related to tumor growth in humans (Sklar and Anisman, 1981). A later study (see Hall and Goldstein, 1986) examined the relationship between attitude towards one's disease and survival rates in female patients who had had mastectomies ten years previously. If the patient's attitude was depressed and hopeless, the ten-year survival rate was only 25 percent. If, however, the patient evidenced a strong will to beat the disease, the ten-year survival rate was 70 percent.

A question of great interest in regard to this finding is how the effects of stress and other psychological factors are mediated. The immune system is the link. It has recently been discovered that there are close, reciprocal connections between the immune system and the nervous system (Hall and Goldstein, 1986; Plotnikoff, et al. 1986; Wechsler, 1987). For example, it is possible to classically condition the immune system (Ader and Cohen, 1985). Lymphocytes, the cells that actually mediate the immune reaction, are now known to have receptors on their surfaces for some of the same chemicals that are neurotransmitters in the brain. Levels of various neurotransmitters are known to change as a function of the emotional state of the individual, and such changes could influence immune system function by changing the type or quantity of neurotransmitter molecules that bind to circulating lymphocytes. Decreased immunological function has been demonstrated in conditions of chronic stress. Kiecolt-Glasser *et al.* (1987) found lowered immune function in divorced and separated women who had been separated for less than one year as compared to a group of married women. Considering only the married women, lowered immune system function was found in those who rated their marriage as of lower quality. Similarly, Arnetz *et al.* (1987) found that unemployed women had lower immune system function when compared to a group of securely employed females.

If stress and depressed, hopeless attitudes toward disease impair immune system function, it seems reasonable to hypothesize that positive attitudes and an absence of stress will result in a more normal immune reaction to disease. This hypothesis is supported by the study of the survival rates of mastectomy patients with different attitudes toward their disease, described above. This sort of finding has encouraged some researchers to see whether changing a patient's attitude about his disease and future can have a beneficial effect on the progress of the disease. The most famous technique involves the use of imagery. Patients are told to imagine their cancer cells as weak and dying, being attacked by vigorous lymphocytes (Simonton, Matthews-Simonton, and Creighton, 1980; Matthews-Simonton, 1984). Unfortunately, the results of the Simonton type of therapy have been at best equivocal (Friedlander, 1985). Nonetheless, numerous practitioners, especially psychologists and those in the holistic medicine movement, are now claiming that cancer can be treated "psychologically" using imagery or several variant therapies that have sprung up.

At this point, the evidence regarding the effectiveness of "psychological" treatments of cancer is simply not sufficient. It is quite reasonable to hypothesize that various psychological procedures might, indeed, be effective. If that turns out to be the case, it will probably be found that almost any procedure that reduces patients' stress and gives them a more positive, hopeful outlook will be effective. In other words, even if the imagery procedure is shown to be effective, it will not have been the imagery per se that was responsible for the effect. Rather, any method that achieves the desired attitude changes will be effective. One problem does exist with the enthusiasm of those using imagery and related techniques. In the breast cancer study, no attempt was made to alter the patients' attitudes toward their cancer. Those attitudes may have been the result of lifelong conditioning. Given this, it may be impossible to produce sufficient attitude change in the short run to alter immune system function in any important way. Finally, it must be kept firmly in mind that the patients in the breast cancer study received conventional therapy. Even if imagery and related techniques are shown to be effective at, for example, increasing the survival rate of cancer patients, the techniques will be effective only when used in conjunction with traditional therapies such as surgery, radiation therapy, and chemotherapy.

Obviously there are a great many unanswered questions in the area of the "psychological" treatment of cancer. Answers can only be obtained from careful, well-designed and -conducted research studies. Unfortunately, those using imagery and related techniques seem uninterested in such rigorous studies, preferring to assert without proof that the methods are effective.

Chelation Therapy

As noted above, quack cures are often claimed to treat numerous different diseases. Chelation therapy is an excellent case in point. In this therapy, the chemical ethylenediamine tetraacetate (EDTA) is given intravenously. EDTA was approved by the FDA in 1953 for use in a few specific conditions: heavy metal poisoning and a disorder in which the body stores too much copper, Wilson's disease (Bennett, 1985). However, chelation therapists now claim that EDTA can be used to treat Alzheimer's disease, Parkinson's disease, blindness, diabetes, multiple sclerosis, atherosclerosis, and the aging process itself, among others. Such claims are unfounded. Chelation therapy, like other quack therapies, can be dangerous and even fatal, if it causes the patient to forego legitimate medical treatment. Further, the therapy, again like many quack therapies, is very expensive. A course of chelation can cost up to $3,000. Since the therapy is, wisely, not covered by medical insurance, the money for this useless treatment comes out of the pocket of the patient.

The elderly become sick more frequently than do younger individuals. While this should not come as a surprise, it does mean that the elderly are at greater risk of being taken in by quack cures and therapies. One such cure is aimed directly at the elderly. This is Gerivitol H-3, a substance "invented" by a Romanian doctor that is said to slow or reverse the aging process and to treat almost every disease of the aged from heart disease and Parkinson's disease to deafness, loss of hair, and impotence. It is promoted by the Romanian National Tourist Office, and one can stay at expensive spas in Romania that "treat" their guests with Gerivitol H-3 and a program of exercise, plus much personal attention from the staff. Given the invigorating effect of the exercise and the pleasantness of the personal attention shown, it is not at all surprising that testimonials about the miraculous effects of Gerivitol H-3 abound. However, studies of the substance's actual effects have shown that there are none. In fact, Gerivitol H-3 contains little more than the local anesthetic procaine.

Homeopathy

Homeopathy was developed in the eighteenth century by the German physician Samuel Hahnemann and became very popular in the nineteenth century. In the last few years, it has made a comeback under the umbrella of *holistic medicine*. The basis of homeopathy is the belief that exceedingly small amounts of certain substances can cure disease by causing the body's natural defenses to fight the agent of disease. The smaller the amount of the substances used, the better. To this end, homeopathic remedies may be diluted in water to such an extent that scarcely a single molecule of the original substance remains in the injection or oral medication that the patient receives. How, then, can the treatment have any effect? Hahnemann was aware of this problem but "believed that the vigorous shaking or pulverizing with each step of the [dilution] process left behind a spirit-like essence of the original substance that helped revive the body's 'vital force'" (*Consumer Reports*, 1987, p. 80). Because of the homeopathic movement's political power as recently as the 1930s, homeopathic remedies were recognized by the 1938 Federal Food, Drug and Cosmetic Act, despite the fact that they are ineffective. Some modern homeopaths use fancy but useless high-tech devices and tests on patients—tests that invariably cost a great deal of money. In addition, some companies use the term "homeopathic" in promoting various quack cancer drugs and cure-alls.

Birth Stress

The allegedly harmful effects of "birth stress" on babies has led, in the past decade or so, to the development of several methods for eliminating such stress. The claim that birth stress is harmful, however, is contradicted by much medical research, nicely summarized in Lagercrantz and Slotkin (1986). Far from being harmful, the stress the infant experiences at birth has several physiological and biochemical effects on the body that are necessary for proper adaptation to the infant's new environment. Birth stress improves breathing by altering lung physiology, increases blood flow to the heart and brain, mobilizes metabolic fuel and may even enhance mother-infant bonding.

Hair Loss Cures and Hair Analysis

A common quack claim is that various "over the counter" products sold without prescription can cure, or at least slow, hair loss in males. These claims are usually accompanied by testimonials and are often made by various fly-by-night companies. It is true that hair can be surgically transplanted; it is also true that the drug minoxidil has recently been approved by the FDA for use in treating hair loss in males. However, the drug is available by prescription only and seems to be far from totally effective (DeGroot, Nater, and Herscheimer, 1987). The commercially advertised baldness cures do not work at all.

Analysis of hair as a method to detect nutritional deficiencies has recently become popular. A sample of hair is sent to a laboratory and analyzed. Barrett (1985) sent samples of the hair of two healthy teenage girls to thirteen different laboratories for their analysis. The laboratories' analyses were inconsistent, mutually contradictory, and very likely to recommend the purchase of unneeded vitamin and mineral supplements. In short, hair analysis of this type is a scam.

Iridology

According to iridologists, diseases can be diagnosed by examining the iris of the eye. They claim that each organ in the body is represented in a specific part of the iris. If an organ is diseased, a change will occur in the appropriate area of the iris. Iridology has a rather long history but has become quite popular lately in the wake of the holistic medicine movement (Worrall, 1982-83). It is often recommended by chiropractors. From a physiological point of view, the claims of iridologists are simply nonsense. There is no representation of the various organs on the iris. This is also true for claims that the different organs and body parts are represented on the sole of the foot, the ear, the palm of the hand, or any other part of the body. Simon, Worthen, and Mitas (1979) conducted a test of iridology, using a total of 143 subjects. All had photographs taken of their iris. Of the total, 95 subjects had no kidney disease and 48 had kidney disease that was rather severe. The photographs of the subjects' irises were given to three iridologists. Their task would have been simple if iridology was valid—they had to separate the photographs of the irises of the sick from those of the healthy patients. They were unable to accomplish this.

Iridology is popular probably because many iridologists use the session as an opportunity to give a cold reading. Further, their presentation is full of the classical multiple outs that make them seem highly accurate.

Worrall (1982-83, p. 34) gives an excellent example of this. A reporter who went to an iridologist was told that "a whitish color emanating from [her] iris shows a lot of acidity and mucus throughout the body and could be from eating a lot of meat." The reporter was a vegetarian. When she so informed the iridologist, he replied that "the acidity could be a reverse effect from eating too much fruit and vegetables." In another case, an iridologist diagnosed a patient as having cancer. The patient did not have cancer, but did have a heart condition, which the iridologist failed to notice (Worrall, 1982-83).

Air Ions

Meteorological variations in air ion levels, specifically increases in positive ion levels associated with hot, dry winds, seem to be associated with increases in socially undesirable behaviors such as criminal activity, suicide, and various sorts of accidents (see Charry and Hawkinshire, 1981, and Brown and Kirk, 1987, for brief reviews). In a laboratory study, Charry and Hawkinshire (1981) found that increased levels of positive air ions resulted in poorer moods, slowed reaction time, and lessened physiological activation or arousal. These changes were not found in all individuals tested, however, and there are large individual differences in susceptibility to the detrimental effects of positive air ions. A complicated pattern of sex differences in the effects of positive ions was also found.

If exposure to positive ions impairs performance and mood, at least in susceptible individuals, it would seem reasonable that exposure to negative ions might improve mood and performance. Just such claims are made by the manufacturers of negative air ion generators. However, the studies on the actual effects of negative air ions paint a very different picture of their effects. Such ions do have effects on human behavior, but they are small, complex, and not always beneficial. Buckalew and Rizzuto (1984) found no effects of exposure to negative ions for three or six hours on various measures of cognitive function and physiological condition. Baron (1987) found that negative ions did have an effect on some, but not all, measures of cognitive function used in his experiments. In some cases, increased negative ion levels increased performance, while in others performance was impaired. Women were generally less susceptible to the effect of negative ions than were men.

The conclusion of research in this area is that changes in air ion levels, positive or negative, can be shown to influence behavior in carefully controlled studies. These effects are certainly of theoretical interest and import. However, they are small and of little practical significance. Surely they do not justify the purchase of a negative air ion generator.

12

Current Trends in Pseudoscience

This chapter consists of a series of short sections on several areas of pseudoscience and the paranormal. It includes a variety of topics that are currently sparking interest both among proponents of pseudoscience and the general public. Some, like firewalking, are of recent vintage, while others, like the Loch Ness monster, have been around for years.

Carlos Castaneda and Don Juan

Carlos Castaneda has become famous through his several best-selling books about Yaqui Indian sorcerer Don Juan, the first being *The Teachings of Don Juan,* published in 1968. These books are said to be based on Castaneda's personal experiences in the Mexican desert as Don Juan's apprentice. This alleged field work formed the basis for Castaneda's doctoral dissertation, for which he was granted the Ph.D. in anthropology by the University of California at Los Angeles. Don Juan's philosophical teachings were perfect for American popular culture in the late 1960s and early 1970s. They involved the use of psychedelic drugs, a belief in real magical (or paranormal) powers, and a thoroughgoing mysticism. The philosophy is still very popular with the "new age" movement and the humanistic psychology movement. Carl Rogers, one of the founders of humanistic psychology, said, "The most vividly convincing documents I have read come from one man, Carlos Castaneda" (quoted in de Mille, 1980, p. 39).

In fact, the entire Don Juan series is a hoax. Careful investigation by Richard de Mille (1978, 1980) has established that Castaneda never did the field work that he claimed to have done. His books contain descriptions of Yaqui culture and practices that are greatly at odds with what is known about Yaqui culture from reports of researchers who have actually studied the Yaqui, incorrect descriptions of the desert environment where his alleged field work took him for years, simple impossibilities about the environment, as well as numerous inconsistencies regarding time and place. Examples can be found in abundance in the de Mille (1978, 1980) books, but consider a few mentioned by Sebald (1980). In his books, Castaneda tells of hiking through the Mexican desert during June, July, and August chatting with Don Juan about various metaphysical topics. Trouble is, it's impossible to do this in the summer, when temperatures soar above 110 degrees for weeks. As Sebald (1980) notes, only foolhardy hikers attempt the desert in the summer—and they die. Sebald (1980) is also most curious about Castaneda's claim to have caught and killed a rabbit with his bare hands during the summer. True, some rabbits are slow during the summer. That's because they have tularemia, an unpleasant disease that humans can catch just from handling an infected rabbit. Apparently ignorant of tularemia, Don Juan tells Castaneda to cook and eat the rabbit he kills. Certainly one would expect Don Juan to know about the dangers of tularemia. Castaneda's and Don Juan's profound ignorance of the environment in which Castaneda allegedly spent several years and in which Don Juan allegedly lived all his life reveal the works of Castaneda to be a hoax, especially when taken in conjunction with the numerous other errors and problems outlined by de Mille (1978, 1980).

The Don Juan hoax has been compared to the 1912 Piltdown man hoax (Truzzi, 1976–77) in which a set of doctored human and orangutan skull bones was passed off as belonging to a previously unknown species of ancient man (see Blinderman, 1986, for the story of the Piltdown hoax). What is most interesting is the response that has greeted the revelation that Castaneda's works are fictional. First, there has been no real attempt to revoke his Ph.D., based as it is on fraudulent "research." Secondly, as de Mille (1978, 1980) documents, the response among many anthropologists and others who share the Don Juan type of philosophical outlook has been neutral. In other words, it doesn't matter if the works are fictional because the underlying philosophy is, in some vague sense, true. An excellent example of this approach is Shelburne's (1987) article titled "Carlos Castaneda: If It Didn't Happen, What Does It Matter?" Shelburne argues that "the issue of whether it [Castaneda's experience] literally happened or not makes no fundamental difference to the truth of the account" (p. 217). Such excuses are little more than intellectual used-car salesmanship.

Collective Delusion

The term *collective delusion*, also known as *mass hysteria*, describes a situation in which a significant part of the population of an area, which can be as small as a single building or as large as a nation, becomes convinced that some strange event is taking place for which there is no immediately obvious explanation. The event—sometimes an outbreak of illness occurring in rapid succession among people working in the same environment—can be attributed to a wide range of causes. Sometimes paranormal or pseudoscientific causes are proposed and accepted. In many, but not all, cases of collective delusion, the media play an important role in spreading the delusion.

A prototypical case of collective delusion, described by Medalia and Larsen (1958), took place in Seattle, Washington, in March and April of 1954. At first a few and then more and more people noticed mysterious tiny pits in their car windshields. Anything that could pit glass, it was reasoned with some justification, could certainly do damage to frail human flesh. Concern grew as did the number of reports. Explanations for the pits were varied and creative. One held that acid pollution was responsible. Another held that fallout from U.S. atomic bomb tests in the Pacific, blown east and falling on Seattle, was causing the damage. On April 15 the mayor of Seattle asked for the assistance of the governor of Washington and the President of the United States. Clearly Seattle was facing a dangerous situation. Or was it? The pits turned out to have a prosaic explanation: They had been caused by pebbles thrown up from the unpaved roads by cars, which then struck the windshield of any car behind. They had simply not been noticed before. Yet, when one person noticed them and pointed them out to someone else who also had not noticed them, but now found them on his or her car and assumed, incorrectly, that they had never been there before, the stage was set for the collective delusion to appear. Medalia and Larsen (1958, p. 180) note that people in this particular episode came up with "evidence" to support what turned out to be clearly incorrect explanations. In the case of the atomic fallout theory, "many drivers claimed that they found tiny, metallic-looking particles about the size of a pinhead on their windows." Other examples of collective delusions involve the sudden outbreak of a mysterious illness, the symptoms of which are nonspecific, such as vomiting, headache, shortness of breath, or fainting (Colligan, Pennebaker, and Murphy, 1982). Small and Borus (1983) present a detailed study of one such case, in which the victims of a mysterious illness were school children in a small Massachusetts town. At rehearsal for a concert children grew ill. Later during the actual concert more children became ill. The illness was at first attributed to environmental pollution, but, as Small and Borus (1983) show, it was a case of mass hysteria.

A case of collective delusion that lasted ten years, beginning about 1969, and covered a large part of the western United States was, and sometimes still is, blamed on UFOs or their occupants. This is the so-called cattle mutilation mystery. Starting in 1969 and gathering steam over the next few years, reports of mysteriously mutilated cattle found on the range in the West became quite common. What was causing these deaths? The deaths could not have been due to natural causes, people believed, because there were surgically sharp incisions on the bodies. And incisions in very strange places—the anus was often cored like an apple, and the eyes, vagina, penis and testicles, tongue, and other soft parts of the body were removed. In addition to the UFO hypothesis, others felt that satanic cults or supernatural forces were at work. As reports increased in numbers, there was a call for the government to take action. In April 1979 the Justice Department funded an investigation of the problem by a former FBI agent. His report (Rommel, 1980) and Kagan and Summer's (1983) book set to rest the claims for paranormal causes of the mutilations. The cattle were dying of natural causes, such as eating poisonous plants, and the bodies were being attacked by scavengers. Scavengers find it difficult to chew through tough cowhide. Instead, they attack the soft areas of the body, and these were just the areas found missing in the "mutilated" cattle. What about the surgical precision of the incisions? In fact the incisions weren't surgically precise at all, as was easily seen when an actual scalpel was used to make an incision on the body of a dead cow, as part of Rommel's investigation. The scavenger-caused wounds simply had a sharper edge than one would expect. Few ranchers, coming on the dead and partly rotted body of one of their cattle, bothered to inspect the wounds for the small tooth marks that would have been visible. Also, as a body decomposes, gases build up within and the body swells. The edges of any wounds are thereby stretched and come to appear sharper than they originally were.

The media played a role in the continued hysteria over the cattle mutilation reports. Sensational reporting that played up the outlandish speculations and ignored the true explanation probably prolonged this particular episode well beyond its natural lifespan.

Creationism

Creationism is one pseudoscience that is much in the public eye of late. Creationists around the country are pressing their demands that something they call "creation science" be taught in the public schools along with the Darwinian theory of evolution. The United States Supreme Court decided by a seven-to-two margin on June 19, 1987, that a Louisiana law that would have required the teaching of "creation science" along with the theory of evolution in biology classes was unconstitutional (Edwards vs. Aguillard, No. 85-1513).

Creation science holds that there is scientific evidence to support the biblical story of creation and to show that theories of evolution (whether strictly Darwinian or not) are wrong. A major piece of evidence cited for years in this regard was the claimed co-occurrence of human and dinosaur tracks in limestone along the Paluxy River in Texas. The coexistence of humans and dinosaurs was said to be proven by these tracks, thereby showing that both were created at the same time and, further, that evolution of humankind never occurred but rather that humankind was created and did not evolve. In actuality, the tracks are those of a small dinosaur (Kuban, 1986; Godfrey and Cole, 1986). Discovered many years ago, the tracks in the limestone along the river did resemble to the untrained eye a crude human footprint. After years of exposure, the softer rock inside the track has weathered away, leaving a much clearer imprint of the foot of a small, three-toed dinosaur. The improvement in definition of a fossilized footprint due to weathering is a well-known phenomenon in paleontology (Thulborn, 1986). Other "man tracks" are the result of the overactive imagination of creationists, who see a human footprint in nearly every small depression in the rocks caused by natural processes of erosion. Finally, blatantly fake human footprints, actually carved in rock, are displayed in creationist museums and offered for sale in the Paluxy River area (Godfrey and Cole, 1986).

Creationists frequently cite the second law of thermodynamics as proof that evolution could not have taken place. The second law states that any closed system will degenerate from whatever order it had at the beginning to a state of greater and greater randomness, or *entropy*. Since evolution results in greater organization over time (i.e., more, not less, complex organisms evolve), it must violate the second law of thermodynamics, which is one of the fundamental laws of nature. This argument is a semantic trick: the second law applies to closed systems— systems in which there is no energy input—but the earth is not a closed system. It is constantly receiving massive amounts of energy from the sun. Therefore, evolution does not contradict the second law at all (Patterson, 1983).

A common tack of creationists is to point to the complexity of some feature of some species and state that such a specialized feature could not have come about through evolution. Thus, evolution is false and creationism is true. A classic example of this tactic concerns the bombardier beetle. Weber (1980) has "exploded" the creationists' use of this interesting beetle as support for creationism. The beetle protects itself from predators in an unusual way: it expels an extremely hot liquid from sacks in its abdomen at any attacker. According to Duane Gish (1977) of the Institute for Creation Research in El Cajon, California, the chemicals that make up the active ingredients of the beetles' defensive fluid, hydrogen peroxide and hydroquinone, are explosive when mixed together. To prevent itself from being blown up, the beetle adds another chemical, a so-called inhibitor, to the mixture to prevent the explosion. When the beetle needs to use its defensive weapon, a fourth chemical, an anti-inhibitor, is added and the explosive mixture is immediately squirted at the attacker. Gish's point is that this complex system could not have evolved through any intermediate steps because the apparatus to make hydrogen peroxide and hydroquinone would have had to evolve before the ability to produce the inhibitor and anti-inhibitor. But, if the ability to produce hydrogen peroxide and hydroquinone evolved first, then the beetle would have blown itself up when the two mixed, so the inhibitor and anti-inhibitor would never have had the chance to evolve. Therefore, Gish and other creationists conclude, the whole system must have been created at the same time.

Gish's (1977) argument might be impressive if it were based on the actual physiology of the bombardier beetle. But he, like many other creationists, gets his facts wrong when discussing scientific evidence. First, hydrogen peroxide and hydroquinone do not explode when mixed. Second, Gish's (1977) description of the biochemistry of the production of the fluid that the beetle emits is wrong. Since the two chemicals that make up most of the fluid do not explode when mixed, there is no need for any "inhibitor" and, not suprisingly, the beetle produces no such chemical. What does happen is that the beetle adds an enzyme to the mixture that produces an "explosive" transformation of the chemicals into oxygen, quinone, and water (Weber, 1980). Thus, Gish mistakes the details of the actual physiological process that underlies the beetles' defense mechanism. Where did the hydrogen peroxide and hydroquinone come from in the first place? The former is found in insects as a normal product of physiological reactions. The latter helps to make insects' cuticle hard and, further, "tastes bad to predators and is the chemical that makes stink bugs stink" (Weber, 1980, p. 5). Given this, it is easy to understand why these two chemicals would evolve separately in an insect.

Weber (1980) notes that although Gish was informed in 1978 of the errors in his presentation of the bombardier beetle, he continued to use it two years later. Creationists often don't let accuracy stand in the way of a good argument against evolution.

A creationist technique related to that used by Gish, as described above, is to present some specific feature of some creature and demand an explanation of how that feature evolved. If no such explanation is immediately forthcoming, it is assumed that the feature must have been created and, therefore, that creationism is correct. On logical grounds this is precisely the same as the argument of the proponents of UFOs as extraterrestrial craft that, if skeptics can't explain away every single UFO sighting, then UFOs must be extraterrestrial in nature. This is a fundamental logical error. In the case of evolution, it will probably never be possible to explain how every feature of every species evolved. We will never have a time machine with which to go back and observe the selection pressures that brought about each feature. The fact that evolutionary theory can explain so many features across numerous species is extremely powerful evidence in its favor.

Creationists believe that all species were specially created by God during creation, as related in the biblical Book of Genesis. If they were specially created, one would expect that the Creator would have produced physiological structures that are perfectly suited to each species' environmental requirements. This is often not the case, as Gould (1980) discusses in his essay "The Panda's Thumb." Although the panda's thumb performs the role of a thumb in primates, allowing the panda to skillfully manipulate objects, especially the bamboo it feeds on, it's really not a thumb at all. Rather, it is a highly modified sesamoid bone, a bone usually found in the wrist. The panda's thumb "wins no prize in an engineer's derby. It is, to use Michael Ghiselin's phrase, a contraption" (Gould, 1980, p. 24). One would not expect the Creator to create slap-dash contraptions, but that is exactly what would be expected of a process of evolution that operates in the way Darwin and his successors have proposed. Another example of such poor engineering is found in the human spinal column. The spinal column gives so many people so much trouble because it is poorly constructed for the bipedal, upright posture of humans. It still shows the anatomical signs of having evolved in an organism that walked on all fours much of the time.

If one is going to contend that the universe was created only some 6,000 years ago, as many creationists do, one must argue against much more than evolutionary biology. One must argue against much of modern science, especially geology, astronomy, and physics, because fundamental findings in all these disciplines point to the great age of the universe. It is therefore not surprising that some of these sciences have lately come under creationist attack. Sheaffer (1982-83, p. 7) quotes one group of creationists as stating that the idea that the earth revolves around the sun "is an anti-Biblical notion and is the precursor of Darwinism." Another problem exists for creationists. If the universe is only 6,000 or so years old and as vast as it is, which most creationists accept, then how could the light of stars billions of light years away have reached earth in the mere 6,000 years the universe has been in existence? The obvious answer is that it couldn't. Another answer given by creationists is that the speed of light has been slowing down since creation. This is but one example of how far the creationists will go to twist the facts to support their pseudoscientific theory.

When pressed by detailed refutations of their arguments, creationists often resort to the ultimate defense of the proponents of pseudoscience, the unfalsifiable hypothesis. One form of the nonfalsifiable defense of creationism is to hold that the evidence for evolution, the age of the earth, or the age of the universe was put there by God to test our faith. A closely related version holds that the evidence was put there by Satan to lead us astray. Note that there is no conceivable piece of evidence that could disprove these hypotheses. No matter what new evidence turned up to support evolution, it could always be explained away by the use of either of these nonfalsifiable hypotheses. As has been noted, such hypotheses can be very seductive because of their seeming power. Their use actually demonstrates only the intellectual bankruptcy of the belief system they are used to support.

This brief discussion has by no means described all the fallacies of the creationists' arguments. Further such discussions can be found in Kitcher (1982) and Godfrey (1983).

Periodically one hears of an expedition to Mount Ararat near the Turkish-Russian border that hopes to find the remains of Noah's ark. Why Mount Ararat? For hundreds of years, it is said, people have reported seeing the remains of the ark on the mountain, which fits, more or less, the biblical description of the place where the ark came to rest. The most dramatic reported ark sighting took place in 1917, when a Russian pilot flying over the mountain not only saw the ark but took photographs of it. His report led to an expedition being sent that located the ark and made a detailed study of the structure. All the documentation of this expedition and the pilot's photographs were lost in the Russian Revolution. Bailey (1978), in an excellent and unfortunately out-of-print book, finds that this story "is almost entirely fiction" (p.55) and that other reports of the ark on Mount Ararat are equally without foundation. More recent photographic evidence, Bailey (1978) finds, is of a highly dubious nature. Moore (1983), in response to creationist claims that the story of Noah and the ark is literally true, has exhaustively catalogued the physical impossibilities in the story, concluding that "such a voyage never took place and could not possibly have ever occurred" (p. 39).

Cryptozoology

Reports of monsters such as the Loch Ness monster, the yeti or abominable snowman, and bigfoot have a great deal in common with reports of UFOs.

First, monster reports are common, although not as common as UFO reports. Second, monsters are reported by sane, reliable witnesses who frequently truly believe that they have seen something huge, mysterious, and frightening. As it does for UFO reports, the honesty of such reports leads many to accept the reports at face value. Third, the case for the existence of monsters relies almost entirely on eyewitness reports, as genuine physical and photographic evidence for their existence is lacking. In fact, some individuals in the UFO movement contend that there is some sort of relationship between UFOs and monsters as the latter are allegedly seen more commonly after UFO sightings (Clark and Coleman, 1978). Given the similarity between UFO and monster reports, what was said in chapter seven regarding the constructive nature of perception and memory applies with full force to reports of monsters.

The Loch Ness monster of Scotland is probably the world's best-known monster, second only to bigfoot in this country. Binns (1984) has carefully examined the Loch Ness monster story, and his excellent book forms the basis for the present discussion. It is widely believed that sightings of the monster date back over a thousand years to one by St. Columba and that sightings have continued on a more or less regular basis since then. This is incorrect. The St. Columba sighting report is an example of the poor scholarship that plagues the Loch Ness mystery. The sighting is taken from a biography of the saint written in 565 A.D., a time when the biographer of a saint was expected to prove his saintliness by telling marvelous stories about strange and miraculous occurrences associated with the saint (Binns, 1984). Such stories can hardly be taken as reliable. Further, St. Columba's "monster" wasn't even seen in Loch Ness, but in the River Ness, a different body of water so shallow that it cannot support navigation, let alone a resident monster.

Reports of sightings made in 1520, 1771, and 1885 first came to light in a letter published in the October 20, 1933, issue of *The Scotsman*. The letter was from one D. Murray Rose who "failed to supply either his address or any specific references to the chronicles or publications wherein his weird and wonderful stories could be found" (Binns, 1984, p. 51). No one has ever been able to find any other reference than Rose's letter to these alleged sightings.

The city of Inverness lies a few miles northeast of Loch Ness, and the first recorded report of the monster appeared in the *Inverness Courier* of May 2, 1933, written by one Alex Campbell. The witnesses were Mr. and Mrs. John Mackay, a local couple who were driving along the loch. Campbell's report of what the Mackays saw is greatly exaggerated. He states, for example, that "the creature disported itself, rolling and plunging for fully a minute, its body resembling that of a whale" (quoted in Binns,

1984, p. 10). In fact, Mr. Mackay, the driver, saw nothing and Mrs. Mackay saw "a violent commotion in the water which seemed to be caused 'by two ducks fighting'" (Binns, 1984, p. 12).

Since 1933 numerous reports of the monster have been made. What prompts them? Loch Ness is a large, long, and deep lake where natural phenomena—like ducks fighting—can provide the stimulus for perception to construct a monster where none exists. For example, the loch contains numerous salmon. On rare occasions, they come to the surface in groups, causing a considerable disturbance. Captain John Macdonald, who had sailed the loch for more than fifty years without ever seeing anything resembling a monster, suggested this type of event as an explanation for the Mackay sighting a few days after Campbell's story was published (Binns, 1984). There are also otter in the loch, which run an average of about four feet in length. When playing together, with several swimming in line, one diving, the next surfacing, and so forth, a group of otter could easily simulate the snake-like aspect that the monster is sometimes said to have. Further, otter are rather rare and so unfamiliar to most people. Otter have been mistaken for "monsters" in other Scottish lochs, as Binns (1984) notes. Deer are common around the loch and have been known to swim across it. A deer swimming in a lake is not something most people expect to see and so, if the lake happens to have the reputation of housing a monster, a monster will likely be perceived. Binns (1984) reports one case in which enlargement of a photograph of the monster revealed a swimming deer. Floating logs and bizarrely shaped pieces of driftwood can also be mistaken for a monster, if that is what one is half-expecting to see. And who could go to the loch without at least half-hoping to get a good view of the monster? Lehn (1979) has demonstrated that atmospheric refraction, associated with a temperature inversion layer (cold air near the surface of the lake, warmer air above), can produce striking illusions in which otherwise well-known objects are visually distorted, both in shape and size. The perfect conditions for such illusion-creating temperature inversions exist at Loch Ness, and many other lakes where monsters are occasionally reported.

Photographs exist that are said to show the monster and, here again, the parallel between monsters and UFOs is striking. Many of the photographs show nothing other than indistinct shapes in the water. They could be anything, and probably are. Further, some of the photos don't include any shoreline in the image and could have been taken anywhere—in a pond in the photographer's back yard, for instance. Given the number of people toting cameras around it is astonishing that more and better monster photos don't exist, if the monster does. Fraud has also played a role in monster photographs. Photos taken in 1934 by R.

A. Wilson that show a reasonably clear dinosaur-like shape are now known to be fakes (Binns, 1984).

The most famous Loch Ness photographs—actually a film—were taken by Tim Dinsdale in the spring of 1960. The film was analyzed by the Royal Air Force Joint Air Reconnaissance Intelligence Center in 1966. The center reported that the moving object in the film was "probably an animate object" (quoted in Binns, 1984, p. 109). This report has received much publicity, but Binns (1984) shows that it faces real problems as proof of the existence of the monster. A careful reading of the report shows that the object's appearance is equivalent to that of a rather fast motorboat. This explanation is rejected because such boats are "normally painted in such a way as to be photo visible at any time" (quoted in Binns, 1984, p. 123), and Dinsdale said it wasn't a motorboat. On the day the film was taken Dinsdale, an ardent believer in the existence of the monster, was greatly fatigued and had already mistaken a floating tree trunk for the monster that same day. The report, then, actually shows that the object could have been a motorboat that was painted an unusual (i.e., dull as opposed to bright) color.

Loch Ness in the 1970s was the site of enormous efforts to obtain, once and for all, proof positive of the monster's existence. Round-the-clock surveillance was maintained for months. Sensitive sonar scanned the loch and sensitive cameras were lowered into it. (One of the problems facing underwater photography in the loch is that the water is extremely murky.) A small underwater submarine spent 250 hours in the loch. The results of all this? Nothing: no surface sightings, no surface photographs, no sonar tracings of a monster, no monster skeletons found on the bottom of the loch, only one photograph, obtained from an underwater camera in the summer of 1972, that showed a clear image of what appeared to be the large flipper of an unknown species. Was this proof at last? Robert Rines, who set up the camera that took the photograph, felt that it did establish the existence of the monster (Rines, Edgerton, Wyckoff, and Klein, 1975-76). The original photograph had been sent to NASA's Jet Propulsion Laboratory in California for computer enhancement, a technique used to clarify photographs, such as those beamed back to earth from space by interplanetary probes. It was the computer-enhanced photo that was allegedly published in the article by Rines et al. (1975-76) and reproduced widely throughout the world. But the published photo was not the computer-enhanced photo. The published photo had been greatly retouched and appears much more obviously to show a flipper, while the actual computer-enhanced photograph could be of almost anything. An investigation by Razdan and Kielar (1984–85) revealed the true nature of the photograph in this case. Razdan and Kielar (1984–85) also point to serious shortcomings in the sonar evidence that Rines *et al.* (1975-76) argue supports their interpretation of the photograph.

The Loch Ness monster has been the object of much searching for more than fifty years. In all that time and with all that effort using some of the most technologically sophisticated devices available, no trace of conclusive evidence has been uncovered that the monster exists. It is most instructive to compare this situation to another where a creature, if by no means a monster, was actually found alive, in spite of the fact that the scientific world believed that it had been extinct for 200 million years. The creature is a fish called a coelacanth which runs to about five feet in length and lives in the Indian Ocean. In 1938 a single specimen was caught, arousing considerable interest among scientists (Smith, 1958). In the next few years, the interest of scientists turned up some additional specimens of this "living fossil." Compare the Loch Ness monster and the coelacanth. The monster is said to be a very large creature living in a lake in a rather heavily populated and traveled area, which is a favorite summer vacation spot with a highway running along it. In the fifty-plus years people have so diligently looked for the monster, no satisfactory evidence for its existence has ever been found. The coelacanth, on the other hand, is a relatively small fish living in a vast ocean. When it was discovered in 1938, the countries bordering on the Indian Ocean were largely primitive colonial states. And yet in just a few years several more examples of the fish were found. It strains credulity to argue that if the coelacanth was found so rapidly and under such unfavorable conditions, the Loch Ness monster has somehow manged to evade its much more persistent and sophisticated searchers for so long.

The evidence for the reality of the yeti in the Himalayas and bigfoot in the Pacific Northwest is little better than that for the Loch Ness monster. Napier (1972) and Wylie (1980) have reviewed the evidence for these two creatures. Regarding the yeti, several large mammals are found in the Himalayas that are mistaken for yeti. These include the woolly wolf and brown and black bears. Bears occasionally stand on their hind feet and in that posture can present a most frightening and unbearlike apparition. So-called yeti tracks are often actually the tracks of one of these animals, sometimes strangely enlarged by melting of the surrounding snow. The Yeti skins that are reported from time to time turn out to be skins of the various mammals that inhabit the Himalayas.

Eyewitness reports, reports of strange large tracks, and even a film help to convince many that bigfoot, or sasquatch, is an actual creature. Initially confined to the Pacific Northwest, bigfoot sightings have become a nationwide phenomenon in the past decade or so. Eyewitness reports, with their notable lack of reliability, can be attributed to misidentification of local species (bears again) and the constructive nature of memory and perception. For example, the Los Angeles *Herald Examiner* reported on May 13, 1982, that a bigfoot-type creature had been spotted in the Los Angeles area. According to eyewitnesses it was between seven and nine feet tall and was "too hairy and smelled too bad to be human" (quoted in Dobson, 1982–83, p. 10). The "creature" turned out to be a bum, of normal height but unwashed and unshaven. Bigfoot footprints have been reported since the 1930s in the Pacific Northwest. Many of these are apparently the work of hoaxers. Dennett (1982-83) reported that Rent Mullens, a retired logger, had confessed to carving eight sets of "bigfeet," one of which he used to produce fake bigfoot footprints. Most of his carved bigfeet ended up in California.

The most famous photographic evidence for bigfoot is a film taken by Roger Patterson on October 20, 1967, which shows a creature walking through brush in front of the camera. Grieve's (1972) analysis of the film shows it to be inconclusive as support for bigfoot, as it could have been the result of a hoax. Occasionally, bits and pieces of alleged bigfoot remains appear. The number of these reported far exceeds the number submitted for scientific testing, perhaps because when the testing is performed it shows the remains to be those of some known species. Kurtz (1980–81) reports that the partly decomposed remains of a bear found in northern New York near the Ontario border caused much excitement as "real proof" of bigfoot in the area until analysis revealed their real origin.

The creatures in Loch Ness, the Himalayas, and the deep woods of the Pacific Northwest are not the only mysterious creatures to intrigue the monster hunters of the world. The recently formed International Society of Cryptozoology has been involved in expeditions to the Congo to hunt for living dinosaurs and to New Guinea to try to find mermaids, called *ri* by the natives, according to the society. These are described as "an air breathing mammal, with the truck, genitalia, arms and head of a human being, and a legless lower trunk terminating in a pair of lateral fins, or flippers" according to Dr. Roy Wagner, of the University of Virginia Anthropology Department (quoted in Sheaffer, 1983–84, p. 117). Why should one believe that such creatures exist? Wagner points to eyewitness reports and says, "I don't think the credibility of some of my informants can be lightly dismissed" (quoted in Sheaffer, 1983–84, p. 117).

Dowsing and the Magic Pendulum

Dowsers claim to be able to find underground water—and sometimes other substances such as oil or gold—by walking over the ground holding a forked stick, known as the "dowsing rod." When the rod is felt to make sudden movements, seemingly on its own, that is an indication that the dowser is above a source of water. Dowsing is an old and venerated folk tradition, especially in northern New England. In addition to predicting where water is, the dowser frequently also predicts the depth at which it will be found. The actions of the rod are vaguely ascribed to some sort of magnetic influence of the water, the psychic abilities of the dowser, or some combination of these. Some more modern dowsers have dispensed altogether with the need to actually walk over the land being dowsed and, instead, dowse over a map of the land in question.

A major factor in convincing people that dowsing works is the seemingly autonomous movements of the rod. As Vogt and Hyman (1979, p. 130) point out, dowsing requires considerable physical effort: "The muscles and body of the diviner are under considerable *tension*. The rod is compressed with great force and this compression is maintained over a considerable period of time." Even under normal conditions of muscle tension, the feedback from the muscles that tells the brain about the degree of muscular movement is far from perfect (Matthews, 1982).

The tension placed on the muscles during dowsing aggravates this situation, so the dowser is unable to feel the small muscle twitches that are responsible for the sudden movements of the rod. It is thus natural, although incorrect, to attribute these sudden movements to the rod itself and to feel that they occur without any intention on the part of the dowser.

Anecdotal eyewitness reports of the success of dowsers are also a major source of evidence for those convinced that dowsing really works. Such reports should be viewed with considerable skepticism because, as has been pointed out previously, they are frequently extremely unreliable. There is an additional factor working to enhance dowsers' "successes" in anecdotal reports: selective memory. To quote Vogt and Hyman (1979, p. 41) once again:

> We know a well-driller in Massachusetts who divines all the wells that he drills. This diviner, in an interview, recounted one success after another in his water witching career; he had not one failure to report. The driller's assistant, however, was skeptical about the value of water witching. He explained it away as "just imagination." In a separate interview, he told one story after another of failures that followed upon a diviner's advice. We had no reason to doubt the honesty or sincerity of either

of these men. One was a believer, and, if we accepted his testimony at face value, water witching was invariably successful. From the skeptic's accounts, however, we would gather that water witching was very unreliable, and successes with it were matters of luck. Both these men were illustrating the tendency to recall only those incidents that are in accord with what we believe or would like to believe.

In addition, there is a large element of the multiple out in dowsers predictions. A dowser may predict that water will be found at several locations. When water is found at any one of these, dowsing seems to have been successful. Since well drilling is likely to stop with the first successful well, later predictions that might well have turned out to be wrong won't be tested. In addition, multiple depths may be predicted or the predicted depth may be very vague, as in "water will be found at a medium depth." In some areas of the country, one will almost invariably find water if one drills deep enough. In these areas, the dowser will almost always be right if the well is drilled deep enough. And, of course, vague depth predictions may be forgotten or "adjusted" to become more accurate after the fact. Finally, geological clues in the land help indicate where underground water may be found. Trained geologists can use these clues to increase their accuracy at predicting where to drill to a level above chance. The dowser may often have picked up these same clues and may use them while dowsing, consciously or unconsciously.

What is obviously needed to evaluate properly the claims of dowsers are controlled studies done either in the laboratory or in the field. Vogt and Hyman (1979) review many such studies. None of them showed any evidence that dowsers could find water at an above-chance level. One very large study (Ongley, 1948) examined a total of fifty-eight dowsers who claimed to be able to find water. None of them performed at a level above chance. More recent studies have had the same result. Vogt (1952) recorded the comparative numbers of dry and successful wells that had been drilled with and without the advice of dowsers. Of the twenty-nine wells drilled with dowsers' advice, twenty-four were successful. That sounds good, until one realizes that of the thirty-two wells drilled without dowsers' advice, twenty-five were successful. There is no statistically significant difference in the relative success rates of wells that were and were not drilled with input from dowsers. Randi (1979-80) tested four Italian dowsers. A pattern of three underground pipes was buried (figure 20). Any one of the pipes could have water flowing through it. The dowsers' task was to trace the route of the one pipe that did have water flowing through it. The dowsers, who didn't know the route of any of the pipes, were totally unable to divine the route of the one with water in it. Smith (1981–82) tested an Australian dowser who claimed to be able to find both water and gold. The dowser failed to find water. During the testing of his ability to find gold, a significant occurrence took place:

> As is traditional in such tests, in full view of Holmes I placed the gold ingot in a box and asked him to see if his powers were working. Instead of going directly to the chosen box (as we expected him to), he walked up and down the row of boxes showing us that he received no reading from the empty boxes. He then mistook the correct box to be the one next to it and promptly divined the wrong box. His wife called out to him to "remember which box it was put in," but to no avail. (Smith, 1981–82, p. 36–37)

Although it would be easy to laugh at this dowser who can't even find something when he's been shown where it is, this incident illustrates an important point. Dowsers' predictions are based on their beliefs. Holmes believed that the gold was in an empty box and the rod promptly pointed to that empty box. If a dowser believes that water is to be found at a particular location, for whatever reason, the small muscular movements that cause the rod to move become more likely to occur at that location. Thus both the movement of the rod and the place where those movements occur are internally generated although, because of the nature of the physiology of the kinesthetic system, the dowser will have no conscious appreciation of this fact.

Some dowsers don't use the traditional rod, but rely on a pendulum, which can be any relatively heavy and small object suspended from a string. A single key will do. The pendulum is usually held at arm's length and is said to swing back and forth, under its own power and with no attempt to induce swinging on the part of the dowser. It swings when the dowser is over water or whatever other substance is being searched for. The pendulum can also be used, it is said, to divine the sex of an unborn child: hold the pendulum over the mother's belly and it will swing one way for a boy, the other for a girl. The pendulum has also been used to determine the guilt or innocence of an accused person and to reveal all sorts of hidden knowledge.

The pendulum seems to be swinging back and forth under its own power and the one holding it claims, quite honestly, to be making no conscious attempts to influence its movement. In reality, as for the dowsing rod, small arm movements, which are not registered in the brain, are responsible for the pendulum's movement. This can be demonstrated quite neatly by having the string that suspends the pendulum draped over some stationary object. Movement stops, even though the person is still holding the string and the pendulum is still free to swing, if there really were psychic forces causing its movement. In an interesting experiment, Easton and Shor (1975) further demonstrated the nature of the pendulum's movement. In one case, subjects could see the pendulum they were holding, in another they couldn't. Movement was greater when they could see it. Movement was even greater, by a factor of ten, when subjects were asked to imagine that the pendulum was moving, as opposed to when they were asked to imagine that it was not. Finally, if they observed some other type of oscillating motion, this also increased the amount of pendulum movement. None of these effects would be expected if the pendulum's movement were caused by some psychic force.

Firewalking

For years people have been amazed, or at least puzzled, by the ability of people in some "primitive" cultures to walk across beds of hot coals, usually during a religious celebration, without burning their feet. This ability is usually attributed to some vague power of "mind over matter." It was one Tony Robbins who popularized firewalking in the United States a few years ago. Robbins, one of numerous self-help gurus based in California, used firewalking as the gimmick in his self-help seminars. He persuaded thousands of people to walk across beds of red-hot coals without suffering burns. This was said to show the amazing power of mind over matter. In other words, it was the sheer power of the mind, perhaps a psychic power, that prevented the feet from being burned as the basic laws of physics surely dictate they must.

In reality, it is the basic laws of physics that prevent people's feet from being burned while firewalking. The power of the mind had nothing to do with it. Leikind and McCarthy (1985–86) have analyzed the physics of firewalking and find that two well-known physical principles account for the rarity of burned feet. First there is the *Leidenfrost effect*. This is the effect seen when a drop of water darts about on a hot skillet. Between the skillet and the drop is a layer of steam that insulates the drop from the full heat of the skillet and prevents it from boiling away almost at once. In the firewalking situation, the soles of the feet are often damp, either from sweat caused by nervousness or from dew on the grass surrounding the bed of coals. In many of Robbins's demonstrations of mass firewalking, the grass is hosed down around the bed of coals. The water on the soles provides the layer of steam that helps to insulate the foot from the full heat of the coals.

But the Leidenfrost effect is not sufficient to explain the lack of burning. The material upon which one walks is a very important factor. Consider an example given by Leikind and McCarthy (1985–86). You're baking something in a pan in the oven at 400 degrees. You open the oven to remove the pan. Naturally, you use a potholder to pick up the pan. If you were to try to pick it up with your bare hands, you'd be burned because it's at a temperature of 400 degrees—but so is the air in the oven, and that certainly doesn't burn your hand, even if you leave it in the oven for a minute or so. Why not? The answer is that "different materials at the same temperature contain different amounts of thermal or heat energy and also have different abilities to carry the energy from one place to another" (Leikind and McCarthy, 1985–86, p. 29). Metal is high in both heat capacity and thermal conductivity, while air is low in both these variables. Thus metal at 400 degrees will burn one badly, while 400-degree air has very little effect. What about the coals one walks on at a Robbins demonstration? Coals are hot (up to 1,200 degrees) but they have low heat capacity and thermal conductivity. Thus, if one walks fairly rapidly over them, no burns will occur. Of course, if one lingers burns can and do occur. Leikind and McCarthy (1985–86) also note that firewalking as practiced by other cultures involves walking on material (coals or porous stone) that is low in both heat capacity and thermal conductance.

Graphology

According to the claims of graphology's proponents, it is possible to determine various characteristics of an individual, especially those relating to personality, from his or her handwriting. It has been estimated that about 3,000 U.S. firms use graphology in employee selection (Rafaeli and Klimoski, 1983). Eighty-five percent of firms in Europe are said to use graphological analyses in making their hiring decisions (Levy, 1979). Van Deventer (1983, p. 74), managing editor of the periodical *United States Banker*, states that "graphoanalysis reveals capabilities and aptitudes in an individual, many of which the applicant may not even be aware of." Given the popularity of graphology and the importance of the decisions that depend, at least in part, on its use, it is important to discover if one's handwriting really does reveal anything about one's personality characteristics.

There is a growing body of empirical research literature on graphology. It is almost uniformly negative as regards graphologists' claims. Most tested among these claims is that job success can be determined or predicted from handwriting. Ben-Shakhar *et al.* (1986), Keinan (1986b), Rafaeli and Klimoski (1983), and Zdep and Weaver (1967) have all found that graphological analysis did not reveal anything about job success. Drory (1986) did find significant positive correlations between job ratings and graphological analysis, but a serious problem with this study is that the handwriting samples used were autobiographical sketches. Thus, the graphologists may have based their judgments on the content of the handwriting rather than on the handwriting itself. That this is the explanation for Drory's (1986) findings is strongly suggested by the fact that studies using such information-filled autobiographical sketches find that when graphologists perform better than chance and a control group of nongraphologists also makes judgments based on the written sketch, the nongraphologists do as well as or better than the graphologists (Ben-Shakhar, Bar-Hillel, and Flug, 1986). Ben-Shakhar, Bar-Hillel, and Flug (1986) showed that nongraphological information (autobiographical information, presence or absence of spelling and grammatical errors, and so forth) in the sketches predicted job ratings as well "as the professional efforts of experienced graphologists" (p. 187).

Studies of graphology have been conducted on variables other than job success. Keinan (1986a) found that graphologists could not distinguish at a level above chance between writing samples provided by soldiers in a highly stressful situation (half an hour before their first night parachute jump) and a nonstressful, relaxed situation. Jansen (1973) found no relation between graphologists' judgments and various personality ratings. Frederick (1965) found that graphologists could not distinguish between mental hospital patients and undergraduate college students.

Some studies have reported positive results in which graphological analysis does allow above-chance discrimination between groups. The differences in the handwriting between the groups studied, however, reflect nonpersonality variables and do not support the graphological claim that personality is reflected in handwriting and can be assessed from it. Sex can be determined from handwriting with about a 70 percent accuracy (Goldberg, 1986). Professional graphologists and nongraphologists are equally accurate at making this judgment (Goldberg, 1986). Goldberg (1986) also found that nongraphologists could distinguish the writing of Americans and Europeans at a level higher than chance. This is presumably due to the different writing styles used and taught in the United States and Europe. Wing and Baddeley (1978) found that drinking alcohol changed some characteristics of handwriting so it should be possible to distinguish the writing of sober from that of intoxicated individuals.

Ratzon (1986) found that handwriting could be used to distinguish Holocaust survivors from psychiatric patients and from a group of "Nazi-persecuted" individuals who escaped the Holocaust by leaving Germany. A subgroup of the Holocaust survivors with organic brain damage could also be distinguished from the other groups by their handwriting. This last finding is not at all surprising, as brain damage can easily be expected to affect, for the worse, almost any type of motor behavior. The finding also gives an important clue to the explanation of the more unexpected finding that the nonbrain-damaged survivors' handwriting differed from those of the Nazi-persecuted group and the psychiatric group. The individuals who suffered through the Holocaust, even if not brain-damaged, were very likely in poorer health, due to their horrendous experience, than were individuals in the other two groups. Poorer health would be expected to result in changes in handwriting.

Nevo (1986) reanalyzed data from a paper by Hönel (1977) in which it was claimed that criminals and noncriminals could be distinguished by their handwriting. Nevo's (1986) reanalysis shows that statistical problems contributed to the large effects that Hönel (1977) reported. The positive effects are greatly reduced when appropriate statistical analyses are performed, but there is still a small ability on the part of a group of graphologists, considered as a whole, to classify the criminal versus the noncriminal. One variable that contributed much to Hönel's (1977) finding was socioeconomic class. Criminals tend to come from lower socioeconomic classes than noncriminals, and socioeconomic class does seem to be reflected in handwriting, perhaps as a function of better education and more emphasis on good handwriting in the upper as opposed to the lower ranges of the socio-economic class structure.

One study exists that seems to demonstrate graphoanalytic ability for which no obvious alternative explanation comes to mind. Frederick (1968) found that graphologists could discriminate between suicide notes written by actual suicides and the same notes copied by normal writers, who copied from typed versions of the notes. Police detectives and secretaries could not make this discrimination. This is an intriguing study and should be replicated.

With the exception of the Frederick (1968) study, the results of studies of graphological claims that handwriting reflects personality variables are entirely negative. Why, then, is graphological analysis so widely used and accepted? The answer is that the fallacy of personal validation, along with the selective nature of memory, accounts for the wide popularity of graphology. Reid (1983, p. 71) provides an excellent example of the fallacy of personal validation as it applies to graphology: "As a reliable first test, I would suggest that you commission a graphological analysis of your own hand-writing and show the report to someone who knows you well, a marriage or business partner. In my case, both I and my wife were satisfied that the assessment was remarkably accurate. It also added to self-knowledge and has since contributed to greater effectiveness in doing my job." This is just the sort of glowing testimonial one receives from a good cold reading.

Reid (1983), who is managing director of an executive search company, also provides excellent examples of selective memory as he recounts instances where graphological analysis has apparently been successful. One case is that of a man recently released from prison after serving a term for embezzlement. The graphological analysis showed that "his declaration that he was reformed needed to be taken with some caution" (p. 71). Thus, he obtained a job where "there was no possibility of his being exposed to temptation" and he has "not trangressed since." This is seen as evidence for graphology. In the situation, the graphological analysis could not be falsified since the man had no opportunity to embezzle again. In another case, an executive was hired by a firm and although a physical exam showed him to be fit, he became seriously ill three months after starting his job and ended up not returning. A graphological analysis carried out after his illness was known on a sample of handwriting taken before he was hired "suggested he had an incipient, serious medical problem" (p. 71).

Functional Differences Between the Two Sides of the Brain

The fact that the two hemispheres of the human brain differ in function has become part of modern popular culture and even turns up in automobile advertising. In the popular view, the differences between the two brain hemispheres are vast. The left hemisphere is thought to control rational, logical, and scientific thought while the right hemisphere is the site of art, music, creativity, and intuition. A related belief is that stable individual differences exist such that people can be classified as left or right hemisphere "dominant." A right hemisphere dominant individual, it is claimed, will be creative, intuitive, and artistic; a left hemisphere dominant individual will be rational, logical, and scientific. Some educators argue that modern education is too "left brain dominant" and that drills and exercises should be used that increase right brain function in the hope that more creative artistic students will result since artistic ability is said to reside "in" the right hemisphere. In the field of management and management training it has been proposed that "which hemisphere of one's brain is better developed may determine whether a person ought to be a planner or a manager" (Mintzberg, 1976, p. 49). Herrmann (1981) has developed a testing and training program that he claims can determine which hemisphere is dominant in an individual and can increase right brain skills, thereby improving managerial abilities. Herrmann's training seminars are extremely expensive; a half-day workshop can cost $2,000

(McKean, 1985). See Hines (1985, 1987) for detailed criticism of pseudoscientific claims about hemispheric differences as they are applied to management and training.

The popular view of and claims made about hemispheric differences outlined above have about as much relationship to the true nature of the differences between the brain hemispheres as astrology has to astronomy. Like many pseudosciences, hemisphere difference pseudo-science contains a grain of truth. In this case, that grain is the fact that there really are differences between the two hemispheres in the way they process information. These differences, however, are unlike those claimed by hemispheric difference pseudoscience.

Hemispheric differences have been the focus of a great deal of research, reviews of which can be found in Gazzaniga and LeDoux (1978), Springer and Deutsch (1985), Bryden (1982), and Young (1983). This research has established that, with one exception, the differences between the hemispheres are small, although real and of considerable theoretical interest in terms of brain function. The actual hemispheric differences are far from the strict dichotomies (e.g., the claim that art is "in" the right hemisphere and that the left hemisphere has no artistic abilities) found in the claims of hemispheric difference pseudoscience. Rather, there is a continuum of function such that one hemisphere is somewhat better than the other at a particular cognitive task, but both hemispheres are able to perform the task.

The research on hemispheric differences shows that, in general, the left hemisphere is better than the right on tasks that involve linguistic stimuli such as visually presented words or auditorially presented speech. This can be shown in brain-damaged subjects when damage to certain specific portions of the left hemisphere, called the language area, results in a disorder known as *aphasia*. This is an inability to speak or understand language and in some cases an inability to do either. Damage to the right hemisphere very rarely produces aphasia. Studies using normal individuals as subjects also show that the left hemisphere is better than the right in processing linguistic stimuli. People make faster judgments when linguistic stimuli are presented to the left hemisphere (via the right visual field or right ear) than to the right hemisphere (via the left visual field or left ear). These differences in speed are small, on the order of 100 milliseconds or less in most studies. The right hemisphere does have the ability to process linguistic information (Searlman, 1977, 1983), it is just not as good as the left hemisphere when dealing with such stimuli.

There is one task that the right hemisphere seems unable to perform in most individuals: speaking. More precisely, the right hemisphere cannot control the muscles of the vocal tract and so is rendered mute. This is the closest thing to an absolute dichotomy of function between the hemispheres that will be found in the research literature. Nonetheless, it provides no support for hemispheric difference pseudoscience because the dichotomy is a motor one dealing with muscle control rather than one dealing with cognitive function, and it is cognitive dichotomies that are proposed by hemispheric difference pseudoscience. A similar dichotomy in terms of motor control of vocalization is found in several species of songbird (Nottebohm, 1979).

Not only does the research on the differences between the hemispheres contradict hemispheric difference pseudoscience in general, it also shows specific claims of the pseudoscience to be false. One major claim is that of *hemisphericity*, the claim that each of us is either left or right hemisphere dominant and that the hemisphere that dominates in an individual can be identified by various types of testing. Beaumont, Young, and McManus (1984) reviewed the concept of hemisphericity and the tests that were claimed to be able to determine it. They concluded that the concept "is a misleading one which should be abandoned" (p. 191). Further, claims for hemisphericity "cannot be supported by current scientific studies of cognitive functions of the cerebral hemispheres, and it is most unlikely that more thorough understanding of the relation between cognitive function and cerebral structural systems will lead to any change in this state of affairs" (p. 206).

Perhaps the best-known claim of hemispheric difference pseudoscience is that creative and artistic abilities reside "in" the right hemisphere. Thus, Edwards (1979) argues that the way to improve artistic abilities is to train the right hemisphere. This is an astonishingly uninformed and simplistic view of brain function. It harkens back to the nineteenth-century pseudoscience of phrenology.

It is possible to examine the effects of brain damage in creative, artistic individuals who suffer from tumors, strokes, or other forms of neuropathology. The results of studies of such individuals show that the claim that art, music, and creativity are "in" the right hemisphere are wrong. Gardner (1982, 1983; Gardner and Winner, 1981) has reviewed this research in some detail. Musical abilities and creativity can be impaired by damage to either hemisphere. The same is true of ability and creativity in the graphic arts. Ability and creativity in writing is much more impaired by damage to the left than the right hemisphere, undoubtedly because the basic units in writing are linguistic.

Additional claims about differences between the two hemispheres are that the right hemisphere is the "dreamer," that it is specialized for mental imagery, and that it is also the emotional hemisphere. None of these claims is true, although some have been presented as fact in introductory psychology texts, for example Haber and Runyon (1983). The actual evidence shows that, if anything, the left hemisphere is more involved with dreaming and mental imagery than the right (Ehrlichman and Barrett, 1983; Farah, 1984; Greenberg and Farah, 1986; Antrobus, 1987). As far as emotions are concerned, both hemispheres are involved in emotional processing but each seems to be more in control of different subsets of emotions, the left hemisphere being biased toward the positive and the right toward the negative emotions (Silberman and Weingartner, 1986).

It is widely believed in hemisphere difference pseudoscience that the predominant direction of people's lateral eye movements (LEMs) can be used to determine whether they are right or left hemisphere dominant. Thus, "left movers" are said to be right hemisphere dominant and "right movers" to be left hemisphere dominant. Ehrlichman and Weinberger (1978) reviewed the literature on LEMs and found that they were not related to hemispheric asymmetry of function. Beaumont, Young, and McManus (1984) reviewed more recent research on this topic and came to the same conclusion. In spite of their lack of validity, a bizarre type of therapy, self-help program, and salesmanship training technique has been built around LEMs, called Neuro-Linguistic Programming (Bandler and Grinder, 1979). The basic idea behind Neuro-Linguistic Programming (NLP) is that LEMs provide a moment-to-moment guide to people's thoughts. Thus, a left LEM indicates the person is remembering sounds or words, while a right LEM indicates sounds or words are being constructed. NLP also interprets—without a shred of evidence to support the interpretation—diagonal eye movements. An upward right eye movement is said to indicate that the person is constructing a visual image. A downward right eye movement is said to indicate that kinesthetic (muscle sense), taste, or smell sensations are being processed (Bandler and Grinder, 1979). Elich, Thompson, and Miller (1985) tested these claims and found no relationship between eye movement direction and the type of image or sensation the subjects were thinking about.

In the more applied realm, Haley (1982) and Dilts (1982), the latter an NLP "trainer," state that NLP can be used to enhance the effectiveness of sales personnel. All one need do is "observe your prospect's eye movement patterns. They hold secrets that sell" (Haley, 1982, p. 24). Since eye movement patterns, in fact, reveal nothing about a person's moment-to-moment thoughts, staring at a prospect's eyes is likely only to annoy him or her.

NLP is also touted as an effective form of psychotherapy and a counseling technique. It is neither. Sharpley (1984, 1987) has reviewed studies of the effectiveness of NLP in this regard and concludes that "research data do not support either the basic tenents of NLP or their application in counseling" (p. 103).

The Hundredth Monkey Phenomenon

There is a species of monkey that lives on several islands off the coast of Japan. The monkeys are often fed by humans and in 1953 one member of one troop on one island learned to wash the sand off sweet potatoes she was given by dunking them in the ocean. Other members of the troop quickly picked up this habit. A controversy has erupted over the manner in which the habit spread to troops on other islands. Watson (1979, p. 147) argues that the "habit seems to have jumped natural barriers and to have appeared spontaneously" on other islands, presumably via some sort of psychic information transmission. Watson (1979) sees the number of monkeys that learned the habit as the important factor. When a sufficient number had learned the trick to produce some sort of mental critical mass, the habit leapfrogged the bounds of space and time and appeared on other islands. The "hundredth monkey" is an aphorism for that critical mass. This concept of mental critical mass has become very popular among occultists, "new age" types, and those in the humanistic psychology movement. It suggests to them that, if only enough people believe something, everyone will begin to believe and the belief will become reality.

Watson's (1979) claims have been examined by Amundson (1984–85) and O'Hara (1985), herself a humanistic psychologist. Both evaluations find that Watson's (1979) report of the transfer of potato-washing behavior is highly inaccurate. There is no need at all to postulate a paranormal explanation for the transfer. Monkeys are extremely clever, and when potatoes were introduced to them in 1952 and 1953, several monkeys on different islands undoubtedly came up with the same idea spontaneously. Further, the islands are close enough that monkeys sometimes swim between them. Watson (1979) doesn't mention this.

Watson (1979) appropriately labels his report "speculation." O'Hara (1985) notes that reports taken from Watson's (1979) book have been even more misleading. In what she terms a "substantial piece of distortion by the editors of *Brain Mind Bulletin*," Watson's speculation is "presented as 'scientific findings'" (p. 65). Such distortions are typical in second- or third-hand reporting of claimed paranormal events.

Kirlian Photography

Psychics and holistic medicine practitioners frequently speak of the human "aura" or the "human energy field." The size, color, and type of vibration of this aura or field is said to reveal much about the individual's health and state of mind. That one could actually photograph these auras was first claimed by one Semyon Davidovich Kirlian in 1937 (Singer, 1981) and so-called Kirlian photography was born. This type of photography has been popular with proponents of the paranormal ever since, as they claim it as physical proof of the existence of a mysterious human aura. Kirlian photographs do show impressive, colorful fringes around the borders of living objects. Nonliving objects do not show such fringes. In humans, emotional arousal enhances the fringe (Singer, 1981). To obtain a Kirlian photograph, it is necessary to place the object to be photographed into an electrical circuit so that it acts like an electrode. Electricity is then passed through the broken circuit.

There is no doubt that Kirlian photos show a real phenomenon. The question is what causes the pattern of fringes. Pehek, Kyler, and Faust (1976) found that the Kirlian effect was due to moisture present on the object to be photographed. Living things (like the commonly photographed fingers) are moist. When the electricity enters the living object, it produces an area of gas ionization around the photographed object, assuming moisture is present on the object. Thus, "during exposure, moisture is transferred from the subject to the emulsion surface of the photographic film and causes an alternation of the electric charge pattern on the film" (Pehek, Kyler, and Faust, 1976, p. 269). If the photograph is taken in a vacuum, where no ionized gas is present, no Kirlian image appears (Cooper and Alt, cited in Singer, 1981). If the Kirlian image were due to some paranormal fundamental living energy field, it should not disappear in a simple vacuum. That the Kirlian image is enhanced by emotional arousal can also be easily explained by the presence of moisture. A basic physiological response to arousal is sweating. Thus aroused individuals will have a greater moisture content on their skin surface and the greater amount of moisture will produce a larger Kirlian image.

Other physical variables also affect the nature of the Kirlian image, including the type of film, the type of electrode used, and various other characteristics of the electricity used—some twenty-five variables in all (Singer, 1981). But, as Singer (1981, pp. 207–08) says, "No mysterious process has been discovered by mainstream scientists investigating the Kirlian process. The paranormal claims about the photographs seem to have resulted from misunderstandings about the physical processes involved, and lack of expertise in conducting rigorous technical measurements."

Plant Perception

Cleve Backster (1968) made quite a splash when he claimed that plants have the ability to feel not only the pain of damage inflicted on them, but to respond, presumably through psychic communication, to pain inflicted on other plants and even to people thinking bad thoughts about plants. To demonstrate his claims, Backster (1968) would hook up potted houseplants to a polygraph (lie detector) and then drop living brine shrimp into boiling water. According to his report, when he did so, the plants showed an electrical response that they did not show when he dropped only water into the boiling water. In other experiments, just thinking about burning the leaf of a plant was said to produce an electrical response in a nearby plant. Backster (1975) later discovered that even yogurt has the ability to sense the distress of fellow yogurts (actually, the tiny organisms that make up the "active cultures" in yogurt). He recorded the electrical response in one cup of yogurt when he killed another cup of yogurt. Sure enough, the cup permitted to live responded to the death of the organisms in the other cup. All of this generated, as might be expected, considerable attention in the popular press and, in 1973, Tompkins and Bird published *The Secret Life of Plants*, in which it was claimed that plants had the ability to perceive and respond to a wide range of emotions, often through psychic abilities. Thus, people began talking to their plants and playing music to them, hoping to encourage them to grow.

Several investigators have taken the time and trouble to attempt to repeat Backster's experiments. They have failed universally to repeat any of the effects that Backster (1968) claimed or to find the abilities that Tompkins and Bird (1973) attributed to plants (Horowitz, Lewis, and Gasteiger, 1975; Kmetz, 1977, 1977–78; Galston and Slayman, 1979, 1981). Kmetz (1977) found that the electrical recording system that Backster (1968) had used was unstable and that his findings were attributable to this lack of stability.

Even in 1973, when *The Secret Life of Plants* appeared, it was obvious to those arguing for plant perception that well-controlled studies would fail to support their claims. A nonfalsifiable hypothesis was promptly constructed: "Hundreds of laboratory workers around the world are going to be frustrated [by failure to find evidence for plant perception] until they realize that empathy between plant and human is a key and learn how to establish it. Spiritual development is essential . . ." (Vogel, quoted in Tompkins and Bird, 1973, p. 27). In other words, any time anyone failed to obtain confirming results, it was not because plants can't perceive emotions and feelings psychically, it was because the experimenters didn't have enough "empathy" or "spiritual development."

Polygraphy

Until quite recently it was accepted as a matter of course that polygraphs, or lie detectors, could in fact determine accurately whether a person was telling the truth. The devices were and still are used not only in criminal investigations but also, much more widely, in employment screening. They have also been used in alleged cases of UFO abductions and sightings where "passing a lie detector test" is said to verify that the UFO encounter actually took place. They are also used in government, both by military and security agencies and by civilian departments. In the past few years, lie detectors and the field of polygraphy have been the subject of increasing skepticism.

The basic principle of the polygraph is simple. It measures an individual's heart rate, respiration rate, and most importantly the electrical conductivity of the skin. All these are measures of physiological arousal, especially skin conductance, which increases when an aroused person sweats. There is little doubt that polygraphs can detect nervousness, which leads to physiological arousal some of the time. However, it is obvious that not everyone is nervous when telling a lie and not everyone is calm when telling the truth. There is no simple correlation between people's physiological state and whether they are telling the truth. Studies carried out both in a laboratory situation and in field situations, sometimes using actual criminals (i.e., Kleinmuntz and Szucko, 1984), have shown that the polygraph is very inaccurate. Reviews of this research can be found in Lykken (1981, along with an excellent history of lie detection), U.S. Office of Technology Assessment (1983), Saxe, Dougherty, and Cross (1985), and Brett, Phillips, and Beary (1986). Lykken (1981) has developed what he terms the "Guilty Knowledge Test," which evaluates an individual's physiological reaction to information that only the criminal could have. In Lykken's (1981) hypothetical example, a double murder has been committed. Police officers photograph the bodies in the actual positions where they were found. Additional photographs are taken of each body after it has been moved about the house to different, but equally plausible locations. An innocent suspect would respond with equal arousal to pictures of the bodies whether they were in the actual or the "posed" positions, assuming that the innocent suspect had not had the opportunity to see the bodies in their correct positions. The murderer, however, Lykken (1981) argued, would respond with greater arousal to the picture that only he or she knew to be correct. Laboratory studies of the Guilty Knowledge Test (see Lykken, 1981 for a review) have shown it to be quite accurate. Unfortunately, it has been adopted hardly at all for actual field use, so whether it will be as accurate in criminal investigations is unknown.

The Guilty Knowledge Test, at least in the laboratory studies that have been conducted, appears to be difficult to beat (Lykken, 1981). The much more common, and crude, form of polygraph test, where the suspect is asked, "Did you kill John Smith on the night of March 4?" is much easier to beat. Voluntary alterations of breathing rate, tensing and untensing of various muscle groups, and even keeping a sharp tack in your shoe and stepping on it to create arousal are all methods of deceiving the device (Lykken, 1981; Biddle, 1986).

By far the most common use of polygraphs is not in criminal investigations but in employment situations. Firms, especially those like jewelry stores and banks where employee theft could be a problem, use polygraphs to assess prospective employees' honesty. Polygraphs may also be used in internal investigations within a company. Use of these devices in the private sector is never justified and should be made illegal. In fact, such use and abuse of polygraphs have attracted legislative attention (Brooks, 1985). A bill that would have outlawed the use of polygraphs in all nongovernmental situations died in the Senate in September 1986 after vigorous opposition from polygraph firms and operators. A similar bill was reintroduced in the 100th Congress. In 1986 the CBS television program "60 Minutes" broadcast an excellent example of why the use of polygraphs should not be permitted. Several polygraph firms were called by CBS and told that there had been a theft of some valuable television equipment and that a number of CBS employees were suspected. Each firm was asked to come and examine the suspects. In fact, there had been no theft and all the "suspects" knew that they were taking part in an experiment. Each polygraph operator was given a hint that one particular suspect was the leading suspect, but the hint concerned a different employee for each operator. The operators in each case identified the "leading suspect" as the guilty party. Not one operator failed to make this incorrect judgment.

The operators that incorrectly identified the different leading suspects as the guilty party in the "60 Minutes" exposé were almost certainly not going along with the hint just to please their client. Rather, they could undoubtedly point to signs in the polygraph output that pointed to the guilt of the party they already suspected was guilty, on the basis of the hint. Those same signs would also have been found, of course, in the results of the tests on the nonleading suspects. But the examiner wasn't looking for them in those records because he or she had not been primed with any hint. The "interpretation" of the results of a polygraph examination is much the same as the interpretation of dreams or tea leaves. If you know what you're supposed to find, you'll find it. Belief in the validity of polygraphs, especially by their operators, is based on the selective nature of memory and constructive perception (in this case, perception of the nature of the lie detector output) that play so large a role in convincing people that psychic predictions, dreams, and hunches are valid. Morand (1976, quoted in Lykken, 1981, p. 126) has described the attitude of polygraph operators when confronted with the evidence that the devices are invalid: "Their response was invariably that the criticisms were not valid because, *in their experience*, the test worked" (emphasis added). This response is nearly identical to that of astrologers or psychoanalysts when they are confronted with the evidence of the lack of validity of their own particular method of divining hidden knowledge.

Closely related to the polygraph is the voice stress analyzer, which had a period of popularity in the 1970s. It was claimed that, by detecting certain frequencies in the human voice, it was possible to determine whether or not people were telling the truth. The beauty of such a system was that the person didn't even have to be present for the method to be used. It could be used on a voice coming in by phone or even on a tape recording of a voice. Highly exaggerated claims for the validity of voice stress analysis were made, largely by representatives of firms selling voice stress analyzers, at up to $4,400 each. Lykken's (1981) review of the research shows that voice stress analysis is useless. Biddle's (1986, p. 25) comment that the polygraph is "an unreliable, pseudo-scientific thingamabob" applies with even greater force to the voice stress analyzer.

Pyramid Power

Influenced apparently by Erich von Däniken's claims that Egyptian mummies had been preserved by some process unknown to science, pyramid power became quite a craze in the world of pseudoscience for a brief time in the mid-1970s. The idea was that the pyramidal shape itself was magical and filled with a mysterious energy and power. In Toth and Nielsen's (1976) *Pyramid Power*, we are told that pyramid power is "the fuel of the future" (frontispiece). The back cover of King's (1977) *Pyramid Energy Handbook* hints that pyramids can "deepen your ESP" and "make your plants grow." MacRobert (1986) reports that it is not unusual to see people walking around with pyramid-shaped hats at "new age" gatherings. I recall seeing an advertisement in a Sunday newspaper supplement for a pyramid-shaped doghouse guaranteed to rid dogs of fleas.

Pyramid power claims have actually been tested. Alter (1973) and

Simmons (1973) showed that pyramid-shaped containers were no more effective than any other shape at preserving organic matter (flowers or meat) placed in them. Nor did putting dull razor blades in a pyramid-shaped holder restore them to sharpness, contrary to a frequent claim of pyramid power promoters. Nonetheless, it was certainly possible to obtain testimonials from people who swore that putting a razor blade under a pyramid made it sharper. How could they believe that? As anyone who has used razor blades knows, even a dull blade can be used if it is needed badly enough. The pyramid power believer puts a dull blade under a pyramid at night and then shaves with it the next morning. Expecting it to be sharper, he perceives it as sharper, but never bothers to make any real measurements of the sharpness. Thus, the belief is perpetuated.

The Shroud of Turin

The Shroud of Turin is said to be the burial cloth of Jesus Christ and to have on it a miraculous image of Christ that could not have been produced by any nonsupernatural method. A Shroud of Turin Research Project claims that scientific analysis of the shroud substantiates its miraculous nature. The claims made for the shroud do not stand up to close inspection. The most reasonable conclusion is that the shroud is a fake that originated in France sometime in the 1300s. The following discussion is based on Nickell's (1983) book-length evaluation of the evidence for the shroud's authenticity.

Where did the shroud come from? If it is genuine, it should be possible to trace its history back to the time of Christ. But this is not possible. The shroud first appeared in France during the 1300s. It was displayed and the claim was made that it was the burial cloth of Christ. As might be expected, it attracted considerable attention—so much attention, in fact, that Henri de Poitiers, the bishop of Troyes, ordered an investigation of the shroud. A report of this investigation was sent to the pope in 1389. Parts of that report are quoted by Nickell (1983, p. 12):

> The case, Holy Father, stands thus. Some time since in this diocese of Troyes the Dean of a certain collegiate church, to wit, that of Lirey, falsely and deceitfully, being consumed with the passion of avarice, and not from any motive of devotion but only of gain, procured for his church a certain cloth cunningly painted, upon which by a clever sleight of hand was depicted the twofold image of one man, that is to say, the back and front, he falsely declaring and pretending that this was the actual shroud in which our Saviour Jesus Christ was enfolded in

the tomb. This story was put about not only in the kingdom of France, but, so to speak, throughout the world, so that from all parts people came together to view it. And further to attract the multitude so that money might be cunningly wrung from them, pretended miracles were worked, certain men being hired to represent themselves as healed at the moment of the exhibition of the shroud, which all believed to be the shroud of our Lord.

Thus the Shroud of Turin came into existence.

Even if this report were not available, one fact would cast strong doubt on the authenticity of the shroud: it's not mentioned in the Bible. The Bible does mention that Christ's body was wrapped for burial, but the type of burial cloth used at the time in Jewish burials was very different from the shroud. The shroud is one fourteen-foot-long piece that would have had to cover the body over the head, according to the position of the images. Jewish burial custom dictated that a separate cloth was used to cover the face of the dead. Further, the Bible does not mention any finding of an image on Christ's burial garments after the Resurrection. Presumably the existence of such a miraculous image would not have escaped the notice of those who entered the tomb following Christ's rising.

One aspect of the image itself poses serious problems for claims that the shroud is authentic. The image shows the hair on the head in fairly well defined curls. But Christ had bled from the application of the crown of thorns to his scalp. The scalp bleeds profusely, and the application of liquid of any kind to the hair causes it to mat down. Thus, the curls in the hair would not be visible, either because of the blood matting the hair or because any fluid used to clean the body for burial would have had the same matting effect.

Red bloodstains are said to be present on the shroud. In fact, there are red markings on the shroud, but they are not blood. For one thing, as blood ages and dries it rapidly (within days) turns black. Precise analysis of the material that makes up the "bloodstains" on the shroud reveals that it is made up of vermilion and a red iron earth, the "two most popular red pigments" used by artists in the 1300s (Nickell, 1983, p. 130). Shroud of Turin Research Project scientists Pellicori (1980) and Heller and Adler (1980) have claimed to find actual blood on the shroud. This finding, even if true, would not prove the shroud authentic, as the artist could easily have added blood, even human blood, to the other pigments used to create the image. However, the tests used that were claimed to indicate the presence of blood are not specific to blood. That is, the tests will react positively in the presence of other organic materials. And organic materials that cause the tests to react positively were widely used by artists of the 1300s. For example, pigments were often put in a solution of egg tempera and then painted on whatever surface was to have an image applied. Egg tempera produces test results similar to those produced by blood in the tests used by Pellicori (1980) and Heller and Adler (1980), as noted by Fischer (1983).

It appears, from Nickell's (1983) analysis, that the image on the shroud was not just painted on. To paint such an image would be very difficult. How, then, was the image produced? A simple rubbing technique was used in which a piece of cloth is placed over a bas relief and pigment is then applied. Using just such a simple technique Nickell (1978, 1983) has been able to produce images that look exactly like the image on the shroud. They even duplicate the "photographic negative" quality of the shroud image that proponents of the authenticity of the shroud state could not have been produced by any artistic means. The rubbing technique was known to artists as early as the 1100s (Mueller, 1981–82), more than 200 years before the shroud appeared.

The shroud appeared at a time when the manufacture, sale, and collection of Christian relics was big business (Nickell, 1983; MacRobert, 1986). It has been said with considerable truth that there were enough pieces of the True Cross floating around Europe at the time to build the ark. Wealthy nobles and merchants collected relics. There were many other shrouds to be found in Europe; the Shroud of Turin is simply the most famous.

The conclusion from the historical and scientific analysis of the shroud is clear: it is a fake relic created sometime in the early or middle 1300s.

Subliminal Perception

Hardly a week goes by that I don't receive in the mail some brightly colored brochure offering "subliminal" audio or videotapes that are promised to improve my sex life or my skill at tennis, make me a better salesman or manager, or help me lose weight. The brochures are usually crammed with testimonials from satisfied customers. Tapes of this type are also offered for sale in many bookstores and other retail outlets. The mass marketing of such subliminal tapes, which started in the early 1980s, is the most recent manifestation of a continued interest in the topic of *subliminal perception*. A *subliminal stimulus* is one presented in such a way that the subject is presumably consciously unaware of either its presence or its content. In spite of this lack of conscious awareness, it is claimed that, under some conditions, the subliminal stimulus can still have an effect on behavior. Subliminal stimuli are believed to be especially effective at influencing behavior because they "bypass" the conscious mind and "go directly into the unconscious." Proponents of the effectiveness of subliminal stimulation adopt a highly Freudian view of the unconscious.

The best-known claims and uses of subliminal perception are in the field of advertising. In 1957 a theater in New Jersey flashed subliminal messages of "Drink Coca-Cola" and "Hungry—Eat Popcorn" during a film (Conner and Conner, 1985). Sales of Coca-Cola and popcorn reportedly increased. The very idea that such attempts to influence buyer behavior had been made understandably produced considerable public outrage. Also related to advertising uses of subliminal stimulation, Key (1973, 1976, 1980) has claimed that a type of subliminal stimulation is frequently used in print advertisements. These are sexually oriented embedded designs hidden in the ad. Examples are said to be a naked woman hidden in the ice cubes of a vodka ad and the word sex hidden in the pattern on a cracker. Such sexually oriented "embeds" are said to increase the effectiveness of the ads that contain them.

A somewhat different use of subliminal techniques has recently attracted much attention in the retail trade, where several companies market subliminal audio tapes as anti-theft and anti-shoplifting devices. Messages such as "I am honest" and "I won't steal" are said to be recorded, at a subliminal level, along with music to be played over a store's public address system.

Several years ago the media gave much play to claims made by several fundamentalist preachers that various rock music groups were putting backward subliminal messages of a Satanic nature into their records, thereby turning the youth of America toward the devil. It was said that such messages could be heard clearly when the records were played backwards.

Finally, psychologist Lloyd Silverman has claimed that subliminal visual messages related to unconscious Freudian constructs such as the Oedipus complex (an example would be the message "Mommy and I Are One") can have effects on both normal and disordered behavior.

As might be expected, there has been a great deal of interest on the part of psychologists in the question of subliminal perception. It is fair to say that subliminal perception has been demonstrated under certain specific and limited conditions. One series of studies dealing with the issue makes use of the well-known phenomenon that with repeated presentations a previously unfamiliar stimulus not only becomes more familiar, but is also rated more favorably (Zajonc, 1968). Several studies (Kunst-Wilson and Zajonc, 1980; Seamon, Brody, and Kauff, 1983a, b; Bonanno and Stillings, 1986) have shown that when unfamiliar random shapes are presented subliminally and repeatedly, these shapes are later rated as more preferable, even though they are not rated as more familiar.

Another type of study examining the effects of subliminal stimulation uses a priming procedure. In such a procedure, which is widely used in experimental psychology to study issues related to memory and perception, two stimuli are presented in succession. Priming occurs when the first stimulus in a pair has some effect—usually speeding reaction time—on the second stimulus in the pair. The lexical decision task (described in chapter four) is an example here. In this task, the subject sees upwards of 200 letter strings and must decide whether each is or is not a real word. Reaction time—the time from the onset of the letter string to the time the subject responds, usually by pressing one of two buttons—is measured. A priming effect is demonstrated in this task when two letter strings in succession are both words and are semantically related. Thus, the response to the stimulus "ROBIN" will be about seventy-five milliseconds faster if the immediately preceding stimulus was "BIRD" than if it was "COIN" (Shoben, 1982). This type of priming is very short-lived and decays rapidly over only a very few seconds (Potter et al., 1984).

Marcel (1980, 1983a,b) has modified a lexical decision task in a manner that permits the examination of whether a subliminal stimulus can generate a priming effect. Basically, Marcel (1980) presented a prime word (like "BIRD" in the example above) but masked it so subjects were not consciously aware of its presence. The mask consisted of a pattern of line segments superimposed on the word after the word had been presented alone for only 10 milliseconds. Marcel found that even the masked, and therefore presumably subliminal, prime word still resulted in a faster reaction time to a succeeding associated word. Studies by other researchers have reported similar effects, but this area of research has recently been seriously challenged on methodological grounds (Holender, 1986).

Earlier studies of subliminal effects used a different approach. The tack was to investigate whether a subliminally presented word affected how subjects rated themselves on some variable. For example, Spence (1964) subliminally presented the word "CHEESE" to subjects to see if they rated themselves as hungrier than subjects who had not been exposed to the subliminal presentation of the word. Sometimes effects of such subliminal stimulation were found (Spence, 1964; Byrne, 1959) and sometimes they were not (Spence and Ehrenberg, 1964; Bernstein and Eriksen, 1965). These studies often suffered from serious methodological flaws that rendered their conclusions unfounded. One major problem was to accept at face value subjects' verbal reports about not consciously perceiving the allegedly subliminal stimulus. Such verbal reports seriously underestimate individuals' actual ability to perceive a stimulus. For example, as Bernstein and Eriksen (1965, p. 37) note, subjects may report not seeing a stimulus because it "saves them the trouble of explaining what they had seen." Further, subjects may not wish to appear to be hallucinating and thus will fail to report a stimulus if they are not sure it was present. The effect of masking a stimulus, as was often done in these early studies and as is done in current studies, may also be to simply lower the subject's willingness to report that a stimulus was present while having minimal effects on the actual ability to perceive that stimulus (Cheesman and Merikle, 1984). Thus, Bernstein and Eriksen (1965) found in one of their conditions that 50 percent of the subjects, when asked, denied having seen a masked stimulus. However, when forced to pick which of two stimuli had been presented, they were accurate between 70 percent and 97 percent of the time. When Cheesman and Merikle (1984) reduced accuracy to chance levels as measured by such a forced-choice procedure, they found no evidence of subliminal effects.

In summary, years of research have resulted in the demonstration of some very limited effects of subliminal stimulation. The question as far as pseudoscience is concerned is whether these findings justify the claims made for the "practical" application of subliminal stimulation for self-improvement, advertising, retail theft control, and so forth. The answer is clearly no. Just as the documented existence of biological rhythms offers no support for pseudoscientific biorhythm theory (see chapter six), so the existence of subliminal effects offers no support for the claims of those promoting subliminal stimulation as an effective technology for behavior control.

One fatal problem faces those who claim that subliminal messages can be used for self-improvement or for theft prevention in retail stores. In the former case, a message like "I am not hungry" is flashed on a television screen by a personal computer. The trouble is that the message is flashed not on a blank screen but during regular programming. Thus, the message will be garbled by the picture on the screen at the time the message appears. In the type of procedure used by Marcel (1980) to study subliminal stimulation, this is equivalent to presenting a word and a mask simultaneously rather than, as Marcel actually did, presenting the word alone and in the clear for ten milliseconds, followed by the mask. If one presents the word and the mask at the same time, no subliminal effect will be found. This same problem occurs in the auditory modality in the case of "Don't steal" messages subliminally presented under recorded music played over a store's public address system. It is impossible for the brain to process the message because the message is never heard at any level, conscious or otherwise. The alleged evidence for the effectiveness of such hidden audio messages (Conner and Conner, 1985) is based on anecdotes and crude uncontrolled classroom "demonstrations." This has not prevented several firms from marketing expensive devices to provide such subliminal messages and making unfounded claims regarding their effectiveness.

Key (1973, 1976, 1980) claims that advertisers are making common use of sexually arousing patterns and designs embedded in print ads in such a way that they are perceived only subliminally unless one looks for them carefully. He condemns this practice which, naturally, advertising agencies deny using. What evidence does Key use to argue that such embedded sexually arousing stimuli are really being used? He can find them everywhere, in almost any print ad he looks at. He even found an entire sexual orgy, complete with a donkey, in a picture of a plate of clams on a Howard Johnson's restaurant menu (Key, 1980). The presence of this subliminal orgy explained why everyone with him ordered clams. This is clearly not evidence; it is merely seeing faces in the clouds.

Key has a unique explanation for how these alleged embedded sexual stimuli achieve their powerful effect. The unconscious brain, it seems, processes information "at the speed of light" (quoted in Creed, 1986-87, p. 359) and can pick out the hidden figures. This is nonsense. A great deal is known about how the brain processes information (for details see any textbook in physiological psychology, neurobiology, or the neurosciences) and it is absolutely clear that no part of the brain processes information at anything close to the speed of light. While this was a common belief in the seventeenth and eighteenth centuries, the actual speed of processing in the brain, as measured by the speed with which nerve impulses travel along neurons, is about forty miles an hour.

Studies have been conducted to see if the types of embedded sexual stimuli Key claims to be all around us have any effect on viewers' responses to advertisements. The results are almost uniformly negative (Gable et al., 1987; Saegert, 1987; Moore, 1982). One study that did claim to show effects of such embedded stimuli (Kilbourne et al., 1985) used as stimuli print ads in which the authors of the study had found, presumably after careful search, embedded sexual stimuli. To "corroborate" the existence of these embedded stimuli, the authors showed the ads to colleagues and students. In a perfect demonstration of the power of suggestion, they report that some people "had difficulty locating the embeds without assistance, once the location of the embeds was pointed out, only one of the observers disputed the existence or nature of the stimuli" (Kilbourne et al., 1985, p. 50). Having found—to their satisfaction, at least—the embedded sexual stimuli, versions of the ads were prepared in which these stimuli had been removed. Subjects were then asked to rate the ads with and without the stimuli on twelve different scales. No consistent results were found. In a second study reported in the same paper, subjects' galvanic skin response (GSR), a measure of physiological arousal, was measured when they observed the ads with and without the alleged embedded stimuli. While the authors claim that they demonstrated a significant effect such that the GSR was greater to the ads with the embedded stimuli, the probability of this effect occurring by chance was .054, greater than the .05 needed for demonstration of significance. Other methodological and statistical problems render this study even less credible.

Vokey and Read (1985) created three sets of stimuli from travel slides by embedding the word "sex," a nonsense word, or nothing in the photographs. Subjects who did not report seeing the embedded words were no better at remembering the slides with "sex" embedded than at remembering either of the other two types of slides, although Key's "theory" clearly predicts that the "sex"-embedded slides should be better remembered than any others.

Advertising researchers have also investigated whether briefly flashed messages can influence behavior. As in the case of studies of embedded stimuli, the results are negative (Saegert, 1987) with the exception of studies flawed by poor methodology or statistical errors. Hawkins (1970) flashed "Coke" or "Drink Coke" for 2.7 milliseconds for a total of 40 times at subjects during a 15-minute period. The subjects then rated how thirsty they were, and these ratings were compared to those of subjects in two control conditions. Hawkins (1970) argued that the results showed a significant subliminal effect; unfortunately, this claim has been accepted rather uncritically by some who have reviewed this area of research (Saegert, 1987). There are three specific statistical problems with the Hawkins (1970) study that render its conclusions unjustified. First, Hawkins reported five different statistical tests of the effects of the subliminal stimuli and up to twelve were possible given the nature of the study. As was discussed in chapter six, making such multiple tests spuriously increases the chance of obtaining statistical "significance" when none in fact is present. Second, Hawkins interpreted as significant results that were not statistically significant. Third, and perhaps most seriously, Hawkins used a dubious statistical procedure, adopting the so-called "one tailed" version of the statistical tests he used, which doubles the chances of obtaining spurious findings of significance. In a second study reported in the same paper, Hawkins could find no effect of subliminal stimulation on brand preference.

In a study with problems very similar to those of the Hawkins (1970) study, Cuperfrain and Clarke (1985) showed pictures of brand-name soaps for seventeen milliseconds a total of five times during a short film. Subjects later rated a series of photographs of different soaps. These authors performed twelve different statistical tests on their results and used the one-tailed version of the test. These errors vastly increased the number of "significant" results that would, in fact, be due to chance.

In summary, although there has been considerable interest in the use of subliminal techniques in the advertising, marketing, and retailing fields, the evidence is clear: subliminal techniques do not work. For a more technical review of this area, the reader is referred to Moore (1982).

In 1982 the charge that reversed subliminal satanic messages were present in recordings of rock music generated a momentary spurt of public interest. All over North America, people were playing records and tapes backwards and listening with great care for the hidden messages. It will come as no surprise that some such messages were found. Fundamentalist preachers seemed to be particularly keen in their ability to detect the hidden messages glorifying the devil. In Arkansas the state legislature passed a bill that required labels on recordings of rock music warning the unwary listener of the dangers of the hidden subliminal messages. The governor did not sign the bill (Vokey and Read, 1985). This flurry of interest spurred Vokey and Read (1985) to undertake some simple but elegant studies to see just how much information was available to subjects in a reversed message, even if it was fully audible. It was found that listeners could determine the sex of the speaker of a backward passage with almost perfect accuracy. Language of the reversed passage could be determined with an accuracy significantly above chance. Listeners could not, however, discriminate between statements and questions. Nor could they say whether two reversed sentences had the same meaning or not. In one experiment, sentences that when played in the normal forward direction fell into one of five categories (Christian, satanic, pornographic, nursery rhymes, or advertising) were played in reverse, listeners could not sort the reversed sentences into their proper categories at a rate different from chance. Only 19.4 percent of the categorizations were accurate, the chance rate being 20 percent. Thus, a reversed Christian sentence ("Jesus loves me, this I know") was just as likely to be classified as satanic or pornographic as Christian. If the brain can't make these distinctions when the reversed sentences are clearly heard, it is inconceivable that such distinctions could be made if the sentences were further obscured by music.

In their paper Vokey and Read (1985) make an important distinction between the issue of the actual presence of reversed, satanic subliminal messages and the effectiveness of such messages even if they exist. Vokey and Read's experiments demonstrated that, even if such messages have been put on recordings, they would have no behavioral effects whatsoever. As to the issue of whether or not such messages have been intentionally placed in recordings, it is technically possible to do so. However, by far the vast majority of the messages of this type that people hear are the result of suggestion and expectations (Vokey and Read, 1985; Thorne and Himelstein, 1984)—the auditory version of seeing faces in clouds.

The final area of subliminal effects to be considered here comes from a long series of experiments by the late Lloyd Silverman and his colleagues (see Silverman, 1983; Silverman and Weinberger, 1985) in which subliminal stimuli, presented visually for four milliseconds, are designed to activate various unconscious mechanisms postulated to exist by psychoanalytic theory. For example, the phrase "Mommy and I are one" is said to reduce unconscious conflicts. The subliminal presentation of the phrase "Beating Dad is OK" is said to improve dart-throwing accuracy of male college students, presumably through some interaction with Oedipal feelings and conflicts. Silverman's work is controversial, and for every positive finding, negative findings have also been reported (see, for example, Fisher et al., 1986; Heilbrun, 1980; Porterfield and Golding, 1985; Oliver and Burkham, 1982)—although the productivity of Silverman and colleagues is such that the absolute number of positive findings is greater than negative ones. The mere number of confirming versus disconfirming results does not measure the validity of the basic finding because of the greater probability of publication of a positive over a negative result.

There are other problems with the work on subliminal psychoanalytic stimulation, as Fudin (1986, 1987) has noted. The statistical analyses in some of the papers are problematic. In published studies the details of the stimuli used and exact procedure are sometimes far from clear. It is just such "minor" details that, in the ESP literature for example, have led to nonexistent phenomena being accepted as real.

Closely related to the claim that subliminal tapes can be used for self-improvement are claims made for some nonsubliminal tapes. A leader in this field is a firm called SyberVision that produces audio and video tapes that, the firm's advertising states, will help the viewer to improve his golf swing, tennis game, skiing skills, or general success in life. The tapes aimed at improving sports skills feature famous athletes demonstrating the proper way to play the game or sport in question. Watching an expert demonstrate the proper way to play and rehearsing that in a sort of "mental practice" can be helpful as a way of increasing one's skill. However, the effects are very small (Feltz and Landers, 1983). Basic to improving any motor skill is actual practice. What pushes SyberVision's claims into the realm of pseudoscience is the fact that it claims that its tapes automatically, and with no effort or practice on the part of the viewer, program the viewer's brain and muscles so that the viewer's skill will be increased. In other words, you need only watch the tapes to greatly improve, say, your tennis game. No sweaty practice, no effort, just stretch out on the couch and watch the tube. For example, the firm says of its skiing tape, "In just 60 minutes, you've received the physical equivalent of several hours of perfect practice." As has been noted previously in this book, a common characteristic of proponents of pseudoscience is to dress up their claims in fancy jargon. SyberVision is no exception, and they use impressive but vacuous neuroscience terms to hype their tapes. Thus, the movements shown on the tapes are "executed at a mathematically precise tempo and rhythm that activates your brain's visual learning mechanism." Further "the neuromuscular impulses repeatedly travel from your brain to your muscles, etching pathways for performance excellence into your memory. Your muscles are being trained to remember perfect form." Another characteristic of a pseudoscience is the reliance on testimonials to support the claim, and SyberVision's ads are full of glowing testimonials.

References

Books and articles particularly useful for additional reading concerning the various topics discussed in this book are indicated by an asterisk in this reference list. Many of the articles cited here that originally appeared in *The Zetetic* or *The Skeptical Inquirer* have been reprinted in two anthologies edited by Kendrick Frazier (1981, 1986), both of which are highly recommended for further reading.

Abell, G., and Greenspan, B. (1979). "Human Births and the Phase of the Moon." *New England Journal of Medicine, 300, 96.*

———. (1981a). "Astrology." In G. Abell and B. Singer (Eds.), *Science and the Paranormal*, pp. 70–94.

———. (1981b). "Moon Madness." In G. Abell and B. Singer (Eds.), *Science and the Paranormal*, pp. 95–104.

* Abell, G., and Singer, B., Eds. (1981). *Science and the Paranormal.* New York: Charles Scribner's Sons.

Adams, R., and Victor, M. (1985). *Principles of Neurology*, 3rd edition. New York: McGraw-Hill.

Ader, R., and Cohen, N. (1985). "CNS-Immune System Interactions: Conditioning Phenomena." *Behavioral and Brain Sciences, 8,* 379–395.

Akers, C. (1984). "Methodological Criticisms of Parapsychology." In S. Krippner (Ed.), *Advances in Parapsychological Research*, vol. 4. Jefferson, N.C.: McFarland, pp. 112–164.

Alcock, J. (1978–79). "Psychology and Near-Death Experiences." *Skeptical Inquirer, 3* (No. 3), 25–41.

* ———. (1981). *Parapsychology: Science or Magic?* Oxford: Pergamon Press.

———. (1985). "Parapsychology: The 'Spiritual' Science." *Free Inquiry, 5* (No. 2), 25–35.

Alter, A. (1973). "The Pyramid and Food Dehydration." *New Horizons, 1,* 92–94.

Amundson, R. (1984–85). "The Hundredth Monkey Phenomenon." *Skeptical Inquirer, 9,* 348–356.

Anastasi, A. (1988). *Psychological Testing*, 6th edition. New York: Macmillan.

Angus, M. (1973). "The Rejection of Two Explanations of Belief in a Lunar Influence on Behavior." Unpublished master's thesis. Simon Fraser University, Burnaby, British Columbia, Canada.

Anonymous (1882). *Confessions of a Medium*. London: Griffith and Farran.

Anson, J. (1977). *The Amityville Horror*. Englewood Cliffs, N.J.: Prentice-Hall.

Antrobus, J. (1978). "Dreaming for Cognition." In A. Arkin, J. Antrobus, and S. Ellman (Eds.), *Mind in Sleep: Psychology and Psychophysiology*, pp. 569–581.

———. (1987). "Cortical Hemisphere Asymmetry and Sleep Mentation." *Psychological Review, 94*, 359–368.

Arkin, A., Antrobus, J., and Ellman, S., Eds. (1978). *The Mind in Sleep: Psychology and Psychophysiology*. Hillsdale, N.J.: Lawrence Erlbaum Associates.

Arnetz, B., *et al.* (1987). "Immune Function in Unemployed Women." *Psychosomatic Medicine, 49*, 3–12.

Atkins, R. (1972). *Dr. Atkins' Diet Revolution*. New York: D. McKay Co.

———. (1982). *Dr. Atkins' Nutrition Breakthrough*. New York: Bantam.

Atkins, T., and Baxter, J. (1976). *The Fire Came By*. Garden City, N.Y.: Doubleday.

Backster, C. (1968). "Evidence of a Primary Perception in Plant Life." *International Journal of Parapsychology, 10*, 329–348.

———. (1975). Verbal presentation at the annual meeting of the American Association for the Advancement of Science, New York.

* Bailey, L. (1978). *Where is Noah's Ark?* Nashville, Tenn.: Abingdon Press.

Bammer, K., and Newberry, B., Eds. (1981). *Stress and Cancer*. Toronto: C. J. Hogrefe.

Bandler, R., and Grinder, J. (1979). *Frogs into Princes*. Moab, Utah: Real People Press.

* Bandura, A. (1969). *Principles of Behavior Modification*. New York: Holt, Rinehart and Winston.

Barker, D. (1979a). Correspondence. *Journal of Parapsychology, 43*, 268–269.

———. (1979b). "Rakesh Gaur: A Case of Reincarnation in India." *Journal of Parapsychology, 43*, 56.

———. (1956). *They Knew Too Much about Flying Saucers*. New York: University Books.

Barnard, M. (1966). *The Mythmakers*. Athens, Ohio: Ohio University Press.

Baron, R. (1987). "Effects of Negative Ions on Cognitive Performance." *Journal of Applied Psychology, 72*, 131–137.

* Barrett, S., Ed. (1980a). *The Health Robbers*, 2nd revised edition. Philadelphia: George F. Stickley.

———. (1980b). "The Mental Health Maze." In S. Barrett (Ed.), *The Health Robbers*, pp. 297–310.

———. (1980c). "The Spine Salesmen." In S. Barrett (Ed.), *The Health Robbers*, pp. 123–145.

———. (1985). "Commercial Hair Analysis: Science or Scam?" *Journal of the American Medical Association, 254* 1041–1045.

* Beaumont, J., Young, A., and McManus, I. (1984). "Hemisphericity: A Critical Review." *Cognitive Neuropsychology, 1*, 191–212.

Becquerel, J. (1934). *Notice sur les travaux scientific de M. Jean Becquerel*. Paris: Gauthier-Villars.

Behar, D., *et al.* (1984). "Sugar Challenge Testing with Children Considered Behaviorally 'Sugar Reactive.'" *Journal of Nutrition and Behavior, 1*, 277–288.

Beloff, J. (1973). *Psychological Sciences.* London: Crosby Lockwood Staples.

Belvedere, E., and Foulkes, D. (1971). "Telepathy and Dreams: A Failure to Replicate." *Perceptual and Motor Skills, 33,* 783–789.

Bender, A. (1985). *Health or Hoax?* Goring-on-Thames: Elvendon Press.

Bennett, D. (1985). "Chelation Therapists: Charlatans or Saviors?" *Science News,* 127, 138–139.

* Ben-Shakhar, G., Bar-Hillel, M., and Flug, A. (1986). "A Validation Study of Graphological Evaluation in Personnel Selection." In B. Nevo (Ed.), *Scientific Aspects of Graphology.* Springfield, Ill.: Charles C. Thomas, pp. 175–191.

Ben-Shakhar, G., *et al.* (1986). "Can Graphology Predict Occupational Success? Two Empirical Studies and Some Methodological Ruminations." *Journal of Applied Psychology, 71,* 645–653.

Berlinger, D. (1977, August). "Project Blue Book." *Science Digest,* 24–28.

Berlitz, C. (1974). *The Bermuda Triangle Mystery.* Garden City, N.Y.: Doubleday.

———. (1977). *Without a Trace.* Garden City, N.Y.: Doubleday.

Berman, J., and Norton, N. (1985). "Does Professional Training Make a Therapist More Effective?" *Psychological Bulletin, 98,* 401–407.

* Bernstein, E. (1982). "Lourdes." *Encyclopeadia Britannica 1982 Medicine and Health Yearbook,* 129–147.

Bernstein, I., and Eriksen, C. (1965). "Effects of 'Subliminal' Prompting on Paired-Associate Learning." *Journal of Experimental Research in Personality, 1,* 33–38.

Bernstein, M. (1956). *Search for Bridey Murphy.* Garden City, N.Y.: Doubleday.

Bettelheim, B. (1967). *Empty Fortress: Infantile Autism and the Birth of the Self.* New York: Free Press.

* Beyerstein, B. (1987–88). "Neuropathology and the Legacy of Spiritual Possession." *Skeptical Inquirer, 12,* 248–262.

Biddle, W. (1986, March). "The Deception of Detection." *Discover,* 24–26, 28–31, 33.

* Binns, R. (1984). *The Loch Ness Mystery Solved.* Buffalo, N.Y.: Prometheus Books.

* Blackmore, S. (1982). *Beyond the Body.* London: Granada.

———. (1983). "Divination with Tarot Cards: An Empirical Study." *Journal of the Society for Psychical Research, 52,* 97–101.

———. (1985). "Belief in the Paranormal: Probability Judgements, Illusory Control, and the 'Chance Baseline Shift.'" *British Journal of Psychology, 76,* 459–468.

———. (1986a). *Adventures of a Parapsychologist.* Buffalo, N.Y.: Prometheus Books.

———. (1986b, April). "Making of a Skeptic." *Fate,* 69–75.

———. (1986–87). "The Elusive Open Mind: Ten Years of Negative Research in Parapsychology." *Skeptical Inquirer, 11,* 244–255.

Blatty, W. (1971). *The Exorcist.* New York: Bantam Books.

Blinderman, C. (1986). *The Piltdown Inquest.* Buffalo, N.Y.: Prometheus Books.

Bonanno, G., and Stillings, N. (1986). "Preference, Familiarity, and Recognition after Repeated Brief Exposures to Random Geometric Shapes." *American Journal of Psychology, 99,* 403–415.

Bootzin, R., Bower, G., Zajonc, R., and Hall, E. (1986). *Psychology Today: An Introduction,* 6th edition. New York: Random House.

Botwinick, J. (1984). *Aging and Behavior*. 3rd edition. New York: Springer.

Boynton, R. (1979). *Human Color Vision*. New York: Holt, Rinehart and Winston.

Brandon, R. (1983). *The Spiritualists*. New York: Alfred A. Knopf.

Breger, L., Hunter, I., and Lane, R. (1971). "Effects of Stress on Dreams," *Psychological Issues*, 7 (No. 3, monograph 27).

Brett, A., Phillips, M., and Beary, J. (1986). "Predictive Power of the Polygraph: Can the 'Lie Detector' Really Detect Liars?" *Lancet, I*, 554–547.

Brierley, J., and Graham, D. (1984). "Hypoxia and Vascular Disorders of the Central Nervous System." In J. Adams, J. Corsellis, and L. Duchen (Eds.), *Greenfield's Neuropathology*, 4th edition. New York: Wiley, pp. 125–207.

Brody, J. (1987, March 25). "Research Lifts Blame from Many of the Obese." *New York Times*, C1, C6.

Brooks, J. (1985). "Polygraph Testing: Thoughts of a Skeptical Legislator." *American Psychologist*, 40, 348–354.

Brown, B., *et al.* (1983). "Dyslexic Children Have Normal Vestibular Responses to Rotation." *Archives of Neurology*, 40, 370–373.

Brown, G., and Kirk, R. (1987). "Geophysical Variables and Behavior, 37: Effects of Ionized Air on the Performance of a Vigilance Task." *Perceptual and Motor Skills*, 64, 951–62.

Brown, R., and McNeill, D. (1966). "The 'Tip of the Tongue' Phenomenon." *Journal of Verbal Learning and Verbal Behavior*, 5, 325–337.

Bryden, M. (1982). *Laterality: Functional Asymmetry in the Intact Brain*. New York: Academic Press.

Buckalew, L., and Rizzuto, A. (1984). "Negative Air Ion Effects on Human Performance and Physiological Condition." *Aviation, Space, and Environmental Medicine*, 55, 731–734.

Buscaglia, L. (1983). *Living, Loving and Learning*. New York: Fawcett.

Byrd, E. (1976). "Uri Geller's Influence on the Metal Alloy Nitinol." In C. Panati (Ed.), *The Geller Papers*. Boston: Houghton Mifflin, pp. 67–73.

Byrne, D. (1959). "The Effect of a Subliminal Food Stimulus on Verbal Responses." *Journal of Applied Psychology*, 43, 249–252.

Campbell, D., and Beets, J. (1978). "Lunacy and the Moon." *Psychological Bulletin*, 85, 1123–1129.

* Carlson, S. (1985). "A Double-Blind Test of Astrology." *Nature*, 318, 419–425.

Castaneda, C. (1968). *The Teachings of Don Juan: A Yaqui Way of Knowledge*. Berkeley, Cal.: University of California Press.

Cerullo, J. (1982). *Secularization of the Soul*. Philadelphia: Institute for the Study of Human Issues.

Chapman, L. (1967). "Illusory Correlation in Observational Report." *Journal of Verbal Learning and Verbal Behavior*, 6, 151–155.

Chapman, L., and Chapman, J. (1967). "Genesis of Popular but Erroneous Psychodiagnostic Observations." *Journal of Abnormal Psychology*, 72, 193–204.

———. (1969). "Illusory Correlation as an Obstacle to the Use of Valid Psychodiagnostic Signs." *Journal of Abnormal Psychology*, 74, 271–280.

Charry, J., and Hawkinshire, F. (1981). "Effects of Atmospheric Electricity on Some Substrates of Disordered Social Behavior." *Journal of Personality and*

Social Psychology, 41, 185–197.

Cheesman, J., and Merikle, P. (1984). "Priming With and Without Awareness." *Perception and Psychophysics, 36,* 387–395.

Child, I. (1985). "Psychology and Anomalous Observations: The Question of ESP in Dreams." *American Psychologist, 40,* 1219–1230.

Cioffi, F. (1970). "Freud and the Idea of a Pseudo-science." In R. Borger and F. Cioffi (Eds.), *Explanation in the Behavioural Sciences.* Cambridge: Cambridge University Press, pp. 471–499.

Clark, J., and Coleman, L. (1978). *Creatures of the Outer Edge.* New York: Warner Books.

Clark, P., and Clark, M. (1984). "Therapeutic Touch: Is There a Scientific Basis for the Practice?" *Nursing Research, 33,* 37–41.

Cohen, B. (1978). "Relative Risks of Saccharin and Calorie Ingestion." *Science, 199,* 983.

Cohen, D. (1981). *The Great Airship Mystery: A UFO of the 1890s.* New York: Dodd, Mead.

Colligan, M., Pennebaker, J., and Murphy, L., Eds. (1982). *Mass Psychogenic Illness: A Social Psychological Analysis.* Hillsdale, N.J.: Lawrence Erlbaum Associates.

Collins, H., and Pinch, T. (1982). *Frames of Meaning: The Social Construction of Extraordinary Science.* London: Routledge and Kegan Paul.

Condon, E. (1969). *Scientific Study of Unidentified Flying Objects.* New York: Bantam Books.

Conner, L., and Conner, L. (1985). *The Midwest Research Report on Subliminal Messages in Retail Stores.* Glen Mills, Pa.: Shoplifters Anonymous.

Consumer Reports (1980). *Health Quackery.* New York: Holt, Rinehart and Winston.

———. (1980). "Foods, Drugs, or Frauds?" *Consumer Reports, 50,* 275–283.

———. (1986). "The Vitamin Pushers." *Consumer Reports, 51,* 170–175.

———. (1987). "Homeopathic Remedies." *Consumer Reports, 52,* 60–62.

Cook, J. (1984, May 21). "Closing the Psychic Gap." *Forbes,* 90–95.

Cooper, J. (1982). "Cottingley: At Last the Truth." *The Unexplained,* No. 117, 2338–2340.

Coren, S. (1972). "Subjective Contours and Apparent Depth." *Psychological Review, 79,* 359–367.

Corinda (1968). *Thirteen Steps to Mentalism.* New York: Tannen Magic Inc.

Costain, T. (1947). *Moneyman.* Garden City, N.Y.: Doubleday.

Coulter, X., Collier, A., and Campbell, B. (1976). "Long-term Retention of Early Pavlovian Fear Conditioning in Infant Rats." *Journal of Experimental Psychology: Animal Behavior Processes, 2,* 48–56.

Creed, T. (1986–87). "Subliminal Deception: Pseudoscience on the College Lecture Circuit." *Skeptical Inquirer, 11,* 358–366.

Crelin, E. (1973). "A Scientific Test of the Chiropractic Theory." *American Scientist, 61,* 574–580.

———. (1985). "Chiropractic." In D. Stalker and C. Glymour (Eds.), *Examining Holistic Medicine,* pp. 197–220.

* Crews, F. (1984, June). "The Freudian Way of Knowledge." *New Criterion,* 7–25. (Reprinted in F. Crews, *Skeptical Engagements* [1986], New York: Oxford

University Press, pp. 43–74.)

Crumbaugh, J. (1966). "A Scientific Critique of Parapsychology." *International Journal of Neuropsychiatry, 5,* 521–529.

Culliton, B. (1987). "Osteoporosis Reexamined: Complexity of Bone Biology is a Challenge." *Science, 235,* 833–34.

* Culver, R., and Ianna, P. (1984). *The Gemini Syndrome.* Buffalo, N.Y.: Prometheus Books.

Cumberland, S. (1975). *A Thought-Reader's Thoughts.* New York: Arno Press. Originally published by Sampson, Low, Marston, Searle, and Rivington, London, 1888.

Cuperfain, R., and Clarke, T. (1985). "A New Perspective of Subliminal Perception." *Journal of Advertising, 14* (No. 1), 36–41.

Dale, A. (1976). *Biorhythm.* New York: Pocket Books.

Dallenbach, K. (1955). Phrenology versus Psychoanalysis. *American Journal of Psychology, 68,* 511–525.

Davidson, R., Schwartz, G., and Rothman, L. (1976). "Attentional Style and the Self-regulation of Mode-Specific Attention: An Electroencephalographic Study." *Journal of Abnormal Psychology, 85,* 611–621.

* Davies, J. (1955). *Phrenology: Fad and Science.* New Haven, Conn.: Yale University Press.

Davis, A. (1954). *Let's Eat Right to Keep Fit.* New York: Harcourt, Brace.

———. (1959). *Let's Have Healthy Children.* New York: Harcourt, Brace.

———. (1965). *Let's Get Well.* New York: Harcourt Brace Jovanovich.

Davis, P., and Schwartz, G. (1987). "Repression and the Inaccessibility of Affective Memories." *Journal of Personality and Social Psychology, 52,* 155–162.

* Dean, G. (1977). *Recent Advances in Natal Astrology.* Subiaco, Western Australia: Analogic.

De Groot, A., Nater, J., and Herxheimer, A. (1987)."Minoxidil: Hope for the Bald?" *Lancet, I,* 1019–1022.

Delaney, J., and Woodward, H. (1974). "Effects of Reading an Astrological Description on Responding to a Personality Inventory. *Psychological Reports, 34,* 1214.

* De Mille, R. (1978). *Castaneda's Journey,* 2nd revised edition. Santa Barbara, Calif.: Capra Press.

* ———, Ed. (1980). *The Don Juan Papers: Further Castaneda Controversies.* Santa Barbara, Calif.: Ross-Erikson Publishers.

Dennett, M. (1981-82). "Bermuda Triangle, 1981 Model." *Skeptical Inquirer, 6* (No. 1), 42–52.

———. (1982-83)."Bigfoot Jokester Reveals Punchline—Finally." *Skeptical Inquirer, 7* (No. 1), 8–9.

* Deutsch, R. (1977). *The New Nuts Among the Berries.* Palo Alto, Calif.: Bull Publishing.

DeWohl, L. (1947). *The Living Wood, a Novel.* Philadelphia: J. B. Lippincott.

Dezélsky, T., and Toohey, J. (1978). "Biorhythms and the Prediction of Suicide Behavior." *Journal of School Health, 48,* 399–403.

Diamond, H., and Diamond, M. (1985). *Fit for Life.* New York: Warner Books.

Dickson, D., and Kelly, I. (1985). "The 'Barnum Effect' in Personality Assessment: A Review of the Literature." *Psychological Reports, 57,* 367–382.

Dilts, R. (1982, February). "Let NLP Work for You." *Real Estate Today,* 21–23.

* Dingwall, E., Goldney, K., and Hall, T. (1956). *The Haunting of Borley Rectory.* London: Gerald Duckworth.

Dobbs, H. (1967). "The Feasibility of a Physical Theory of ESP." In J. Smythies (Ed.), *Science and ESP.* New York: Humanities Press.

Dobson, B. (1982-83). "On the Trail of the Buena Foot 'Monster.'" *Skeptical Inquirer, 7* (No. 4), 8–10.

Doman, G. (1974). *What to Do About Your Brain-Injured Child, or Your Brain-Damaged, Mentally Retarded, Mentally Deficient, Cerebral-Palsied, Emotionally Disturbed, Spastic, Flaccid, Rigid, Epileptic, Autistic, Athetoid, Hyperactive Child.* Garden City, N.Y.: Doubleday.

———. (1984). *How to Multiply Your Baby's Intelligence.* Garden City, N.Y.: Doubleday.

Dombovy, M., Sandok, B., and Basford, J. (1986). "Rehabilitation for Stroke: A Review." *Stroke, 17,* 363–369.

Dommeyer, F. (1975). Book review. *Parapsychology Review, 6,* 11–12.

Dowling, S. (1984). "Lourdes Cures and Their Mental Assessment." *Journal of the Royal Society of Medicine, 77,* 634–638.

Doyle, A. (1922). *The Coming of the Fairies.* New York: George H. Doran Co.

Drory, A. (1986). "Graphology and Job Performance: A Validation Study." In B. Nevo (Ed.), *Scientific Aspects of Graphology.* Springfield, Ill.: Charles C. Thomas, pp. 165–173.

Dunninger, J. (1967). *Dunninger's Complete Encyclopedia of Magic.* Secaucus, N.J.: Lyle Stuart.

Durlak, J. (1979). "Comparative Effectiveness of Paraprofessional and Professional Helpers." *Psychological Bulletin, 86,* 80–92.

Dywan, J., and Bowers, K. (1983). "The Use of Hyponosis to Enhance Recall." *Science, 222,* 184–185.

Easton, R., and Shor, R. (1975). "Information Processing Analysis of the Chevreul Pendulum Illusion." *Journal of Experimental Psychology: Human Perception and Performance, 1,* 231–236.

Edwards, B. (1979). *Drawing on the Right Side of Your Brain.* Los Angeles: Tarcher.

Edwards, F. (1956). *Strangest of All.* New York: Citadel.

———. (1959). *Stranger Than Science.* New York: Lyle Stuart.

* Edwards, P. (1986). "The Case Against Reincarnation: Part 1." *Free Inquiry, 6* (No. 4), 24–34.

* ———. (1987a). "The Case Against Reincarnation: Part 2." *Free Inquiry, 7* (No. 1), 38–47.

* ———. (1987b). "The Case Against Reincarnation: Part 3." *Free Inquiry, 7* (No. 2), 38–49.

* ———. (1987c). "The Case Against Reincarnation: Part 4." *Free Inquiry, 7* (No. 3), 46–53.

Effron, E. (1984). *The Apocalyptics.* New York: Simon and Schuster.

Egeland, J., *et al.* (1987). "Bipolar Affective Disorders Linked to DNA Markers on Chromosome 11." *Nature, 325,* 783–787.

* Ehrlichman, H., and Barrett, J. (1983). "Right Hemispheric Specialization for Mental Imagery: A Review of the Evidence." *Brain and Cognition, 2,* 55–76.

* Ehrlichman, H., and Weinberger, A. (1978). "Lateral Eye Movements and Hemispheric Asymmetry: A Critical Review." *Psychological Bulletin, 85,* 1080–1101.

Eisenbud, J. (1967). *The World of Ted Serios: Thoughtographic Studies of an Extraordinary Mind.* New York: William Morrow.

Eisendrath, D. (1967, October). "An Amazing Weekend with Ted Serios: Part II." *Popular Photography,* 85–87, 131–33, 136.

Elich, M., Thompson, R., and Miller, L. (1985). "Mental Imagery as Revealed by Eye Movements and Spoken Predicates: A Test of Neurolinguistic Programming." *Journal of Counseling Psychology, 32,* 622–625.

Ellis, A. (1984). *Reading, Writing and Dyslexia: A Cognitive Analysis.* Hillside, N.J.: Lawrence Erlbaum Associates.

Ellis, L., and Ames, M. (1987). "Neurohormonal Functioning and Sexual Orientation: A Theory of Homosexuality-Heterosexuality." *Psychological Bulletin, 101,* 233–258.

Emery, C. (1982–83). "Rhode Island UFO Film: Fact or Fantasy?" *Skeptical Inquirer, 7* (No. 4), 54–57.

Englund, C., and Naitoh, P. (1980). "An Attempted Validation Study of the Birthdate-based Biorhythm (BBB) Hypothesis." *Aviation, Space, and Environmental Medicine, 51,* 583–590.

Erwin, E. (1980). "Psychoanalytic Therapy: The Eysenck Argument." *American Psychologist, 35,* 435–443.

———. (1986). "Psychotherapy and Freudian Psychology." In S. Modgil and C. Modgil (Eds.), *Hans Eysenck: Consensus and Controversy.* Philadelphia: Falmer Press, pp. 179–203.

Everson, T., and Cole, W. (1966). *Spontaneous Regression of Cancer.* Philadelphia: W. B. Saunders Co.

Eysenck, H. (1952), "The Effects of Psychotherapy: An Evaluation." *Journal of Consulting Psychology, 16,* 319–324.

Eysenck, H., and Nias, D. (1982). *Astrology: Science or Superstition?* New York: St. Martin's Press.

* Eysenck, H., and Wilson, G., Eds. (1973). *Experimental Study of Freudian Theories.* London: Methuen and Co.

Faraday, M. (1853, July 2). "Experimental Investigation of Table-moving." *The Athenaeum,* pp. 801–802.

Farah, M. (1984). "The Neurological Basis of Mental Imagery: A Componential Analysis". *Cognition, 18,* 245–272.

Feingold, B. (1975). *Why Your Child Is Hyperactive.* New York: Random House.

Feinleib, M., and Fabsitz, R. (1978). "Do Biorhythms Influence Day of Death?" *New England Journal of Medicine, 298,* 1153.

Feltz, D., and Landers, D. (1983). "The Effects of Mental Practice on Motor Skill Learning and Performance: A Meta-analysis." *Journal of Sport Psychology,*

5, 25–57.

* Festinger, L., Riecken, H., and Schachter, S. (1956). *When Prophecy Fails.* New York: Harper and Row.

Fields, H., and Levine, J. (1984, August). "Placebo Analgesia—A Role for Endorphins?" *Trends in the Neurosciences,* 27–29.

Fischer, J. (1983). "A Summary Critique of Analysis of the 'Blood' on the Turin 'Shroud.'" In J. Nickell, *Inquest on the Shroud of Turin,* pp. 149–152.

Fisher, C., Glenwick, D., and Blumenthal, R. (1986). "Subliminal Oedipal Stimuli and Competitive Performance: An Investigation of Between-Groups Effects and Mediating Subject Variables." *Journal of Abnormal Psychology, 95,* 292–294.

Fodor, N. (1964). *Between Two Worlds.* West Nyack, N.Y.: Parker Publishing.

Forlano, G., and Ehrlich, V. (1941). "Month and Season of Birth in Relation to Intelligence, Introversion-Extroversion and Inferiority Feelings." *Journal of Education Research, 32,* 1–2.

Foulkes, D. (1985). *Dreaming: A Cognitive Psychological Analysis.* Hillsdale, N.J.: Lawrence Erlbaum Associates.

Foulkes, D., *et al.* (1972). "Long Distance 'Sensory-Bombardment' ESP in Dreams: A Failure to Replicate." *Perceptual and Motor Skills, 35,* 731–734.

Frank, B. (1976). *No Aging Diet.* New York: Dial Press.

Franklin, W. (1976). "Metal Fracture Physics Using Scanning Electron Microscopy and the Theory of Teleneural Interactions." In C. Panati (Ed.), *The Geller Papers.* Boston: Houghton Mifflin, pp. 83–106.

———. (1977, September/October). Letter. *The Humanist,* pp. 54–55.

Franks, C. (Ed.) (1969). *Behavioral Therapy: Appraisal and Status.* New York: McGraw-Hill.

* Franks, F. (1981). *Polywater.* Cambridge, Mass.: MIT Press.

Frazier, K. (1979–80). "Amityville Hokum: The Hoax and the Hype." *Skeptical Inquirer,* 4 (No. 2), 2–4.

———. (1980–81). "Mummy's Curse Tut-tutted." *Skeptical Inquirer,* 5 (No. 1), 13.

* ———, Ed., (1981). *Paranormal Borderlands of Science.* Buffalo, N.Y.: Prometheus Books.

———. (1981–82). "Judge Rebuts Tut Suit." *Skeptical Inquirer,* 6 (No. 4), 12.

———. (1982–83). "Psychics' 1982 Predictions." *Skeptical Inquirer,* 7 (No. 3), 8–9.

———. (1983–84). "Media Awake to Psychics' Failed Predictions for 1983." *Skeptical Inquirer, 8,* 296–298.

———. (1984–85). "California Intact, Psychics Too, Despite Flubs on '84 Predictions." *Skeptical Inquirer, 9,* 307–310.

———. (1985–86). "Psychics' '85 Forecasts: Slightly Off the Mark." *Skeptical Inquirer, 10,* 197–198.

* ———. (Ed.), (1986). *Science Confronts the Paranormal.* Buffalo, N.Y.: Prometheus Books.

Frazier, K., and Randi, J. (1981–82). "Prediction after the Fact: Lessons of the Tamara Rand Hoax." *Skeptical Inquirer,* 6 (No. 1), 4–7.

Frederick, C. (1965). "Some Phenomena Affecting Handwriting Analysis." *Perceptual and Motor Skills, 20,* 211–218.

―――. (1968), "An Investigation of Handwriting of Suicidal Persons through Suicide Notes." *Journal of Abnormal Psychology, 73,* 263–267.

Freud, S. (1950). *The Interpretation of Dreams* (A. Brill, trans.). New York: Modern Library. Original English edition published in 1913.

―――. (1916). *Leonardo da Vinci* (A. Brill, trans.). New York: Moffat, Yard.

Fried, J. (1975). *The Vitamin Conspiracy.* New York: Saturday Review Press.

* ―――. (1984). *Vitamin Politics.* Buffalo, N.Y.: Prometheus Books.

Friedhoff, A., and Chase, T., Eds. (1982). *Gilles de la Tourette's Syndrome.* New York: Raven Press.

Friedlander, E. (1985). "Dream Your Cancer Away: The Simontons." In D. Stalker and C. Glymour (Eds.), *Examining Holistic Medicine,* pp. 273–285.

Friedman, G., *et al.* (1986). "Serum Retinol and Retinol-Binding Protein Levels Do Not Predict Subsequent Lung Cancer." *American Journal of Epidemiology, 123,* 781–789.

Fudin, R. (1986). "Subliminal Psychodynamic Activation: Mommy and I Are Not Yet One." *Perceptual and Motor Skills, 63,* 1159–1179.

―――. (1987). "Subliminal Psychodynamic Activation: Note on Illumination and the Bleaching Hypothesis." *Perceptual and Motor Skills, 64,* 1223–1230.

Fuller, J. (1966). *The Interrupted Journey.* New York: Dell.

―――. (1974). *Arigo: Surgeon of the Rusty Knife.* New York: Crowell.

Gable, M., *et al.* (1987). "An Evaluation of Subliminally Embedded Sexual Stimuli in Graphics." *Journal of Advertising, 16* (No. 1), 26–31.

Gaddis, V. (1965). *Invisible Horizons.* Philadelphia: Chilton.

Galbraith, G., Cooper, L., and London, P. (1972). "Hypnotic Susceptibility and the Sensory Evoked Response." *Journal of Comparative and Physiological Psychology, 80,* 509–514.

Galston, A., and Slayman, C. (1979). "The Not-So-Secret Life of Plants." *American Scientist, 67,* 337–344.

Galston, A., and Slayman, C. (1981). "Plant Sensitivity and Sensation." In G. Abell and B. Singer (Eds.), *Science and the Paranormal,* pp. 40–55.

Gardner, H. (1982). *Art, Mind and Brain.* New York: Basic Books.

―――. (1983). *Frames of Mind.* New York: Basic Books.

Gardner, H., and Winner, E. (1981). "Artistry and Aphasia." In M. Sarno (Ed.), *Acquired Aphasia.* New York: Academic Press, pp. 361–384.

* Gardner, M. (1957). *Fads and Fallacies in the Name of Science.* New York: Dover.

―――. (1966). "Mathematical Games." *Scientific American, 215* (No. 1), 108–112.

―――. (1981a). "Geller, Gulls, and Nitinol." In M. Gardner, *Science: Good Bad and Bogus.* Buffalo, N.Y.: Prometheus Books. (Reprinted from *The Humanist,* May/June, 1977).

―――. (1981b). "Parapsychology and Quantum Mechanics." In G. Abell and B. Singer (Eds.), *Science and the Paranormal,* pp. 56–69.

―――. (1984, August). "Cruel Deception in the Philippines." *Discover,* 8.

―――. (1986). *The Wreck of the Titanic Foretold?* Buffalo, N.Y.: Prometheus Books.

―――. (1987a). "Isness Is Her Business." *The New York Review of Books, 34* (No.

6), 16–19.

———. (1987b). "Science-Fantasy Religious Cults." *Free Inquiry, 7* (No. 3), 31–35.

* Garelik, G. (1984, November). "The Great Hudson Valley UFO Mystery." *Discover*, 18–24.

* ———. (1986, December). "Exorcising a Damnable Disease." *Discover*, 74–84.

Gauquelin, M. (1979). *Dreams and Illusions of Astrology*. Buffalo, N.Y.: Prometheus Books.

Gazzaniga, M., and LeDoux, J. (1978). *The Integrated Mind*. New York: Plenum.

Geschwind, N. (1983). "Interictal Behavioral Changes in Epilepsy." *Epilepsia, 24* (Supp. 1), S23–S30.

Ghez, C., and Fahn, S. (1985). "The Cerebellum." In E. Kandel and J. Schwartz (Eds)., *Principles of Neural Science*, 2nd edition. New York: Elsevier, pp. 502–522.

* Gilovich, T., Vallone, R., and Tversky, A. (1985). "The Hot Hand in Basketball: On the Misperception of Random Sequences." *Cognitive Psychology, 17*, 295–314.

Gish, D. (1977). *Dinosaurs: Those Terrible Lizards*. San Diego, Calif.: Creation-Life Publishers.

Gittelson, B. (1982). *Biorhythm: A Personal Science*. New York: Warner Books.

Gleick, J. (1986, June 3). "Moon's Creation Now Attributed to Giant Crash." *New York Times*, C1, C3.

* Glick, P., and Snyder, M. (1986). "Self-fulfilling Prophecy: The Psychology of Belief in Astrology." *The Humanist, 46* (No. 3), 20–25, 50.

Globus, G., *et al.* (1968). "An Appraisal of Telepathic Communication in Dreams." *Psychophysiology, 4*, 365.

* Godfrey, L., Ed. (1983). *Scientists Confront Creationism*. New York: Norton.

* Godfrey, L., and Cole, J. (1986, August). "Blunder in Their Footsteps." *Natural History*, 4–12.

Goldberg, L. (1986). "Some Informal Explorations and Ruminations about Graphology." In B. Nevo (Ed.), *Scientific Aspects of Graphology*. Springfield, Ill.: Charles C. Thomas, pp. 281–293.

* Goldsmith, D., Ed. (1977). *Scientists Confront Velikovsky*. Ithaca, N.Y.: Cornell University Press.

Goodman, L. (1968). *Linda Goodman's Sun-Signs*. New York: Bantam Books.

———. (1971). *Linda Goodman's Sun-Signs*. New York: Bantam Books.

———. (1982). *Love Signs*. New York: Fawcett.

Gould, R. (1944). *The Stargazer Talks*. London: Geoffrey Bles.

Gould, S. (1980). "The Panda's Thumb." In S. Gould, *The Panda's Thumb*. New York: Norton, pp. 19–26.

Goy, R., and McEwen, B. (1980). *Sexual Differentiation of the Brain*. Cambridge, Mass.: MIT Press.

Gracely, R., *et al.* (1983). "Placebo and Naloxone Can Alter Post-surgical Pain by Separate Mechanisms." *Nature, 306*, 264–265.

Greeley, A. (1987, January/February). "Mysticism Goes Mainstream." *American Health*, 47–49.

Green, R. (1987). *The "Sissy Boy Syndrome" and the Development of Homosexuality.* New Haven: Yale University Press.

* Greenberg, M., and Farah, M. (1986). "The Laterality of Dreaming." *Brain and Cognition, 5,* 307–321.

Griaule, M., and Dieterlen, G. (1954). "The Dogon." In D. Forde (Ed.), *African Worlds.* London: Oxford University Press, pp. 83–110.

Grieve, D. (1972). "Report on the Film of a Supposed Sasquatch." In J. Napier, *Bigfoot,* pp. 217–222.

* Gross, M. (1978). *The Psychological Society.* New York: Random House.

* Grosser, M. (1962). *The Discovery of Neptune.* New York: Dover.

* Grunbaum, A. (1984). *Foundations of Psychoanalysis: A Philosophical Critique.* Berkeley: University of California Press.

Gruneberg, M., and Sykes, R. (1978). "Knowledge and Retention: The Feeling of Knowing and Reminiscence." In M. Gruneberg, P. Morris, and R. Sykes (Eds.), *Practical Aspects of Memory.* London: Academic Press, pp. 189–196.

Guerin, P. (1970, November–December). "The Warminster Photographs: A Tentative Interpretation." *Flying Saucer Review, 16,* 6.

Haber, A., and Runyon, R. (1983). *Fundamentals of Psychology,* 3rd edition. Reading, Mass.: Addison-Wesley.

Haber, R., and Hershenson, M. (1973). *The Psychology of Visual Perception.* New York: Holt, Rinehart and Winston.

* Hadingham, E. (1987). *Lines to the Mountain Gods.* New York: Random House.

Haley, M. (1982, February). "The Eyes Have It." *Real Estate Today,* 24–27.

Hall, C. (1954). *Primer of Freudian Psychology.* New York: New American Library.

———. (1963). "Strangers in Dreams: An Empirical Confirmation of the Oedipus Complex." *Journal of Personality, 31,* 336–345.

Hall, C., and Van de Castle, R. (1965). "An Empirical Investigation of the Castration Complex in Dreams." *Journal of Personality, 33,* 20–29.

Hall, F., Davis, M., and Baran, D. (1987). "Bone Mineral Screening for Osteoporosis." *New England Journal of Medicine, 316,* 212–214.

Hall, N., and Goldstein, A. (1986). "Thinking Well." *The Sciences, 26* (No. 2), 34–40.

Hall, R. (1972). "Sociological Perspectives on UFO Reports." In C. Sagan and T. Page (Eds.), *UFOs—A Scientific Debate.* Ithaca, N.Y.: Cornell University Press, pp. 213–223.

Hall, T. (1978). *Search for Harry Price.* London: Gerald Duckworth.

———. (1985). "A Note on Borley Rectory: 'The Most Haunted House in England.'" In P. Kurtz (Ed.), *A Skeptic's Handbook of Parapsychology,* pp. 327–338.

Han, J., and Terenius, L. (1982). "Neurochemical Basis of Acupuncture Analgesia." *Annual Review of Pharmacology and Toxicology, 22,* 193–220.

Hansel, C. (1966). *ESP: A Scientific Evaluation.* New York: Charles Schribner's Sons.

* Hansel, C. (1980). *ESP and Parapsychology: A Critical Re-evaluation.* Buffalo, N.Y.: Prometheus Books.

Hapgood, C. (1966). *Maps of the Ancient Sea Kings.* New York: Chilton.

Hare, R. (1855). *Experimental Investigation of Spirit Manifestations, Demonstrating the Existence of Spirits and Their Communion with Mortals: Doctrine of the spirit world respecting heaven, hell, morality, and God: Also, the influence of scripture on the morals of Christians.* New York: Partridge and Brittan.

Hargrave, C. (1966). *History of Playing Cards and a Bibliography of Cards and Gaming* New York: Dover Publications. Originally published by Houghton Mifflin Co., Boston, 1930.

Harris, J., and Weeks, K. (1973). *X-Raying the Pharaohs.* New York: Charles Scribner's Sons.

Harris, M. (1986). "Are 'Past-Life' Regressions Evidence of Reincarnation?" *Free Inquiry, 6* (No. 4), 18–23.

Hattie, J., Sharpley, C., and Rogers, H. (1984). "Comparative Effectiveness of Professional and Paraprofessional Helpers." *Psychological Bulletin, 95,* 534–541.

Hawkins, D. (1970). "The Effects of Subliminal Stimulation on Drive Level and Brand Preference." *Journal of Marketing Research, 7,* 322–326.

Hegstad, R. (1974). *Rattling the Gates.* Washington, D.C.: Review and Herald Publishing Association.

Heilbrun, K. (1980). "Silverman's Subliminal Psychodynamic Activation: A Failure to Replicate." *Journal of Abnormal Psychology, 89,* 560–566.

Heller, J., and Adler, A. (1980). "Blood on the Shroud of Turin." *Applied Optics, 19,* 2742–2744.

Hendry, A. (1979). *The UFO Handbook.* Garden City, N.Y.: Doubleday.

Hennekens, C. (1986). "Micronutrients and Cancer Prevention." *New England Journal of Medicine, 315,* 1288–1289.

Henry, J. (1982). "Circulating Opioids: Possible Physiological Roles in Central Nervous Function." *Neuroscience and Biobehavioral Reviews, 6,* 229–245.

Herbert, V. (1980). "The Health Hustlers." In S. Barrett (Ed.), *The Health Robbers,* pp. 49–68.

———. (1986a). "Diet and Cancer." *Science, 233,* 926.

———. (1986b). "Questionable Cancer Remedies." In A. Holleb (Ed.), *American Cancer Society's Complete Book of Cancer.* Garden City, N.Y.: Doubleday, pp. 238–247.

Herrmann, N. (1981, October). "The Creative Brain." *Training and Development Journal,* 10–16.

Hersey, R. (1931). "Emotional Cycles in Man." *Journal of Mental Health, 77,* 151–169.

———. (1932). *Workers' Emotions in Shop and Home.* Philadelphia: University of Pennsylvania Press.

———. (1955). *Zest for Work.* New York: Harper and Row.

Hilgard, E. (1977). *Divided Consciousness.* New York: Wiley.

———. (1980–81). "Hypnosis Gives Rise to Fantasy and Is Not a Truth Serum." *Skeptical Inquirer, 5* (No. 3), 25.

Hilgard, E., Atkinson, R., and Atkinson, R. (1979). *Introduction to Psychology,* 7th edition. New York: Harcourt Brace Jovanovich.

Hines, T. (1976). "Attended and Unattended Processing in Hemispheric

Activation." Unpublished master's thesis, University of Oregon, Eugene, Ore.

———. (1979). "Biorhythm Theory: A Critical Review." *Skeptical Inquirer, 3* (No. 4), 26–36.

———. (1985, November). "Left Brain, Right Brain: Who's on First?" *Training and Development Journal*, 32–34.

* ———. (1987). "Hemispheric Difference Mythology in Management and Training." *Academy of Management Review, 12*, 600–606.

Hines, T., and Dennison, T. (1988). "A Reaction Time Test of Extrasensory Perception." Vol. 13, p. 161–165.

Hines, T., Lang, P., and Seroussi, K. (1987). "Extrasensory Perception Examined Using a Reaction Time Measure." *Perceptual and Motor Skills, 64*, 499–502.

Hintzman, D., Asher, S., and Stern, L. (1978), "Incidental Retrieval and Memory for Coincidences." In M. Gruneberg, P. Morris, and R. Sykes (Eds.), *Practical Aspects of Memory*. London: Academic Press, pp. 61–68.

Hobson, J., Lydic, R., and Baghdoyan, H. (1986). "Evolving Concepts of Sleep Cycle Generation: From Brain Centers to Neuronal Populations." *Behavioral and Brain Sciences, 9*, 371–448.

Hobson, J., and McCarley, R. (1977). "Brain as a Dream State Generator: An Activation-Synthesis Hypothesis of the Dream Process." *American Journal of Psychiatry, 134*, 1335–1348.

Hodgkinson, S., *et al.* (1987). "Molecular Genetic Evidence for Heterogeneity in Manic Depression." *Nature, 325*, 805–806.

Hoebens, P. (1981–82a). "Croiset and Professor Tenhaeff: Discrepancies in Claims of Clairvoyance." *Skeptical Inquirer, 6* (No. 2), 32–40.

———. (1981–82b). "Gerald Croiset: Investigation of the Mozart of 'Psychic Sleuths.'" *Skeptical Inquirer, 6* (No. 1), 17–28.

———. (1982–83). "Modern Revival of 'Nostradamitis.'" *Skeptical Inquirer, 7* (No. 1), 38–45.

Hoggart, S. (1984, November 25). "The Ghostbusters." (London) *Observer*, pp. 21–22.

Holden, P. (1977, October 26). "Biorhythms: The Flow of Energy." (Eugene) *Oregon Daily Emerald*, p. 5.

Holender, D. (1986). "Semantic Activation without Conscious Identification." *Behavioral and Brain Sciences, 9*, 1–66.

Holmes, D. (1974). "Investigations of Repression: Differential Recall of Material Experimentally or Naturally Associated with Ego Threat." *Psychological Bulletin, 81*, 632–653.

Holzer, H. (1974). *The Ghosts That Walk in Washington*. New York: Ballantine.

Hönel, H. (1977). "Grundrhythmus und kriminelle Disposition in der Handschrift." *Zeitschrift für Menschenkunde, 41*, 1–55.

Hong, W., *et al.* (1986). "13-cis-retinoic Acid in the Treatment of Oral Leukoplakia." *New England Journal of Medicine, 315*, 1502–1505.

Hopkins, B. (1987). *Intruders*. New York: Random House.

Horowitz, K., Lewis, D., and Gasteiger, E. (1975). "Plant 'Primary Perception': Electrophysiological Unresponsiveness to Brine Shrimp Killing." *Science, 189*,

478–480.

Houdini, H. (1924). *Magician among the Spirits.* New York: Harper and Row.

Howard, I., and Templeton, W. (1966). *Human Spatial Orientation.* New York: Wiley.

Howe, G., Birch, J., and Miller, A. (1977). "Artificial Sweeteners and Human Bladder Cancer." *Lancet, II,* 578–581.

Huber, P. (1977). "Early Cuneiform Evidence for the Existence of the Planet Venus." In D. Goldsmith (Ed.), *Scientists Confront Velikovsky,* pp. 117–144.

Hunter, K., and Shane, R. (1979). "Time of Death and Biorhythmic Cycles." *Perceptual and Motor Skills, 48,* 220.

* Hyman, R. (1976–77). "'Cold Reading': How to Convince Strangers that You Know All About Them." *Zetetic, 1* (No. 2), 18–37.

———. (1980–81). "Further Comments on Schmidt's PK Experiments." *Skeptical Inquirer, 5* (No. 3), 34–40.

———. (1985a). "A Critical Historical Overview of Parapsychology." In P. Kurtz (Ed.), *A Skeptic's Handbook of Parapsychology,* pp. 3–96.

* ———. (1985b). "The Ganzfeld Psi Experiment: A Critical Appraisal." *Journal of Parapsychology, 49,* 3–49.

Hynek, J. (1972). *The UFO Experience.* New York: Ballantine Books.

———. (1976–77). Comments. *Zetetic, 1* (No. 2). 77–79.

Hynek, J., and Vallee, J. (1975). *The Edge of Reality: A Progress Report on Unidentified Flying Objects.* Chicago: Henry Regnery Co.

* Irwin, H. (1985). *Flight of Mind.* Metuchen, N.J.: Scarecrow Press.

Iverson, J. (1977). *More Lives Than One?* London: Pan Books.

* Jacobs, D. (1975). *The UFO Controversy in America.* Bloomington, Ind.: Indiana University Press.

Jacobson, M. (1978). *Developmental Neurobiology.* 2nd edition. New York: Plenum.

James, A. (1984). "The Validity of 'Biorhythmic' Theory Questioned." *British Journal of Psychology, 75,* 197–200.

Jansen, A. (1973). *Validation of Graphological Judgments: An Experimental Study.* The Hague, Netherlands: Mouton.

Janssen, W. (1980). "The Gadgeteers." In S. Barrett (Ed.), *The Health Robbers,* pp. 93–107.

Jerome, L. (1977). *Astrology Disproved.* Buffalo, N.Y.: Prometheus Books.

Jung, C., and Pauli, W. (1955). *The Interpretation of Nature and the Psyche.* New York: Pantheon.

* Kagan, D., and Summers, I. (1983). *Mute Evidence.* New York: Bantam Books.

* Kahneman, D., Slovic, P., and Tversky, A. (Eds.) (1982). *Judgment Under Uncertainty: Heuristics and Biases.* Cambridge, England: Cambridge University Press.

Kalat, J. (1987). *Biological Psychology,* 3rd edition. Belmont, Calif.: Wadsworth.

* Keene, M. (1976). *Psychic Mafia.* New York: St. Martin's Press.

Keinan, G. (1986a). "Can Graphologists Identify Individuals Under Stress?" In B. Nevo (Ed.), *Scientific Aspects of Graphology.* Springfield, Ill.: Charles C. Thomas, pp. 141–151.

———. (1986b). "Graphoanalysis for Military Personnel Selection." In B. Nevo (Ed.), *Scientific Aspects of Graphology.* Springfield, IL: Charles C. Thomas, pp.

193-201.

Kelly, D., Ed. (1986). *Stress Induced Analgesia.* New York: New York Academy of Sciences (*Annals,* Vol. 467).

Kemper, T. (1984). "Asymmetrical Lesions in Dyslexia." In N. Geschwind and A. Galaburda (Eds.), *Cerebral Dominance: The Biological Foundations.* Cambridge, Mass.: Harvard University Press, pp. 75-89.

Kennedy, J. (1939). "A Methodological Review of Extra-Sensory Perception. *Psychological Bulletin 36,* 59-103.

Key, W. (1973). *Subliminal Seduction.* Englewood Cliffs, N.J.: Prentice-Hall.

———. (1976). *Media Sexploitation.* Englewood Cliffs, N.J.: Prentice-Hall.

———. (1980). *The Clam-Plate Orgy.* Englewood Cliffs, N.J.: Prentice-Hall.

Kiecolt-Glaser, J., *et al.* (1987). "Marital Quality, Marital Disruption, and Immune Function." *Psychosomatic Medicine, 49,* 13-34.

Kilbourne, W., Painton, S., and Ridley, D. (1985). "The Effects of Sexual Embedding on Responses to Magazine Advertisements." *Journal of Advertising,* 14 (No. 2), 48-56.

King, S. (1977). *Pyramid Energy Handbook.* New York: Warner Books.

King, T. (1973). *Love, Sex, and Astrology.* New York: Harper and Row.

* Kitcher, P. (1982). *Abusing Science: The Case Against Creationism.* Cambridge, Mass.: MIT Press.

* Klass, P. (1974). *UFOs Identified.* New York: Random House.

———. (1977-78). Review of C. Berlitz, *Without a Trace. Zetetic,* 2 (No. 1), 97-102.

———. (1978-79). "The Gallup UFO Polls." *Skeptical Inquirer, 3* (No. 2), 5-7.

———. (1980-81). "Hypnosis and UFO Abductions." *Skeptical Inquirer, 5* (No. 3), 16-24.

———. (1981). "UFOs." In G. Abell and B. Singer (Eds.), *Science and the Paranormal.* pp. 310-328.

* ———. (1983). *UFOs Explained.* New York: Random House.

———. (1984-85). "Radar UFOs: Where Have They Gone?" *Skeptical Inquirer,* 9, 257-260.

———. (1987-88). "Intruders of the Mind." Review of B. Hopkins, *Intruders. Skeptical Inquirer,* 12, 85-89.

* ———. (1988). *UFO Abductions: A Dangerous Game.* Buffalo, N.Y.: Prometheus Books.

Kleinmuntz, B., and Szucko, J. (1984). "A Field Study of the Fallibility of Polygraphic Lie Detection." *Nature, 308,* 449-450.

Kline, P. (1968). "Obsessional Traits, Obsessional Symptoms and Anal Erotism." *British Journal of Medical Psychology, 41,* 299-305.

Klotz, I. (1980). "The N-Ray Affair." *Scientific American, 242* (No. 5), 168-175.

Kmetz, J. (1977). "A Study of Primary Perception in Plant and Animal Life." *Journal of the American Society for Psychical Research, 71,* 157-169.

———. (1977-78). "Plant Primary Perception: The Other Side of the Leaf." *Skeptical Inquirer, 2* (No. 2), 57-61.

Knight, G. (1980). "The Confused Crusaders." In S. Barrett (Ed.), *The Health Robbers,* pp. 160-172.

Knowles, L., and Jones, R. (1974, November). "Police Altercations and the Ups and Downs of Life Cycles." *Police Chief*, 51–54.

Kolata, G. (1985). "Why Do People Get Fat?" *Science, 227*, 1327–1328.

* ———. (1986, January). "Weight Regulation May Start in Our Cells, Not Psyches." *Smithsonian*, 91–97.

Kosok, P., and Reiche, M. (1949). "Ancient Drawings on the Desert of Peru." *Archaeology, 2*, 206–215.

Krieger, D., Peper, E., and Ancoli, S. (1979). "Therapeutic Touch, Searching for Evidence of Physiological Change." *American Nurses' Association, 79*, 660–662.

* Krupp, E. (Ed.) (1978). *In Search of Ancient Astronomies*. Garden City, N.Y.: Doubleday.

———. (1981). "Recasting the Past: Powerful Pyramids, Lost Continents, and Ancient Astronauts." In G. Abell and B. Singer (Eds.), *Science and the Paranormal*. pp. 253–295.

Kuban, G. (1986). "A Summary of the Taylor Site Evidence." *Creation/Evolution, 6* (No. 1), 10–18.

Kunst-Wilson, W., and Zajonc, R. (1980). "Affective Discrimination of Stimuli That Cannot Be Recognized." *Science, 207*, 557–558.

Kurtz, P. (1976–77). "The Aims of the Committee for the Scientific Investigation of Claims of the Paranormal." *Zetetic, 1* (No. 1), 6–7.

———. (1980–81). "Bigfoot on the Loose: Or How to Create a Legend." *Skeptical Inquirer, 5* (No. 1), 49–54.

* ———, Ed. (1985a). *A Skeptic's Handbook of Parapsychology*. Buffalo, N.Y.: Prometheus Books.

———. (1985b) "Spiritualists, Mediums, and Psychics: Some Evidence of Fraud." In P. Kurtz (Ed.), *A Skeptic's Handbook of Parapsychology*, pp. 177–223.

———. (1986). "Does Faith-Healing Work?" *Free Inquiry, 6* (No. 2), 30–36.

Kurtz, R., and Garfield, S. (1978). "Illusory Correlation: A Further Exploration of Chapman's Paradigm." *Journal of Consulting and Clinical Psychology, 46*, 1009–1015.

Kurtzke, J. (1968). "Clinical Manifestations of Multiple Sclerosis." In J. Kurtzke (Ed.), *Epidemiology of Multiple Sclerosis*. Springfield, Ill.: C. C. Thomas, pp. 161–216.

* Kusche, L. (1975). *The Bermuda Triangle Mystery—Solved*. New York: Harper and Row.

———. (1977–78a). "Critical Reading, Careful Writing, and the Bermuda Triangle." *Zetetic, 2* (No. 1), 36–40.

———. (1977–78b). Review of C. Berlitz, *Without a Trace*. *Zetetic, 2* (No. 1), 93–97.

———. (1979–80). Review of W. Moore and C. Berlitz, "The Philadelphia Experiment: Project Invisibility." *Skeptical Inquirer, 4* (No. 1), 58–62.

———. (1980). *The Disappearance of Flight 19*. New York: Harper and Row.

———. (1981). "The Bermuda Triangle." In G. Abell and B. Singer (Eds.), *Science and the Paranormal*. New York: Charles Scribner's Sons, pp. 296–309.

LaBruzza, A. (1978). Letter to the editor. *American Journal of Psychiatry, 135*, 614–

615.

Lachman, R., Lachman, J., and Butterfield, E. (1979). *Cognitive Psychology and Information Processing: An Introduction.* Hillsdale, N.J.: Lawrence Erlbaum Associates.

Lagercrantz, H., and Slotkin, T. (1986). "The 'Stress' of Being Born." *Scientific American, 254* (No. 4), 100–107.

Latman, N. (1977). "Human Sensitivity, Intelligence and Physical Cycles and Motor Vehicle Accidents." *Accident Analysis and Prevention, 9,* 109–112.

Latman, N., and Garriott, J. (1980). "An Analysis of Biorhythms and Their Influence on Motor Vehicle Fatalities." *Accident Analysis and Prevention, 12,* 283–286.

Lawrence, J., and Perry, C. (1983). "Hypnotically Created Memory Among Highly Hypnotizable Subjects." *Science, 222,* 523–524.

Lazarus, A. (1986). "On Sterile Paradigms and the Realities of Clinical Practice: Critical Comments on Eysenck's Contribution to Behavior Therapy." In S. Modgil and C. Modgil (Eds.), *Hans Eysenck: Consensus and Controversy.* Philadelphia: Falmer Press, pp. 247–257.

Lehn, W. (1979). "Atmospheric Refraction and Lake Monsters." *Science, 205,* 183–185.

Leichty, E. (1975). *The Omen Series Shumma Izbu.* Locust Valley, N.Y.: J. J. Augustine.

Leikind, B., and McCarthy, W. (1985-86). "An Investigation of Firewalking." *Skeptical Inquirer, 10,* 23–34.

Leonard, G. (1976). *Somebody Else Is on the Moon.* New York: David McKay.

* Leoni, E. (1982). *Nostradamus and His Prophecies.* New York: Bell Publishing Co. Originally published by Exposition Press, New York, 1961.

Levine, M., and Shefner, J. (1981). *Fundamentals of Sensation and Perception.* New York: Random House.

Levinson, H. (1980). *A Solution to the Riddle Dyslexia.* New York: Springer-Verlag.

———. (1984). *Smart But Feeling Dumb.* New York: Warner Books.

Levinson, H., and Carter, S. (1986). *Phobia Free: A Medical Breakthrough Linking Ninety Percent of All Phobias and Panic Attacks to a Hidden Physical Problem.* Beaumont, Tex.: M. Evans.

Levinthal, C. (1983). *Introduction to Physiological Psychology,* 2nd edition. Englewood Cliffs, N.J.: Prentice-Hall.

Levy, L. (1979). "Handwriting and Hiring." *Dun's Review, 113,* 72–79.

Lieber, A. (1978). *The Lunar Effect: Biological Tides and Human Emotions.* Garden City, N.Y.: Doubleday.

Lieber, A., and Sherin, C. (1972). "Homicides and the Lunar Cycle: Toward a Theory of Lunar Influence on Human Emotional Disturbance." *American Journal of Psychiatry, 129,* 69–74.

Liebeskind, J. (1976). "Pain Modulation by Central Nervous System Stimulation." *Advances in Pain Research and Therapy, 1,* 445–453.

Lim, R. (1975). "Zodiacal Sign Polarities as an Index of Introversion Extroversion." Unpublished master's thesis. San Francisco State University.

Lind, K. (1982). "A Synthesis of Studies on Stroke Rehabilitation." *Journal of Chronic Disease, 35,* 133–149.

Linn, R. (1976). *The Last Chance Diet.* Secaucus, N.J.: Lyle Stuart.

Loftin, R. (1980-81). "A Maltese Cross in the Aegean?" *Skeptical Inquirer,* 5 (No. 4), 54-57.

Loftus, E. (1979). *Eyewitness Testimony.* Cambridge, Mass.: Harvard University Press.

Loftus, E., Miller, D., and Burns, H. (1978). "Semantic Integration of Verbal Information into a Visual Memory." *Journal of Experimental Psychology: Human Learning and Memory, 4,* 19-31.

Loftus, E., and Palmer, J. (1974). "Reconstruction of Automobile Destruction: An Example of the Interaction between Language and Memory." *Journal of Verbal Learning and Verbal Behavior, 13,* 585-589.

Lorenzen, J., and Lorenzen, C. (1970). *Abducted! Confrontations with Beings from Outer Space.* New York: Berkley.

Lowell, P. (1908). *Mars as the Abode of Life.* New York: Macmillan.

* Lykken, D. (1981). *A Tremor in the Blood.* New York: McGraw-Hill.

MacDougall, C. (1983). *Superstition and the Press.* Buffalo, N.Y.: Prometheus Books.

MacKay, C. (1980). *Extraordinary Popular Delusions and the Madness of Crowds.* New York: Bonanza Books. Originally published by Richard Bentley, London, 1841.

MacRobert, A. (1982, September 3). "A Skeptic's Guide to New Age Hokum. *Vermont Vanguard Press,* 46-49, 62.

* ———. (1986). "Reality Shopping: A Consumer's Guide to New Age Hokum." *Whole Earth Review,* no. 52, 4-14.

Makarec, K., and Persinger, M. (1985). "Temporal Lobe Signs: Electroencephalographic Validity and Enhanced Scores in Special Populations." *Perceptual and Motor Skills, 60,* 831-842.

Mallardi, V. (1978). *Biorhythms and Your Behavior.* Philadelphia: Running Press.

* Mandell, A. (1980). "Toward a Psychobiology of Transcendence: God in the Brain." In J. Davidson and R. Davidson (Eds.), *Psychobiology of Consciousness.* New York: Plenum Press, pp. 379-464.

Mann, J., and Stanley, M., Eds. (1986). *Psychobiology of Suicidal Behavior.* New York: New York Academy of Sciences. (*Annals,* Vol. 487.)

Marcel, T. (1980). "Conscious and Preconscious Recognition of Polysemous Words: Locating the Selective Effects of Prior Verbal Exposure." In R. Nickerson (Ed.), *Attention and Performance VIII.* Hillsdale, N.J.: Lawrence Erlbaum Associates, pp. 435-457.

———. (1983a). "Conscious and Unconscious Perception: An Approach to the Relation between Phenomenal Experience and Perceptual Processes." *Cognitive Psychology, 15,* 238-300.

———. (1983b). "Conscious and Unconscious Perception: Experiments on Visual Masking and Word Recognition." *Cognitive Psychology, 15,* 197-237.

* Marks, D., and Kammann, R. (1980). *Psychology of the Psychic.* Buffalo, N.Y.: Prometheus Books.

Marks, D., and Scott, C. (1986). "Remote Viewing Exposed." *Nature, 319,* 444.

Markwick, B. (1978). "The Soal-Goldney Experiments with Basil Shackleton: New Evidence of Data Manipulation." *Proceedings of the Society for Psychical*

Research, 56, 250-277.

———. (1985). "Establishment of Data Manipulation in the Soal-Shackleton Experiments." In P. Kurtz (Ed.), *A Skeptic's Handbook of Parapsychology*, pp. 287-311.

Maslow, A. (1966). *The Psychology of Science: A Reconnaissance*. New York: Harper and Row.

Matsumoto, S., Nogami, Y., and Ohkuri, S. (1962). "Statistical Studies on Menstruation: A Criticism of the Definition of Normal Menstruation." *Gumma Journal of Medical Science, 11*, 294-318.

Matthews, P. (1982). "Where Does Sherrington's 'Muscle Sense' Originate? Muscles, Joints, Corollary Discharges?" *Annual Review of Neuroscience, 5*, 189-218.

Matthews-Simonton, S. (1984). *The Healing Family*. New York: Bantam Books.

Mayo, J., White, O., and Eysenck, H. (1978). "An Empirical Study of the Relation between Astrological Factors and Personality." *Journal of Social Psychology, 105*, 229-236.

McCarley, R., and Hobson, J. (1977). "The Neurobiological Origins of Psychoanalytic Dream Theory." *American Journal of Psychiatry, 134*, 1211-1221.

McKean, K. (1985, April). "Of Two Minds: Selling the Right Brain." *Discover*, 30-41.

McKhann, G. (1982). "Multiple Sclerosis." *Annual Review of Neuroscience, 5*, 219-239.

Medalia, N., and Larsen, O. (1958). "Diffusion and Belief in a Collective Delusion: The Seattle Windshield Pitting Epidemic." *American Sociological Review, 23*, 180-186.

Medhurst, R. (1971). "The Origin of the 'Prepared Random Numbers' Used in the Shackleton Experiments." *Journal of the Society for Psychical Research, 46*, 39-55. (Note: A short correction to this paper appeared in the same journal, vol. 46, p. 203.)

Megargie, E. (1972). *The CPI Handbook*. San Francisco: Jossey-Bass.

Melzack, R. (1973). *The Puzzle of Pain*. New York: Basic Books.

Menger, H. (1959). *From Outer Space*. New York: Pyramid Books.

Menkes, M., *et al.* (1986). "Serum Beta-Carotene, Vitamins A and E, Selenium, and the Risk of Lung Cancer." *New England Journal of Medicine, 315*, 1250-1254.

Menzel, D. (1972). "UFOs—The Modern Myth." In C. Sagan and T. Page (Eds.), *UFOs—A Scientific Debate*. Ithaca, N.Y.: Cornell University Press, pp. 123-182.

Menzel, D., and Taves, E. (1977). *The UFO Enigma*. Garden City, N.Y.: Doubleday.

Mertz, B. (1978). *Temples, Tombs and Hieroglyphs*. New York: Dodd, Mead.

Meyer, P. (1986, March-April). "Ghostboosters: The Press and the Paranormal." *Columbia Journalism Review*, 38-41.

Meyskens, F., and Prasad, K., Eds. (1986). *Vitamins and Cancer*. Clifton, N.J.: Humana Press.

Milich, R., and Pelham, W. (1986). "Effects of Sugar Ingestion on the Classroom and Playgroup Behavior of Attention Deficit Disordered Boys." *Journal of Consulting and Clinical Psychology, 54,* 714–718.

Milich, R., Wolraich, M., and Lindgren, S. (1986). "Sugar and Hyperactivity: A Critical Review of Empirical Findings." *Clinical Psychology Review, 6,* 493–513.

Millar, K., and Watkinson, N. (1983). "Recognition of Words Presented during General Anaesthesia." *Ergonomics, 36,* 585–594.

Miller, L. (1986, December). "In Search of the Unconscious." *Psychology Today,* 60–64.

Mintzberg, H. (1976). "Planning on the Left and Managing on the Right." *Harvard Business Review, 54* (No. 4), 49–58.

Mishkin, M., and Appenzeller, T. (1987, June). "The Anatomy of Memory," *Scientific American,* 80–89.

Moertel, C., *et al.* (1985). "High-Dose Vitamin C Versus Placebo in the Treatment of Patients with Advanced Cancer Who Have Had No Prior Chemotherapy." *New England Journal of Medicine, 312,* 137–141.

Money, J. (1987). "Sin, Sickness, or Status? Homosexual Gender Identity and Psychoneuroendocrinology." *American Psychologist, 42,* 384–399.

Montgomery, R. (1965). *A Gift of Prophecy: The Phenomenal Jeane Dixon.* New York: William Morrow.

———. (1985). *Aliens Among Us.* New York: Putnam.

Moody, R. (1976). *Life After Life.* New York: Bantam Books.

Moore, R. (1983). "The Impossible Voyage of Noah's Ark." *Creation/Evolution,* 4 (No. 1), 1–43.

Moore, T. (1982). "Subliminal Advertising: What You See Is What You Get." *Journal of Marketing, 46* (No. 2), 38–47.

Moore, W., and Berlitz, C. (1979). *The Philadelphia Experiment: Project Invisibility.* New York: Grossett and Dunlap.

Moore-Ede, M., Sulzman, F., and Fuller, C. (1982). *The Clocks That Time Us: Physiology of the Circadian Timing System.* Cambridge, Mass.: Harvard University Press.

Moran, R., and Jordan, P. (1978, May). "The Amityville Horror Hoax." *Fate,* 43–47.

Morris, L. (1979). *Extroversion and Introversion.* Washington, D.C.: Hemisphere Publishing Co.

Morris, R. (1977–78). Review of *The Amityville Horror. Skeptical Inquirer, 2* (No. 2), 95–102.

* ———. (1978). "Survey of Methods and Issues in ESP Research." In S. Krippner (Ed.), *Advances in Parapsychological Research, 2, Extrasensory Perception.* New York: Plenum Press, pp. 7–58.

———. (1982). "An Updated Survey of Methods and Issues in ESP Research." In S. Krippner (Ed.), *Advances in Parapsychological Research 3.* New York: Plenum Press, pp. 5–40.

Mueller, M. (1981–82). "The Shroud of Turin: A Critical Appraisal." *Skeptical Inquirer, 6* (No. 3), 15–34.

Napier, J. (1972). *Bigfoot.* New York: Dutton.

* Nash, M. (1987). "What, If Anything, Is Regressed about Hypnotic Age Regression? A Review of the Empirical Literature." *Psychological Bulletin, 102,* 42-52.

Neepe, V. (1983). "Temporal Lobe Symptomatology in Subjective Paranormal Experiments." *Journal of the American Society for Psychical Research, 77,* 1-29.

Nelson, G. (1970). "Preliminary Study of the Electroencephalograms of Mediums." *Parapsychologica, 4,* 30-35.

Nelson, T. (1978). "Detecting Small Amounts of Information in Memory: Savings for Nonrecognized Items." *Journal of Experimental Psychology: Human Learning and Memory, 4,* 453-468.

Nevo, B. (1986). "Basic Rhythms and Criminal Disposition in Handwriting, by H. Hönel: Critical Review and Reanalysis." In B. Nevo (Ed.), *Scientific Aspects of Graphology.,* Springfield, Ill.: Charles C. Thomas, pp. 203-215.

Nickell, J. (1978). "The Shroud of Turin—Solved!" *The Humanist, 38* (No. 6), 30-32.

———. (1982-83). "The Nazca Drawings Revisited: Creation of a Full Sized Duplicate." *Skeptical Inquirer, 7* (No. 3), 36-44.

* ———. (1983). *Inquest on the Shroud of Turin.* Buffalo, N.Y.: Prometheus Books. Updated edition: Prometheus Books, 1987.

Nogrady, H., McConkey, K., and Perry, C. (1985). "Enhancing Visual Memory: Trying Hypnosis, Trying Imagination, and Trying Again." *Journal of Abnormal Psychology, 94,* 195-204.

* Nolen, W. (1974). *Healing: A Doctor in Search of a Miracle.* New York: Random House.

Norvell (1975). *Astrology—Your Wheel of Fortune.* New York: Harper and Row.

* Nottebohm, F. (1979). Origins and Mechanisms in the Establishment of Cerebral Dominance. In M. Gazzaniga (Ed.), *Handbook of Behavioral Neurobiology, Vol. 2: Neuropsychology.* New York: Plenum, pp. 295-344.

* Nye, M. (1980). "N-Rays: An Episode in the History and Psychology of Science." *Historical Studies in the Physical Sciences, 11* (No. 1), 125-156.

Oberg, J. (1977a, February). "Astronauts and UFOs: The Whole Story." *Space World,* 4-28.

———. (1977b, fall). "Modern Moon Myths and UFO Folklore," *Search Magazine,* 5-8, 52-62.

———. (1978-79a). "Astronaut 'UFO' Sightings." *Skeptical Inquirer, 3* (No. 1), 39-46.

———. (1978-79b). "Tunguska Echoes." *Skeptical Inquirer, 3* (No. 2), 49-57.

* ———. (1982). *UFOs and Outer Space Mysteries.* Norfolk, Va.: Donning Co.

Oberg, J., and Sheaffer, R. (1977-78). "Pseudoscience at *Science Digest.*" *Zetetic, 2* (No. 1), 41-44.

O'Hara, M. (1985). "Of Myths and Monkeys: A Critical Look at the Theory of Critical Mass." *Journal of Humanistic Psychology, 25,* 61-78.

Oliver, J., and Burkham, R. (1982). "Subliminal Psychodynamic Activation in Depression: A Failure to Replicate." *Journal of Abnormal Psychology, 91,* 337-342.

Omarr, S. (1972). *Astrology, You, and Your Love Life.* New York: Pyramid Books.

Omohundro, J. (1976-77). "Von Däniken's Chariots: A Primer in the Art of Cooked Science." *Zetetic, 1* (No. 1), 58-68.

Ongley, P. (1948). "New Zealand Diviners." *New Zealand Journal of Science and Technology, 30,* 38-54.

Osis, K., and Haraldsson, E. (1977). "Deathbed Observations by Physicians and Nurses: A Cross-cultural Survey." *Journal of the American Society for Physical Research, 71,* 237-259.

Otani, D., and Dixon, P. (1976). "Power Function between Duration of Friendly Interaction and Conformity in Perception and Judgments," *Perceptual and Motor Skills, 43,* 975-978.

* Palmer, J. (1978). "Extrasensory Perception: Research Findings." In S. Krippner (Ed.), *Advances in Parapsychological Research 2: Extrasensory Perception.* New York, Plenum Press, pp. 59-243.

———. (1982). "ESP Research Findings: 1976-1978." In S. Krippner (Ed.), *Advances in Parapsychological Research 3.* New York: Plenum Press, pp. 41-82.

Patterson, J. (1983). "Theromdynamics and Evolution." In L. Godfrey (Ed.), *Scientists Confront Creationism,* pp. 99-116.

Paul, G. (1969a), "Outcome of Systematic Desensitization, I: Background Procedures, and Uncontrolled Reports of Individual Treatment." In C. Franks (Ed.), *Behavior Therapy: Appraisal and Status,* pp. 63-104.

———. (1969b). "Outcome of Systematic Densensitization II: Controlled Investigations of Individual Treatment, Technique Variations, and Current Status." In C. Franks (Ed.), *Behavior Therapy: Appraisal and Status,* pp. 105-159.

Pauling, L. (1980). "Vitamin C Therapy of Advanced Cancer." *New England Journal of Medicine, 302,* 694.

Pehek, J., Kyler, H., and Faust, D. (1976). "Image Modulation in Corona Discharge Photography." *Science, 194,* 263-270.

Pellicori, S. (1980). "Spectral Properties of the Shroud of Turin." *Applied Optics, 19,* 1913-1920.

* Pepper, C. (1984). *Quackery: A $10 Billion Scandal.* Washington, D.C.: U.S. Government Printing Office (U.S. House of Representatives Document 98-262).

Persinger, M. (1983). "Religious and Mystical Experiences as Artifacts of Temporal Lobe Function: A General Hypothesis." *Perceptual and Motor Skills, 57,* 1255-1262.

———. (1984a). "Propensity to Report Paranormal Experiences Is Correlated with Temporal Lobe Signs." *Perceptual and Motor Skills, 59,* 583-586.

———. (1984b). "Striking EEG Profiles from Single Episodes of Glossolalia and Transcendental Meditation." *Perceptual and Motor Skills, 58,* 127-133.

Persinger, M., and DeSano, C. (1986). "Temporal Lobe Signs: Positive Correlations with Imaginings and Hypnosis Induction Profiles." *Psychological Reports, 58,* 347-350.

Persinger, M., and Makarec, K. (1987). "Temporal Lobe Epileptic Signs and Correlative Behaviors Displayed by Normal Populations." *Journal of General Psychology, 114,* 179-195.

* Pfungst, O. (1956). *Clever Hans: The Horse of Mr. von Osten.* New York: Holt, Rinehart and Winston. Originally published by Henry Holt and Co., New York, 1911.

Pincus, J., and Tucker, G. (1985). *Behavioral Neurology,* 3rd edition. New York: Oxford University Press.

Pirke, K., and Ploog, D., Eds. (1984). *Psychobiology of Anorexia Nervosa.* Berlin: Springer-Verlag.

Pittner, E., and Owens, P. (1975, April). "Chance or Destiny? A Review and Test of the Biorhythm Theory." *Professional Safety,* 42–46.

Plotnikoff, N., *et al.,* Eds. (1986). *Enkephalins and Endorphins: Stress and the Immune System.* New York: Plenum Press.

Plummer, M. (1986). "Current Investigations." *The Skeptic* (Australia), 6 (No. 2), 2–5.

Pollack, J. (1964). *Croiset the Clairvoyant: The Story of an Amazing Dutchman.* Garden City, N.Y.: Doubleday.

Porterfield, A., and Golding, S. (1985). "Failure to Find an Effect of Subliminal Psychodynamic Activation upon Cognitive Measures of Pathology in Schizophrenia." *Journal of Abnormal Psychology,* 94, 630–639.

Posey, T., and Losch, M. (1983–84). "Auditory Hallucinations of Hearing Voices in 375 Normal Subjects." *Imagination, Cognition and Personality,* 3, 99–113.

* Posner, M. (1978). *Chronometric Explorations of Mind.* Hillsdale, N.J.: Lawrence Erlbaum Associates.

Potter, M. *et al.,* (1984). "Lexical and Conceptual Representations in Beginning and Proficient Bilinguals." *Journal of Verbal Learning and Verbal Behavior,* 23, 23–38.

Pratt, J. (1978). Statement. *Proceedings of the Society for Psychical Research,* 56, 279–281.

Price, H. (1940). *The Most Haunted House in England: Ten Years' Investigation of Borley Rectory.* London: Longmans, Green and Co.

Price, H. (1946). *The End of Borley Rectory.* London: G. G. Harrap.

Prioleau, L., Murdock, M., and Brody, N. (1983). "An Analysis of Psychotherapy *Versus* Placebo Studies." *Behavioral and Brain Sciences,* 6, 275–310.

Rachman, S. (1971). *The Effects of Psychotherapy.* New York: Pergamon Press.

* Rachman, S., and Wilson, G. (1980). *The Effects of Psychological Therapy.* Oxford: Pergamon Press.

* Radner, D., and Radner, M. (1982). *Science and Unreason.* Belmont, Calif.: Wadsworth Publishing Co.

Rae, A. (1986, November 27). Extrasensory Quantum Physics. *New Scientist,* 36–39.

Rafaeli, A., and Klimoski, R. (1983). "Predicting Sales Success through Handwriting Analysis: An Evaluation of the Effects of Training and Handwriting Sample Content." *Journal of Applied Psychology,* 68, 212–217.

Randall, J. (1975). *Parapsychology and the Nature of Life: A Scientific Appraisal.* London: Souvenir Press.

Randi, J. (1978). "King Tut's 'Revenge.'" *The Humanist,* 28 (No. 2), 44–47.

———. (1979–80). "A Controlled Test of Dowsing Abilities." *Skeptical Inquirer,*

4 (No. 1), 16–20.

* ———. (1980). *Flim-Flam!* New York: Lippincott and Crowell.

* ———. (1982). *The Truth about Uri Geller*. Buffalo, N.Y.: Prometheus Books.

———. (1982–83a). "Allison and the Atlanta Murders: A Follow-up." *Skeptical Inquirer, 7*, (No. 2), 7.

———. (1982–83b). "Nostradamus: The Prophet for All Seasons." *Skeptical Inquirer, 7* (No. 1), 30–37.

———. (1982–83c). "Project Alpha Experiment: Part 1. The First Two Years." *Skeptical Inquirer, 7* (No. 4), 24–33.

———. (1983–84). "Project Alpha Experiment: Part 2. Beyond the Laboratory." *Skeptical Inquirer, 8*, 36–45.

———. (1984–85). "The Columbus Poltergeist Case: Part I." *Skeptical Inquirer, 9*, 221–235.

———. (1986a). "An Answer to Peter Popoff." *Free Inquiry, 6* (No. 4), 46–48.

———. (1986b). "'Be Healed in the Name of God!' An Exposé of the Reverend W. V. Grant." *Free Inquiry, 6* (No. 2), 8–19.

———. (1986c). "Peter Popoff Reaches Heaven via 39.17 Megahertz." *Free Inquiry, 6* (No. 3), 6–7.

* ———. (1987). *The Faith Healers*. Buffalo, NY: Prometheus Books.

Randolph, G. (1984). "Therapeutic and Physical Touch: Physiological Response to Stressful Stimuli." *Nursing Research, 33*, 33–36.

Rao, K. (1978). "Theories of Psi." In S. Krippner (Ed.), *Advances in Parapsychological Research 2. Extrasensory Perception*. New York: Plenum Press, pp. 245–295.

Rapoport, J. (1986). "Diet and Hyperactivity." *Nutrition Reviews, 44* (Supplement), 158–162.

Ratzon, H. (1986). "Handwriting Analysis of Holocaust Survivors." In B. Nevo (Ed.), *Scientific Aspects of Graphology*. Springfield, Ill.: Charles C. Thomas, pp. 127–139.

Rawlings, M. (1978). *Beyond Death's Door*. New York: Thomas Nelson.

Razdan, R., and Kielar, A. (1984–85). "Sonar and Photographic Searches for the Loch Ness Monster: A Reassessment." *Skeptical Inquirer, 9*, 147–158.

Rehm, L., Ed. (1981). *Behavior Therapy for Depression: Present Status and Future Directions*. New York: Academic Press.

Reid, J. (1983, October). "Use of Graphology." *Personnel Management, 71*.

Reilly, T., Young, K., and Seddon, R. (1983). "Investigation of Biorhythms in Female Athletic Performance." *Applied Ergonomics, 14*, 215–217.

Reiser, M., *et al.* (1979). "An Evaluation of the Use of Psychics in the Investigation of Major Crimes." *Journal of Police Science and Administration, 7*, 18–25.

Revzin, P. (1986, December 22). "If He Existed at All, Nicholas of Myra Was the First Santa." *The Wall Street Journal*, pp. 1, 13.

Reynolds, C. (1967, October). "An Amazing Weekend with Ted Serios. Part I." *Popular Photography*, 81–84, 136–140, 158.

Rhine, J., and Pratt, J. (1962). *Parapsychology: Frontier Science of the Mind*. Oxford: Blackwell.

Rhine, J., and Rhine, L. (1929). An Investigation of a Mind-Reading Horse. *Journal of Abnormal and Social Psychology, 23*, 449–466.

Richmond, R. (1985-86). "The Claws That Catch." *Skeptical Inquirer, 10,* 83-85.

Ridpath, I. (1978-79). "Investigating the Sirius 'Mystery.'" *Skeptical Inquirer, 3* (No. 1), 56-62.

Righter, C. (1977, February 8). "Your Astrological Signs Tell If You've Picked the Right Mate." *National Enquirer,* 49.

Riis, B., Thomsen, K., and Christiansen, C. (1987). "Does Calcium Supplementation Prevent Postmenopausal Bone Loss?" *New England Journal of Medicine, 316,* 173-177.

Rines, R., *et al.* (1975-76). "Search for the Loch Ness Monster." *Technology Review, 78* (No. 5), 25-40.

Ring, K. (1980). *Life at Death: A Scientific Investigation of the Near-Death Experience.* New York: Coward, McCann and Geoghegan.

* Robbins, R. (1959). *Encyclopedia of Witchcraft and Demonology.* New York: Crown Publishers.

Rogo, D., and Bayless, R. (1979). *Phone Calls from the Dead.* Englewood Cliffs, N.J.: Prentice-Hall.

Rogo, D. (1986, April). "Making of Psi Failure." *Fate,* 76-80.

Rommel, K. (1980). *Operation Animal Mutilation.* Albuquerque, N.M.: District Attorney, First Judicial District, State of New Mexico.

Rorschach, H. (1942). *Psychodiagnosis: A Diagnostic Test Based on Perception.* New York: Grune and Stratton.

Rose, L. (1968). *Faith Healing.* London: Penguin.

* Rosen, R. (1977). *Psychobabble.* New York: Atheneum.

Ross, J., and Persinger, M. (1987). "Positive Correlations between Temporal Lobe Signs and Hypnosis Induction Profiles: A Replication." *Perceptual and Motor Skills, 64,* 828-830.

Rotton, J., and Kelly, I. (1985). "Much Ado about the Full Moon: A Meta-analysis of Lunar-Lunacy Research." *Psychological Bulletin, 97,* 286-306.

Rush, J. (1982). "Problems and Methods in Psychokinesis Research." In S. Krippner (Ed.), *Advances in Parapsychological Research 3,* New York: Plenum Press, pp. 83-114.

Russell, D., and Jones, W. (1980). "When Superstition Fails: Reactions to Disconfirmation of Paranormal Beliefs." *Personality and Social Psychology Bulletin, 6,* 83-88.

Sacks, O. (1985). *Migraine: Understanding a Common Disorder.* Berkeley, Calif.: University of California Press.

Saegert, J. (1987). "Why Marketing Should Quit Giving Subliminal Advertising the Benefit of the Doubt." *Psychology and Marketing, 4,* 107-120.

Sagan, C. (1972). "UFOs: The Extraterrestrial and Other Hypotheses." In C. Sagan and T. Page (Eds.), *UFOs—A Scientific Debate.* Ithaca, N.Y.: Cornell University Press, pp. 265-275.

———. (1981). "An Analysis of *Worlds in Collision.*" In G. Abell and B. Singer (Eds.), *Science and the Paranormal.* New York: Charles Scribner's Sons, pp. 223-252.

Sagan, C., and Fox, P. (1975). "The Canals of Mars: An Assessment after Mariner

9." *Icarus, 25,* 602–612.

Sanderson, I. (1970). *Invisible Residents.* New York: World Books.

Sanduleak, N. (1984–85). "The Moon Is Acquitted of Murder in Cleveland." *Skeptical Inquirer, 9,* 236–242.

Satz, P., and Bullard-Bates, C. (1981). "Acquired Aphasia in Children." In M. Sarno (Ed.), *Acquired Aphasia.* New York: Academic Press, pp. 399–426.

Saunders, D. (1975, August). "To Steven Soter and Carl Sagan." *Astronomy,* 20.

Saxe, L., Dougherty, D., and Cross, T. (1985). "The Validity of Polygraphy Testing.'" *American Psychologist, 40,* 355–366.

Saxon, K. (1974). *Keeping Score on Our Modern Prophets.* Eureka, Calif.: Atlan Formularies.

Schaumburg, H., *et al.* (1983). "Sensory Neuropathy from Pyridoxine Abuse: A New Megavitamin Syndrome." *New England Journal of Medicine, 309,* 445–448.

Schmidt, E., *et al.* (1978). "Laetrile Toxicity Studies in Dogs." *Journal of the American Medical Association, 239,* 943–947.

Schmidt, S. (1970). *Astrology 14.* New York: Pyramid Books.

Schneider, E., and Reed, J. (1985). "Life Extension." *New England Journal of Medicine, 312,* 1159–1168.

Schur, M. (1966). "Some Additional 'Day Residues' of the Specimen Dream of Psychoanalysis." In R. Loewenstein, *et al.* (Eds.), *Psychoanalysis, a General Psychology: Essays in Honor of Heinz Hartmann.* New York: International Universities Press, pp. 45–85.

Schwartz, B. (1956). "An Empirical Test of Two Freudian Hypotheses Concerning Castration Anxiety." *Journal of Personality, 24,* 318–327.

Scott, C., and Haskell, P. (1973). "'Normal' Explanations of the Soal-Goldney Experiments in Extrasensory Perception." *Nature, 245,* 52–54.

———. (1974). "Fresh Light on the Shackleton Experiments?" *Proceedings of the Society for Psychical Research, 56,* 43–72.

Seabrook, W. (1941). *Doctor Wood.* New York: Harcourt, Brace.

Seamon, J., Brody, N., and Kauff, D. (1983a). "Affective Discrimination of Stimuli That Are Not Recognized: Effects of Shadowing, Masking, and Cerebral Laterality." *Journal of Experimental Psychology: Learning, Memory, and Cognition, 9,* 544–555.

Seamon, J., Brody, N., and Kauff, D. (1983b). "Affective Discrimination of Stimuli That Are Not Recognized: II. Effects of Delay between Study and Test." *Bulletin of the Psychonomic Society, 21,* 187–189.

Searlman, A. (1977). "A Review of Right Hemisphere Linguistic Capabilities." *Psychological Bulletin, 84,* 503–528.

* Searlman, A. (1983). "Language Capabilities of the Right Hemisphere." In A. Young (Ed.), *Functions of the Right Cerebral Hemisphere,* pp. 87–111.

Sebald, H. (1980). "Roasting Rabbits in Tularemia of the Lion, the Witch, and the Horned Toad." In R. De Mille (Ed.), *The Don Juan Papers: Further Castaneda Controversies,* pp. 34–38.

Sebeok, T., and Rosenthal, R., Eds. (1981). *The Clever Hans Phenomenon:*

Communication with Horses, Whales, Apes, and People. New York: New York Academy of Sciences (*Annals*, Vol. 364).

Shapiro, A., and Shapiro, E. (1982). "Tourette Syndrome: History and Present Status." In A. Friedhoff and T. Chase (Eds.), *Gilles de la Tourette Syndrome*, pp. 17-23.

Sharpley, C. (1984). "Predicate Matching in NLP: A Review of Research on the Preferred Representational System." *Journal of Counseling Psychology, 31*, 238-248.

———. (1987). "Research Findings on Neurolinguistic Programming: Nonsupportive Data or an Untestable Theory?" *Journal of Counseling Psychology, 34*, 103-107.

Sheaffer, R. (1977-78). "Do Fairies Exist?" *Zetetic, 2* (No. 1), 45-52.

———. (1978, June). "The Cottingley Fairies: A Hoax?" *Fate*, 76-81.

———. (1978-79). Review of J. Hynek's *Hynek UFO Report*. *Skeptical Inquirer, 3* (No. 2), 64-67.

* ———. (1981). *The UFO Verdict*. Buffalo, N.Y.: Prometheus Books.

———. (1982-83). "Creationist Cosmology." *Skeptical Inquirer, 7* (No. 1), 7-8.

———. (1983-84). "Psychic Vibrations." *Skeptical Inquirer, 8*, 117-120.

Shelburne, W. (1987). "Carlos Castaneda: If It Didn't Happen, What Does It Matter?" *Journal of Humanistic Psychology, 27*, 217-227.

* Shepherd, G. (1987). *Neurobiology*. New York: Oxford University Press.

Shinn, E. (1978). "Atlantis: Bimini Hoax." *Sea Frontiers, 24*, 130-141.

Shoben, E. (1982). "Semantic and Lexical Decisions." In C. Puff (Ed.), *Handbook of Research Methods in Human Memory and Cognition*. New York: Academic Press, pp. 287-314.

* Shumaker, W. (1972). *Occult Sciences in the Renaissance*. Berkeley: University of California Press.

* Siegel, R. (1980). "The Psychology of Life after Death." *American Psychologist, 35*, 911-931.

Siegel, R., and West, L. (Eds.) (1975). *Hallucinations: Behavior, Experience, and Theory*. New York: Wiley.

* Silberman, E., and Weingartner, H. (1986). "Hemispheric Lateralization of Functions Related to Emotion." *Brain and Cognition, 5*, 322-353.

Silverman, L. (1983). "The Subliminal Psychodynamic Activation Method: Overview and a Comprehensive Listing of Studies." In J. Masling (Ed.), *Empirical Studies of Psychoanalytic Theory*, vol. 1. Hillsdale, N.J.: Lawrence Erlbaum Associates, pp. 69-100.

Silverman, L., and Weinberger, J. (1985). "Mommy and I Are One: Implications for Psychotheraphy." *American Psychologist, 40*, 1296-1308.

Simmons, D. (1973). "Experiments on the Alleged Sharpening of Razor Blades and the Preservation of Flowers by Pyramids." *New Horizons, 1*, 95-101.

Simon, A., Worthen, D., and Mitas, J. (1979). "An Evaluation of Iridology." *Journal of the American Medical Association, 242*, 1385-1389.

Simonton, O., Matthews-Simonton, S., and Creighton, J. (1980). *Getting Well Again*. New York: Bantam Books.

Simpson, D. (1979-80). "Controlled UFO Hoax: Some Lessons." *Skeptical Inquirer*,

4 (No. 3), 32–39.

Singer, B. (1981). "Kirlian Photography." In G. Abell and B. Singer (Eds.), *Science and the Paranormal*, pp. 196–208.

Skeptical Eye (1980, December). "Extrasensory Deception." *Discover*, 8.

Sklar, L., and Anisman, H. (1981). "Stress and Cancer." *Psychological Bulletin*, 89, 369–406.

Slater, E. (1985a). "Conclusions on Nine Psychologies." In R. Westrum (Ed.), *Final Report on the Psychological Testing of UFO "Abductees."* Mt. Rainier, MD: Fund for UFO Research, pp. 17–31.

Slater, E. (1985b). "Addendum to 'Conclusions on Nine Psychologies.' " In R. Westrum (Ed.), *Final Report on the Psychological Testing of UFO "Abductees."* Mt. Rainier, Md.: Fund for UFO Research, pp. 32–40.

* Small, G., and Borus, J. (1983). "Outbreak of Illness in a School Chorus: Toxic Poisoning or Mass Hysteria?" *New England Journal of Medicine*, 308, 632–635.

Smith, D. (1981–82). "Two Tests of Divining in Australia." *Skeptical Inquirer*, 6 (No. 4), 34–37.

Smith, J. (1956). *The Search Beneath the Sea: The Story of the Coelacanth*. New York: Holt.

* Smith, M. (1983). "Hypnotic Memory Enhancement of Witnesses: Does It Work?" *Psychological Bulletin*, 94, 387–407.

Smith, M., Glass, G., and Miller, T. (1980). *The Benefits of Psychotherapy*. Baltimore: Johns Hopkins University Press.

Smith, W., Dagle, E., Hill, M., and Mott-Smith, J. (1963). "Testing for Extrasensory Perception with a Machine." *Data Sciences Laboratory Project 4610*, AFCRL-63-141, May.

Snodgrass, J., Levy-Berger, G., and Haydon, M. (1985). *Human Experimental Psychology*. New York: Oxford University Press.

Snyder, C., and Shenkel, R. (1975, March). "The P. T. Barnum Effect." *Psychology Today*, 52–54.

Soal, S., and Goldney, K. (1943). "Experiments in Precognitive Telepathy." *Proceedings of the Society for Psychical Research*, 47, 21–150.

———. (1960). Correspondence. *Journal of the Society for Psychical Research*, 40, 378–381.

Sommer, B. (1973). "Effect of Menstruation on Cognitive and Perceptual-Motor Behavior: A Review." *Psychosomatic Medicine*, 35, 515–534.

Soter, S., and Sagan, C. (1975, July). "Pattern Recognition Zeta Reticuli." *Astronomy*, 39–41.

Spear, N. (1979). "Experimental Analysis of Infantile Amnesia." In J. Kihlstrom and F. Evans (Eds.), *Functional Disorders of Memory*. Hillsdale, N.J.: Lawrence Erlbaum Associates, pp. 75–102.

Spence, D. (1964). "Effects of a Continuously Flashing Subliminal Verbal Food Stimulus on Subjective Hunger Ratings." *Psychological Reports*, 15, 993–994.

Spence, D., and Ehrenberg, B. (1964). "Effects of Oral Deprivation on Responses to Subliminal and Supraliminal Verbal Food Stimuli." *Journal of Abnormal and Social Psychology*, 69, 10–18.

Spiegel, D., Cutcomb, S., Ren, C., and Pribram, K. (1985). "Hypnotic

Hallucination Alters Evoked Potentials." *Journal of Abnormal Psychology, 94,* 249–255.

Spring, B., Chiodo, J., and Bowen, D. (1987). "Carbohydrates, Tryptophan, and Behavior: A Methodological Review." *Psychological Bulletin, 102,* 234–256.

Springer, S., and Deutsch, G. (1985). *Left Brain, Right Brain,* 2nd edition. San Francisco: Freeman.

Squire, L. (1986). "Mechanisms of Memory." *Science, 232,* 1612–1619.

Stalker, D., and Glymour, C., Eds. (1985). *Examining Holistic Medicine.* Buffalo, N.Y.: Prometheus Books.

* Stannard, D. (1980). *Shrinking History.* Oxford: Oxford University Press.

Steiner, R. (1986–87). "Exposing the Faith-Healers." *Skeptical Inquirer, 11,* 28–31.

Stevenson, I. (1974). *Xenoglossy: A Review and Report of a Case.* Charlottesville, Va.: University Press of Virginia.

———. (1975). *Cases of the Reincarnation Type. Vol. 1. Ten Cases in India.* Charlottesville, Va.: University Press of Virginia.

———. (1977). *Cases of the Reincarnation Type. Vol. 2. Ten Cases in Sri Lanka.* Charlottesville, Va.: University Press of Virginia.

Stiebing, W. (1984). *Ancient Astronauts, Cosmic Collisions and Other Popular Theories about Man's Past.* Buffalo, N.Y.: Prometheus Books.

Stillman, I., and Baker, S. (1983). *The Doctor's Quick Inches-Off Diet.* New York: Dell.

* Story, R. (1976). *The Space-Gods Revealed.* New York: Harper and Row.

———. (1977–78). "Von Däniken's Golden Gods." *Zetetic, 2* (No. 1), 22–35.

———. (1980). *Guardians of the Universe?* New York: St. Martin's.

Strieber, W. (1978). *Wolfen.* New York: Bantam Books.

———. (1987a). *Communion.* New York: Morrow.

———. (1987b, May). Open letter to Dr. Swords. *MUFON UFO Journal,* 7–8.

Stunkard, A., et al. (1986). "An Adoption Study of Human Obesity." *New England Journal of Medicine, 314,* 193–198.

Sulloway, F. (1979). *Freud: Biologist of Mind.* New York: Basic Books.

* Swan, R. (1983). "Faith Healing, Christian Science, and the Medical Care of Children." *New England Journal of Medicine, 309,* 1639–1641.

Swords, M. (1987, May). "Communion: A Reader's Guide." *MUFON UFO Journal,* 3–6.

Talbot, N. (1983). "The Position of the Christian Science Church." *New England Journal of Medicine, 309,* 1641–1644.

Targ, R., and Puthoff, H. (1974). "Information Transfer under Conditions of Sensory Shielding." *Nature, 251,* 602–607.

Targ, R., and Puthoff, H. (1977). *Mind Reach.* New York: Delacorte Press.

Tarnower, H., and Baker, S. (1981). *The Complete Scarsdale Medical Diet.* New York: Bantam Books.

Tart, C. (1976). *Learning to Use Extrasensory Perception.* Chicago: University of Chicago Press.

Tart, C., Puthoff, H., and Targ, R. (1980). "Information Transmission in Remote Viewing Experiments." *Nature, 284*, 191.

Taylor, S. (1987). "The Origin of the Moon." *American Scientist, 75*, 468–477.

Tellegen, A., and Atkinson, G. (1974). "Openness to Absorbing and Self-altering Experiences ('Absorption'), a Trait Related to Hypnotic Susceptibility." *Journal of Abnormal Psychology, 83*, 268–277.

Temple, R. (1976). *The Sirius Mystery*. London: Sidgwick and Jackson.

Templer, D., Brooner, R., and Corgiat, M. (1983). "Geophysical Variables and Behavior: 14. Lunar Phase and Crime—Fact or Artifact?" *Perceptual and Motor Skills, 57*, 993–994.

Templer, D., Veleber, D., and Brooner, R. (1982). "Geophysical Variables and Behavior: 6. Lunar Phase and Accident Injuries—A Difference between Night and Day." *Perceptual and Motor Skills, 55*, 280–282.

Teyler, T., and DiScenna, P. (1986). "Hippocampal Memory Indexing Theory." *Behavioral Neuroscience, 100*, 147–154.

Thomason, S. (1984). "Do You Remember Your Previous Life's Language in Your Present Incarnation?" *American Speech, 59*, 340–350.

———. (1986–87). "Past Tongues Remembered?" *Skeptical Inquirer, 11*, 367–375.

Thommen, G. (1973). *Is This Your Day?* New York: Avon Books.

Thorndike, L. (1923). *History of Magic and Experimental Science, Vols. 1 and 2: The First Thirteen Centuries*. New York: Columbia University Press.

Thorne, S., and Himelstein, P. (1984). "The Role of Suggestion in the Perception of Satanic Messages in Rock-and-Roll Recordings." *Journal of Psychology, 116*, 245–248.

Thouless, R. (1974). "Some Comments on 'Fresh Light on the Shackleton Experiments.'" *Proceedings of the Society for Psychical Research, 56*, 88–92.

Thulborn, T. (1986). "On the Tracks of Men and Money." *Nature, 320*, 308.

Tompkins, P., and Bird, C. (1973). *The Secret Life of Plants*. New York: Harper and Row.

Toth, M., and Nielsen, G. (1976). *Pyramid Power*. New York: Warner Books.

Truzzi, M. (1976–77). Review of R. de Mille, *Castaneda's Journey*. *Zetetic, 1* (No. 2), 86–87.

Turnbull, C. (1961). "Some Observations Regarding the Experiences and Behavior of the Bambuti Pygmies." *American Journal of Psychology, 74*, 304–308.

Tyler, H. (1977). "The Unsinkable Jeane Dixon." *The Humanist, 38* (No. 3), 6–9.

U.S. Office of Technology Assessment (1983, November). *Scientific Validity of Polygraph Testing: A Research Review and Evaluation*. (OTA-TM-H-15). Washington, D.C.: Office of Technology Assessment.

Vallee, J. (1975). *The Invisible College: What a Group of Scientists Has Discovered about UFO Influences on the Human Race*. New York: E. P. Dutton.

Van der Waerden, B. (1974). *Science Awakening II: The Birth of Astronomy*. New York: Oxford University Press.

Van Deventer, W. (1983, November). "Graphoanalysis as a Management Tool." *United States Banker*, 74–76.

Velikovsky, I. (1950). *Worlds in Collision.* Garden City, N.Y.: Doubleday.

———. (1952). *Ages in Chaos.* Garden City, N.Y.: Doubleday.

———. (1955). *Earth in Upheaval.* Garden City, N.Y.: Doubleday.

———. (1960). *Oedipus and Akhnaton: Myth and History.* Garden City, N.Y.: Doubleday.

——— (1977). *Peoples of the Seas.* Garden City, N.Y.: Doubleday.

Vitaliano, D. (1973). *Legends of the Earth.* Bloomington, Ind.: Indiana University Press.

Vogt, E. (1952, September). "Water Witching: An Interpretation of a Ritual Pattern in a Rural American Community." *Scientific Monthly,* 175–186.

* Vogt, E., and Hyman, R. (1979). *Water Witching U.S.A.,* 2nd edition. Chicago: University of Chicago Press.

* Vokey, J., and Read, J. (1985). "Subliminal Messages: Between the Devil and the Media." *American Psychologist, 40,* 1231–1239.

Von Däniken, E. (1970). *Chariots of the Gods?* New York: Putnam.

———. (1984). *Pathways to the Gods.* New York: Berkley.

Von Franz, M.-L. (1964). "The Process of Individuation." In C. Jung (Ed.), *Man and His Symbols,* Garden City, N.Y.: Doubleday, pp. 158–229.

Waldfogel, S. (1948). "The Frequency and Affective Character of Childhood Memories." *Psychological Monographs, 62,* No. 291.

Wallace, A. (1878). "Psychological Curiosities of Skepticism: A Reply to Dr. Carpenter." In A. Wallace *et al.* (Eds.), *Psycho-physiological Sciences and Their Assailants.* Boston: Colby and Rich.

Waller, R., and Keeley, S. (1978). "Effects of Explanation and Information Feedback on the Illusory Correlation Phenomenon." *Journal of Consulting and Clinical Psychology, 46,* 342–343.

Walzer, E. (1984, November 1). "Mystery UFOs Are Identified." (White Plains, N.Y.) *Reporter Dispatch,* A1, A5.

Watkins, L., and Mayer, D. (1982). "Organization of Endogenous Opiate and Non-opiate Pain Control Systems." *Science, 216,* 1185–1192.

Watkins, L., and Mayer, D. (1986). "Multiple Endogenous Opiate and Non-opiate Analgesia Systems: Evidence of Their Existence and Clinical Implications." In D. Kelly (Ed.), *Stress-Induced Analgesia,* pp. 273–299.

Watson, L. (1979). *Lifetide: The Biology of the Unconscious.* New York: Simon and Schuster.

Weber, C. (1980). "The Bombardier Beetle Myth Exploded." *Creation/Evolution, 1* (No. 3), 1–4.

Wechsler, R. (1987, February). "A New Prescripton: Mind over Malady." *Discover,* 50–61.

Welch, P. (1967, September 22). "A Man Who Thinks Pictures." *Life,* 112–114.

Welford, A. (1976). *Skilled Performance: Perceptual and Motor Skills.* Glenview, Ill.: Scott, Foresman.

Wernli, H. (1961). *Biorhythm.* New York: Crown Publishers.

Westrum, R. (1985). "Introduction: Putting Abduction Reports into Perspective." In R. Westrum (Ed.), *Final Report on the Psychological Testing of UFO "Abductees."* Mt. Rainier, Md.: Fund for UFO Research, pp. 1–5.

Whelan, E. (1980). "The Fear of Additives." In S. Barrett (Ed.), *The Health Robbers,* pp. 35–48.

Whelan, E., and Stare, F. (1976). *Panic in the Pantry.* New York: Atheneum.

* ———. (1983). *The 100% Natural, Purely Organic, Cholesterol-Free, Megavitamin, Low-Carbohydrate Nutrition Hoax.* New York: Atheneum.

White, S., and Pillemer, D. (1979). "Childhood Amnesia and the Development of a Socially Accessible Memory System." In J. Kihlstrom and F. Evans (Eds.), *Functional Disorders of Memory.* Hillsdale, N.J.: Lawrence Erlbaum Associates, pp. 29–73.

Wilhelm, J. (1976). *Search for Superman.* New York: Pocket Books.

Williamson, T. (1975, March). "Cancel Today and Save Tomorrow!" *Airscoop,* 18–20.

Wilson, I. (1982). *All in the Mind.* Garden City, N.Y.: Doubleday.

Wing, A., and Baddeley, A. (1978). "A Simple Measure of Handwriting as an Index of Stress." *Bulletin of the Psychonomic Society, 11,* 245–246.

Winter, D. (1985). *Faces of Fear.* New York: Berkley Books.

Wood, L., Krider, D., and Fezer, K. (1979). "Emergency Room Data on 700 Accidents Do Not Support Biorhythm Theory." *Journal of Safety Research, 11,* 172–175.

Worrall, R. (1982–83). "Iridology: Science or Delusion?" *Skeptical Inquirer, 7* (No. 3), 23–35.

Wylie, K. (1980). *Bigfoot: A Personal Inquiry into a Phenomenon.* New York: Viking Press.

Yetiv, J. (1986). *Popular Nutritional Practices: A Scientific Appraisal.* Toledo, Ohio: Popular Medicine Press.

Young, A. (Ed.) (1983). *Functions of the Right Cerebral Hemisphere.* New York: Academic Press.

Young, J. (1967). *The Medical Messiahs.* New Haven: Yale University Press.

Zajonc, R. (1968). "Attitudinal Effects of Mere Exposure." *Journal of Personality and Social Psychology Monograph Supplement, 9* (No. 2, part 2).

Zdep, S., and Weaver, H. (1967). "The Graphoanalytic Approach to Selecting Life Insurance Salesmen." *Journal of Applied Psychology, 51,* 295–299.

Zusne, L., and Jones, W. (1982). *Anomalistic Psychology.* Hillsdale, N.J.: Lawrence Erlbaum Associates.

Author Index

Index